P9-CPY-664

Relics and Writing in Late Medieval England

Relics and Writing in Late Medieval England

ROBYN MALO

UNIVERSITY OF TORONTO PRESS
Toronto Buffalo London

Toronto Buffalo London
www.utppublishing.com
Printed in Canada

ISBN 978-1-4426-4563-9

Printed on acid-free, 100% post-consumer recycled paper with vegetable-based inks.

Library and Archives Canada Cataloguing in Publication

Malo, Robyn, 1975–, author
Relics and writing in late medieval England / Robyn Malo.

Includes bibliographical references and index.
ISBN 978-1-4426-4563-9 (bound)

I. English literature – Middle English, 1100–1500 – History and criticism. 2. Relics in literature. 3. Religion and literature – England – History – To 1500. I. Title.

PR275.R4M34 2013 820.9'382 C2013-903493-5

University of Toronto Press acknowledges the financial assistance to its publishing program of the Canada Council for the Arts and the Ontario Arts Council.

University of Toronto Press acknowledges the financial support of the Government of Canada through the Canada Book Fund for its publishing activities.

Contents

Acknowledgments

It takes a village to write a book – or at least to write this one. I have incurred too many debts to pay, not the least of which is to my colleagues and friends at Purdue University, whose support has been instrumental in seeing this project to its end. I am grateful to colleagues who read and commented on drafts of various chapters, especially Dorsey Armstrong, Nush Powell, and Chris Lukasik; Paul White and Shaun Hughes both offered support and gave good advice. I also wish to thank my department head, Nancy Peterson, and Dean Bud Weiser for their investment in my career and work. Purdue University generously provided a subvention to defray the costs of publication. I wish to thank the interlibrary loan staff at Purdue for securing whatever obscure book I happened to need, as well as the libraries at Indiana University (IU) and the University of Illinois – Urbana-Champaign (UIUC) for allowing me access to their stacks. The librarians at IU and UIUC were always helpful and friendly; they made the time I spent in these places a delight. Small portions of chapters 4 and 5 appeared in *The Chaucer Review* and in *Wycliffite Controversies* (Brepols, 2011); I am grateful for permission to reproduce this material here.

Many medievalists generously read and commented on this book, and it is the stronger for their input. I wish especially to thank my colleague and friend, Shannon Gayk, who read in detail most of this book, offering thoughtful and gracious comments; working weekends in Bloomington were always punctuated by wine, good food, and friendship. I am lucky to know her. David Aers read the entire book at the drop of a hat; I am deeply grateful for his generosity and input. Other scholars have also been similarly generous and unstinting in giving me feedback at various stages of the process. I thank in particular Kathleen

Ashley, Mishtooni Bose, Andrew Cole, Patrick Hornbeck, Drew Jones, Ethan Knapp, Lisa Kiser, Rachel Koopmans, Bobby Meyer-Lee, Jenny Sisk, Fiona Somerset, Nicholas Watson, and the anonymous readers for University of Toronto Press. Suzanne Rancourt has been patient and kind from start to finish, and I thank her for her guidance throughout this process; thanks as well to Shoshana Wasser, Emily Johnston, and the copyeditors for the Press.

I owe a special debt of thanks to Paul Szarmach and Dee Dyas, whose NEH Summer Seminar in 2007, Cathedral and Culture in Medieval York, was central to finishing the research for this book. Austin College, my first tenure-track home, provided financial support for this trip, and I remain grateful to my colleagues there for their encouragement of my work. While in York, Louise Hampson and Andrew Morrison facilitated my viewing William of York's fifteenth-century shrine at the Yorkshire Museum. The shrine was not on display, and I thank them very much for taking the time to show it to me. I am also especially grateful to John Crook, who in July 2007 took me on a private tour of St Swithun's various resting places at Winchester Cathedral. Dr Crook spent an entire day showing me the very architectural details that have been so seminal to this project, and he has proven a quick and generous email correspondent in the years since, sharing his expertise whenever I have had questions and sharing with me his photographs of some of England's monuments. Figures 2 and 3 are pictures he took, and I am thankful indeed for his permission to reproduce them here.

My friends have offered support in ways great and small, and I am so pleased to know them: Kelly Bradbury, Jen Camden, Cat Gubernatis Dannen, Kathleen Griffin, Julie Liu, Stacey Mickelbart, Dana Oswald, Preeti Sivasankar, and Monica Willemsen – and a very special shout-out to all members of our book group. Thanks also to Davy Bowker, Erin Charters, Chip Comery, and Doug Sprenkle. I also wish to thank my family for their support over the years it took this project to emerge: Paul Malo and Elizabeth Cohoe, Jacquie Taylor and John Henderson, Kit Malo, and Stephen Malo. Thanks as well to my extended family, Bob, Sue, and Maggie Johnston. I am above all grateful to Michael Johnston, who has read more versions of this book than I remember having written. There is no question that I could not have seen this project through without his constant support, intellectual curiosity, and rigor. He would often ask the very questions I was avoiding, and the book is the better for it. He also tolerated, more than anyone should ever have to, dinner-table conversations about, for example, Latin relic lists.

But if this book took a village, my teachers and mentors are the most important people who live there. They have been instrumental to my intellectual and even personal development; it has been a joy and a privilege to know them. Over the years and in various ways, Tom St Amand, Fraser Cameron, Tom Adamowski, Suzanne Conklin Akbari, and Alastair Minnis have been on the sidelines, both cheering me on and challenging me when I needed it most.

In particular, I am overwhelmed by Alastair's enthusiastic support over the past ten years. I wish to thank him for his encouragement, guidance, and endless patience in reading and commenting on my work. It is safe to say that he taught me how to be a scholar, how to write, and that whatever tics remain are entirely my own. He models at once scholarly rigor and human empathy; I can only hope to advise my own students half so well. I am humbled to have worked with him so closely and count myself lucky to have had such a wonderful advisor, mentor, and friend. I dedicate this book to him.

Unless otherwise noted, all translations are my own.

Relics and Writing in Late Medieval England

Introduction: Relic Discourse

Sometime on Monday, 13 June 2011, a parishoner whom witnesses describe as "unusually aggressive in trying to see or touch" a relic of St Anthony of Padua allegedly stole the holy object for herself. The irony of this theft – St Anthony's patron duty is to find things – was not lost on reporters.[1] In the wake of the 2008 economic crash, Rev. Jose Magaña, pastor of the parish in Long Beach, California, decided in June 2011 to display the relic for the first time since 2002. He hoped that this object would reassure parishioners, many of whom had experienced economic devastation first-hand. As Magaña told his congregation, St Anthony "can restore your faith in God, your trust in the system, in yourself." After Sunday Mass on 12 June, the faithful gathered before the reliquary, which Jennifer Medina describes as about sixteen inches high and adorned with angel-shaped handles.

By the next morning, the relic had disappeared. For many, the theft was a deeply upsetting event: upon discovering that the very object meant to offer hope for something better was gone, parishioners wept openly, as did Magaña himself. On the advice of police, Father Magaña did not describe the relic, instead focusing on its ability to restore or test the faith of his congregation. And, seemingly justifying the pastor's assurances, the police recovered the relic several days later in the home of Maria Solis, whom they charged with burglary and arrested.[2] Desire for the relic, an object that returns faith to the beleaguered, is thus at once laudable and deeply suspect. For while Father Magaña assured everyone of St Anthony's ability to comfort them, he also reminded them not to touch this relic. In fact, several ushers guarded the reliquary in order to keep the devout at a safe distance. It may well be justified to characterize the thief as "aggressive," but doing so nevertheless presents as fundamentally disordered any who, by attempting to touch the object, subvert the common practices of a relic cult, which included pilgrims keeping their distance.

Even though our society is radically different from the medieval cultures this study examines, this newspaper article reproduces medieval modes of speaking about relics. In the twelfth century, for instance, Eadmer of Canterbury emphasized that translating the body of St Oswald would keep it away from lay pilgrims:

> God [deigned] to direct [Ealdwulf] in a vision to raise the holy body of his beloved Oswald from its place of burial, and when it had been elevated to bury it elsewhere in a more worthy place ... [Ealdwulf] recognized that there was easy access to him [Oswald] – more than was just – for these men and those and perhaps men less worthy than was suitable,[3] and because of this he had determined in his mind to move Oswald from that place, should the opportunity be granted him. But now, since a divine revelation had just fortified him for the task, he determined without delay the day on which he would fulfil his wish, that is to raise up the limbs of this preeminent father from the earth and to set them down in a place free of the bustle of secular persons and removed from access by the irreverent.[4]

Eadmer uses the word "access" ("accessus," "accessu") twice in this passage, and both instances have to do with preventing those who are unworthy ("minus dignis") from approaching Oswald's shrine too closely. Eadmer explicitly associates "secular persons" with the undeserving and with the irreverent; according to Eadmer, Eadwulf seems to think that none of these groups should be in close proximity to relics. The passage suggests that keeping the average "secular person" away from Oswald's relics is the primary benefit of translating them. Whether Eadwulf simply wanted to keep the body safe from theft is largely beside the point: the translation of relics to enormous (and largely secluded) shrines, which began in earnest in the twelfth century, had a lasting effect on the way medieval (and modern) writers describe these holy objects.

We are still compelled to speak about relics in this distinctive way. The *New York Times* article focuses not on the relic itself, but on on what this pastor says about this devotional totem. By describing the relic as an object that can restore or test the faith of his congregation, Magaña echoes medieval assurances that faith in the healing (or retributive) power of relics would yield miraculous results. Likewise, in an article detailing the touring blood relic of Pope John Paul II, an onlooker connects lack of faith in a relic with, in this case, negative results: "They talk about how he [John Paul II] has returned [to Mexico] to bring us peace … There has been so much blood lost here. Will there be peace? No. Because not many people believe."[5] So, too, Magaña's comment that the relic may restore faith in "the system" squares with a medieval discourse that yokes together the material holy and institutional politics. In this context, what people say about the relic affirms the order of things, that all is as it should be. And congruous with many relic cults of the later Middle Ages, ordinary parishioners were not permitted to approach or touch the relic. Like medieval relic custodians, the ushers guarding this relic regulated contact with the holy body, protecting it from overly exuberant devotees who might steal or defile it somehow. Both medieval and contemporary narratives, that is, suggest that it is essential to worship at a distance. Medieval miracles of punishment are not much different than the depiction of the Long Beach thief as "aggressive," portraying those whom the saint heals as always already deserving of divine mercy and those whom the saint punishes as refusing to abide by the regulations of a relic cult: unwavering faith, devotion to the shrine, attentiveness to figures of authority.

In opening this study with a contemporary narrative, I do not mean to suggest that that twenty-first-century journalism mirrors medieval discourses exactly. But in the case of the Long Beach theft, as in the medieval narratives this book examines, we begin to see how, in the absence of physical contact or, sometimes, even visual contact, narrative plays a crucial role in affirming the relic's sanctity and what it can do (restore faith, and so on). To be sure, these qualities of relics come from narratives of the devout. But in our investigations of the past, we have reproduced some of these conventions, characterizing relics as metaphorical bridges between heaven and earth, for instance.[6] Such assertions are interesting and important; but, as I will argue throughout this book, considering *how* relics came to signify a bridge is equally important to our understanding of these objects and their place in late medieval devotional culture. Taking into account how relics come to mean something more than relics themselves, this study examines the language that describes relics, the distinctive set of literary conventions that I here call "relic discourse": how, rather than exclusively what, relics signify.[7] By "relic discourse" I mean the technical terminology, together with the metaphors and commonplaces, that writers in the later Middle Ages drew upon to construct the meaning of relics, usually – but, as we will see, not always – to affirm their importance. Many of the medieval writings about relics that I consider in this study, in fact, highlight the potentially deceptive nature of shrines, indirectly suggesting that, when pilgrims cannot see these objects directly, language is critical in explaining what they are.

Relics and Writing

For instance, the author of the *Fasciculus morum*, a fourteenth-century preacher's handbook, compares the deceptive language used within the confessional to a shrine. In so doing, he emphasizes that a reliquary hides as surely as represents its contents and, by extension, might mislead those who valued it for the wrong reasons:

> We should thus know that people who veil their sins in this fashion are like these false pardoners, who show their relics in some golden vessel that is decorated with precious gems, or else wrapped in cloths of gold and silk, so that they may look truly precious before the people. But as it often happens, when they open them up, you will find nothing but the bones from a farm animal that have been pulled out of a ditch, stinking and dried up and worthy of every abomination. In the same [w]ay, when such people ought to show their sins frankly and truthfully in confession, they put so many excuses around them like wrappers, as if they wanted to make of their sins relics to be worshipped, whereas in truth they stink horribly before God and his angels.[8]

It is an odd comparison, of language to a material object: the "golden vessel" and "precious gems" are analogous to prevarication – to the "veiled sin." And yet, perhaps *not* an odd comparison. For a reliquary, like language, can both signify and mislead. To be sure, the passage is didactic: it teaches how *not* to go to confession. But insofar as it interrogates the relationship between a beautiful shrine and its contents, the passage also invokes the discourse of relics. By contending that ornate and opaque shrines enable the presentation of fake relics as "truly precious," the *Fasciculus* presents the shrine as potentially incommensurate with its contents. The shrine thus poses an interpretative problem, for it does not necessarily signify an authentic relic and may, in fact, hide what the object really is (in this case, a fake).

As the *Fasciculus* passage indicates, the meaning of a shrine may not be immediately apparent. Although the function of a shrine is the creation of difference (the saint's body is no ordinary body), there is no absolute sense in which a bejewelled casket denotes the ethereal or miraculous. Instead, relic discourse explains and enforces what the shrine and its holy object signify. In the case of the Long Beach relic, Father Magaña's sermon surely helped to create the subsequent atmosphere of devotion. This book will argue that relic discourse provides the interpretative framework for "reading" relics and reliquaries, that language constructs the meaning of relics – and that, in writings about relics, there is a contest of sorts over what this meaning should be. "Relic discourse" comprises both mainstream and reformist versions of how best to represent what relics stand for and what they do. The meaning of relics is therefore (and crucially) polyvalent. Meaning is created through technical vocabulary that specifies certain kinds of relic, using a term like "corpus" (body) to describe what was only a head ("caput"), a procedure that could be (and was) misapplied in the interests of "creating" a different kind of relic than was actually there. Meaning was also created through metaphor, one of the most common being the designation of relics as "treasure." Various other commonplaces of the discourse played their part, including: the superior ability of shrines over relics per se to represent the saint's holiness and the subsequent necessity of lavish spending on shrine monuments; the importance of limiting access to major relics; the unworthiness of supplicants and the moral superiority of relic custodians.

Finally, and perhaps most obviously, the literalized metaphor ostensibly tells us how to construe a relic: here I refer to the shrine itself, the monumentally material treasury (indeed, a treasure in itself) that contained the saint's body. But, as the passage from the *Fasciculus* demonstrates, there could be a shocking gap between exterior sign and interior meaning. Of course, material treasure was supposed to affirm the spiritual value of authentic relics. It represented the relics' heavenly significance; hiding the saint's body in a reliquary ostensibly helped to achieve the expression of this value. But the crucial distinction in the passage from the *Fasciculus morum* is not between decaying bodily matter and a sumptuous shrine. After all, a beautiful shrine could also contain the stinking and dried up body of a genuine saint (though the bodies of at least some saints were said to be incorrupt), in which case the outward opulence of the shrine corresponded to the actual worth of its contents, which comprised heavenly "treasure." But in denigrating the bones not merely as "stinking and dried up," but also as those of farm animals rather than saints, the *Fasciculus* author emphasizes the degree to which a reliquary could both conceal and even, to outward appearances, make its contents seem different, more precious, than they actually were. In comparing fake relics with dissembling sinners, then, the author's unspoken assumption is that there was no guarantee a lavish reliquary contained a genuine saint – and that even when the relic was genuine, the shrine might not convey precisely what it was. This "treasure" metaphor, in other words, often needed some explanation.

Three issues in particular inform the trajectory of this study and are important to mention here. First, both religious and rhetorical translation are at the centre of this project.[9] In the context of saints' cults, *translatio* commonly means the moving of a relic from one place to the other – and more specifically, from one container (say, a tomb) to another (say, a shrine). In medieval *artes poetriae*, however, *translatio* is a term for metaphor, which includes under its umbrella *denominatio* (metonymy), a trope which substitutes for the "thing contained" the name of "that which contains it."[10] Translation is thus, as Carolyn Dinshaw has pointed out, a "hermeneutic gesture" involving the "act of discovering, interpreting, and carrying over"[11] and enabling the expression of the value or meaning of one thing in terms of something else. The translation of relics functioned similarly, the intent being to substitute the reliquary for the relic. Thiofrid of Echternach, an early twelfth-century Benedictine whose treatise on relics chapter 1 examines in detail, "insists that relic and reliquary are truly a single unit."[12] His *Flores epytaphii sanctorum* seeks to collapse the distinction between relic and its container. The physical translation of a reliquary thus shares a close relationship with the construction of metaphor and metonym, both of which also replace "the thing contained" with "that which contains it." Translation equates the vehicle (the reliquary) with its tenor (the relic); and there is a sense in which the vehicle displaces the tenor altogether, leading to metonymic slippage in which reliquary comes to signify relic.[13] In a sense, both literal and metaphorical *translatio* obscure the means by which relics come to signify, presenting this meaning as always already present in the relic. But as Paul de Man has argued so persuasively, metaphor and metonymy are both contingent: both depend on accidental, not essential, connections.[14] The question then becomes how treasure (and that cluster of words) and literal treasure come to express the meaning that is then read back into the relic as if it were there in the first place.

So: both metaphorical language and the act of translation are meant to explain the relic's meaning. And yet, metaphor and translation themselves require commentary and explanation and are themselves dependent on contingent associations between, say, light and holiness, or between treasure and holiness. Cynthia Hahn is surely right to suggest that reliquaries "teach meanings and prepare the audience for the proper reception and treatment of holy objects" and "that reliquaries and their presentation propose a complex instruction of the body and the senses, the teaching of *reverentia*."[15] But as we will see, many writers, including Chaucer, Wyclif, Malory, and Lydgate, also raise questions about the orthodox insistence on translating and enshrining prestigious relics: What are the consequences of building a lavish and beautiful shrine? What does such a monument really signify? Does this act falsely portray the shrine's (dead and rotting) contents? Does such a construction place the poor at a disadvantage? Does disguising a relic imply that the laity cannot access God's grace without clerical mediation? These questions were frequently subtended by an interest in the similarities between relic cults and representational language, which shared a common vocabulary (translation, ornamentation). In this book, I use the term "translation" primarily to denote the physical movement of the saint's body from one place to another; but I also draw on the idea of rhetorical translation, which highlights the importance of relic discourse in generating the meaning of relics after they were enshrined.

Second, while I remain alert to the interplay between the written record and oral tradition, my use of the term "language" throughout the book is more attentive to the written record. The written record is always contentious in that it both expresses and represses certain viewpoints; as Anne Hudson, Norman Tanner, and others have demonstrated, even in well-documented cases such as heresy trials and canonization proceedings, the proscriptive nature of such events means that we cannot always be sure of what was actually said.[16] And as Rachel Koopmans explains so beautifully, the procedure of recording oral stories could be a "stiffening and deadening one ... English writers were engaged in imprisioning and pinning down stories, not setting them free."[17] Nevertheless, though I am alive to the fragmentary nature of written evidence, I am interested precisely in how the written record acts as a kind of preservative, in how it is shaped by clerical viewpoints, and in how it cannot necessarily offer a perfect window onto lay practices. In its attempts to homogenize and stabilize demotic practices, the written record can provide a witness to otherwise unrecorded tension and disagreement.[18]

Third, the fundamental and driving idea of this book is that in late medieval England, writing often filled the gap created by the material occlusion of certain major relics – and that writings about these relics must be understood in the context of what their shrines looked like. Each and every chapter is informed by this basic principle. Readers of this book may have seen certain shrines and reliquaries, extant in European churches or on display in modern museums, which are designed to exhibit relics, rather than hide them. One such example is a travelling exhibit, "Treasures of Heaven: Saints, Relics and Devotion in Medieval Europe," which I visited at the British Museum on 13 July 2011. The statement on the Web page for this exhibit – that the objects included illustrate "the emergence and transformation of several key types of reliquary, moving from an age in which saintly remains were enshrined within closed containers to an era in which relics were increasingly presented directly to the viewer" – importantly describes many reliquaries.[19] At the same time, this description depends both on the era (certainly relics were displayed openly by the eighteenth and nineteeth centuries) and on the type of reliquary. Nevertheless, the predominant narrative is that *all* medieval reliquaries functioned in this way and indeed were built, as Seeta Chaganti remarks of late medieval cathedral renovations, "in order to showcase relics."[20] On the one hand, this is absolutely correct: large cathedral feretories advertised the sanctity of their contents, much as a highway billboard "showcases" and narrates its product. But in addition to thinking about these monuments as showcasing relics, I would invite us to consider how these feretories, enormous in size and particular to England,[21] occluded their relics as well,[22] and to ask the question: Might such reliquaries have had the effect of distancing pilgrims from both bodies and saints?[23]

In England, the end of the twelfth century saw a "fashion for translations,"[24] from the tomb shrines of the earlier period to the gargantuan cathedral feretories of the later English Middle Ages. These reliquaries were opaque, enormous in size, and kept the holy bodies they contained completely hidden. This trend continued into the late fifteenth century, when in the 1470s, St Swithun and St William of York were translated from already-imposing shrines to monuments nearly fifteen feet high.[25] The technical terminology, metaphors, and commonplaces of relic discourse afford a glimpse inside such a shrine, as it were, describing in detail relics that most would never see. The implications of occluding relics and constructing their meaning through language are enormous: the relic is not an obviously numinous object. This statement is not a confessional admission that I do not believe bodies can be holy. Rather, the point is that precisely because we all have bodies, constructing their holiness is a very tricky business. As I have worked on this book, I have come to regard the relic as in many respects an empty signifier, its meanings produced, in some sense, by narrative (whether that narrative is linguistic or, as Seeta Chaganti has shown, produced by certain reliquaries themselves). The power of the relic in a way exists somewhere else – with God, in heaven, in abstract concepts of resurrection and redemption – and this power has to be shifted to the reliquary, and by extension to the relic, in some way. (Thiofrid of Echternach in fact makes this very claim, though of course he also wants it to cut both ways: the power of the relic is, for him, both a priori and transferred.) It is the argument of this book that relic discourse effects this shift, and that without the discourse in its myriad forms, even the most holy object might not be terribly easy to understand.

This book therefore examines the emergence and use of relic discourse in England over the course of the four hundred years from the twelfth to sixteenth centuries, during which period the shrines of England's major saints underwent such a dramatic transformation. But while this study keeps diachronic change in view, it also focuses on thematic consistency. Commonplaces that emerged early in the period and partly as a result of newly built feretory shrines nevertheless inform later, fifteenth- and sixteenth-century depictions of relics. Often, what is shocking in the twelfth century (the secret exhumation of the saint's body under the cover of night) is typical, not worthy of comment – an implicit part of the discourse – by the fifteenth.

My study calls attention to how the changing historical and architectural contexts of shrines in England led to the emergence of relic discourse, and in turn to how writing, how relic discourse, shaped the cultural meaning of relics themselves.[26] Seeta Chaganti's recent *The Medieval Poetics of the Reliquary* takes a theoretical approach to the cult of relics, focusing on the relationship between enshrinement and poetic practice.[27] This relationship is central to thinking about how relics signify, but it is in a sense limited; if we also take up the specific historical contexts of relics and relic cults in fourteenth- and fifteenth-century England, the result is a better understanding both of the wide range of relics' meanings and the extent to which these meanings were constructed and sometimes contentious. We have certainly been hindered by the almost total disappearance of such artefacts in England due to the iconoclasm associated with the Reformation.[28] This lack of evidence has meant in part that, when literary critics investigate relics, we often do so from the basis of theory, conceptualizing their semantic range in ways that, while fruitful, nonetheless remain both abstract and largely dependent on medieval theology – implicitly assuming that this theology is univocal and normative, when instead it participated in a complex discourse. Such approaches often take relics' meaning as self-evident, reproducing the medieval discourses that *created* this meaning. For instance, the ideas that relics function as metaphors for a paradoxically unified fragmentation, or for an absent presence, govern Chaganti's understanding of medieval relics, as well as that of Carolyn Dinshaw.[29] But in theorizing relics as fragments that somehow express what is simultaneously there, but not there – as emblems for lack and for desire – these approaches take as a basic premise that relics signified in a way that did not necessarily need explanation, that their very instability or fragmentary nature was somehow stable. Put another way, in conceiving of the relic as the consummate fragment, scholars have assumed this meaning to be always already there in the relic. Counterintuitively, then, even the most theoretical study of the relic often presupposes what the relic means, relying heavily on both the medieval and contemporary theology of relics.[30] And again, the questions I would like to ask here are – *How* does the relic come to signify what we think it does? And what is at stake in this complex process?

In arguing that the meaning of relics, like that of other religious devotional objects and practices, derives from context and from language – and is therefore polyvalent and unstable – my study draws from and extends the productive work, over the past twenty-five years, on discourses of popular piety in England. This body of scholarship has revised earlier and romanticized ideas of mysticism, affective piety, and the cult of the saints, showing how, as Sarah Beckwith comments of Christ's body, these practices and objects "have an ideological dimension" and are "unimaginable outside the context of social relations."[31] Rather than conceiving of medieval religion only in terms of medieval theology, studies by David Aers and Lynn Staley, Kathleen Ashley and Pamela Sheingorn, Sarah Beckwith, Gail McMurray Gibson, Miri Rubin, and James Simpson reimagined medieval piety and religious devotion as both shaping and shaped by the late medieval cultures of which they were a part.[32] In investigating communities rather than individuals in isolation;[33] engaging with the political importance of religious practices;[34] identifying the multiple meanings of religious symbols like the Eucharist and Christ's body;[35] and showing how different contexts and discourses affect and even generate this meaning, these studies challenge us all to think in more complex ways about medieval religious objects, symbols, and practices and what they signify.

Likewise, I seek to move beyond theological definitions of relics towards a more complex understanding of how these objects, as Beckwith says of Christ's body, "do not so much express meaning as encourage the creative attribution of multiple meanings to themselves."[36] We should not assume that just because Victricius of Rouen is enthusiastic about the signifying potential of even the smallest fragment of a relic, medieval religious belief always held all relics everywhere to be equal.[37] Victricius – far removed from late medieval England, and yet one of the most commonly cited authorities on the topic of relics – surely had his own ends in mind in composing his treatise.[38] One wonders whether, in so assiduously defending fragments, he addresses an undocumented complaint that possessing such fragments was not as impressive as having the entire body, or a bigger part of it. Understood in this context, his response sounds almost defensive, not unlike a parent offering a child fruit for dessert instead of chocolate. It is not necessary to point out that, parental desires to the contrary, not all children like apples. Reading Victricius as representing a ubiquitous and uncontested attitude, in other words, is only one way of reading him. And yet, relying only (or primarily) on medieval theological treatises such as Victricius's *In Praise of the Saints* for our understanding of relics is relatively commonplace. Part of my point, however, is that in a religious world of "extraordinary heterogeneity,"[39] in which religious discourse "belonged to everyone," as Miri Rubin has pointed out, systems of power also ensured its dissemination and potency.[40] Although it is now widely accepted that the religious culture of the late Middle Ages was shaped by both clerical power and lay innovation, this scholarly commonplace has not yet influenced investigations of relics, which frequently enough reproduce and idealize, rather than interrogate, ideas of medieval devotion.[41]

This book considers how systems of power and discourse influenced medieval (and, frankly, modern) understandings of relics, and how relics, like other medieval religious objects and symbols, were also sites of contested meanings. That is, while the master narrative of "an harmonious pre-Reformation Merry England, a consensual garden of Eden" has largely fallen away,[42] we tend still to speak of relics as we no longer speak of Christ's body, nor of the cult of saints more generally[43] – with very little nuance, adopting the language of medieval theologians without taking into account the culturally specific ways in which the cult of relics evolved (and was understood) over time. Drawing largely from the magisterial studies of Peter Brown, Caroline Walker Bynum, and Patrick Geary,[44] scholars of late medieval England frequently describe relics as signs able to erase "the line between the material and the spiritual,"[45] as equally powerful no matter how fragmentary,[46] as "both in heaven and ever-present," stretching "across the spaces between life and death, heaven and earth."[47] This reliance on such a small set of secondary sources has led to a closed loop in English literary criticism: scholars frequently cite each other citing Brown, Bynum, and Geary.[48] But this continued appropriation of medieval idealism is only part of the story. Of course, relics did signify these things. The problem is not that these sorts of observations about relics are incorrect, but rather that they are incomplete. The significance of relics in late medieval England sometimes diverges widely from simpler versions of these objects as bits of heaven on earth.

Indeed, taken in concert, relic lists, hagiographies, and architectural history tell the story of a wide-ranging discourse and more complex practices than we have hitherto imagined. These sources reveal a contentious attitude to relics as holy objects. Unlike relics of Christ and Mary – which comprised matter both the same and, in their divinity, inherently distinct from the pilgrims who visited them – and unlike the Eucharist or other holy objects and images,[49] pilgrims had something fundamental in common with body-part relics of saints. Any pilgrim had a body, too.[50] Relics of saints, in other words, had the potential to communicate the possibility of lived sanctity. Relics of Christ's blood, devotion to the suffering Christ, and devotion to Mary signalled redemption, but not sameness. As Langland imagines it in Passus 18 of *Piers Plowman*, Christ wears the costume of humanity; he is equally and also God.[51] Saints, on the other hand, were entirely human. Hagiographies describe these individuals as doing extraordinary things, feats perhaps impossible for regular people; and their bodies sometimes changed or developed an effusive productivity after death. But they were nevertheless human bodies, endowed with grace that, theoretically, any other body could access, too. As I have worked on this book, I have often thought that this sameness contributes to the difficulty of representing relics and to our own nostalgic attachment to what they signify. Does *having* a body make it trickier – or, perhaps, intensely desirable – to envision a body, or a fragment of it, as holy? In any case, by enshrining these objects in monuments that few, if any, had the privilege of touching, and by describing relics in metaphorical terms that distance them from their human origins, both the practices of enshrinement and the discourse of relics ultimately characterize holy remains as foreign, objects of heaven, even as they are completely familiar.

While this book has much in common with the scholarship that has challenged us to rethink our approaches to medieval material and religious culture, then, it also seeks to emphasize that relics, insofar as they comprise human remains (and what has been in contact with human remains), are profoundly different from – and were frequently treated differently from – other medieval devotional objects. I began this book with the basic assumption that relic cults and the language associated with them would correspond to the broader trends in medieval lay piety, particularly those associated with lay involvement in shaping religious discourse and engaging in relationships with patron saints. On the one hand, relics are clearly part of what Gail Gibson identified as the late medieval "incarnational aesthetic."[52] Their importance responds to lay preference as much as it arises from clerical impetus. But on the other hand, while lay patronage influenced the production of images in the fourteenth and fifteenth centuries and contributed to what Michael Camille famously called the "image explosion" of that period,[53] lay patronage did not shape the development of major relic cults at cathedral centres in quite the same way. Clerics composed relic lists and determined which relics to display (inside of reliquaries) and which to keep in relic cupboards. It seems unlikely that clerics made these choices based entirely on lay preference. So, too, clerics often composed narratives of incorrupt saints and crafted the metaphors that became common for describing relics (treasure and light). This is not to suggest that lay involvement in cults had no effect on relic discourse or the cult of relics – according to the Waltham chronicler, in the eleventh century Harold Godwinson was instrumental in donating some relics to Waltham Priory and had some pointed opinions about how best to display them (he would have preferred not to)[54] – but it seems clear that the laity cannot have had as direct an effect as they did on other late medieval religious practices. What is more, the surviving evidence is almost entirely clerical. This fact is inevitable, of course, given the provenance of much of the written record for the Middle Ages; but it is difficult to supplement this record with information from lay wills, for instance, for while many owned small relics or donated funds for a shrine's upkeep, none owned the entire body of a major saint or commissioned the building of a new cathedral shrine.[55]

Relics and relic discourse, like other discourses of popular piety, illuminate our understanding of the dynamic relationships between religious performances, rituals, and objects – but the narrative commonplaces that arise as a result are, curiously, removed from the piety that shaped many other religious practices in late medieval England. So while this is a book about a discourse of popular piety, it is nevertheless interested in clerical, as well as lay, discourses. So, too, I wish to identify clerical discourses *as clerical*, considering how mainstream relic discourse in many ways circumscribed lay behaviour at shrines, rather than assuming the records we have always record the spontaneous behaviour of the lay devout. Records of cathedral offerings and archaeological evidence (of worn stairs, for instance) tell us that shrines sites were hugely popular, but they do not offer an unadulterated glimpse of what went on at these places. Miracle narratives are frequently invested, however earnestly, in creating a pious and dynamic version of their cult centre.[56] Whether these clerical descriptions of lay behaviour are always accurate is less important than their use of commonplaces to describe the experience at any shrine as, somehow, universal.

What is more, the enshrinement of relics at England's major cathedrals belies the commonplace that the lay faithful were always able to interact with religious objects. Caroline Walker Bynum comments of medieval images that "[t]hey invited touch and taste as well as sight."[57] Sarah Stanbury similarly points out that in late medieval England, the desire for sight and touch dovetailed with the circulation and popularity of alabaster images, books of hours, and so on – material objects that were, Stanbury argues, part of medieval commerce and hence important as *things*.[58] But the body-part relics of major saints were treated differently: they were enshrined, hidden from view, and, apart from translation ceremonies, it is not clear whether even the relic custodian ever saw or touched them. Lay interaction with these major cathedral relics would not necessarily have resembled devout interaction with a depiction of the *arma Christi*, for instance – the tools of the crucifixion, depicted in late medieval images[59] – or even with the statue of a saint at a local parish.

The discourse of relics thus helps not only to construct narratives of sanctity, but also of social hierarchy; not only narratives of bodily redemption, but also of bodily decay. Relics and relic discourse, in other words, have something profound to say about medieval attitudes to the body and to death. By encasing England's premier saints in beautiful reliquaries, and referring to such objects as treasure, light, and so on, the religious culture of the time presented a narrative of stasis in place of horrifying change: the end of this life and bodily decomposition. This practice also communicated, however implicitly, a surprisingly positive attitude about the body, which carried with it the promise of glorified flesh in the Resurrection.[60] It is perhaps to be expected, in this context, that few theologians or narrators of miracle stories could determine precisely how relics themselves signified – for to do so would be to determine not the importance of the divine and heavenly other (like Christ), but the more immediate and complicated embodied present, the day-to-day life of every person living in England at the time.

Relics and relic discourse are also important insofar as they inform our understanding of the uneasy relationship between text and image or devotional totem. I do not wish to imply that language is only important to envisioning the relics of England's premier saints, for continental saints clearly enjoyed a rich literary tradition as well.[61] But the increasing size and inaccessibility of shrines in England suggest the importance of written descriptions and highlight the fraught relationship between text, image, and devotional object in late medieval England. Words increasingly served as guides to and descriptions of what opaque and large feretory shrines kept hidden. Relic discourse, that is, not only emerges from but also illuminates a moment in England when many problematized the simple "sisterhood of visual and verbal signs," arguing that vernacular religious texts ought to replace images as the "libri laicorum."[62] The tension between relic, shrine, and language enriches and complicates how we understand the operation of image and text on the eve of the Reformation, as the relic itself is *not* made by human craft and thus comprises a different kind of devotional object than an image or statue – an issue Wycliffite authors take up in some detail. A relic's relationship to language is hence all the more complex. We need to think more reflectively about how writing has mediated our experience of medieval relic cults because it is the primary evidence that remains of them.

Writing is particularly important in the case of relic cults in England, where, due to the iconoclasm of the Reformation, the physical monuments of pilgrimage have all but disappeared. This destruction provides a temporal bookend for my study: 1538, when, under the aegis of Henry VIII, the dissolution of the monasteries began in earnest. Even before this profound loss, the practices of enshrinement in England differed widely from those of the continent, particularly in France, where tomb shrines and table shrines were common throughout the period, and Catalonia, where major saints were often enshrined in crypts under the high altar (St Eulalia's fourteenth-century shrine at the cathedral in Barcelona is one surviving example).[63] Throughout this study, I hope to draw attention to the importance of language in generating the meaning of these holy objects during the period in question. This book deals in large part with understanding the parameters of such relic discourse: what it is, who was using it, and why.

Addressing theologians, hagiographers, and chroniclers from the twelfth through sixteenth centuries, Part I, "Relic Discourse and the Cult of Saints," outlines the "what," the components of relic discourse: technical terminology and metaphor (chapter 1) and commonplaces (chapter 2). chapter 1 examines texts from Guibert of Nogent's twelfth-century *De sanctis et eorum pigneribus* and Thiofrid of Echternach's twelfth-century *Flores epytaphii sanctorum* to fourteenth-century relic lists and fifteenth- and sixteenth-century descriptions of the incorrupt bodies of Werburge, Cuthbert, and Æthelthryth. Guibert and Thiofrid are both critically important in that they offer two of the only explicit treatises on relics that survive from the Middle Ages.[64] A Benedictine and friend of Anselm of Bec (who became Anselm of Canterbury), Guibert was connected to England through his study: he was well aware of the travelling relic quests to England that were becoming all too common (for his taste) in the early twelfth century. And while his treatise survives in only one manuscript copy which likely did not enjoy a wide circulation in the Middle Ages,[65] it nevertheless shares much in common with the "critically-minded clerics and laymen" who, like Harold Godwinson, found some of the changing practices at relic cults distasteful.[66] Henry of Huntington is one such cleric: in the prologue to his book on miracles, compiled in the 1140s, Henry complains about inauthentic relics and their cults: "The religious have grown accustomed to this kind of deception and falsehood for their own personal enrichment and [accustomed] *to enlarge the shrines of their saints beyond what is reasonable.*"[67] So goes one complaint (possibly) about the burgeoning practice of translating relics to large feretory shrines. Guibert's treatise may not have circulated, in other words, but it nontheless remains an important sign of the times, both in its emphasis on the (evils of) translation and on the importance of the written tradition. Thiofrid of Echternach's twelfth-century treatise, *Flores epytaphii sanctorum*, one of the only other surviving works to focus extensively on the theology of relics, comprises a snapshot of relic cults at the moment when relic discourse was beginning to emerge. It engages extensively with an issue of concern in England: the justification of ornamented and lavish shrines.[68] Both his treatise and that of Guibert of Nogent comprise two of the only witnesses to the momentous changes taking place at the beginning of the twelfth century in England: the movement of major relics from tomb shrines to cathedral feretories. And both works address the issue of lavish enshrinement in detail.

Chapter 2 focuses on texts that are explicitly about the cult of saints – particularly British Library MS Harley 2278, which contains John Lydgate's fifteenth-century *Lives of Ss Edmund and Fremund* – detailing how the many commonplaces of relic discourse emphasize the central importance of the shrine. A monk of Bury and a prolific writer, Lydgate (*c.* 1370–1449) in many respects exemplifies mainstream culture of the fifteenth century: in his commitment to Chaucerian imitation, to the English court, and to the monastic jurisdiction of Bury. In concert with works such as Henry Bradshaw's *Life of St Werburge* (1513), as well as twelfth-, thirteenth-, and fourteenth-century translation accounts, Lydgate's text provides an instructive example of mainstream relic discourse at work, showcasing the wholesale adoption of commonplaces that emerged centuries earlier.

Part II, "The Trouble with Relic Discourse," takes up the "who" and "why," showing that rather than using relic discourse to propagate a saint's cult, some late medieval poets drew upon it to ask complex questions about the implications of certain kinds of representation, primarily rhetorical artifice and metaphor. Many writers, including Malory (chapter 3), Chaucer (chapter 4), and Wycliffite authors (chapter 5), deployed relic discourse in order both to uphold *and* to challenge the premises of some mainstream religious practices. Chapter 3, for instance, "Relic Discourse in English Grail Legends," demonstrates that the fourteenth-century alliterative *Joseph of Arimathie*, Henry Lovelich's fifteenth-century *The History of the Holy Grail*, and Thomas Malory's late fifteenth-century *Le Morte d'Arthur* all treat the Grail as a relic of the Holy Blood. In depicting the Grail knights as supplicants, Malory's narrative vividly exposes purveyors of relic discourse as making promises (e.g., that any supplicant will be healed if he is penitent) they cannot keep. In Malory's text, then, while relic discourse serves as an indicator of good devotional conduct, it also illustrates that good devotional conduct could be, as in Lancelot's case, irrelevant to achieving a miracle. In a way, *Le Morte d'Arthur* reveals the limitations of relic discourse, from Lancelot's failures to the Grail's disappearance at the end of the narrative. Chaucer's *Troilus and Criseyde* and the Pardoner's Tale, as well as the many Wycliffite texts I discuss in chapter 5, examine the efficacy of devotional conduct, the consequences of enshrining prestigious relics, the degree to which translation resembles rhetorical dissimulation, and the effects of these practices on pilgrims. Relic discourse hence afforded the writers in this study an avenue for exploring the significance of metaphor – of presenting one thing as if it were something else – and, by extension, of hierarchical structures, bodily difference, and the effect on the socially disadvantaged of lavish expenditure on shrines.

Can Shrines Signify Saints? Relic Discourse and *Praesentia*

Focusing on the specific developments in relic cults and relic discourse in England troubles received wisdom about the medieval cult of relics. Many of these notions – that all the faithful perceived a saint's *praesentia*, or heavenly presence, to inhere even in the smallest fragment of a relic, for instance[69] – are accurate, of course, but only up to a point. Crystal reliquaries, particularly for relics of Christ and Mary, indeed survive; but these are not the *only* kind of reliquary. Nor is the fragment of a saint the only kind of relic. To wit, medieval relic lists and hagiographies establish a discursive hierarchy of relics: usually, bigger is better (chapter 1). We have, I think, become fascinated by the aspect of the theology of relics that posits the part as equal to the whole, without recognizing that medieval practices (insofar as we are able to perceive them from other sources) do not always accord with it.

The commonplace that fragments are equivalent to entire bodies – that all relics are, in some sense, the same – stems in part from what Christopher A. Jones identifies as the substantial influence of Peter Brown, Caroline Walker Bynum, and Patrick Geary on literary scholars of medieval England.[70] Most commonly, scholars pick up on Brown's discussion of *praesentia* and Bynum's consideration of resurrection theology. But this foundational work cannot always explain the frequent emphasis not only on the saint's presence (or *praesentia*) at his or her shrine, and the spiritual importance of relics, but also (and more insistently) how relics were displayed, materially used, and discursively constructed. The saint's power was derived from his or her remains, as has persuasively been shown – but also from words.[71]

The meaning of relics and shrines was thus not inherently obvious, a point that some medieval texts intimate in their concern that opaque and lavish shrines might sabotage, rather than facilitate, a supplicant's experience of the saint's *praesentia*. For instance, in his twelfth-century account of Harold Godwinson's gift of relics to Waltham abbey,[72] the Waltham chronicler outlines the potential ill effects of opaque and ornate reliquaries:

> I fear that, if these precious relics of the saints are entrusted to these reliquaries of gold and silver ["capsis istis aureis et argenteis"], something 'far

> more valuable than gold or precious stones and sweeter than honey and the honeycomb' may, through the prevailing madness of wicked men, be stolen from the church, and in these man-made vessels these holy things may be alienated through the greed of evil men in later generations, and put to the use of sinners.[73]

Harold goes on to request that the relics be hidden, instead – in this impulse he is not unlike Guibert of Nogent, as chapter 1 demonstrates. More important for my present purpose, however, is that the Waltham chronicler depicts Harold as concerned that opulent reliquaries *make viewers forget about saints*. The chronicler thus challenges – albeit indirectly – arguments that shrines were the best way to manifest saintly glory, that the shrine absorbs the power of the relics and manifests the saint's presence. Instead, we get the impression that sumptuous reliquaries, which proliferated in late medieval England, may have had the opposite effect: as the chronicler would have it, Harold seems concerned with the degree to which shrines might alienate the pilgrim from the saint and detract from a pilgrim's perception of holy *praesentia*.

The Waltham chronicler's worry about a shrine's possible usurpation of its saint is borne out by fourteenth-, fifteenth-, and sixteenth-century depictions of Thomas Becket's cult at Canterbury, which rarely – almost never, in fact – mention Becket's relics, focusing instead on the lavish reliquary.[74] So, too, an English relic list from Coventry, *c.* 1500, focuses on reliquaries rather than relics, illustrating that, even in documents that recorded a cathedral's holdings, writers sometimes elided relics and their containers.[75] Henry Knighton's chronicle account of a fourteenth-century theft similarly demonstrates that shrines, and not saints' bones, often received the most attention. For Knighton records that in 1364, thieves "robbed churches, and the shrines of saints, and carried off relics" ("spoliauerunt ecclesias, feretra sanctorum, et reliquias asportauerunt").[76] On the face of it, Knighton's account suggests that these robbers understood the relics as having spiritual value – as having *praesentia* – and might even have been enacting *furta sacra* (a holy and divinely sanctioned theft, as opposed to a regular, unauthorized theft).[77] But Knighton's narration of the theft of the head of St Hugh of Lincoln tells a different story. In this case, the thieves, having stolen Hugh's head, successfully remove the gold, silver, and precious stones adorning it ("captis argento et auro lapidibusque preciosis"), at which point they unceremoniously pitch the head itself into a nearby field ("capud proiecerunt in quodam campo").[78] One hopes that Knighton's thieves were not thinking of St Hugh as their personal patron as they did so. In portraying the thieves as having no regard for this relic, Knighton's narrative, which he may well have intended to illustrate how *not* to treat relics, confirms the Waltham chronicler's fears that a pricey reliquary would distract viewers from its contents. In these instances, it does seem that the reliquary eclipses the relic, and it is difficult to imagine that all gem-encrusted and enormous shrines encouraged a personal relationship with the saint. In fact, the degree to which elaborate shrines detract from both the saint and the poor is one of the most common Wycliffite critiques of late medieval English relic cults (chapter 5). For Wyclif and many subsequent religious reformers and dissidents, treasure is not a functional metaphor; it points primarily to itself and not to what it supposedly signifies – i.e. spiritual rather than earthly value.

Of course, more conventional writers often did emphasize the effectiveness of shrines in rendering a saint's *praesentia*. In Lydgate's *Miracles of St Edmund*, the shrine functions as an important sign for Bury's communal identity and Edmund's prowess.[79] All the same, by focusing on the shrine and not on the relics, Lydgate implicitly presents the literalized metaphor (the shrine) as able to signify better than relics. Lydgate depicts those close to a drowned two-year-old as deciding

> Alle of assent with reuerence we shal seke
> Thyn hooly place, oold and yong of age,
> With greet avys, lowe our selff and meke,
> Contryt of herte, sobre of our visage.
> With this avowh come on pylgrymage
> Affor thy shryne to thy royal presence,
> Prostrat afor the with ffeithfful hool corage,
> To our prayere tyl thou yive audience.[80]

In this stanza, Lydgate credits the pilgrims with having penitence and humility. Some who used relic discourse emphasized these qualities as necessary prerequisites to securing any miracle (chapter 2). Lydgate also depicts these characters as locating Edmund's "royal presence" *at his shrine*. Moreover, Lydgate offers us the shrine as a perfect metaphor for Edmund himself: lying prostrate before the shrine is to lie prostrate before the saint. Hence, while Lydgate trumpets Edmund's mystical power, he presents this power as inhering not in Edmund's relics, but rather in the shrine. Lydgate's text thereby complicates the received wisdom about medieval perceptions of relics. He does not quite follow the model we might expect – emphasizing the potency even of the smallest fragment of Edmund's body, or presenting the entire body as the unmediated spot for accessing God's grace. Instead, Lydgate subordinates the body itself to the monument at Bury.

We cannot know whether pilgrims tended to respond in the way Lydgate liked or, on the contrary, manifested Harold Godwinson's worst fears (according to the Waltham chronicler). The intention here is not to problematize the value of *praesentia* at a saint's cult, or to question the extent to which a given shrine was regarded as a holy sign within late medieval religion. My point is that we have overlooked how the opulent nature of many shrines led at least some writers to doubt whether the physical manifestations of relic cults invariably encouraged a personal relationship between supplicant and saint. In late medieval England, Wycliffite writers, the Waltham chronicler, those who described Becket's shrine (from Matthew Paris to Erasmus and John Stow), and Knighton indicate that a given saint's *praesentia* was sometimes perceived to be in competition with the gold and gems at a shrine. The vehicle (the shrine), as Waltham's Harold points out, could distract visitors from the tenor (the saint). The death of the three ne'er-do-wells of the Pardoner's Tale– whom I argue to be on a pilgrimage of sorts – can be seen to illustrate precisely this point (chapter 4). It does not follow from Lydgate's portrayal of Edmund's *praesentia* that his view of late medieval cults represents that of all his contemporaries. It would be more productive, I think, to take into account the writings that seem to question the efficacy of lavish shrines, thereby acknowledging that there were competing versions of what late medieval shrines signified: the saint, on the one hand; and avarice, on the other.

Discourse and Practice

No discourse can be understood as perfectly shaping or reflecting (inevitably diverse and complex) practices; the business of displaying and accessing relics in late medieval England is no exception. In this book I am not claiming to uncover with certainty what medieval people did or what they believed about relics. As cultural phenomena, pilgrimage and relic cults were widespread and difficult to monitor – with great gaps between theological theory (which maintained that relics ought to be carefully regulated)[81] and demotic practice (which at its most extreme included physically assaulting a holy body in order to obtain a relic).[82] Relics themselves were similarly diverse and difficult to monitor. They came in different sizes and types – and these sizes and types were frequently treated, and written about, differently. So, too, reliquaries were many and varied, from the opaque and seemingly impenetrable cathedral-shrine monuments to small phylacteries and personal totems.

In this study, I wish to outline how one particular and widespread discourse functioned: the various ways in which certain writers depicted relics, and how they used this discourse to engage with (among other things) matters relating to hierarchy, money, and power. (Both Chaucer and Malory *explicitly* associated pilgrims' inability to access relics with their not having the "power" to do so.[83]) Relic discourse emerged from the contest over what relics could and should signify – it provided a model for the valuation of relics, the attempt to fix (or to complicate) their meaning and articulate their use. And as will become clear, not everyone believed that relics provided a simple, material representation of salvation. The discursive strategies were much more complex than that. This complexity is the subject of this book.

PART ONE

Relic Discourse and the Cult of Saints

Chapter One

Representing Relics

Both this and the next chapter take up works from the early twelfth century, when translating the relics of major cathedral saints to bigger and more ornate shrines became popular, to the early sixteenth century, when encasing such relics in a feretory shrine was the common practice. It would be imprudent to suggest that relic discourse suddenly appeared with the first such translation; examples of relic custodians, for instance, or pious supplicants, survive from Wulfstan's tenth-century Anglo-Latin poem, *Narratio metrica de S. Swithuno*, with which John Leland, a sixteenth-century antiquary, was familiar.[1] But it does seem clear that the later development from tomb to feretory shrines influenced the emergence of relic discourse because the very shrines that became popular prohibited, to a large degree, intimate pilgrim access to major saints' relics (and sometimes to the shrine itself). In this context, relic discourse became a critical way to understand and shape the value and meaning of objects that were largely hidden.

The twelfth-century Renaissance in England has been characterized as a period of heightened literary productivity and heightened skepticism; it was also a period of monastic reform, focused in part on reclaiming the holy past.[2] English monks began to compile miracle collections in unprecedented numbers.[3] The twelfth century also witnessed the consolidation of papal authority and control: the papal mandate to canonize saints came into being in 1171, and though this mandate was followed unevenly until 1230, when it was incorporated into canon law, it clearly influenced both the growing popularity of translating major saints and the emphasis on written accounts of them.[4] It is not necessarily surprising that practices of enshrinement began to change alongside more stringent criteria for sanctity, on the one hand, and a more rational approach to the world, on the other: as the emphasis shifted from the miraculous to the natural, showcasing the miraculous by building shrines seems the necessary, and corresponding, response. In a way, the material treasure of a feretory monument expressed a metaphorical objection to the dismissive complaints of scholars like William of Conches, a twelfth-century canon at St Paul's cathedral in London, who remarked that the religious mainstream were ignorant "of the forces of nature" and that they placed "more reliance on their monkish garb than on their wisdom."[5] Relic discourse is partly a product of this era, a monastic (and conservative) response to scholastic inquiry and to papal requirements for a demonstrable sanctity.

But unlike miracle collections, which declined in the thirteenth century, the commonplaces of relic discourse proliferated in the late Middle Ages. While the practices of enshrinement changed radically during this period, many of the commonplaces and metaphors evident in twelfth-century texts are still present in narratives from the thirteenth, fourteenth, and fifteenth centuries. Later texts often include such topoi as an afterthought, suggesting how demotic practice might influence relic discourse. What is shocking in the twelfth century (secret exhumation of the saint's body, for instance) is often taken for granted by the fourteenth or fifteenth. Across the period in question, the conventions of relic discourse both changed and remained the same. Although by the late fifteenth and early sixteenth centuries, it was simply no longer surprising not to see the body of a major saint, it was still necessary – perhaps even more so – to explain and create the meaning of that body through language.

The organization of this and the following chapter hence keeps in view both synchronic and diachronic axes, both consistency and change. I introduce material thematically, rather than chronologically, for while there are clear developments over the course of four hundred years, the longevity of some of the commonplaces, terms, and metaphors of relic discourse demands careful attention. Such an approach means, necessarily, placing side by side authors from different periods. In addition to highlighting convergent ways of thinking about and describing relics, this method also illustrates the many and varied responses to and uses of relic discourse, not all of which square with the mainstream. For instance, Guibert of Nogent and the Waltham chronicler in the twelfth century, and the author of the *Fasciculus morum* and William Langland in the fourteenth, express similar anxiety about the possible consequences of enshrining saints. In the C-Text of *Piers Plowman*, Conscience rails in part against offerings at shrines that contain fake relics:

> Ydolatrie ye soffren in sondrye places manye
> And boxes ben yset forth ybounde with yren
> To vndertake the tol of vntrewe sacrefice.
> In menynge of myracles muche wex hangeth there:
> Al the world wot wel hit myghte nought be trewe,
> Ac for it profiteth yow into pursward ye prelates soffren
> That lewed men in mysbileue lyuen and dyen.[6]

This "wex" denotes votive offerings, often in the shape of the afflicted body part, which pilgrims left at shrine sites.[7] Conscience describes such places as encouraging idolatry because a shrine's appearance might not be commensurate with its contents – "hit myghte nought be trewe." Conscience also gestures towards the importance of language and rhetorical manipulation in maintaining this deception: to solicit donations at false sites of pilgrimage, clerics must behave or speak as though the objects of veneration are legimate. They must, in other words, employ relic discourse. The readings in these opening chapters outline the conventions of this discourse as they developed over four hundred years, enabling the presentation of both authentic and illegitimate relics as holy things.

This chapter will discuss two conventions of relic discourse that developed alongside the movement in England from tomb to feretory shrines: technical terminology and metaphor. The technical terminology of relic discourse explains what is inside (or what is supposed to be inside) such reliquaries. What emerges from the relic lists and hagiographies I discuss in this chapter – including fourteenth-century relic lists from religious houses in medieval England, fifteenth-century hagiographies of Æthelthryth and Cuthbert, an early sixteenth-century life of Werburge, and Reginald Pecock's fifteenth-century *The Repressor of Overmuch Blaming of the Clergy* – is a discursive hierarchy of relics. While it has been common to insist on the importance and prestige of fragmentary relics, it is clear that these texts place more value on entire bodies than on body parts (particularly small ones). Indeed, this specialized vocabulary privileges the very relics that cathedral monuments kept hidden. Writing may thus provide a substitute for seeing the relic – and, sometimes, for seeing the shrine, as in the case of a proclamation list, read aloud at

Salisbury Cathedral to parishioners unable to attend the procession on Relic Sunday.[8]

Just as technical terminology ostensibly explains what the relic is, the treasure metaphor explains what it is like. And while such terms as "corpus" or "caput" render saints' bodies as *like* supplicants, inasmuch as they draw attention to body parts shared by all human beings, the treasure metaphor presents relics as consisting of matter different from that of the lay pilgrims who visit shrines. In fact, Guibert of Nogent objects to enshrinement precisely because it presents saintly bodies as different from other bodies, not because he rejects the practice of relic veneration outright. Guibert – who was connected to England through his friendship with Anselm of Canterbury, once Anselm of Bec – provides evidence for a more complex attitude to relics than we typically allow.[9]

Thiofrid of Echternach, unlike Guibert, who rejects translation outright, argues that relics in fact derive their meaning from enshrinement and through metaphor. His defence of encasing relics in gilded and gem-encrusted containers is one of the earliest and most detailed of its kind, and, like Guibert's treatise, the arguments of Thiofrid's early twelfth-century treatise, *Flores epytaphii sanctorum*, share much in common with – without necessarily having influenced directly – attitudes that were widespread in England once translation to cathedral feretory shrines became the common practice. We may think of Thiofrid's argument as anticipating (and indeed advocating for) the development of the ornate architectural monuments that became popular in the decades and centuries immediately after he wrote his tract.[10] These two works are hence critically relevant to the cultural and religious contexts of relic cults in medieval England.

Late Medieval Shrine Architecture: Lavish Reliquaries and Occluded Relics

Envisioning all medieval relics as having been accessible and visible is more a product of our own assumptions than a reflection of medieval practice. As many of the texts I discuss in this and the next chapter make abundantly clear, it was common to conceal the major relics at cathedral shrines. The twelfth-century Waltham chronicler, for instance, depicts the eleventh-century Earl Harold Godwinson – who endowed Waltham abbey with many relics – as advocating that relics

> be buried in the ground, sealed with clay, to lie hidden in a secret place concealed from all mankind ["in loco secreto omni homini occulto"] except

for the one man alone who is to be entrusted with the task of hiding this great treasure ["tantum thesaurum"].[11]

Here, then, is a clear call for the occlusion of relics – and by a layman. He had much support among medieval clerics. Eadmer of Canterbury, for instance, went so far as to suggest that the primary benefit of translating relics was to keep them away from pilgrims.[12]

By the fourteenth century, the physical surroundings at English relic sites were promoting an encounter that was characterized by deferral and distance.[13] Indeed, as this chapter argues, many of the relics at major cult centers were enclosed in their containers and rarely exposed; the average pilgrim or cleric could not simply peek inside a reliquary. What is more, recent architectural and historical scholarship suggests that getting close to these major relics was not as easy as we have often supposed. English cathedral shrines changed substantially from the twelfth to fifteenth centuries, from the tomb shrines of the earlier period to the lavish and enormous feretories of the later Middle Ages. Moreover, these reliquaries did not necessarily resemble the body parts they contained, the result being that language was necessary to "read" a shrine. Gabled reliquaries, for instance, looked like houses rather than bodies. We would do well to remember Cynthia Hahn's discussion of early medieval body-part or shaped reliquaries (sometimes called "speaking reliquaries") such as golden arms, which supposedly resembled their contents exactly.[14] Hahn observes that "the proposition that reliquaries explicitly reveal their contents ... not only rashly underestimates medieval ability to handle complex sign systems, but is, as well, contrary to fact."[15] This criticism applies to cathedral feretories as well as to the "shaped" reliquaries that Hahn discusses, for the monuments of England's premier saints, like speaking reliquaries, participated in "complexly metaphorical systems of meaning."[16] Language is hence a necessary component of creating a relic's meaning, especially in the case of the major relics at cathedral shrines – for these were the relics most carefully guarded and difficult, if not impossible, to see. Writing filled the gap created by the occlusion of these major relics.

Literary scholars ought to consider this development from tomb to feretory shrines because, compared to tomb shrines, the design and location of cathedral feretories inhibited lay interaction with relics. So, too, understanding the physical setting of these feretories – which were opaque and hence "displayed *and yet at the same time concealed*" relics[17] – is essential to appreciating the importance of relic discourse in constructing the meaning of relics. In contemporary sources such as writings by Lydgate, Chaucer, and Malory, relic discourse is used to create meaning for an object that was, unlike the tomb shrines that were popular before the thirteenth century, comparatively distant from the supplicants who visited it.

Often constructed over the saint's burial site, these earlier tomb shrines consisted of two main parts: the tomb, and the shrine monument, which was either built directly over the tomb or, in some cases, may have served as the shrine base.[18] Both Edward the Confessor's and Thomas Becket's early tomb shrines included portholes in the sides, apertures known as *foramina* or *fenestellae* and intended, possibly, to enable pilgrims to reach in and touch the top (or bottom) of the sarcophagus.[19] Compared to the behemoth structures of the later period, these monuments were quite small: Lantfred and Wulfstan both describe St Swithun's tenth-century tomb shrine as about the size of the coffin itself.[20] Neither do the early tomb shrines of St Thomas of Canterbury or St Edward the Confessor appear to have been especially large. An illumination from Edward's thirteenth-century *vita*, in Cambridge University Library MS Ee. 3.59, features pilgrims crawling in and out of the portholes of Edward's tomb shrine, itself about three feet high (judging from the height of standing pilgrims) [Figure 1].[21] The stained glass at Canterbury similarly suggests that Becket's twelfth-century tomb shrine, located in the crypt, was about three feet high. Moreover, at least some of these monuments were situated in or close to the nave, where any pilgrim would have had easy and unfettered access to the shrine.[22] William of York's sarchopagus, in the nave at York Minster,[23] is a well-known example, and the miracle stories of 1177 include many cures "ad tumulum."[24] Even if we grant that the spaces around these shrines may have been crowded, and that in a throng of many pilgrims those at the back would not have been able to see the tomb, it seems equally reasonable to imagine that given the height of these shrines, their portholes and even possible locations (in naves or transepts, as opposed to within or behind the choir), tomb shrines were, in many respects, easier for pilgrims to touch and approach than late medieval feretories.

John Blair, Nicola Coldstream, John Crook, Tim Tatton-Brown, and others have made it clear that the end of the twelfth century saw a "fashion for translations."[25] As a result, tomb shrines, widespread in England in the eleventh and twelfth centuries, were uncommon by the fourteenth century.[26] Coldstream argues that the move from tomb shrines to feretories, frequently modelled on the 1220 and 1269

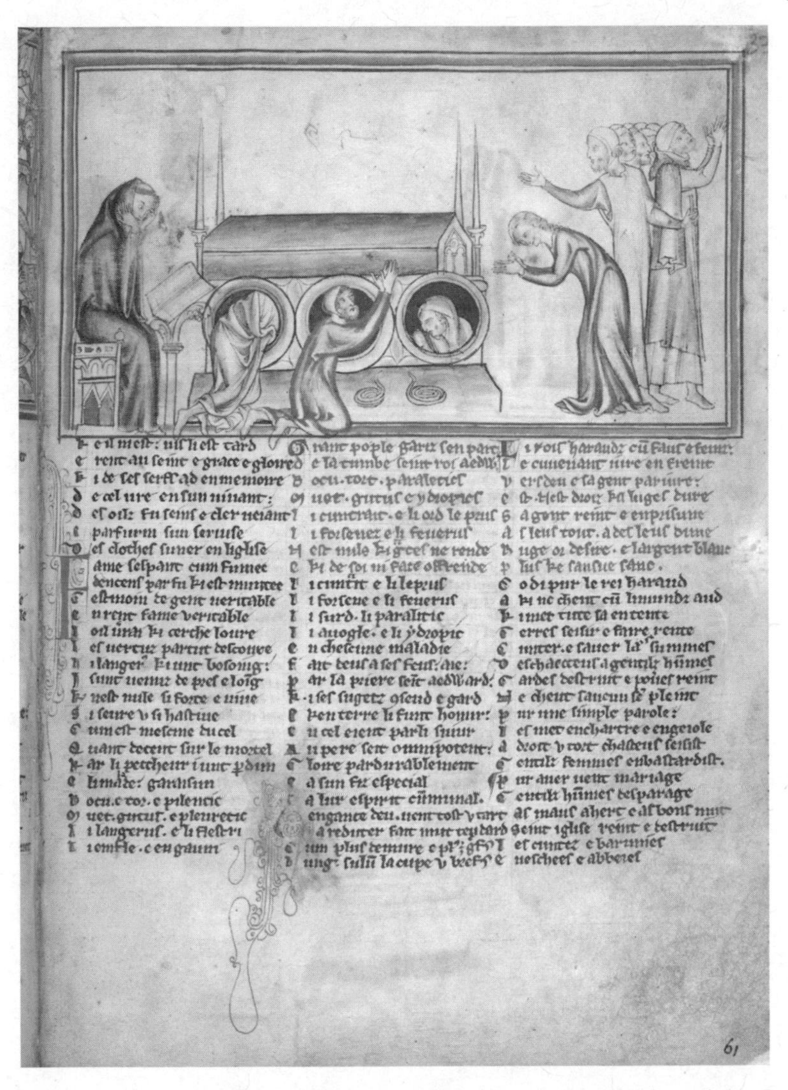

Figure 1. Cambridge Library MS Ee. 3.59 (fol. 33r). Image of Edward the Confessor's thirteenth-century tomb shrine, depicting pilgrims crawling in and out of the *foramina* (also called *fenestellae*), or holes in the side of the monument. These shrines were usually constructed *over* the putative saint's original tomb site. The snake-like objects to the right of the praying pilgrim are in fact trindles, or wax votive candles. These were often cut to the length of a supplicant's body and then left at the shrine site. Edward was translated from this monument to a feretory shrine in 1269 (depicted in Figure 2). Reproduced by kind permission of the Syndics of Cambridge University Library.

translations of St Thomas at Canterbury and St Edward at Westminster, reached its height at the beginning of the fourteenth century.[27] By the time Chaucer wrote *The Canterbury Tales*, neither St Thomas nor St Edward were to be found in tomb shrines, but rather in cathedral feretories in the retrochoirs of Canterbury and Westminster: for envisioning Becket's shrine as Chaucer would have known it, *pace* Eugene Vance, the illuminations in Edward's *vita* are irrelevant [Figure 1].[28]

Unlike tomb shrines, built over the resting place of the saint and relatively modest in height, these cathedral feretories (from the technical term *feretrum* or *feretra*) consisted of both a tall shrine base and the shrine itself. In the early fourteenth century, such bases were, on average, eight feet tall, eight feet long, and three feet wide; and they usually took the form of a box-like base with niches [Figures 2 and 3].[29] Theoretically, the pillars would enable pilgrims to pray underneath the shrine, while the niches provided a place to kneel at the base of the shrine. In both cases, the shrine base elevated the shrine far above the height of earlier tomb shrines, presenting the saint at a much greater distance than had been the case at earlier shrines. To be sure, neither shrine type exposed the saint's relics, and both early and late reliquaries made some provisions for pilgrim access: architectural historians identify the portholes of tomb shrines and the feretory niches of the later period as facilitating intimacy with the saint.[30] But I would suggest that insofar as the later shrines are elevated above supplicants, they convey literal and figurative distance: the saint is raised up above the pilgrim; the saint is, in some sense, presented as absolutely different. Moreover, by the thirteenth and fourteenth centuries, many shrines, such as Becket's, had been moved to a position behind the high altar, sometimes in chapels or retrochoirs newly designed for this purpose.[31] At Winchester and York, the shrines of Ss Swithun and William were both located *inside* the quire until the late fifteenth century, a position that, practically speaking, made access nearly impossible for many, if not most, pilgrims.

In the fifteenth century, two other alterations contributed to the increasing distance of cathedral feretories from pilgrims. First, shrine bases continued to "develop upward."[32] The late fifteenth-century shrines of William and Swithun, by then situated behind the high altar as was common, were not simply opaque but enormous. William of York's shrine *base*, built in 1472 and representative of fourteenth- and fifteenth-century bases, is eleven feet high.[33] Swithun's base, *c.* 1476, may have been as tall as fourteen feet.[34] Though it has been suggested that the height of shrine bases was meant to allow a pilgrim to get "as

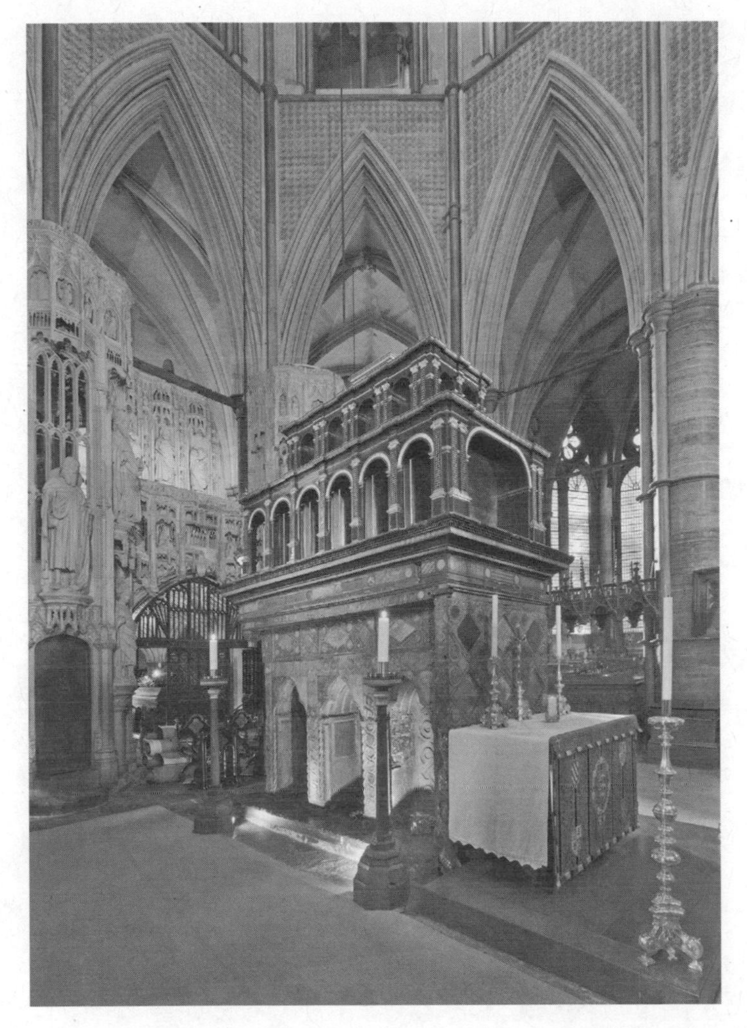

Figure 2. Westminster Abbey. The niche-base feretory shrine of Edward the Confessor, from the northwest. Depicted is the sixteenth-century reconstruction of the shrine to which Edward was translated in 1269, illustrating the sheer size of late medieval feretory shrines. The reliquary itself would have rested on top of this already-tall structure. The niche base is representative of English medieval high shrines; its construction and use of Purbeck marble are "emphatically local," as John Crook explains. Even today, this shrine is difficult to access or see. Image courtesy of John Crook.

Figure 3. St Alban's Abbey. The fourteenth-century shrine of St Alban. Constructed of Purbeck marble (typical of English niche-base shrines like this one), this shrine base for St Alban's was completed in the early fourteenth century and restored in the 1990s. It is a large monument, measuring 8.5 by 3.1 feet; including the gabled reliquary, its height is about 13.1 feet. These dimensions are about average for feretory shrines in the fourteenth and fifteenth centuries in England; some of the niche bases, as at Winchester and York, were even taller. Image and dimensions courtesy of John Crook.

close as possible to the object of his devotions,"[35] we should consider the possibility that these enormous bases also deferred access to the shrine (while preserving the illusion of intimacy). At these major shrine sites, the closest most pilgrims would ever get to the relics would have been eleven feet away from a *feretrum* that kept the saints' bones completely hidden.

Second, while Coldstream argues that late medieval elevated shrines would have been visible from the nave, Crook, Ben Nilson, and Tatton-Brown have all suggested that by the fourteenth and fifteenth centuries, screens surrounding cathedral feretories became gradually more common. Though we may construe imposing feretories as enabling pilgrims to view the shrines from the nave, to do so would have been all but impossible at York or Winchester, where fifteenth-century choir screens and reredoses (at Winchester, forty feet high) entirely divided the eastern from the western end of the cathedral. At Canterbury, a series of screens partially blocked the shrine, isolating it from the nave. Both these screens and the royal tombs around the shrine would have made it difficult to see the shrine even from the ambulatory; and very few were admitted to the shrine area itself.[36] By the fifteenth century, even the most elevated reliquary may not have been visible from the western end of a cathedral – a point Nilson and Tatton-Brown take up in some detail.[37]

Many of these feretories were also subject to a sort of "Russian nesting doll" effect: the gilded and gem-encrusted shrines were themselves often contained by shrine canopies – that is, wooden structures that operated on a pulley system and could hide even the shrine from view.[38] And in at least some cases, the *feretrum* itself contained not the saint's body, but rather his coffin or earlier reliquary. At Bury, for example, any who viewed the elaborate shrine base and *feretrum* were still twice removed from Edmund's body, which may have been encased within a coffin within the shrine.[39] At Westminster, Edward the Confessor's feretory may not have contained his relics at all.[40] The shrines themselves were usually locked (and infrequently opened).[41] Many other reliquaries at Canterbury and elsewhere were similarly opaque and difficult to reach;[42] Erasmus's account testifies to the predominance of opaque, gilded, and gem-encrusted reliquaries at Canterbury, where even he was not allowed the privilege of seeing Becket's bones.[43] As Tatton-Brown explains in his description of the fourteenth- and fifteenth-century pilgrim route at Canterbury, the average visitor would not have been permitted in the north quire aisle, the location of Canterbury's relic cupboard, which contained the "sudarium" and other relics. Finally, Becket's many relic custodians would have participated in the occlusion of his relics by the way in which they controlled pilgrim behaviour at the shrine.[44] In short, we must revisit the notion that all relics were easy to get at, for by the later Middle Ages, many shrines – let alone their contents – were probably not that easy to see or touch. Hence, while in some respects we may think of the ambulatories (or walkways) surrounding these cathedral feretories as facilitating pilgrimage, I think we should also consider the effect both of a feretory's size and of the occlusion of its holy bones on the meaning of relics.[45]

This strategy of material occlusion calls into question assertions that, as in the anonymous *Tale of Beryn*, "the holy relikis [at Canterbury], ech man with his mowith / Kissid, as a goodly monke þe names told & tauȝt."[46] I wonder what relics the *Beryn* poet had in mind: were these "holy relikis" supposed to be those of Becket? If so, his account probably plays fast and loose with the actual practice. It seems unlikely that these (quite average) pilgrims would have had such unfettered access to them when even Erasmus, who certainly saw more than most, did not. Erasmus and his companion did kiss what was probably Thomas of Canterbury's bloodied "face-cloth," or "sudarium," and were offered an arm (with bits of flesh still attached) to kiss; at least some (prestigious, privileged) supplicants, then, occasionally managed intimate physical contact with certain relics, perhaps most usually anonymous or non-notable ones.[47] Nevertheless, given that what we know of historical practices disagrees with the *Beryn* poet's literary presentation of events, I suspect that the *Beryn* poet imagined the pilgrims kissing the ornamented containers of relics rather than the precious contents themselves.

Based on what we know about shrine monuments, we should approach with skepticism the idea that every pilgrim always had easy access to these monuments and their relics. In making this point, I wish to correct a common misconception that in the later Middle Ages in England, *all* shrines became more, rather than less, accessible. The accuracy of this claim depends largely on the kind of relic and the kind of shrine: relics of Christ and Mary were often kept in crystal reliquaries or monstrances, as relic lists suggest. Many such glass reliquaries, often ornamented with gold, silver, and/or precious stones, survive from the later Middle Ages.[48] But as the lists also indicate, these relics were not always displayed openly; it can be difficult to tell how, when, and whether a supplicant would have seen even these less prestigious relics.[49] Certainly the design and architectural context of major cathedral shrines of the later Middle Ages in England would have prohibited most pilgrims from approaching these monuments very closely – or perhaps even seeing them from a position as far removed as the nave. Given this limited access, relic discourse ensured that pilgrims could imagine what the relic inside the shrine looked like. Terms like "caput" and "corpus" denote both a relic's importance (relative to the other saintly bodies in a cathedral's collection) and enable us to envision the relic itself.

The Technical Terminology of Relic Discourse; Or, Why Bigger is Better

Many late medieval writers categorized precisely the relics they knew were all around them. And several modern scholars have followed that lead. Having made a detailed examination of Canterbury's medieval relic lists and the writings of Gervase of Canterbury, nineteenth-century historians John Wickham Legg and W. H. St John Hope identify four classes of relics: greater relics of saints and archbishops in standing shrines or tombs; lesser relics of saints and archbishops in portable or moveable shrines; the relics of former archbishops and pious layfolk, buried or placed near altars; and miscellaneous objects enclosed in reliquaries.[50] Legg and Hope are not alone in ranking such items (usually in precisely this order). The leading historians of the architectural and written history of relics in medieval England all suggest categories of relics as well, which correspond to those Legg and Hope develop.[51] Of these, Mark Spurrell's claim is perhaps the most forceful: he points out that, contrary to the theory which posits "even the smallest relic" as sacramental and powerful, in medieval English practice, "a knuckle bone of one of the apostles was not accorded the care and reverence which the whole relic of a much lesser saint attracted, nor was it as potent as a miracle worker."[52] Spurrell's claim is absolute, but as he and others make clear, discerning how different kinds of relics were used and displayed can tell us a lot about whether the smallest fragment of a saint was considered equivalent to an incorrupt body. Usually, the answer is no. Perhaps not surprisingly, these distinctions were never codified; but they were nevertheless implicit within discourse and practice. In late medieval England, the part was rarely portrayed to be as prestigious as the whole.

Many literary scholars have nonetheless persisted in characterizing all relics as equivalent.[53] This assumption subtends some arguments that the (small and fake) relics of Chaucer's Pardoner pose a threat to the (large and ostensibly authentic) ones at Canterbury.[54] But in the context of relic discourse, size matters. This is true despite the oft-repeated claim that in partial relics ("minutiae"), we find the "plenitude of flesh" ("plenitudo carnalis"), that "wherever [there is any part of a saint's body, there is the] whole" ("ubi est aliquid ibi totum est").[55] Body-part relics are better than other kinds of relics, a point Carolyn Dinshaw, but few others, emphasizes. But *pace* Dinshaw, some body-part relics are better than others.[56] Written accounts of relics privilege complete bodies and larger parts of bodies (e.g., heads and arms) over "holy fragments."[57] Authors sometimes describe one kind of relic as something more prestigious, as the author of a fourteenth-century Canterbury relic list, who identifies Swithun's head as "corpus," rather than "caput" – the entire body being even more impressive than the head. St Alphege brought Swithun's head to Canterbury in 1006; the rest of Swithun's body remained at Winchester.[58] The language of the Canterbury relic list thus creates a relic they did not actually have and strongly suggests that whole bodies are better than heads – better than "fragments."[59] Moreover, in identifying one relic as something else, purveyors of relic discourse expose the tenuous relationship between a relic's container (replete with imagery, gold, and gems) and what it contains (a rotting body? A head? A foot?).[60]

I will discuss some of this technical terminology ("caput," "corpus," etc.) in detail at the end of this section. For now, I will borrow two terms – notable and non-notable relics – from nineteenth-century canon law.[61] These terms are useful because they describe the relics of the Middle Ages in a more specific way than adjectives such as "greater," "lesser," or even "major." Notable relics must always consist of a body part, and, as a rule, they must be bigger (and better) than their non-notable counterparts. Non-notable relics extend to include the smaller or less important body parts of saints, as well as the material objects associated with the saints. Moreover, while all notable relics are body-part relics, not all body-part relics are large enough to be considered notable – a point Reginald Pecock makes clear.

Pecock, probably born in Wales *ca.* 1390, is best known for his energetic written defence of mainstream church practices against heretical challenges. Educated at Oxford, Pecock garnered national attention in 1447 for having preached a controversial sermon in London; his vernacular apologia for orthodoxy was treated, thereafter, as suspect.[62] Kirsty Campbell identifies Pecock as a key part of the "capacious" vernacular theology of fifteenth-century England; in her reading, Pecock "thinks big" and wishes to launch a "mass educational program" for the laity.[63] In this context, Pecock's defence of relics, which directly engages with dissent, has much to tell us about the construction of relics' symbolism and about resistance to this symbolism. In chapter 8, supposition 3 of *The Repressor of Overmuch Blaming of the Clergy* (*c.* 1449) – part of the section on pilgrimage – Pecock takes up different aspects of material devotional culture (images, shrines, and relics) and constructs them as distinct.[64] As he works to justify relics' presence in shrines in churches across England, he allows that

> In a cuntrey where that of a Seint can not be had his bodi or bonis or eny relik of him, it is resonable and worthi that an ymage of him be mad and be sett vp in place into which peple mai come forto it biholde ... And sithen of Crist crucified and of Marie his modir we han not the bodies or bonis, neithir in ech cuntre is eny relik had of hem, therfore it muste needis be more resonable and more worthi that in dyuerse placis of cuntrees be maad ymagis of Crist crucified and of his modir Marie. (I 183)

Pecock alludes to supply and demand, for certainly not every church or even every cathedral had a major saint or shrine. A simple enough point; but in making it, Pecock asserts a hierarchy of devotional objects, one that privileges saints' bodies over images, and one that privileges some kinds of relics over others. After all, images are most appropriate "in a cuntrey where that of a Seint can not be had his bodi or bonis or eny relik of him" (I 183). Pecock does not speak of a relic as a kind of image; rather, he presents an image as a worthy substitute when no relic can be had.

What is more, Pecock delineates several different kinds of relics: the "bodi," the "bonis," and "eny relik." He thereby anticipates later canon law in constructing three categories of relics: Pecock presumably means "bodi" to denote whole ("notable") relics; "bonis" would seem to designate piecemeal relics, a tooth perhaps, or a finger ("non-notable," or lesser body-part relics, though it is possible that a bone could be larger – a thighbone, say – and hence notable); and "eny relik" functions much like the Latin "reliquiae" in relic lists[65]: as a catch-all term for miscellaneous relics. In keeping with many mainstream and reformist thinkers, Pecock rejects the notion of "eny relik" of Christ or Mary (though passion relics elsewhere appear in a category of their own in, for example, Flete's relic list of Westminster Abbey).[66] The text sets up a causal relationship between the absence of relics and the need for images: "*sithen* of Crist crucified and of Marie his modir we han not the bodies ... *therfore* it muste needis be ... maad ymagis of Crist crucified and of his modir Marie" (I 183; emphasis added). In discounting the possibility of relics of Jesus and his mother, Pecock again emphasizes the function of images: they serve when no relic can be had. Pecock's discursive hierarchy thus runs as follows: notable body-part relics; non-notable body-part relics; other, non-notable, non-body-part relics; and last, images, which will do the trick in a pinch.

This tendency to treat different kinds of relics as distinct does not begin in the fifteenth century.[67] The language of a thirteenth-century relic list from Durham Cathedral similarly presents a hierarchy of devotional objects. This list affirms that not all relics were viewed equally – not every part was understood to be as good as the whole.[68] Cuthbert's body leads off this list, and it is described as follows: "The body of St Cuthbert, with its flesh and bones and totally whole, as if it were living" ("Corpus sancti Cuthberti cum carne et ossibus, et totum integrum, quasi adhuc esset vivus").[69] The author describes no other relic in this list as if it were alive. Moreover, the appositive "et totum integrum" differentiates between Cuthbert's body and the other "bone" ("os") and "flesh" ("carnis") relics on the list, which are neither incorrupt nor entire. This single clause creates a separate class of relic, as it were: the whole body relic, set apart from other body-part relics. By using such specific language, the author presents Cuthbert's incorrupt and lifelike body as having greater value than, say, "the relics of St Edward, Martyr" ("reliquiae sancti Edwardi martiris"),[70] which are not described in exact terms.

In some instances, authors of relic lists present partial relics as if they were whole: in a 1315 relic list from Canterbury Cathedral, for example, Swithun's head is listed not as "head" ("caput") (as are other head relics, which immediately follow Swithun's entry), but rather as "body" ("corpus").[71] In this instance, language confers value on what should have been, according to the next section of relics, a less prestigious body part than many of the relics in the "corpus" category.[72] Similarly, in the sixth century, Wilfrid attempted to present what were very likely *brandea* – pieces of cloth that had been placed in close proximity to a saint – as if they were bodies.[73] Wilfrid thus imparts to contact relics the prestige associated with full-body relics: in a manner of speaking, rather than building shrines for the relics he had, Wilfrid invents relics for the shrines he built. So, too, the lexicon of these thirteenth- and fourteenth-century lists sets whole bodies – and other body-part relics, such as heads and arms – apart from the various "ossa" and "reliquae" included in most relic lists.[74]

As should be obvious by this point, relic lists are not merely descriptive. Throughout the fourteenth-century Canterbury list, in which we find Swithun's head listed as "corpus," the author presents relics in such a way as to suggest relative value: it begins with whole bodies (e.g., "corpus sancti Thome Martyris"), the locations of which are stipulated. It is worth quoting the first few, to gain a sense of how this list constructs their importance:

> The body of St Thomas the Martyr, in his feretory.
> The body of St Alphege, in his feretory next to the high altar.
> The body of St Dunstan, in his feretory next to the high altar, facing the south.
>
> (Corpus sancti Thome Martyris In feretro suo.
> Corpus sancti Aelphegi In feretro suo juxta magnum altare.
> Corpus sancti Dunstani In feretro suo juxta magnum altare versus austrum.)[75]

And so on. The author here presents other whole-body relics (and indeed, all other relics) of Canterbury Cathedral as having value relative to that of Thomas Becket – simply to write "in feretro suo" was sufficient. The author describes the location of no other body so simply. The rest of the relics are subdivided into categories depending both on their location and type. Heads (e.g., "Caput santi Blasij") "are stored in the great reliquary chest next to the high altar" ("in magno armariolo reliquiarum juxta magnum altare continentur").[76] The list moves on to "arms of saints" ("Brachia sanctorum"), also stored in the relic cupboard with the heads. After this, we have a list of cross reliquaries and their contents. These contain multiple (and presumably, necessarily, smaller) relics. All of the relics in this inventory were kept in a cupboard of some kind, and while a few were stored "in a crystal phylactery" ("in filacterio cristallino"), such as Mary's hair or St Edmund's blood,[77] many more were kept in wooden or golden crosses and other reliquaries. Moreover, of the relics kept in a crystal reliquary, none are among the most prestigious relics of the cathedral, instead consisting of, for example, some "bones of the Holy Innocents" ("de ossibus sanctorum Innocentium"), or "A finger and tooth of St Alban" ("Digitus et dens sancti Albani").[78] It is unlikely that any of these would have been displayed openly; they would be stored instead in Canterbury's great relic cupboard or in reliquary chests kept on the reredos.[79] While some pilgrims may have valued their small and personal relics, there seems little doubt as to how – lexically and visually – the pilgrim experience at Canterbury was *constructed*: as one in which not all relics were equal.

Authors of relic lists categorize these lesser relics using words as varied and specific as "os," "carnis," "dens," and "reliqua."[80] It is frequently (though not always) the case that relics designated "corpus," "brachium," or "caput" are more highly valued than the fragmentary or smaller relics, many of which are not accorded a category as precise as "dens," for instance.[81] Richard of Sedgebrook, Cuthbert's custodian at the time he wrote Durham Cathedral's 1383 relic list, usually describes the kind of relic, with the exception of unidentified "diverse" relics: "Item capsa argentea cum cathena argentea cum diversis reliquiis beate Marie Magdalene" ("Item, a silver case with pure silver, containing many relics of Blessed Mary Magdalene")[82], or the more frequent "reliquiis sine billis" ("relics without writing").[83] Relics without writing may even be considered meaningless, undefined. Certainly such relics are not portrayed as having the same value as Cuthbert's body.

Constructing the Relic in Saints' Lives: The Incorrupt Body

For the most part, then, written accounts tend to privilege relics that are large and, better still, undecayed. Later medieval lives and miracles of Ss Æthelthryth, Werburge, and Cuthbert emphasize the incorrupt bodies of these saints, similarly foregrounding the importance of the complete body, "totum integrum." These accounts indicate the pervasive influence of relic discourse in late medieval England, and in presenting whole and inaccessible bodies as the consummate objects, they also suggest a clear difference between the cult of relics and other devotional objects to which the lay faithful had greater access. Henry Bradshaw, for instance, a sixteenth-century monk imbricated in the local politics of early sixteenth-century Chester, was invested in Werburge insofar as she manifested both the Anglo-Saxon past and the local politics of the present.[84] For Cynthia Turner Camp, the "unchanging nature of [incorrupt] bodies" – like that of Werburge herself – demonstrates "how these miraculously preserved cadavers belie not only the process of decay, but also the passage of time. Existing in its own never-ending present, the incorrupt corpse can continuously manifest its historical moment, providing the present with a direct, unmediated encouter with the past."[85] But at the same time, encounters with relics as noteworthy as those of Werburge were often heavily mediated both by shrines and by relic discourse.[86] Even before her body decays, then, Werburge's relics do not necessarily offer unmediated access to the past – though, as Camp suggests, Bradshaw clearly values Werburge's body more highly before it decomposes than after. That said, when Bradshaw spends time depicting the virgin saint's incorrupt body, he participates in the same discursive activity as when, after the body decays, he elides her body with the shrine that contains it. In both cases, relic discourse subsumes the body of this saint to metaphor and to the shrine, while maintaining the integral body as the ideal object.

In his early sixteenth-century *The Life of Saint Werburge of Chester* (before 1513), Bradshaw describes the discovery of Werburge's incorrupt body as follows:

> And as eche man thought by naturall reason
> Nothyng shulde remayn of that blessed body
> But the bare boones / all els to resolucion:
> The couerture remoued by the sayd clergy,
> The corps hole and sounde was funde, verely,
> Apperyng to them / on slepe as she had ben,
> Nothyng depaired / that ther coude be seen.
> Her vesture appered hole, clere and white,
> No parte consumed / for all the longe space,
> Fragrant in odoure / repleit with delite,
> As at the fyrst season whan she buried was;
> But whan discouered was her swete face,
> Beauty appered more white than the lile,
> Mixt with rose colour, / moost faire for to se.[87]

Like the description of Cuthbert's body in the relic list, the passage gives us Werburge's body as if it were alive – as if it were "on slepe," not dead, so beautiful that it is "more white than the lile." Bradshaw indicates that this state is a surprise to the onlookers, who "thought by naturall reason" that only her "bare boones" will be left – "all els to resolucion." As Bradshaw would have it, those present fully expect her flesh ("all els") to have decayed. But her "corps" is found "hole and sounde," the contrast merely emphasizing Werburge's virtue. The author of a fifteenth-century redaction of his life and miracles describes Cuthbert's body similarly. There, as at the translation of Werburge's body, those present expect to find "þat [Cuthbert's] flessh' rotyn had bene" (3882), only to discover the body "all' hale," "As a man were leuand, / To a slepand man mare lyke / Þan to a dede man."[88] Though Bradshaw does not explicitly mention Werburge's flesh, the thwarted expectations of "ech man" – that there will be no flesh, only bones – tell us that, just as Cuthbert's body is said to survive "cum carne et ossibus, et totum integrum, quasi adhuc esset vivus" (or as in his fifteenth-century *vita*, "all' hale,"), Werburge's body defies nature by surviving "cum carne et ossibus." It is clearly an important point to Bradshaw: he spends five stanzas describing her body, which is beautiful and fragrant in death.

Even Bradshaw's explanation for Werburge's eventual decay privileges the entire body over bones or dust. Her incorrupt body only succumbs to "naturall resolution" in order to preserve her honour from the Vikings, who threaten to touch and defile "her body / by indignation" (1.3474). (The corollary is that, if the Vikings had never arrived, the body would have remained whole.) In this section, Bradshaw must therefore affirm that it *is* acceptable *not* to have Werburge's body. God preserved many English saints; but many others, Bradshaw allows, were slain or devoured by beasts. Early martyrs – including St Stephen – worked miracles even in the absence of their entire corpses. So, too, Bradshaw avers, Werburge will work greater miracles "in her body resolued to naturall consumption" (1.3509). Bradshaw thus avers that Werburge's decayed body will be even more potent than her incorrupt body had been. Bradshaw spends six stanzas on this issue, one more than he allotted to describing the undefiled body in the first place. His insistence that it is *not* problematic to have only bones or ashes – that these kinds of relics are just as good as Werburge's entire body had been – both reveals a need to defend the efficacy, indeed, the sanctity, of Werburge's decayed remains and reaffirms the superiority of the whole body. That Bradshaw must defend Werburge's ability to perform miracles suggests that there were those who took her decayed body as a sign that she no longer could.

Like Bradshaw's *Werburge*, an early fifteenth-century life of Æthelthryth, *Vita S. Etheldredae Eliensis* (*c.* 1420) – based largely on the twelfth-century *Liber Eliensis* – constructs a discursive hierarchy of relics, in which the saint's incorrupt and whole body is the consummate object.[89] The *Etheldreda* poet offers exquisite detail of Æthelthryth's seventh-century translation, when all who are present see the body, which is said to look the same as it did in life. But in contrast to Bradshaw, who admits openly that Werburge's body eventually decomposes, the

Etheldreda poet insists that Æthelthryth remained incorrupt in the tenth century, when some doubted the integrity of her body. He does so without giving the reader (or any character) a glimpse of the body itself. Instead, the poem relies on a punishment miracle included in the *Liber Eliensis*, wherein a canon suffers for attempting to see whether Æthelthryth's body has in fact decayed. The *Etheldreda* poet thus understands what Æthelthryth's body is from *what is written about it*. And in turn, insofar as the *Vita* – not the body itself – enables us to interpret the relic, Æthelthryth's body exists as a discursive object: writing confirms its transcendent status.

In his rendition of Æthelthryth's seventh-century translation, the *Etheldreda* author highlights the continued importance of the saint's body, expanding upon descriptions of it in the *Liber Eliensis* and employing many of the same topoi Bradshaw uses. The result is a blazon to Æthelthryth's perfection. Her body is said to be

> As whyte, as rody and as freysshe
> Hurre fayre body was þer as hit þo lay,
> And with-ouȝt ony corrupcione of hurre fleysshe,
> Ryȝt as þaw hit hadde ben leyde with-in þe chest þat same day;
> Hurre lures weron white as ony lely floure,
> …
> Hurre body lay þer as semely in euerichemonnus syȝt,
> Ryȝt a-lyue as þaw hit ȝet were. (838–42, 850–1)

The text yokes together Æthelthryth's purity in life with her body after death. As this poem would have it, Æthelthryth's relic is unique because it is not really like most relics: it appears as though it were "ryȝt a-lyue"; it is, like the love object in a courtly blazon, "semely," "rody," "freysshe," and "fayre." Having detailed her beauty, and elaborating on the passage found in the *Liber Eliensis*, the *Etheldreda* poet then insists that everyone *saw* the body. After a procession to the abbey, those present are said to lay the body on the high altar, where the relic is displayed

> Opynliche … in eueriche monnus syȝt,
> Þat euery mon myȝt clereliche & welle loke þer-vpone,
> To merueylle vpone hurre colour so bryȝt.
> And when eueryche mon hadde rediliche y-sey þat fayre body,
> Ryȝt at hurre owne plesauns & at hurre owne wylle … (867–71)

Adverbs such as "opynliche," "clereliche," and "rediliche" foreground the action of this passage and allow the poet to emphasize that onlookers catch more than a glimpse of the body. Repetition functions similarly: "eueriche monnus syȝt, / Þat euery mon"; and again, "eueryche mon" in the next stanza. According to the text, no monk contests the body's incorruption; all see it.

In placing such an emphasis on the need to see a body to verify its state, the *Etheldreda* author inadvertently sets up the possibility that by the tenth century, it is no longer whole and perfect. The *Etheldreda* author follows his source, the *Liber Eliensis*, in describing Æthelthryth as incorrupt ("intentata"), even though no one sees her body ("inconspecta").[90] Both accounts presuppose Æthelthryth's body to be whole, even though, in contrast to the earlier period, it is never exposed. Writing instantiates the incorrupt relic: the punishment narrative of a "seculere chanoun" (987), Cerdyke, who attempts to ascertain the body's state, affirms the wholeness of Æthelthryth's hidden body in a way the occluded relic itself cannot. In this punishment miracle, the *Etheldreda* narrative is at odds with itself, suggesting simultaneously that the canon should accept the saint's incorruption on authoritative tradition, but also that perhaps he (like his seventh-century forbears) has a right to see.

According to the *Etheldreda* poet, Cerdyke lets his curiosity get the better of him: rather than respecting Æthelthryth's privacy (and the authority of the institution of which he is a part), he visits the saint's tomb and peers through a hole he chisels in its side. But he does not stop there: he attempts, even once he can see the relic, to move aside Æthelthryth's clothing, the better to see whether her body is really incorrupt (998–1007). He fails; his candle goes out, and Æthelthryth herself ensures that he sees "no-thyng y-wys" (1015). The *Etheldreda* poet makes two important alterations to the text of the *Liber*, both of which emphasize vision.[91] First, according to the *Liber*, the offending party dies;[92] in the *Vita S. Etheldredae* Cerdyke is merely struck blind (1020). Second, the *Liber* author blames invading Vikings for having bored a hole in Æthelthryth's shrine in the ninth century.[93] By contrast, as the *Etheldreda* author would have it, Cerdyke is himself responsible for the hole and even sets up a candle, the better by which to see Æthelthryth.[94] Juxtaposed with the poem's account of "eueryche mon" seeing the body – and given the punishment, which is far less severe than in the *Liber* – Cerdyke's fate reminds the reader about the importance of vision, implying that some things may need to be seen in order to be believed. The unarticulated corollary is that, in spite of his transgressive behaviour, Cerdyke is on to something: is the occluded body really whole? Does the *Etheldreda* poet worry that the body had decayed and therefore suggest that only the morally corrupt, like Cerdyke, would try to see it? At the same time, given both Cerdyke's failure to see and the author's *written* insistence on Æthelthryth's incorruption, it seems clear that this text presents authoritative and written tradition as perfectly sufficient for interpreting a relic.

As these examples suggest, whatever the practices – which included, inter alia, giving small relics as gifts to ecclesiastical and royal dignitaries who attended a translation – written accounts often privilege the undefiled and intact body. Elaborate and opaque shrines, while disassociating the shrine from the saint, simultaneously affirmed that his or her body remained whole (or, at the least, capable of working miracles). As will become apparent in the following discussion of Guibert and Thiofrid, shrines were either ideal or entirely inappropriate symbols – in both cases because the shrine could figure forth something that might not be, something that language *had to affirm was there*. While for Guibert, relics comprise human matter, for Thiofrid, relics supersede the human matter they comprise. These theologians thus offer two of the most radical approaches to representing relics: as absolutely other, or as human. Yet, while Thiofrid and Guibert hardly see eye to eye on the question of reliquaries, they both address the relationship between relics and the written tradition and would agree that, without writing, it is nearly impossible to interpret a reliquary or relic.

Writing Relics: The Treasure Metaphor in Guibert of Nogent and Thiofrid of Echternach

This section argues for the symbiotic relationship between Guibert's critique of enshrinement, on the one hand, and his privileging of the written tradition, on the other. Unlike Thiofrid, Guibert views treasure as antithetical to body parts. In *De sanctis et eorum pigneribus*, *c.* 1119, he therefore rejects treasure as an appropriate metaphor for holiness or for relics.[95] What disturbs Guibert, in other words, "are pointless wonderworks perpetrated through obvious fraud and spread by clerics mainly anxious to collect cash."[96] His invective against the monks of Soissons, who laid claim to a baby tooth of Christ, inspires him to expound against abuses in general; from Guibert's perspective, gold, silver, and gems cannot easily signify a decaying body:

> As far as I know, God has not said to anyone yet living or to come: "You are gold or silver, and to gold or silver you shall return." ["aurum vel

> argentum es, in aurum vel argentum ibis."] So why, I ask, should a human being be removed from the natural elements (still less by the order of God) and be enclosed in gold or silver cases ["aureis vel argenteis conculis inseratur"], which are not required for purposes of preservation ... Surely if the bodies of the saints remained in the places assigned them by nature – that is, in their graves ["sua iuxta naturae debitum loca, id est sepulcra"] – then errors of the sort I have encountered would not exist. But, as it is, these bodies are removed from their tombs ["tumulis eruuntur"], their limbs carried in every direction, and, under the pretext of piety, opportunities arise to display them.[97]

In this passage, Guibert argues that the elevation and translation of relics occlude the common fate we all share and deserve ("commereri humana natura" [I 604]): the return to dust. As Wyclif would later object, Guibert suggests that an opulent reliquary enables the creation of relics out of "pars persona empte" – just about anything.[98] As Guibert puts it, by enabling the "replacement of common bones for holy relics" ("ossa vulgaria pro sanctorum pigneribus" [I 598]),[99] enshrinement encourages fraud. His concern is clearly with abuses and with the proliferation of non-notable and fake relics, for if no body were exhumed or translated, there would be no error. His premise is nevertheless that saints' bodies share the same nature as all other bodies, none of which consist of gold and silver. In this context, the adornment of reliquaries is entirely incommensurate with what is inside. Translation and enshrinement thus efface what the relic has in common with the supplicant: the body, the inevitability of decay, and the promise of resurrection.

According to this logic, none would ever see a saint's relic, for the body would always remain undisturbed, in the ground – "sua iuxta naturae debitum loca, id est sepulcra." But while Guibert disparages opulent reliquaries, he does not present as a solution that relics be exposed to view. Instead, Guibert maintains that relics derive their meaning largely from "being interpreted through a text," from "a variety of textual proofs," in Brian Stock's turn of phrase.[100] For Guibert, writing and "timeworn tradition" (Head 406) comprise the only definitive ways to discern whether a saint is legitimate. But not any narrative will do. It must be accurate; it must not "ring falsely" nor contain "inanities" (407); it must "strengthen ... the faith" (406). Guibert thus complains about having to "reread with utter loathing" an account claiming sanctity for a man who, having "drunk past the point of being sober,

[had] fallen down a well, and thus died" (407). Only these accounts – only language – reveals the *vita* as fabricated. This instance illustrates not only Guibert's frustration with the circulation of fake relics, but also his unstated argument that one need never view a body in order to know whether it is genuinely holy. In a way, this emphasis on authoritative and linguistic tradition subtends his argument against translation: no ceremony, no body, generates meaning for a relic as effectively as writing.

Just as such a false narrative might impugn a putative saint (408), an authoritative narrative confirms a saint and his relic as holy. Guibert thus derives the meaning of relics from language – specific kinds of writing and eyewitness testimony (417), to be sure, but language all the same. Such is Guibert's stance in discussing the supposed body of St Firminus:

> When my predecessor ... transferred what he thought to be the body of St Firminus the martyr from one casket to another, he failed to discover any document inside, not even a single letter of testimony as to who lay there ... For which reason the bishop [of Amiens] forthwith had an inscription made on a leaden plate, which would lie in the reliquary: "This is Firminus the martyr, bishop of Amiens." Not long afterward, the incident was repeated in a similar manner at the monastery of Saint-Denis. Relics were taken forth from their resting place in order to be placed in a more ornate shrine ... When the skull was unwrapped along with the bones, a slip of parchment was found in the martyr's nostrils, on which it was written that *this* body was Firminus ... [But] does [this] claim become valid merely by being written down? (417–18; I 551–67)

When relics themselves are hidden (as Guibert advocates they should be, "sua iuxta naturae debitum loca, id est sepulcra"), written descriptions of relics are crucial for determining the value of any relic. It is not acceptable to have a body with *no* written identification, as the behaviour of the bishop of Amiens makes clear. We all know that the practical purpose of such identification is to ensure authenticity and curb the circulation of fakes.[101] But these written documents also indicate that it is very difficult (if not impossible) to *interpret* a relic without language. Authenticity is not, in other words, the only issue.

In privileging textual tradition, Guibert predicates his treatise on the idea that relics are not intelligible on their own – they require interpretation. As Stock observes of Guibert's logic, "a 'body' covers a relic's 'spirit,' which is then interpreted by a text ... And this requires an interpreter."[102] Paradoxically, in *De pigneribus*, because relics comprise human bodies, they should remain hidden – the corollary being that writing is the best and even the only way to generate their meaning. I think it is thus inaccurate to say that Guibert is anti-relic, possessed of "a general revulsion at the body,"[103] though he is clearly enraged by clerical abuses.[104] Instead, Guibert worries about abuses that stem from associating relics too closely with the (literal and figurative) treasure that stands for sainthood and heaven.

Shrines as Metaphors for Saints: Thiofrid of Echternach

In one of the longest surviving (and yet most neglected) treatises on relics, Thiofrid of Echternach – a contemporary of Guibert's – argues for the absolute difference between saints' bodies and other bodies and for the consequent need to enshrine relics in opulent monuments.[105] These monuments are, for Thiofrid, the ideal way to figure forth the privileged status of God's chosen. Thiofrid wrote this treatise, *Flores epytaphii sanctorum*, sometime between 1098 and 1105.[106] Divided into four *libri*, each of which deals thematically with an aspect of relics, the *Flores* survives in only two copies. In Book I, Thiofrid explains the status of relics as privileged matter sanctified by Christ, as the treasure ("thesaurus") of Christ, in Books III and IV, the significance of non-notable contact relics (such as clothing or instruments of torture). In Book II, the focal point for the following discussion, Thiofrid insists that elaborate shrines are the only appropriate way to convey the value of this treasure. In advancing an argument for the importance of shrines, the *Flores* paradoxically affirms the contingent relationship between reliquaries and relics: there is no essential sense in which the one stands for the other.

Here, I will demonstrate that for Thiofrid, relics derive their meaning not just from enshrinement but, specifically, from metaphor. Lavish metaphors enable the supplicant to interpret and understand the relic. Enshrinement thus facilitates (rather than inhibits, as Guibert would argue) the interpretation of relics. And yet, Thiofrid also presupposes that relics are always already possessed of a stable meaning; in order to comprehend a relic's power, one need only look at a shrine. Nevertheless, in order to explain the relic's authority, Thiofrid relies on the metaphoric relationship between the holy object and the monument that contains it. Thiofrid claims to be talking about the relic, but in the end, he tells us only what the relic *resembles*, depending on figurative language to convey a reality he simultaneously takes to be self-evident.

The relic per se is not intelligible without figurative language (what it is like) and negation (what it is not). In one conceit, Thiofrid describes the relic, which is not the soul, as *like* the soul:

> And so, just as the soul is not visible in the body and nevertheless does wondrous things through the body, so the treasure of this precious dust, even though it cannot be seen or touched, nevertheless … transfers the abundance of its holiness into all the materials that conceal it both inside and outside [scil. the reliquary]. (II 3.12–16)
>
> (Atque ut ipsa anima in corpore non uidetur et tamen mira per corpus operatur sic preciosi pulueris thesaurus licet non uideatur, licet non tangatur sanctitatis tamen affluentiam … transmittit in omnia in quibus intra et extra occultatur.)

In this extended simile, Thiofrid explains that, just as the soul is hidden ("occultatur") in the body, the "precious dust" is concealed by the reliquary. He thus renders the relationship between the reliquary and relic intelligible in terms of something else. While the purpose of this argument is to describe the relic as something that always already has miraculous power, this passage works instead to *instill* this power in the relic. Thiofrid's own repeated emphasis on transference underscores the degree to which interpreting relics depends on the generative power of metaphor. In this process, the relic takes on the qualities of its metaphor – relics are treasure ("thesauri," "tanti thesauri," "tanti precii thesaurus," and so on), not souls, not even saints.[107] As each transference takes place, the heavenly mysteries of the relic are further removed from the viewer, who sees not the soul, nor the relic, but the reliquary.

In the context of the *Flores*, this deferral is necessary. Thiofrid argues that relics are more precious than gold or gems; gem-encrusted reliquaries thus offer the best metaphoric approximation of the merits of the saints. Gold comprises the best (temporal) way to demonstrate that the "paltry dust [of saints' relics] is more precious than worldly gold" ("preciosior est puluis exiguus auro mundo") (II 2.37). The reliquary thereby takes on the status of the relic, displacing the saint's body altogether. The common human nature, which Guibert emphasizes, is lost. Thiofrid creates in the relic a distinct substance, characterized by superlative metaphors. In one such comparison, Thiofrid likens a relic to the substance of the Eucharist (blood and flesh), and reliquaries to the accident (the bread). In this paradigm, the host is an impenetrable reliquary, whose contents are visible only in the context of a Eucharistic miracle. The shrine, like the Host itself, expresses the mystery of its substance:

> If with the touch of faith one feels [a relic's] outer enclosure of gold and silver leaf ... [it is] as if one were touching the very thing hidden within, in this way the power of divine majesty works "salvation in the midst of the earth" [cf. Ps. 73:12]. (II 3.18–22)

> (Si constantissimae manu fidei exterior eius attrectetur clausula auri ac argenti bratea ... ac si hoc tangatur quod interius occultatur, sic diuinae maiestatis potentia salutem in medio terrae suae operatur.)

While Thiofrid elsewhere suggests that the saint's soul empowers the relic, in this passage he would seem to acknowledge that instead, the metaphor (the shrine) enables us to interpret the relic. In this context, to perceive the vehicle (the shrine) is to comprehend the power of the tenor (the relic). The power of the relic resembles that of the Eucharist; it also resembles that of the saintly soul. But what is it, *in itself*? With each metaphor, Thiofrid's treatise affirms (even as it denies) that relics pose a hermeneutic challenge. The need to occlude major relics in elaborate shrines merely emphasizes this challenge. Whether Thiofrid was concerned with the practical side of such occlusion – keeping pilgrims at a distance – is difficult to say. But there is no doubt that Thiofrid regards such occlusion as a necessary component of expressing the meaning of relics. In insisting that relics stand for something other than what they are (bodies and body parts), Thiofrid eschews the possibility of interpreting the bodies *themselves*.

And yet, Thiofrid justifies the enshrinement of relics by arguing for relics' latent potency – by suggesting, in other words, that power emanates from the relic itself:

> Thus the power of that holy soul which already reigns with God is miraculously conveyed from its innermost recesses to the outermost things that pertain to it, both while it is imprisoned in the flesh and after it has been elevated to citizenship in the heavenly Jerusalem; and whatever miraculous quality [that soul] bears through flesh and bone by virtue of those merits that go before it and intercede on its behalf, more wondrously still does it transfer ["transfundit"] that quality from its decomposed remains ["de

dissoluto puluere"] into all the substances, of whatever material or worth, used to cover or adorn dust so great as this (II 3.3–11).

(Sic sanctae uis animae cum Deo iam regnantis ab intimis ad extima ad se cum in carnis carcere clausam tum in caelestis Hierusalem municipatum translatam pertinentia se mirifice diffundit, et quicquid sanctis preuenientibus ac intercaedentibus meritis per carnem et ossa mirabile gerit idem mirabilius de dissoluto puluere in omnia tam exteriora quam interiora cuiuscumque materiae uel precii tantae fauillae ornamenta et operimenta <scil. corporum sanctorum> transfundit.)[108]

In this configuration, the soul of the saint – not the language, nor the shrine – confers power and sanctity on the relic. The relic then imbues the shrine with its *virtus* and meaning. Given that this power resides in the relic itself, it stands to reason that one should be able to identify any relic as holy just by looking at it. Nevertheless, as Thiofrid's language here suggests, the relationship between shrine and relic, between relic and soul, is constituted through transference ("transfundit"). In this respect, the relic acts as the mechanism for imparting the saint's *virtus* to the shrine. While Thiofrid presents the shrine as an important, even a priori representation of sanctity, he nonetheless reveals that to understand this sanctity, one must understand what the reliquary signifies (the saint in heaven) and how (through transference). Even as this section posits the latent *virtus* of the relic (actualized by the soul, "conveyed from its innermost recesses to the outermost things that pertain to it"), it also relies on the notion that, without an explanation – a gloss of what the metaphor means, if you will – whatever is in the "innermost recesses" will remain hidden. Without this explication, even the shrine – let alone the relic – cannot be understood.

Relics are thus unlike images in that frequently, what pilgrims saw was at two removes from what the relic was supposed to represent. In a way, images did not need representation; they themselves signified the communion of saints. Whether such images really could serve as "libri laicorum" was a subject for debate.[109] But while an image or statue was often decorated to resemble its saint[110] – so much so that, as Kathleen Kamerick comments, images "remained the focus of mistrust and anxiety that the simple laity would worship the art itself, rather than the holy people it represented"[111] – major relics were usually ensconced in feretories that did not necessarily tell the story of the relic, let alone of the saint, heavenly rewards, and resurrection.[112] Representing relics, the title and subject of this chapter, was a tricky business. The prominence of metaphor and technical terminology in descriptions of relics is thus not surprising, as writers struggled to make sense of these devotional objects. Indeed, Thiofrid invokes medieval discussions of translation (and, by extention, of metaphor and metonym) when he explains enshrinement using a common image to explain translation (the clothed body) and when he presents the relic's power as transferring ("transfundit") to the shrine.[113] He presents the reliquary as a "skillfully wrought garment" ("arteque elaboratas uestes"; II 1.59). Here, to be translated is to be clothed in "the softest and finest garments" available ("mollibus et exquisitissimus uestiantur"; II 1.75–81). At every juncture, Thiofrid privileges the signifying power of the container over the "thing contained." As in the relic lists and hagiographical accounts with which I opened this chapter, relic discourse enables Thiofrid to construct the relative value of different bodies and body parts.

In presenting some relics as more valuable and powerful than others, the texts considered thus far both shape and reflect religious practice at relic sites. We should keep the various kind of relics in mind when supplicants succeed or fail to access relics in medieval literary texts, for often enough, the circumstances under which a given character (virtuous, chaste) accesses a relic are prescribed by the discourse itself. Characters such as Chaucer's Pardoner offer access to non-notable (and fake) relics; and very often, as the next chapter will demonstrate, only supplicants depicted as paradigms of virtue approach notable relics with impunity. Cult centers made use of discourse to construct the value of the relic as other, as superhuman (even while the relic itself comprised human remains), as having far greater power and value than that possessed by any of the supplicants who visited it, no matter how high their social status. By extension, writings about the social meaning and function of relics are often also about the social meaning and function of the shrine. For, as chapter 2 takes up, relic discourse enables the presentation of shrines *as* relics, complicating any simple understanding of just what the term "relik" might designate – and challenging us to rethink our assumption that medieval relics consist primarily of "holy fragments."

Chapter Two

The Commonplaces of Relic Discourse: The Pilgrim at the Shrine

A miracle story from John Lydgate's *Extra Miracles of St Edmund*, *c*. 1444, suggests that Lydgate instills in his supplicants a willingness to recognize St Edmund's shrine both as Edmund's miracle-working centre and as Edmund himself:[1]

> Alle of assent with reuerence we shal seke
> Thyn hooly place, oold and yong of age,
> With greet avys, lowe our selff and meke,
> Contryt of herte, sobre of our visage.
> With this avowh come on pylgrymage
> Affor thy shryne to thy royal presence,
> Prostrat afor the with ffeithfful hool corage,
> To our prayere tyl thou yive audience. (*EM* 313–20)[2]

This passage predicates the need to go on pilgrimage on the desire to be close to the saint – as both the neighbours and the parents of the drowned child articulate in unison, to be in his "royal presence." John Lydgate (*c*. 1370–1449), monk of Bury and closely associated with the Lancastrian regime,[3] gives these pilgrims an unwavering belief in *praesentia*, or the saint's absolute and powerful presence at the place of his relics. But insofar as Lydgate emphasizes Edmund's shrine and its location at the abbey, he effaces the relics themselves and associates *praesentia* with the shrine, instead. We are left with a question: what establishes a saint's *praesentia* and heavenly power? The occluded relic? The lavish shrine? The written history of the saint's prowess? Throughout his narrative – with the exception of his description of the discovery and rejoining of the saint's head and body – Lydgate seldom refers to the relics themselves. The text does not, that is, generate *praesentia* only from Edmund's relics. Instead, the interplay and tension between text and image in Harley 2278 create the *praesentia* that is often imagined, instead, simply to emanate from the saint's body.

This chapter will argue that, just as relic discourse creates the significance of relics through technical terminology and metaphor, it also establishes a relic's *praesentia* – a crucial part of the relic's meaning – through certain important commonplaces. I have organized these commonplaces into two broad categories. The first group comprises descriptions of shrines and relics that make little or no linguistic distinction between these two material objects; the second, the role of relic custodians in encouraging this association between reliquary and saint. I begin by addressing the commonplaces of the first group, including the necessity of translating a saint at night, the elision of shrine and saint, and the supplicant's (bad or good) behaviour. The chapter ends with an examination of how the relic custodian both affirms and sometimes even produces the technical terminology, metaphors, and commonplaces of relic discourse. By restricting access to the saint (as Cynthia Hahn has speculated relic custodians may have done) or creating "certain expectations" at the shrine,[4] custodians communicated the saint's importance and miracle-working presence. Relic custodians thereby helped to create a saint's *praesentia*, just as pilgrim behaviour helped to affirm it.

My contention here is ultimately that the relationship between the container and the contained depends largely upon individual points of view. The reliquary does not necessarily have the intrinsic value that we have assumed. *Praesentia*, for instance, is surely a manufactured rather than inherent attribute of saints' cults in medieval England – an attribute generated both by the written descriptions of relics I discussed in chapter 1 and by the accounts of translations and shrines I examine here.[5] Put another way, the occlusion of major relics in feretory shrines contributed to the linguistic and literary construction of sanctity. This linguistic construction – relic discourse – shares much in common with physical shrines. Both the reliquary and the discourse ostensibly signify both the relic and what it represents: both contain, literally or figuratively, the relic. These issues are critical to our understanding not only of the development of saints' cults from the twelfth through sixteenth centuries in England, but also how this development reflected some of the same concerns as the image debate. Writings about relics, as about images, foreground the issue of what the shrine represents and (implicitly or explicitly) whether this material form would be distracting to the laity. A central question of both the image debate and relic discourse, in other words, is the proper representation of heavenly sanctity. The commonplaces of relic discourse suggest the difficulty in figuratively signifying a relic. In displacing the relic entirely, for instance, the elision of shrine and saint implies that the relic itself cannot generate meaning. Translation, on the other hand, suggests that to be understood, relics must be hidden, both in their shrines and by the language clerics use to describe them.

The translation narratives I consider here are from English chronicles and miracle stories from the twelfth through fourteenth centuries and from stand-alone hagiographies from the fifteenth and sixteenth centuries. These sources are records of English saints and holy places from precisely the period when cathedral shrines evolved from the earlier, smaller tomb shrines to the gargantuan feretories of the later English Middle Ages.[6] My choice of material represents both Latin and English translation accounts throughout the period in which English shrine architecture radically changed. Both narratives of translation and the elision of shrine and saint express the close connection between shrine and rhetoric: both shrine and rhetoric create distance between the viewer (or reader, or audience) and the relic (or, in the case of rhetoric, the signified). Part II of this book takes up this dynamic: Chaucer, Malory, and others capitalize on how relic discourse enables conversations about the function of representational language, images, and devotional objects in general – and about how this discourse circumscribes (without necessarily rewarding) pilgrim behaviour. The commonplaces of relic discourse, then, are important both in themselves and in how, in some vernacular poetry of the fourteenth and fifteenth centuries, they facilitate explorations of rhetorical dissimulation and serve as indicators of good devotional conduct.

The twelfth and thirteenth centuries are crucial in that they witnessed the uptick in translations John Blair and others have noticed. As chapter 1 demonstrated, these translations were typically of major relics to much larger, more opaque, and more ornate reliquaries than ever before. During this period, written accounts became crucial to envisioning the relic.[7] So, too, many narratives of translation explain both a relic's importance and what it looked like, attributes that would not always be obvious after the relic was hidden. Both Simeon of Durham and Jocelin of Brakelond, a monk at Bury, highlight this difficulty in their twelfth-century records of the translations of St Cuthbert and St Edmund of

Bury. Simeon and Jocelin describe viewing the saint's body as an exclusive event and acknowledge the frustration of those who were not permitted to see the relics. Both accounts present a kind of metaphorical seeing, describing the bodies in ekphrastic detail and offering written rather than corporeal proof of incorruption. The attendant controversies – angry monks at Bury, disbelieving prelates at Durham – highlight the newness of this kind of subterfuge.[8] As Jocelin says, the monks at Bury are devastated in part because they all expected Edmund's body to be displayed openly. While Jocelin and Simeon ultimately present their accounts as evidence for the status of the saintly bodies, that writing is merely a substitute for viewing is abundantly clear.

These early narratives are in contrast to John Capgrave's fifteenth-century *Life of St Gilbert*. Capgrave includes the commonplace of viewing the body at night, but he does not present the secrecy of such an event as unusual, nor does he identify widespread desire to see and touch the relics. So, too, John Lydgate's and Henry Bradshaw's later accounts of Edmund and Werburge indicate that by the fifteenth and sixteenth centuries, the elision of saint and shrine had itself become commonplace.[9] In these narratives, both authors present the shrine as if it were in fact the saint, and writing about the shrine – and, in Harley 2278, both writing and images – takes the place of viewing or touching the relics. Even when Capgrave describes the prelates who handle Gilbert's relics, his detached tone contrasts with Jocelin's impassioned narrative and conveys, as Antonia Gransden observes of many such accounts, "no impression of a real event."[10] Moreover, while both Jocelin and Simeon wrestle with the need to affirm the status of a relic for those who cannot determine its state for themselves, Capgrave presents writing as the best evidence of all, presenting the written charters enclosed with Gilbert's body as proof positive of the ascetic's holiness. The idea of saintly remains was still important, as Bradshaw makes clear in his description of Werburge's relics. And yet the argument that a written description can stand in place of the saint's body is no longer necessary. In the centuries following the move from tomb to feretory shrines, in other words, there does seem to be a corresponding shift in emphasis from wanting to see the way a body looked to relying on the way authors of translation and miracle stories described it.[11]

Each commonplace of relic discourse thus helped to endow the shrine site with power and saintly presence, enabling pilgrims and readers alike to interpret the shrine as representing, absolutely and completely, the saint. In the passage I opened with, for instance, Lydgate constructs the ideal supplicant, who goes on pilgrimage of his or her own "assent" and "with reuerence"; she or he is humble, sober, faithful, and, perhaps most importantly of all, "contryt." Doubtless many pilgrims embraced this ideal and behaved in the manner Lydgate outlines, lying "prostrat" before the reliquary. And of course, not every good supplicant was rewarded with a miracle – such things were not automatic. But as a *literary* commonplace, the fiction of perfect supplicant makes the point that *only* the scurrilous fail to secure a miracle, implicitly ascribing a saint's inaction not to clerical or heavenly shortcomings, but rather to the moral failings of pilgrims. In other words, the commonplace of the virtuous pilgrim affirms the saint's *praesentia* in his or her relics, even in the absence of a miracle. Accounts of the relic custodian, a character whose importance the final section of this chapter addresses, present him as the instrument of mediation at a cult site, providing the textual and linguistic basis for interpreting (and controlling) the relic. This role is suggestively depicted in the early fourteenth-century canonization proceedings of St Thomas Cantilupe of Hereford, as well as Thomas of Monmouth's twelfth-century *Life and Miracles of St William of Norwich*, with which the chapter ends.

Nighttime Exhumation and Narrative "Seeing" in Translation Accounts

Medieval narratives of Cuthbert, Edmund of Bury, Gilbert, Thomas Becket, Frideswide, William of Norwich, and Erkenwald foreground the necessity of exhuming and moving a holy body at night.[12] One might go so far as to say that darkness operates like a shrine, occluding and protecting the body from potential spectators. The author of the fifteenth-century *Gilte Legende*, for example, suggests that clerics exhumed Thomas Becket at night in order to avoid bedlam: "At Cauntur-bury was so greet prese that the bisschoppys and the lordys wyste not how for to do thys dede to haue the bones owt of the erthe. But Richard bisschop of Salisbury counseylid that *it schulde be do by nyght whyle the peple slepte*, and so yt was doon."[13] In his fourteenth-century *Festial*, John Mirk similarly identifies Becket's exhumation as having taken place at "nyght," and Mirk details the vigil kept by the clerics who "hyllyd [þe scryne] wyth cloþes of golde, and cetton torches brennyng aboute tyl on þe morowon and lafton men wyth to kepe and wakynne."[14] Erkenwald's 1326 translation was also conducted at night ("in media nocte"), allegedly to avoid the "mass hysteria that would have resulted if the relics had been exposed during the daytime" ("propter tumultum populi evitandum").[15] Even these brief narratives, describing the clandestine exhumation of a saint's body, indicate that translating a body under the cover of night and in secret was not uncommon.[16] This convention, which justifies preventing others from seeing the saint's relics, suggests the importance of written descriptions in the absence of seeing a holy body. As the following accounts show, when very few see the relic before the translation, language becomes the primary way to confirm what the shrine contains.

In his twelfth-century account of Cuthbert's 1104 translation, Simeon of Durham foregrounds the controversy and skepticism attending Cuthbert's nighttime exhumation. He thereby anticipates and then resolves doubt about whether Cuthbert's relics are incorrupt – and presents his written description of the event as a way to view, metaphorically, Cuthbert's body. St Cuthbert, a seventh-century monk and bishop of Lindisfarne, was one of the most popular saints of northern England throughout the Middle Ages.[17] His body, said to have been found incorrupt in the seventh century, became over time the focal point for debates over whether it indeed remained whole. Simeon's narrative is no exception. There, disbelief about the status of Cuthbert's remains stems from how few monks initially examine the body: nine monks ("numero novem") conduct an investigation of the relic at night ("IX. kal. Septembris noctis").[18] Simeon records in detail their careful exploration ("diligenter explorarunt") of the body (251), which in its flexibility and integrity is more like a sleeping man than a dead corpse ("tota sui integritate artuumque flexibilitate dormientem magis repraesentabat quam mortuum" [252]). Simeon's narrative creates a vivid word picture of a fragrant and pliable body ("suavissimi odoris fragrantiam" [252]); though we merely read about, rather than see, this body, these comparisons make it seem almost visible. Simeon thereby substitutes writing for viewing: he offers us an ekphrastic description that affirms what the object *looks like*. This description is both necessary and important because others do not get the chance to see the body, which these select nine uncover before dawn.

But this account is also, in a sense, too good to be true, too conventional; and too few witness the miraculous event. Simeon allows for these objections. He writes cynicism into his narrative, acknowledging that not everyone will accept as fact what only nine monks saw. Bishop Ranulf, one skeptical interlocutor, questions the initial report that Cuthbert remains incorrupt (254). His disbelief, as well as the insistence of neighbouring monks that they, too, should have been involved in the investigation ("quod etiam nos ipsi oculis perspeximus" [256]), suggest the difficulty in examining a saint's body at night and in secret: those who do not see the body might not believe what they hear about it.

At the same time, this secrecy empowers Simeon's narrative, which both allows for and then eradicates the doubt about Cuthbert's relic. As Simeon would have it, to settle the dispute, leading clergy, as well as Alexander, brother of the king of Scotland (258), agree to examine the relics. The result – that Abbot Ralph declares the body to be incorrupt ("Ecce! … fratres, hoc corpus [est] sanum et integrum" [259]), thereby corroborating the testimony of the nine monks – also instills authority in Simeon's writing. For Abbot Ralph, one of Simeon's own characters, ratifies Simeon's version of events (that the body was incorrupt in the first place). In Simeon's version of the translation, disinterring the saint at night ultimately means subordinating the body to language: to what those who were there say – and to what Simeon writes – about what they saw.

In his narrative of Edmund of Bury's 1198 translation, Jocelin of Brakelond similarly depicts Edmund's corpse as a bendable, lifelike body.[19] Like Simeon, Jocelin incorporates monks who object to not having been included in the initial examination of the body; he also describes exhuming the body at night and in secret: Abbot Samson "told the Convent betimes to make themselves ready to transfer the body in the night."[20] In this case, only a select few see the actual body, the coffin itself having been placed within the feretory.[21] As Jocelin tells it, the monks all expect the abbot to "display the coffin to the people during the octave of the feast, and to carry back the holy body in the presence of them all; but we were sorely deceived" (113).[22] In Jocelin's account, Samson's decision disappoints not just the hopes but expectations ("putabamus omnes") of the monks. The monks' frustration – and presumably, Jocelin's own, as he includes himself among those who are "deceived" ("seducti *sumus*") – highlights the importance of Jocelin's description of Edmund's body as seen through the eyes of Abbot Samson and those who accompany him, at night, "to behold [their] patron" ("uidere patronum suum") (113). If the monks may not see the relic, they may at least read about what it looked like.

While Jocelin's description presumably does not entirely assuage the grief of those who are sorrowful ("doluerunt") at being excluded from this moment (115), it approximates in narrative detail what it might have been like to "see such things" (116). Edmund's body is wrapped in linen "of wondrous whiteness"; the "head lay united to the body" (114). Samson, like the nine monks in Simeon's account, experiences "joy mixed with fear" ("gaudium mixtim cum pavore" [Simeon 250]); he is unwilling to unwind the linen cloth to "see the sacred flesh unclothed" (Jocelin 114). Both Jocelin and Simeon emphasize the power – and the potential danger – of viewing the saint's naked and incorrupt flesh. Here, Abbot Samson dares only

> to touch the eyes and the nose, which was very large and prominent, and afterwards he touched the breast and arms and, raising the left hand, he touched the fingers and placed his fingers between the fingers of the saint; and going further he found the feet turned stiffly upwards as of a man dead that self-same day, and he touched the toes of the feet and counted them as he touched them.
>
> (Tetigit oculos et nasum ualde grossum et ualde eminentem, et postea tetigit pectus et brachia, et subleuans manum sinistram digitos tetigit et digitos suos posuit inter digitos sanctos. Et procedens inuenit pedes rigide erectos tanquam hominis hodie mortui, et digitos pedum tetigit, et tangendo numerauit.) (114)

It is an extraordinary narrative, presenting us with minutiae that call attention both to Edmund as mortal king (Edmund's "large and prominent nose," for instance) and saint (his body appears as that "of a man dead that self-same day"). In foregrounding Samson's tactile encounter with the body ("tetigit"; "digitos suos posuit inter digitos sanctos"), the passage invites us to experience the body with the abbot, to envision Edmund and Samson's interlocked fingers or Samson's exploratory touch. This passage renders Edmund's body as something Samson interprets – "reads," in a sense – with his hand, as if Samson were blind and the body were Braille. In this passage, we thus "see" Edmund through touch. This narrative seeing takes the place of actual seeing; and given that Jocelin includes the detail that Samson does not permit most of the monks to see the actual relic, we may even think of Jocelin as positioning his account to stand in for the body itself.

John Capgrave's fifteenth-century *Life of St Gilbert* (1451), composed for the Gilbertine nuns at Sempringham, is not concerned with whether Gilbert's body is incorrupt, but Capgrave's rendition of Gilbert's translation, like the earlier accounts of Jocelin and Simeon, nevertheless includes the conventional disinterment at night.[23] An Augustinian canon and prior of the Lynn convent by 1446, Capgrave was an innovative thinker who shared in common with Reginald Pecock the idea that "orthodoxy must, and could, be grounded in reason and knowledge."[24] He, like Lydgate – whom Karen Winstead in fact suggests as a literary "inspiration" for Capgrave[25] – composed and translated his works during a period when East Anglian religious culture flourished, the fifteenth century of "concrete and incarnational devotions."[26] And yet, Capgrave's *Life of St Gilbert* reveals the cult of the saints to operate differently than the devotional practices surrounding other holy things: the account presents the non-viewing of the body as hardly worthy of comment and written documents as in a sense more important than relics. Such an account is at odds with Gail McMurray Gibson's description of the other, more concrete devotional practices of the East Anglian laity, who commissioned statues in their churches and owned books of hours – objects they would, in other words, have been able to handle, to touch.[27] In the case of Gilbert's body, though, writing is more important than tactile contact. While Jocelin and Simeon register surprise at the relatively private examination of the saint's body, both Capgrave and his thirteenth- and fourteenth-century sources take this topos for granted, suggesting that by the thirteenth century, conducting private examinations of relics was the norm.[28]

Gilbert of Sempringham, founder of the Gilbertines and known for his rigid asceticism, was canonized in 1202. According to Capgrave, on

> the nyth of [St Gilbert's] translacion, þat is to sey, þe nyth be-twix þe Satirday and þe Sunday, þe noble man, þe archbishop with oþir bischoppes and ministres came on-to þe graue wher þe holy membres of Gilbertes body was hid, and with grete worchep þei lifte up þat holy uessel of God, þat, so waschid and arayed þe next day aftirward, he myte with lesse tariing be laid in his schrine. (115)

Capgrave later iterates that these events transpire at night: "Whan all þese relikes were lift fro þe ground and waschid þe archbischop went a-gayn to chambyr for to take a rest, *for it was fer fro day*" (116; emphasis added). While Capgrave offers an explanation for carrying out this work at night – to expedite the translation the next day ("with lesse tariing") – those in attendance are members of the clerical elite. And yet, unlike Jocelin and Simeon, Capgrave offers no specifics about the number or precise rank of those who were present: exhuming the body is apparently not a controversial affair and does not warrant corroborating testimony. Neither does Capgrave dwell on whether a certain prelate or Gilbertine bristled at having been excluded from the ceremony. The account is in many respects ahistorical, derived more from convention, and from the straightforward depiction of the event in his sources, than from the views of individuals.

The *Life of St Gilbert* nevertheless highlights the parallels between translation, darkness, and relic discourse. Translation and enshrinement, as I have already suggested, are analogous to figurative language insofar as they present the signified (the relic) in terms of something else (the shrine). So, too, relic discourse presents the relic in terms of something else (commonplaces, metaphors, technical terminology). The night before the translation ceremony, bishops and priests gaze upon the saint's flesh and affirm his chastity: they discover the "fayre red pouder of his flesch, swech as þei sey as virgines haue whan þei ar ded" (116). Even this brief description is figurative, presenting Gilbert's decomposed flesh as *like* that of a virgin. The moment is clearly meant to convey Gilbert's chastity and asceticism, but it nevertheless reminds us that the clerics who are present *interpret* the signs of the relics (the colour of the powder) and then record this interpretation in written form. Enshrining the saint is thus all the more complex, assuming the need to communicate not only his sanctity, but also his virginity. The clerics proceed to verify that the cloth in which Gilbert was buried is "hool with-oute corrupcion" (116), in this way emphasizing their founder's own moral incorruptibility. In this instance, the cloth stands for abstract qualities: Gilbert's virtue, and so on. There is extended touching in the handling and washing of these sacred objects. Capgrave's account of these moments enables us to imagine what the remains looked like, imaginatively to interact with it just as the archbishop did when he views the "fayre red pouder of [Gilbert's] flesch." In describing the miraculous attributes of the relics, this section constructs Gilbert's *praesentia*, and it does so largely metaphorically. It also reminds us that this viewing is secretive, conducted under the cover of darkness. The very nature of such an examination requires a written account – and in his version of the translation ceremony itself, Capgrave emphasizes just such narratives.

By night, that is, we learn, albeit figuratively, what the relic looks like; by day, we learn that some documents describe it.[29] Capgrave portrays Gilbert's body only in the context of the nighttime exhumation; he does not include specific details about the state of the relic in his rendition of the daytime translation. This description of the translation festivities, which take place the day after they exhume Gilbert's body, then, highlights the distance between the relic, the shrine, and the language used to describe both. Once the clerics enclose the relics in silk and place them in the reliquary,

> Thei layde eke with him a grete chartour in whech was wretyn al his lif, his canoniȝacion eke, and his translacion seled with þe seles of þe bischoppis & abbotes whech wer þere present. Ther was put in with him eke a plate of led, in whech plate was wrytyn al þis þing more compendiously, as I suppose, þat þe rememberauns of al þis werk schuld last euyr. (117)

In place of a written description of the body's appearance – the focal point of the disinterment the night before – this passage gives us only the clerical "seles" of those who were present. Capgrave gestures towards the importance of writing in creating the meaning of the thing itself, which is now enclosed ("sperd") within the shrine: descriptions of Gilbert's life, canonization, and translation ensure that his body will not be, like many relics in the fourteenth-century relic list from Durham Cathedral, "sine billis"[30] – and hence, at best, interpreted as anonymous and, at worst, inauthentic. Capgrave highlights the official capacity of the writing enclosed with Gilbert's body: the plate of lead bears the seals of all who "were þere present"; the charter includes the papal canonization document. Insofar as he, too, is creating a written account of the saint's life, miracles, canonization, and translation, Capgrave aligns his own *Life of St Gilbert* with these authoritative records. Both his *Life* and these other written accounts memorialize Gilbert's life, works, and relics. They also permit all who come after to experience the body through narrative and to understand the sanctity of the place where Gilbert is buried.

These stories of Cuthbert, Edmund, and Gilbert present viewing relics openly as, paradoxically, an occluded, secret – even dark – affair. By contrast, reading or hearing about relics often occurs in the open as part of a ritual; at Gilbert's translation, for example, "Ther saide þe archbischop a ful notable sermone grounded al up-on þe holynesse and þe myracles of þis holy man Gilbert," including the details of his canonization proceedings (117). For Jocelin, narrative provides an antidote to deception and trickery ("male seducti"). His account expounds openly what Abbot Samson hid from most of Bury's monks. In these cases, language supplies meaning for what remains unseen and can even, in the detailed bodily examinations Simeon and Jocelin record, constitute a kind of "seeing" and create the saint's *praesentia* – for the accounts confirm, as neither the body nor even the reliquary itself can, that the saint's shrine is a powerful and miracle-working place.

The Elision of Shrine and Saint in Lydgate's *Edmund and Fremund* and Bradshaw's *Werburge*

The translation of a saint's body frequently meant that, while few saw or handled the relics before the ritual, fewer still would view the relics after the ceremony ended.[31] The feretory – rather than the actual relics – thus expresses and even constitutes the saint's *virtus* and *praesentia*; and narrative accounts explain, often figuratively, the power of the feretory and the bodily remains. In the *Extra Miracles of St Edmund*, for instance, Lydgate closely associates Edmund's miracle-working powers with his shrine, presenting enshrinement as a prerequisite for late medieval miracle-working: "To seyntes shryned or set in tabernacles, / God hath mervaylles wrought many moo than oon" (*EM* 167–8).[32] Carl Horstmann renders this clause nonrestrictive, implying grammatically that God works miracles through saints: "To seyntes, shryned or set in tabernacles, / God hath mervaylles wrought many moo than oon."[33] Anthony Bale and A.S.G. Edwards's transcription (cited above) does more justice to the sense of what I also take as a restrictive clause. Their version of the line conveys the idea that enshrined saints do what relics (or even saints) alone cannot. While Lydgate invokes the technical terminology of relic discourse in affirming the wholeness of Edmund's body (*EF* 1982–95), as well as the primary metaphor of relic discourse in referring to Edmund's head as "this holy tresour, this relik souereyne" (*EF* 1983), both the *Extra Miracles* and the text in Harley 2278 elide Edmund's body with – even subordinate it to – the lavish feretory.[34]

The representative function of the shrine was hence a flashpoint for many writers of the period. If the reliquary were to be understood as the relic, and, by extension, as the saint, it must convey this figurative relationship appropriately. Wycliffite texts, as but one example, indicate that by the fourteenth and fifteenth centuries, some viewed as problematic the correlation between relic and lavish shrine.[35] Harley 2278, by contrast, presents the shrine as the best way to represent Edmund's holiness. That Lydgate presents Edmund and his relics as equivalent to the shrine indicates, on the one hand, his commitment to emphasizing Bury's political importance: Edmund's shrine was located at Bury, and thus respecting the shrine was in some sense to respect Bury St Edmunds. But on the other hand, this elision of shrine and saint also points towards the difficulty of – and controversy over – expressing the holy in terms of images, an issue to which I will return at the end of this section.

By the 1430s, John Lydgate was one of England's most prominent poets;[36] as Derek Pearsall – who remains both Lydgate's most famous critic and also, as Maura Nolan has dubbed him, "the reluctant hero of Lydgate studies"[37] – writes, Lydgate "achieved an extraordinary pre-eminence in his own day."[38] And to be sure, Lydgate was not simply a monastic poet. Though he was confined to the cloister, it seems clear that his impressive list of patrons – a veritable who's who of fifteenth-century Lancastrian power, including Henry V and Humphrey, duke of Gloucester – sought him out.[39] His *Lives of Ss Edmund and Fremund* shares with this regime an interest in upholding mainstream religious practice.[40] For unlike some other poems in Lydgate's ouevre, *Edmund and Fremund* is relatively mainstream and orthodox; it does not necessarily, as Nolan notes of some of Lydgate's other works, "indulge in literary practices that seem inimical to the ends of propaganda."[41] And yet, Lydgate's depiction of Edmund's shrine in particular does reveal the mechanisms that justified orthodox practices: while Lydgate trumpets Edmund's mystical power, he presents this power as inhering not in Edmund's relics, but rather in the shrine. This emphasis suggests that by the fifteenth century, shrines in fact eclipsed the bodies of saints – and by foregrounding the shrine, Lydgate's text reveals the constructedness of the idea that God's grace, via the saint's body, effected the miraculous.

Produced sometime after Henry VI's Christmas visit to Bury in 1433, Harley 2278 contains this important work.[42] Of late, the poem and manuscript have garnered critical attention for having possibly been written, as Jennifer Sisk has put it, to "register [Henry VI's] royal potential."[43] So, too, Fiona Somerset argues that the *Lives of Ss Edmund and Fremund* is to Henry VI what Lydgate's *Siege of Thebes* or *Troy Book* is to Henry V;[44] John Ganim articulates that *The Life of St Edmund* "contains its own account of its writing as a token specifically meant to remind Henry VI of his visit to the monastery."[45] Sisk turns to the form of the manuscript, suggesting that with the *Lives*, Lydgate ultimately created "generic dissonance that reflects the historical uncertainty he faced."[46] Here, I wish to redirect our attention from the didactic and political elements of this poem to the images and text depicting the translation and miracles of St Edmund. The illuminations that accompany the narrative of Edmund's translation from Bury to London, for example, highlight

Edmund's shrine, even as the written account emphasizes the "many myracle[s]" St Edmund *himself* works both in London and en route to Bury (*EF* 3374). The resulting tension between the text and images of Harley 2278 helps to generate the *praesentia* that we often imagine to emanate from Edmund's relics and shows that paradoxically, words such as "martir" or even "body" could function as metonyms for a reliquary.

As the illuminations in Harley 2278 make clear, Lydgate refers to the shrine as if it were the body itself. In one such instance, though the bishop of London agrees that Edmund belongs in Bury, he attempts to "translate [Edmund] into Powlys cherche" (*EF* 3395). Needless to say, Edmund demurs, and when the dissembling clerics attempt "with the *body* to Poulis for to gon," they find it "as fyx as a gret hill off ston" (*EF* 3401–2; emphasis added), "like a mont" (*EF* 3409). These lines suggest that the London bishop and the "multitude" (*EF* 3403) are trying to move Edmund's actual body (rather than the shrine which contains it). "Body" is, after all, the only grammatical antecedent for "yt" (*EF* 3402). Until the end of the next stanza, when Lydgate implies that the bishop is dealing specifically with the shrine (*EF* 3406–8), the "body" of line 3401 would seem to suggest that the monks are handling Edmund himself. However, the illuminations that accompany this section depict only the shrine. Fol. 113v [Figure 4], for instance, features the "multitude" endeavouring to dislodge Edmund from his resting place. In this image, five clerics, having placed their hands at the base of the shrine, encircle it. The bishop looks on in the bottom left corner of the page, apparently instructing those who "dyde ther force and besy peyne" (*EF* 3404) on how better to accomplish his goal. Of course, they cannot move Edmund's shrine; and as the written text would have it, they cannot move Edmund himself, his "body" (*EF* 3401). The image both reminds us that Edmund's body is in the shrine and that we are to interpret this shrine metaphorically, as representing the relics themselves. So, too, while Lydgate reminds us that the reliquary contains Edmund's body – Ayllewyn "Took the chest, wher the kyng lay cloos" (*EF* 3419) – the images accompanying Ayllewyn's journey to Bury with the saint highlight the shrine itself. As the text would have it, "Alle syke ffolk that for helpe souhte / To the martir … / Were maad hool. Myracles euer he wrouhte" (*EF* 3424–6). In this case, the illumination features the sick prostrate before the *shrine*, which is itself on a wagon (fol. 115r). Lydgate informs us that the reliquary chest encloses Edmund's body (*EF* 3419); but at the same time, the image reminds us that no one can

Thre yeer/ the martir/ heeld ther resydence
Tyl Ayllewyn/ be reuelacion
Took off the bysshop/ vpon a day licence
To leede kyng Edmund/ ageyn to bury toun
But by a maner/ symulacion
The bysshop graunteth/ and vnder that gan werche
Hym to translate/ in to Powlys cherche

Figure 4. This illumination features monks attempting to move Edmund in order "hym to translate in to Powlys cherche." The monks encircle the gabled and gilded reliquary, attempting to move it. By contrast, Lydgate consistently uses the terms "body," as in this miracle, or "martir," rather than "shrine." © The British Library Board. (British Library MS Harley 2278 [fol. 113v].)

see the body, subsumed by its container. The illustrations depict what is actually visible – the shrine – even as the text consistently presents the reliquary as Edmund himself, as the "martir."

The images of Edmund's 1095 translation in fact illustrate how the reliquary functions in place of the relics. This image portrays the reliquary chest hovering above the saint, who appears as one sleeping inside the shrine (fol. 117r). (This illumination is historically accurate: 1095 is the last translation at which Edmund's body was said to have been displayed openly.[47]) In this case, the accompanying text describes the monks carrying Edmund's body to the shrine: "They took the martir on ther shuldres squar / And to the shryne deuoutely they it bar" (*EF* 3499–500). When the narrative gives us Edmund's literal body, the image corresponds, depicting the body itself. By contrast, Lydgate usually refers to both the saint and the shrine as "the martir" (*EF* 3425, 3457, 3499), regardless of whether Edmund's actual body is exposed. By foregrounding the shrine even when the narrative emphasizes Edmund, these illuminations reveal the workings of metaphor: because they depict the shrine even when Lydgate says "martir" or other body-related words, the images show the word "martir" to be in its own way figurative, just as the treasure-related metaphors deriving from the shrine are metaphorical for the saint.

Harley 2278 suggests that by the fifteenth century, relic discourse might not always describe the relic so much as a set of conventions: the elision of shrine and saint, the operation of metonym, and the circumscribing of pilgrim behaviour. The same can be said of Henry Bradshaw's early sixteenth-century poem, *The Life of Saint Werburge of Chester*.[48] Unlike Jocelin and Simeon, who were writing at the beginning of the transition from tomb to feretory shrines, Bradshaw assumes as obvious the immediate interpretation of the shrine as Werburge.[49] Bradshaw's sources are diverse and include Bede, William of Malmsbury, Ranulf Higden, Alfred and Gerald of Wales, and, as Bradshaw notes, "mo in deed."[50] In spite of this myriad of sources, Bradshaw is solely responsible for the sections eliding saint and shrine, situating his depiction of the saint's cult squarely within his own cultural and historical milieu. Additions to his poem include the description of the procession of Werburge's relics into Chester (2.267–350), the great fire at Chester (2.1598ff), and the descriptions of war that I discuss in the section on miracles of punishment.[51] These additions reflect the status of Werburge's shrine in the context of Chester: depicting it as a protective totem is a commonplace of hagiography. But these sections of text also emphasize Werburge's shrine, even grammatically, to the extent that it becomes, in the words of George Orwell, a "worn-out metaphor," which has "lost all evocative power."[52] Among Orwell's examples are familiar phrases – "toe the line," "stand shoulder to shoulder with," "no axe to grind," and so on. While the term "shrine" (and its other designators, such as "treasure") perhaps does not belong in quite this "huge dump," as Orwell says, we might nonetheless think of it in terms of yet another Orwellian phrase: the "dead" metaphor, which reverts to being an "ordinary word."[53] In other words, a fascinating element of Bradshaw's piece is that while we assume the shrine to stand in for the saint, the text so frequently focuses on the shrine itself that the word "shrine" becomes "ordinary" – that is, referring to itself – and not figurative.

At the same time, Bradshaw's text resists the impotence of the word "shrine," reminding us grammatically that it represents both the relic *and* the saint. In explaining the reasons for moving Werburge's body from Hanbury to Chester – locals fear the Viking threat – Bradshaw explains that the general concern is "for the shryne specially" (2.248), going on, a few lines later, to emphasize prayers "To preserue the countrey / the relique / the shryne / From daunger of enmite and miserable ruyne" (2.251–2). Anxiety for the shrine in particular ("specially") implies the citizens worry about financial loss and not about Werburge's relics: the Danes may well, after all, destroy the shrine and steal anything of monetary value attached to it. This possibility, for a moment, allows us to think of the word as one of Orwell's "dead metaphors," referring not to the saint but only to itself. The very next lines remind us, however, of the elision of shrine and saint – remind us that, in fact, the shrine is meant to signify Werburge. (Whether or not the shrine always does so successfully is another question.) In juxtaposing the terms "relique" and "shrine," and in doing so appositively, the phrase sets up a series of representational connections: denizens of Hanbury worry about the country, that is, about their relic, that is, about their shrine. In this series of appositives, the shrine is the final designator, signifying both the relic *and also* the surrounding country.[54] To threaten the physical monument is thus symbolically to threaten not only Werburge's relics, but also Hanbury.[55] The line serves another purpose, however: in using the shrine as an appositive to "relique," Bradshaw explains and to some degree constructs the figurative relationship between these two objects. This move alone reveals, I think, that it was not simply intuitive to understand the shrine as standing for, or in some sense existing as, the relic. Instead, Bradshaw spells out this association, surely not necessary if his contemporary audience simply envisioned the shrine as taking on both literal and cultural significance (as the relic, as the city).

The shrine in *The Life of Saint Werburge*, in other words, is as tricky a metonym as the terms "martir" and "body" in Harley 2278. The relationship between shrine and relic is simply not clear cut and easily intelligible. While we are obviously meant to understand those from Hanbury as taking Werburge herself when Bradshaw comments that the "holy goost inspired theyr mynde / To take the shryne ... / And brynge it to Chestre" (2.258–9), the preceding lines have to some degree separated this signifier from what it represents. Hence, though Bradshaw continues to use the terms "relique" and "shryne" interchangeably throughout this passage – for instance, when the citizens and clerics of Chester come "afore this relique" and then kneel, "[s]alutynge the shryne" (2.296, 298) – there is a sense in which the one is in fact separate from the other. Why, for instance, are the citizens before the relic and saluting the shrine? Were the shrine to function simply as the designator for Werburge, it would make a lot more sense to have the crowd before the shrine and saluting the relic. This arrangement would explain the shrine's significance more clearly in that one venerates the relic for what it represents – not the shrine, made by craftspeople and opulent. Neither term is an end rhyme, and exchanging them would affect the metre by only one syllable. To be sure, both words are metaphorical. But in these lines, the veneration of the shrine – that the people kneel before and salute the shrine, specifically – nevertheless portrays the reliquary as having a more unstable relationship to its relic and to Werburge than we might assume.

This instability is apparent in Bradshaw's account of the fire in Chester, as well. When a vicious fire threatens to consume the entire city, and the labour of the citizens is entirely "in vayne" (2.1623), the abbots of the monastery process around the city with the "holy shryne in prayer and deuocion" (2.1650). As in the instance of Werburge's translation, Bradshaw explains a few lines later that by the shrine, he means Werburge, as the abbots trust "in Werburge for helpe, aide and grace" (2.1653). All the same, the passage instills in the saint's shrine the protective power that saves Chester: "The fire began to cesse – / a myracle clere – / Nat passyng the place / where the holy shryne / Was borne by the bretherene / as playnly dyd appere" (2.1662–4). As this passage would have it, wherever the abbots take it, the *shrine* prevents the fire from spreading and puts it out. Calamity averted, "Vnto her shryne the people all went, / The clergie before, in maner of procession, / Thankyng the virgin with loue feruent" (2.1675–7). By the end of the near tragedy, then, Bradshaw does present the shrine as Werburge's somewhat indeterminate location. In doing so, however, he does not necessarily resolve his direct reference to the shrine throughout the section, or indeed a mere thirty lines later, when Bradshaw explains that "Sith the holy shryne came to their presence, / It hath ben their comfort and gladnes, truly" (2.1711–12). In this instance, at the beginning of the section on Werburge's miracles at Chester, Bradshaw does not even supply the feminine pronoun, as he frequently does elsewhere. Instead, he refers to the shrine as "it," thereby distancing the relic, and Werburge herself, even further from both monument and metonym. By presenting the "holy shryne" as the comfort of all Chester, Bradshaw momentarily obfuscates the presence of Chester's saint. Or, at the very least, he complicates the use of the term "shrine" and how it was commonly deployed in this period.

Clearly, then, terms for shrine sometimes designated something other than or in addition to the saint, to the point of simply denoting the shrine itself or material treasure in general. Bradshaw's frequent explanations of this word thus make a good deal of sense. Just as a difficult metonym might require a gloss, the behaviour and depiction of misbehaving pilgrims in Harley 2278 imply that eliding the shrine and saint similarly requires a explanation. One such miracle features Osgothus, a Dane who hates the "martyr" and "lyk a wood man ferde, / The myraclis off Edmund whan he herde" (*EF* 3296–7). Worse still, Osgothus "despysed his myracles whan he herde hem reede" (*EF* 3300). Such moments present Edmund's sanctity and *praesentia* as constructed through discourse – Osgothus does not witness miracles, but rather hears literary accounts of them. These lines also underscore Lydgate's presentation of Edmund's shrine as Edmund himself, for we know, having read the account of Edmund's miracles, that Lydgate frequently depicts supplicants as encountering the "martir" when they in fact encounter the shrine. So, too, Lydgate explains of Osgothus's behaviour that "Whan ffolk off pryde lyst haue no reward, / To hooly seyntis for to do reuerence, / God punyssheth hem" (*EF* 3291–3). Yet again, what Lydgate denotes as "hooly seyntis" amounts to Edmund's shrine, as the illuminations in this section make clear. For the Dane directs his scorn not precisely at Edmund's relics but at the lavish monument at Bury, demonstrating a clear disregard for his religious, social, and political betters. It is perhaps no surprise, then, that Osgothus's problem lies in his failure to "do reuerence" to Edmund's reliquary. In keeping with his approach throughout this text, Lydgate once again elides Edmund's shrine and relics, metaphorically substituting one ("hooly seyntis") for what is literally there (the shrine).

The poem thereby provides the template for interpreting the punishment miracle from the beginning: Osgothus's failure to respect *Edmund's shrine*. Lydgate insists upon the pagan's distaste for Edmund, but the descriptions of Osgothus nevertheless suggest that the problem is with Osgothus's attitude and even his fashion choices, which vies with the splendor of Edmund's shrine. Members of the community, for instance, see Osgothus "[n]ext to the kyng with gold and perlys rounde, / Rychely beseyn, and statly off array, / Aboute the shryne walkyng al the day" (*EF* 3302–4). Lydgate contemns the physical bearing and costume of this Dane, who is dressed "rychely" in "gold and perlys," who does not kneel or fall prostrate before the reliquary, but rather *walks* about Edmund's monument all day. This is a character who mistakes his own splendor as exceeding that of Edmund. In the context of Harley 2278, Osgothus's gold and pearls are in competition with the lavish decoration at Edmund's shrine, which Lydgate specifies is

> prouyded for the nonys
> With clothis off gold arrayed, and perre,
> And with many ryche precyous stonys
> Longyng vnto his [Edmund's] roial dignyte. (*EF* 3501–4)

Put another way, this heathen dresses himself as if *he* were a saint. His strutting about the shrine similarly demonstrates that, from Lydgate's perspective, this Dane refuses, either through his costume or bodily attitude, to acknowledge the shrine as representing something different, and better, than him.

The next stanza affirms, even as it disparages, Osgothus's view of himself as Edmund's equal:

> Off coryouste and presumpcion
> His look he caste toward that hooly kyng,
> Off fals dysdeyn voyd off deuocion,
> Depraued his vertues, his passion, his lyuyng. (*EF* 3305–8)

As I pointed out earlier, when Lydgate supplies "hooly seyntis" for Edmund's shrine (*EF* 3292), Osgothus is said to look with disdain at that "hooly kyng" (*EF* 3306). Of course, the Dane is looking at Edmund's shrine, not at Edmund himself, nor even at the relics. Yet again, Lydgate does not simply substitute the reliquary *for* the saint, but gives us the reliquary *as* the saint. Osgothus's offence is absolute: he holds Edmund himself, not the trappings of the cult, in contempt. Insofar as we learn that Osgothus "toward the martyr ... bar old hatrede" (*EF* 3298), we are led to understand that Osgothus disdains the shrine because he hated Edmund. Lydgate's construction of this character, along with the insistence that the shrine *is* the "hooly seynt," thus delimit our interpretation of this moment. It cannot be that Osgothus venerates Edmund but views the lavish shrine as problematic.[56] It cannot be that he just doesn't understand what the shrine signifies. We are meant to understand, instead, that Osgothus – scornful, depraved, presumptuous; who hated Edmund; who stalks around the shrine like a member of the nouveau riche at the most prestigious event – objects to and disrespects Edmund. At the same time, in the absence of an interpretative key, it is difficult not to pity Osgothus. Lydgate merely interprets his actions; but is it really possible that this character, so far removed from the discourse upon which the meaning of a shrine depended, could possibly understand Edmund's shrine as the martyr himself – or the martyr as the shrine?

The image and text in the manuscript show no patience for Osgothus's behaviour or acknowledgement that, in the absence of some explanation, the shrine might not be terribly easy to interpret. Indeed, the illumination on fol. 110v juxtaposes Osgothus's subsequent "furye" (*EF* 3334) with the unchanging splendor of Edmund's reliquary [Figure 5], suggesting both Edmund's own static divinity and the pagan's lack of understanding. The image accompanies Lydgate's warning that pilgrims who fail to "do reuerence" to "hooly seyntis" will pay the price (*EF* 3292), and it depicts Osgothus's punishment:

> This lord off Denmark, for al his gret bost,
> For al his tresour, his gold, and his perre,
> As a demonyak, vexyd with a gost,
> Ful offte turnynge in his infirmyte ... (*EF* 3319–22)

In the illumination, the Dane – portrayed in Persian garb as a Saracen pagan – indeed appears to lie "dystreyned, / In his furye walwying up and don" (*EF* 3333–4). He is at the front of the illumination at one end of Edmund's shrine; the "furye" is strong enough to have caused

Whan ffolk off pryde lyst haue no rewarde
To hooly seyntis for to do reuerence
God punysshith hem wrong on seynt Edward
Whilom at Couentre beyng in presence
Whan Osgothus off hatful necligence
A lord off Denmark lyk a wood man ferde
The myracles off Edmund whan he herde

Figure 5. The torment and healing of Osgothus the pagan Dane (depicted here in decidedly Saracen clothing). To the left, Osgothus writhes in pain; on the right; the healed pagan and monks pray in thanksgiving at the shrine monument. The illumination clearly shows the niche base common in late medieval England, on top of which sits Edmund's lavish gabled reliquary. © The British Library Board. (British Library MS Harley 2278 [fol. 110v].)

him to lose his turban.[57] His body faces *away* from the shrine, as indicated by the position both of his feet and the way his falchion hangs at his side; but, perhaps in his frenzy, he contorts his upper body back towards the reliquary so that we can see his face. His suffering contrasts with the shrine itself, static and splendid; and it contrasts with the resolution of his ailment, as well, depicted on the right side of the illumination, in which the healed Dane and the monastic community pray at the shrine. This image does not portray Osgothus's recovery and subsequent behaviour as having very much, if anything, to do with Edmund himself or with the "hooly seyntis." Rather, the Dane's bad behaviour and subsequent conversion affirm the primacy of Bury, of Edmund's shrine – and of the sanctity of Edward the Confessor, who is present, pities Osgothus's state, and asks Leofstan to pray for the misguided pagan (*EF* 3335–46). Even as the poetic line suggests that Osgothus's offence is against the saint, the miracle narrative colludes with this image to emphasize the pagan's pride and accoutrements (his gold, his pearls) – his disrespect for the monument.

While this narrative of punishment presents the shrine as a lightning rod for God's retributive power, its depictions of how *not* to behave at a shrine nonetheless suggest an alternative model for interacting with a reliquary. As I will suggest in the next section, accounts of misbehaving pilgrims demonstrate that some do not regard the shrine as commensurate with sanctity – one can bite the shrine, regard it with derision, try to steal it, even ignore it.[58] In depicting these offenders as distinctly Saracen, the manuscript illuminations of Harley 2278 imply that anyone who misinterprets the shrine is fundamentally misguided in his or her religious beliefs. Nevertheless, the corollary is that without some interpretive aid, not everyone will understand the shrine in the same way: these would-be supplicants demonstrate that the shrine, in and of itself, does not unequivocally signify St Edmund's importance. Moreover, as Arcoid's twelfth-century *Miracula Sancti Erkenwaldi* shows, many non-Saracen supplicants are similarly confused about the appropriate behaviour in the presence of apparently *any* shrine and its relic. The commonplaces of relic discourse ensure the appropriate interpretation of Edmund's and Erkenwald's reliquaries. And yet, this interpretation hinges on understanding the representative function of those commonplaces in the first place.

The dependence of relic cults on language recalls the point I made at the beginning of this section: that the commonplace of elided shrine and relic has much in common with a basic premise of the image debate.

Both apologists for images and those who critiqued mainstream church practice were preoccupied with how and what images represented and with what kind of response they might invoke in the viewer.[59] That is, does the image represent God? If so, how? Through the figurative use of splendid details, such as gilding, meant to signify the glory of heaven? If so, will the viewer understand these images, or will they inspire in the viewer the desire for sumptuous material goods? Or confuse the supplicant to the extent that she or he takes the image for its prototype? Even Lydgate's implicit defence of lavish shrines problematizes the appearance of these shrines, which those ill-versed in the Christian system of belief – the pagan Osgothus, for instance – might not know how to interpret. If the shrine so completely displaces the relic that terms reserved for the relic – "martyr," "body," and so on – describe the shrine instead, does the relic itself signify anything at all? The elision of shrine and saint, in other words, obliquely raises some of the driving questions of the image debate, particularly those of appropriate representation and how best to convey sanctity to the unlearned. In the case of Harley 2278, if we are to imagine Osgothus as unlearned (which in a Christian context, he surely is), the shrine does not fare very well as a representative object. For as much as Lydgate wishes us to understand Osgothus rejecting Edmund, it is difficult to sustain that reading in the face of the images depicting Osgothus at the shrine site. The primary difference between relic and image is that an image or statue ostensibly refers directly to its saint; the relic, ever hidden, at a remove from what the pilgrim sees, points more to a man-made object (the shrine) than to God. The relic, then, functions recursively, gesturing back to this world rather than to the next. Lydgate's *Edmund and Fremund*, as it is rendered in Harley 2278, suggests that as books for the unlearned, shrines are nothing if not inadequate.[60]

Affirming *Praesentia* I: Depraved Supplicants, Miracles of Punishment

St Erkenwald, bishop of London and of the East Saxons from 675 to 693 A.D., was the patron saint of medieval London. His cult, devoted primarily to the veneration of his relics, flourished from the seventh through the sixteenth centuries.[61] Correspondingly, Erkenwald was translated in 1140, 1148, and on 1 February 1326, when another shrine had been completed. Arcoid's twelfth-century *Miracula Sancti Erkenwaldi* (c. 1140–1), like the twelfth-century accounts of Jocelin and

Simeon, emphasizes enshrinement in such a way as to intimate the newness of translating saints to large feretory shrines.[62] Arcoid, canon of St Paul's and apologist for mainstream orthodoxy, wished to secure funding for Erkenwald's new shrine. While Jocelin and Simeon write from the perspective of monks denied the viewing of their saint's body, Arcoid writes as a shrewd fundraiser and publicist: under his direction, the miracles read as an affirmation not only that the shrine represents Erkenwald, but also that the community should, therefore, support the shrine financially. That said, Arcoid's impatience with those who challenged the authenticity of the miraculous or the practices of relic cults suggests a commitment to rendering orthodox practices not merely as normal, but as the only acceptable possibilities.[63]

Two punishment miracles in particular emphasize the conflation of Erkenwald with his reliquary – and of Arcoid's narrative in explaining the importance of this shrine and thereby constructing Erkenwald's *praesentia*.[64] In one of these instances, Arcoid showcases the central role of the laity in donating money for the construction of Erkenwald's new reliquary chest: "When it pleased God … that a silver shrine be made for Erkenwald ["deo parare argenteum erkenwaldo ferculum placuisset"], although the wealthy citizens contributed little or nothing, the generous hand of the poor set up collecting stations."[65] Arcoid uses the heroic poor to present financial support of Erkenwald's shrine as a moral absolute: if even the poor contribute, no one has an excuse for failing to do so. Hence, when a certain woman wishes to donate, "but her husband rebuked her bitterly and she was unable to do what she had proposed" (135), Arcoid has prepared the reader to view this husband as transgressive and immoral. The husband is subsequently afflicted with stomach problems until he, newly repentant, is carried "to the saint's sepulcher" ("ad ipsius mausoleum" [135]). While his offence is against the future object that will hold Erkenwald's remains, he must seek forgiveness from Erkenwald himself. The miracle thus conflates Erkenwald with his future shrine, suggesting in no uncertain terms that the proper attitude towards the shrine is one of careful respect and financial support.

Miracle 10 similarly narrates the consequences of lay misbehaviour, in the process endowing the shrine with the power that ought to be associated with Erkenwald's relics. This punishment miracle involves Eustace, a silversmith who pays "silly visit[s]" to the construction site of Erkenwald's silver reliquary ("theca"). Erkenwald has yet to be translated to this monument, which nevertheless exacts revenge for

Eustace's behaviour. Arcoid depicts Eustace as a drunkard who distracts the other silversmiths from their important task, which is to cover the "wooden sepulcher" ("sepulchrum ligneum") with "silver and gold" ("argento et auro") (143). Arcoid records that Eustace

> beg[a]n to make disgraceful remarks about the wooden shrine but also with wild presumption and daring he raised the wooden lid and hid himself inside as though he were the saint's body at rest; and thus he spoke: "I am the most holy Erkenwald: bring me gifts; ask for my help; make me a sepulcher of silver!" (143)

I find it impossible to read this passage and not think of Monty Python. But of course Arcoid finds nothing amusing in Eustace's actions. As an *exemplum*, the miracle seems superfluous – who else would attempt such a thing? – but as a commentary on *how* the shrine conveys the saint's power, this miracle is critically important. By enclosing himself within the shrine, Eustace's action complicates the idea that *praesentia* emanates from the relics. Instead, his behaviour suggests that the shrine creates saintly presence and power: in order to wield this power, all one need do is step inside. In fact, to take Eustace at his word, the shrine creates Erkenwald out of anyone: "*I am the most holy Erkenwald.*" Eustace does not say he is like Erkenwald, after all, but rather that, as soon as he climbs inside the reliquary, he and the saint are interchangeable. We are obviously meant to understand this moment as blasphemous, and Eustace dies "within a few days, by the stroke of divine judgement," because of his transgression (143). But Eustace's derisive attitude towards the shrine nevertheless reveals the necessity of language to understand its signifying power: once the wooden lid closes, who is to say what (or who) is inside? Is it Erkenwald, merely by virtue of the shrine itself? Eustace's attitude suggests both the possibility that some may (however drunkenly, however much in jest) take the shrine for saint – and, more problematically, that the saint is understood as powerful only because of his shrine. In this *exemplum*, in fact, Erkenwald's relics are nowhere to be seen.

On some level, Arcoid must have meant the narrative of Eustace to intimidate the locals into compliance. But this miracle is also suggestive of one lay attitude: Eustace is clearly having a bit of fun, and yet his actions also suggest that he thinks enshrinement is kind of silly, that not everyone regarded with measured seriousness the use of gold, silver, and gems in conveying a saint's holy power. At the same time, such a miracle, as I have already said, holds considerable importance for understanding the significance of shrines in this period. First, Arcoid simultaneously divorces Erkenwald from and unites him with the shrine. This move, of course, further emphasizes the commonplace of eliding saint and shrine and demonstrates the degree to which authors often presented the one as the other. But this aspect of relic discourse is only part of the story. For, second, Arcoid's narratives illustrate a fundamental problem with all types of representational language and objects, in that both metaphors and images have the potential to obscure what they signify. Hence, on the one hand, the repeated insistence that viewers understand the shrine as the saint (don't forget what this really is, in other words); but on the other hand, the clear instability of the shrine as a signifying object. An absent relic obviously complicates the signifying potential of a shrine. There is no question that, for Eustace, this absence creates the opportunity for some horsing around. In his absurd behaviour, Eustace illuminates how the reliquary generates meaning (by its splendour) but indicates that this particular metaphor could, in fact, refer to many things (including himself!). In more general terms, Eustace's blundering suggests that what one person understands by figurative language – treasure, for instance – might not be the same as what someone else understands by the very same term. By its very nature, translation – of relics, of language, of concept into metaphor – troubles meaning.

Hence, though in *The Life of St Werburge of Chester* Bradshaw presents Werburge as inseparable from her shrine, the failure of some to understand the shrine's significance confirms that as a sign, a reliquary is elusive. Bradshaw, like Arcoid, similarly derives Werburge's presence and agency in part from her ability to punish those who disrespect her shrine. And as in Lydgate, those who disrespect the shrine fall outside of the Christian English hegemony and have no way of anticipating what the shrine signifies. In one punishment narrative, Bradshaw explains Werburge's protective power when the Welsh besiege Chester. The canons "Toke the holy shryne of theyr patrones, / Set it on the towne-walles for helpe and tuicion, / Trustynge on her to be saued from distres" (2.710–12).[66] Ignorant of this divine object, one Welshman "with great wyckednes / Smot the sayd shryne in casting of a stone" (2.713–14). The subsequent miracle illustrates both the retributive power of the saint and the importance of respecting her shrine:

> Anone great punysshement vpon them all lyght:
> The kyng and his host were smytten with blyndnes …

And he that smote the holy shryne, doubtles,
Was greuously vexed with a sprite of darkenes,
And with hidous payne expired miserably. (2.716–17, 719–21)

Bradshaw specifies that the shrine is so damaged by the assault that it is "piteous to loke vpon" (2.715). And while Bradshaw describes the soldier as attacking not Werburge, but "the holy shryne," the Welsh king lives the rest of his life attempting to please "*this virgin* / for drede of punysshement" (2.729; emphasis added). These details, which elide the difference between Werburge, her relics, and the reliquary, anthropomorphize the shrine, presenting it as Werburge herself. We might understand Werburge as responding to an affront to her domicile rather than to her person. But there is also value in understanding the Welsh king's subsequent devotion to this holy virgin – and not, say, political and religious authorities of Chester – as equating Werburge with her reliquary. While the miracle affirms the importance and authority of Chester, the immediate punishment and the Welsh king's obsequious attitude combine to designate the shrine as the saint.

So, too, Harley 2278 includes a long section devoted to narrating the various consequences for those who do not appropriately venerate the container for Edmund's remains. For those who misbehave in this section do so – hardly a surprise, by this point – at Edmund's shrine. No one blasphemes Edmund, though Lydgate presents the one as if it were the other. In fact, Lydgate aligns Edmund both with his shrine and, as importantly, with narratives about the shrine. Leoffstan, like Osgothus, is a character without scruples: he dislikes Edmund himself and hates to hear anything about the saint:

[Leoffstan] hadde no deuocion
To here off hym, froward by dysdeyn,
Off his myracles ful small affeccion,
To heere hem rad the tyme spent in veyn. (*EF* 3165–8)

As in his account of Osgothus, Lydgate emphasizes written accounts of Edmund, which Leoffstan cannot tolerate to "heere … rad." Lydgate presents Edmund himself as commensurate with what is written about him; but in the retelling of why Edmund punishes Leoffstan, Lydgate highlights the shrine, too. In this case, a woman takes sanctuary at Edmund's shrine[67]: "For dreed off deth, socour for to fynde / Off blyssyd Edmund entred is the place, / Lowly besechyng he on hir wo taue mynde" (*EF* 3173–5). The criminal thus exemplifies the appropriate attitude at the site of a relic cult: one of humility, as I will discuss in detail in the following section.

Leoffstan, by contrast, has no regard for Edmund's "libertes" (*EF* 3169).[68] He arrests the woman and drags her away "with force and violence, / Vnto the seynt doyng no reuerence" (*EF* 3177–8). It is clear that Leoffstan disrespects the location of Edmund's shrine and the protection the shrine site traditionally afforded the criminally accused. This power-mad "tirant" (*EF* 3210) has no "reuerence" for Edmund's "seyntuarye" (*EF* 3200) – and as Lydgate makes clear, no reverence for "the seynt" himself.[69] So, too, the image on fol. 106r foregrounds Edmund's shrine, which occupies the central position of the illustration. Leoffstan, sporting a turban, appears as a Saracen judge, further emphasizing his refusal to listen to narratives of Edmund's power and his inability to interpret the importance of Edmund's shrine. Lydgate presents this incapacity as the direct cause of Leoffstan's fate: he fails to do reverence to the saint or to sanctuary (to, in other words, the "ffranchise" of the "hooly chirch" [*EF* 3181]), and at the woman's execution, a demon possesses and, in the end, kills him (*EF* 3212).

One could almost take from this miracle the moral "respect the metaphor!" By extension, the urgency of the situation – a woman, her life in danger, fleeing to the presence of the saint – presents one, and only one, appropriate interpretation for the shrine. And yet, for Leoffstan, then "shyrreue" (sheriff) (*EF* 3164), the primary difficulty seems to be that he values secular over religious law. As a result, Leoffstan interprets the shrine through the lens of legal discourse. In order to arrest the offending women, his bailiffs overpower Bury's clerks; Lydgate describes this action as violating the "boundis" of Bury St Edmunds (*EF* 3171). The binary opposition in this scene is clearly between secular and religious power. The manner in which the woman addresses Edmund is similarly suggestive: "Help blissid Edmund!" she says – "Keep and conserue thy iurediccion" (*EF* 3191, 3193). But Leoffstan fails to observe the rights of the church and enters with "al his court … / In the cherche to sitte in iugement" (*EF* 3198–9). The vocabulary throughout this punishment miracle derives from legal terminology: judgment, jurisdiction, court, sherrif, franchise. So though Leoffstan does not correctly interpret let alone respect the idea that Edmund's shrine is, metaphorically, Edmund, the passage also presents him as viewing the scene from a completely different perspective than Lydgate would perhaps wish.

In the end, Leoffstan earns his comeuppance not because of how he interprets or enacts the law, but because he disrespects both Edmund's shrine and his "libertes" (*EF* 3169). His punishment thus emphasizes how to interpret the reliquary: as Edmund, a tool of the mainstream church, not a tool for rabble-rousing officers of the secular court. Of course, Leoffstan functions in part as an example of what not to do. He and characters like him thus provide a model for pilgrim conduct. In the context of relic discourse, immoral pilgrims demonstrate that, without some kind of (usually written) guidance, not everyone will know how to behave at a shrine. By providing the occasion for miraculous, if punitive, intervention, Leoffstan affirms that the shrine is a holy and important place and that the saint himself is present and active. But insofar as his frame of reference is legal, not relic, discourse, this miracle challenges the simple operation of figurative language, presenting the relationship between container and contained as dependent on individual points of view. From the perspective of the woman whom Leoffstan executes, figurative representation is even dangerous.

Affirming *Praesentia* II: Exemplary Supplicants

As a convention of relic discourse, the misguided supplicant exposes the degree to which relics depended upon shrines and, ultimately, upon writing for their meaning. Even as such narratives affirm the relic's sanctity, they also showcase the degree to which this sanctity is not always evident just by looking at the reliquary. On the one hand, Lydgate, Arcoid, and Bradshaw all suggest that *only* the sinful fail to perceive the saint's *praesentia*, or to abide by the saint's wishes. On the other, the sinners in these narratives are frequently only horrible insofar as they fail to interpret the shrine; Leoffstan is a scrupulous and perhaps unintelligent judge, but it is difficult to see how precisely his supposed hatred for Edmund informs his actions at Bury. By contrast, the perfect supplicant – the one who secures a miracle, even for a bevy of sinners – exemplifies perfect understanding of what the shrine is, what the saint can do, and how to behave. In the twelfth-century *Miracula Sancti Erkenwaldi*, Arcoid describes one successful pilgrim praying "on bended knees ["flexis genibus"] ... with groans that would make one weep, with contrite heart and looks of humility" (132–3).[70] This woman earns her miracle "at the saint's tomb" ("ad sancti tumulum"). So, too, in the sixteenth century, Henry Bradshaw portrays the grateful citizens of Chester, on the arrival of Werburge's relics, as kneeling all down "afore this relique" (by which Bradshaw actually means Werburge's shrine: "The relique, the shryne full memoratyue" [2.296, 529]):

> The lordes / the cite3ins / and all the commons
> Mekely submytted them-selfe to the shryne,
> With manyfolde prayses and humble supplicacions,
> With interiour loue / and morall discipline" (2.302–5)

Werburge also heals those who come to her shrine "wepynge" (899, 916), "humble" (915), with a "hert full penitent" (933). So, too, the saint comes to the aid of a falsely accused man, who is in fact "Honest in maners / and of good conuersacion, / Disposed to vertue and humilite" (948–9). He prays "humblie" that Werburge save him from death, and when she rescues him from hanging (966–74), all visit "the shryne thc virgin thankyng" (987). Many early Christian writers outline the qualities of such a supplicant: unwavering faith, hope, charity, and often penitence and confession. Victricius of Rouen, Gregory of Tours, Guibert of Nogent, Wulfstan, Gerald of Wales, and John Mirk (among others) emphasize faith and penance as especially crucial.[71] In *Legendys of Hooly Wummen*, Osbern Bokenham similarly specifies that "good deuocyounn" is necessary to obtain a miracle from the foot relic of St Margaret.[72] So, too, in "The Lyfe of Ioseph of Armathia" printed by Richard Pynson in 1520, pilgrims are exhorted to

> Gyue your attendaunce
> Saynt ioseph there to serue with humble affectyon,
> At Glastenbury for to do hym reuerence;
> Lyft vp your hertes with goostly deuocyon.[73]

In his twelfth-century *Sententia de memoria sanctorum quos veneraris*, Eadmer of Canterbury urges the monks to behave as archetypal virtuous supplicants.[74] Eadmer describes explicitly what this physical and spiritual attitude ought to be:

> For when those ones [that is, the supplicants], by day or night, stand in praise of God for their glory, truly it must be believed that they, through each and every moment, offer praise to God for their salvation.[75]
>
> The supplicants prostrate their bodies before the saints' relics, they grovel on the ground on bended knees, they bend their faces to the floor – and we are to believe that the saints stand before God rigidly indifferent to these prayers, that they refuse to listen, that they care nothing for them? Who could say such a thing? The devotion of these suppliants will not be useless, it will not be in vain, it will not go unrewarded.[76]

Eadmer here characterizes not simply devout but, more specifically, successful supplicants. Such people venerate the saint day and night. Eadmer is clear about who will benefit from such devotion: the supplicants ("isti") will ("pro salute istorum"). Their suffering ("compatiantur"), that is, will be for their own benefit, since the truly devout and selfless supplicant, who knows himself to be in need of God's grace ("dei misericordia indigere cognoscunt"),[77] finds respite in saintly intercession.

Hence, the bodily attitude of Eadmer's ideal supplicants must be obvious and easy to spot. These supplicants prostrate themselves on the floor; they await divine mercy on bended knee; they "bend" ("incuruantur") their faces to the floor. The physical attitude of such supplicants shows them to be in need ("indigere") because it shows them to be, on some level, unworthy ("indigni") of the saint's attentions. They are on the ground; they not only kneel, but press their bodies, and even their faces, to the floor. For these kinds of supplicants, Eadmer promises, the saints will not "refuse to listen" ("auditum auerterent"). So, too, as Eadmer narrates in the *Sententia*, the supplicant ought to have faith, "by which it may be believed that the saints are able to help"; unfailing hope of the saints' goodness, which "anticipates that they want to help"; and "charity that does not grow lukewarm in love and devotion for the joy and praise of the saints."[78] Good – successful – supplicants have faith that is unwavering (even in the face of contrary evidence), unabashed hope that the saints will help, and enthusiastic devotion to the memory and relics of the saints.

For Guibert of Nogent, as for Eadmer, appropriate behaviour included faith and penitence, and Guibert emphasizes these virtues even as he argues against translation and enshrinement. From Guibert's point of view, the supplicant who puts her faith in an authentic relic transcends the base abuses of relic cults. The moral state of the supplicant is so important to Guibert that, in *De sanctis et eorum pigneribus*, he narrates several miracles that centre primarily on faith. In the first of these, Guibert recounts the story of a young man and woman who embark upon an incestuous affair. The woman becomes pregnant, and the two flee, fearing that their neighbours will discover their union (and its fruits). Before they leave, however, the young woman – beset by guilt and shame – confesses "with deep sorrow" ("altissimi dolore") to the local priest.[79] As far as Guibert is concerned, her confession, along with her faith, saves her life: when the young man pushes her into a well and bombards her with rocks in an attempt to kill her (thereby keeping his crime a secret), the woman survives in the well for "almost forty days, with no other nourishment than" drops of water (411). Guibert makes the moral of the story clear:

> Behold how much value lies in faith in doing penance, as well as in persevering in the desire to correct oneself. A person who places faith in doing penance, having accepted the grace of confession and with it a trustworthy forgiveness, will never have to despair concerning indulgence ... The faith of this young woman seems to me to be particularly important, in that she faithfully and unswervingly turned to God in the moment of her need ["fidelis et irreverberatus in sua ad deum necessitate concursus"]. (trans. Head 411–12; I 292–300)

Guibert's treatise as a whole argues against what he sees as the more outrageous abuses of relic cults, but in this moment, Guibert articulates the primary conventions of the successful supplicant, instead: faith and penitence.

Lydgate includes one such supplicant in his *Lives of Ss Edmund and Fremund* and many such petitioners in the *Extra Miracles*. In the *Lives of Ss Edmund and Fremund*, Lydgate narrates Sweyn's invasion of England, which continues "ful ten yere" (*EF* 2976). This instance distills the consequences of bad kingship, for Etheldredus, unable to defend the realm from Sweyn's tyrrany, flees the island. More importantly for my purposes, however, the virtuous subjection of Ayllewyn, Lydgate's ideal supplicant, precipitates Edmund's miraculous intervention. Ayllewyn is not the only character who models humility and penitence, however. Many tormented people

> lay prostraat knelyng aboute his shryne.
> Women go barfoot pitously wepyng.
> With letanyes preestis dede enclyne.
> By abstynence the peeple long fastyng.
> Men off religioun, be prayer and wakyng,
> Besouhte the martir ther fredam to renewe,
> And off his mercy on ther wo to rewe. (*EF* 2983–9)

These "peeple" behave according to the dictates of literary convention: they lie prostrate before the shrine; the women weep (presumably in penance). Others fast, acknowledging their sin and demonstrating humility. Ayllewyn himself "Afforn his shryne vpon the pauement lay"

(*EF* 2998), refusing to depart "nyht nor day" (*EF* 3000); his "perfeccion" was so "couth" that all expect him to secure a miracle (*EF* 3004). Edmund ultimately grants the prayer of Ayllewyn, the perfect supplicant – the one who, like the other tearful penitents, treats the shrine as the saint. The *Extra Miracles of St Edmund* similarly emphasizes miracle working as part of a spiritual economy: Edmund restores a boy to a bereaved mother, who vows to "halwe ... the day / Off thy martir, kyng of Estyngelond, / With devout herte" (*EM* 121–3) – provided that Edmund resurrect her son.

Creating *Praesentia*: Relic Custodians

The mother's exemplary attitude precipitates her son's recovery, just as the depraved behaviour of Osgothus and Leoffstan precipitates their punishments. In both cases, Lydgate directly associates the moral state of the individual with how Edmund responds. This approach instills the shrine with Edmund's *praesentia*: just as Edmund punishes those who denigrate his reliquary, he rewards those who, like the rejoicing supplicants from the opening of this chapter, travel "Affor thy shryne to thy royal presence, / Prostrat afor the with ffeithfful hool corage" (*EM* 318–19). Both rewards and punishments presuppose that Edmund resides in the shrine, and while the saint's retribution demonstrates that the shrine is a complex and even confusing sign for the saint, miracles of healing and reward construct the shrine as easy to understand, downplaying its presence as a complex representational object. Relic custodians, on the other hand, establish a shrine's holy power by their very presence. Often called *custodes tumuli, tumbarii*, feretrars, or *custodes pignorum*, relic custodians (or shrine keepers) are understudied and neglected literary and historical characters. Shrine keepers were fixtures at many popular shrines, such as that of Thomas Becket at Canterbury; the unsanctioned cults of Richard Scrope at York and, at Lincoln, of Robert Grosseteste and John Dalderby all had custodians.[80] There were keepers of Scrope's tomb at York long after ecclesiastical and secular powers delegitimized it: John Stytenham appears as custodian in 1421 and William Haiton in *c.* 1468.[81] In these cases, relic custodians provide evidence for a shrine's popularity, even when ecclesiastical and secular authorities officially contemned the would-be saint. Custodians appear at parochial shrines, too, as the keepers of St Modwen's bones and image in the Abbey of Burton upon Trent.[82] Sometimes, guardians were appointed for especially important images – that of Our Lady at Caversham or Our Lady of Walsingham, for instance.[83] At Durham Cathedral, both relic custodians and sacristans cared for Cuthbert's and many other relics. Dom. Richard de Sedgebrook, a late fourteenth-century sacristan at Durham, compiled an important relic list and was apparently responsible for the relics in Durham's cupboard;[84] sacristans at Durham were responsible for Cuthbert's relics from at least the twelfth century, when Reginald of Durham records Elfred Weston, a sacristan, as guardian of the shrine.[85] Durham had a sacristan who served as shrine keeper in the fifteenth century as well, when Alfred the sacristan took on the position. So, too, sacristans at Bury cared for Edmund's relics; Islwyn Geoffrey Thomas suggests that their "eminent position" indicates the importance of relics to Bury.[86]

The duties of these keepers and sacristans included caring for the shrine itself. As Jocelin of Brakelond's account makes clear, before the fire in 1198 necessitated Edmund's translation, the custodians at Bury had special access to the saint by means of a "hole in the coffin-lid through which the guardians of the feretory used of old to thrust their hands that they might touch the holy body" (112).[87] The keepers themselves were asleep when the fire broke out ("cum ergo dormirent custodes" [106]), and according to Jocelin, Edmund himself complains that his shrine was badly guarded ("neggligenter custodiri") (110); the abbot iterates this accusation, citing "neggligenciam custodum" as the reason for the fire (116). Once the body was translated, the abbot appointed "new guardians ... and [made] rules for them, that they might guard the shrines more honourably and with greater diligence [than those who were on duty when the fire started]" (116).[88] Samson's desire to have honest keepers is commensurate with a late thirteenth-century document from Worcester outlining the desirable qualities of a relic custodian: "The convent for its part, will choose to their liking honest clerics or monks as custodians" ("et conventus pro parte sua, quos voluerint custodes honestos clericos vel monachos deputabit").[89]

Clearly, protecting the shrine was a central duty of the relic custodian, who might also become a focal point for blame in the event of a tragedy, such as Bury's 1198 fire. Elsewhere, Reginald of Durham credits the virtue and diligence of twelfth-century relic custodians as saving Cuthbert's shrine from fire: "How Saint Cuthbert appeared in a vision to a certain sacristan [the custodian], and he advised him to extinguish the candle, lest his vestments be burned."[90] Throughout the narrative, Reginald highlights Cuthbert's close relationship to his shrine keepers, regularly appearing to them in visions to instruct them on how to care for and protect his remains.[91]

Insofar as they emphasize this intimate contact with the saint, Reginald and Jocelin depict shrine keepers as members of the select group who were permitted direct access to the saint's body (a practice that frustrated Jocelin of Brakelond).[92] This privilege enabled custodians to corroborate, even construct, the saint's efficacy and presence. The *Customary of the Shrine of St Thomas* describes some of the Canterbury custodial duties, including ringing the bell to announce the opening of the shrine, keeping pilgrims out of the shrine area during lunch, reopening the shrine after lunch, and ensuring that pilgrims behave appropriately.[93] So, too, by sleeping at shrines, or supervising pilgrims from observatory booths – frequently located above the feretory – the keeper was an embodied reminder that the shrine was a special place.[94] Some custodians relied directly on shrine offerings to pay their yearly stipend; their very livelihood thus depended upon advertising the saint's *praesentia*.[95] Obviously, if the saint were perceived as impotent, pilgrims and offerings would be few and far between. Thus, while the job of a custodian was in some sense practical – to prevent theft, as Patrick Geary and others have suggested – it also involved rhetorical performance, the manipulation of language in order to convey the importance of a relic and shrine.

Indeed, some custodians generated the very written accounts that endowed their monuments (and relics) with meaning and potency. In one famous manuscript illumination of the *Life of Edward the Confessor*, a shrine keeper watches over the early tomb shrine of Edward. As he does so, he is poised over a book in which he is writing, possibly recording the miracles Edward works for the pilgrims who are crawling in and out of the tomb's "foramina" [Figure 1].[96] Relic lists (such as those I discuss in chapter 1) were themselves often used and/or composed by shrine keepers or sacristans.[97] These lists sometimes include relics that a cathedral did not in fact have, as when the author of a fourteenth-century Canterbury relic list includes Swithun's body ("corpus") when it is clear that Canterbury could lay claim only to Swithun's head ("caput").[98] Portraits of immoral relic custodians show the potential of language to misidentify such objects, featuring custodians whose expert rhetorical skill enables them to present just about any object as wonderous.[99] But even honest keepers participated in generating the commonplaces that imparted value to a relic and shrine. Keepers such as Benedict of Peterborough at Canterbury, and Gilbert of Chevening at Hereford, narrated the miracles that legitimized their cults.[100] In his twelfth-century *The Life and Miracles of St William of Norwich*, Thomas of

Monmouth, William's primary guardian in the 1150s, does not merely affirm his saint's *praesentia* – his prose account generates it.[101] So, too, by offering testimony during Thomas Cantilupe's fourteenth-century canonization proceedings, Gilbert of Chevening, Cantilupe's shrine keeper from 1287 to 1303, helps to create a saint.

The canonization investigation of Thomas Cantilupe, a late thirteenth-century bishop of Hereford, took place in London and Hereford from July to November 1307. The written record of this event introduces a historical relic custodian: Gilbert of Chevening, who was custodian of St Thomas Cantilupe's shrine in 1287 and possibly later. Gilbert was a canon of Hereford Cathedral until at least 1307, after which point he disappears from recorded history.[102] He provides a fascinating test case of the role of an actual relic custodian in the official process of declaring someone a saint. For in the hearings, Gilbert is both curator of the shrine and advocate for Thomas's sanctity. The document refers to both "domino Gilberto procuratore capituli Herefordiensis" and Gilbert, "presbyter, perpetuus vicarius ecclesiae de Magna Markele."[103] This is the same person: Gilbert of Cheveninge, vicar of Much Markle parish, is also a postulator for Thomas Cantilupe, as is attested by a reference to Gilbert, "dominus ... vicarius de Magna Marcle, & Thomas de Guynes, procuratores in isto negotio capituli Herefordiensis" (*AASS* 641). Gilbert of Cheveninge is also "ipso existente custode tumuli dicti domini Thomae" (622). It is therefore likely that Gilbert of Cheveninge played one of the most instrumental roles in the canonization of Thomas Cantilupe, as both relic custodian and postulator to the papal curia.[104]

Gilbert of Chevening appears in several documents of the early fourteenth century, including *The Register of Richard de Swinfield* and Thomas Cantilupe's 1307 canonization proceedings. It is not known when Gilbert was born, though it seems clear that he was from Chevening, in northwestern Kent, twenty-two miles from London. The Chevening parish register, St Botolph, dates from 1561, and there is no record of Gilbert's participation in his local parish, nor of his parentage.[105] He appears for the first time in Bishop Richard Swinfield's register in the entry for 6 April 1283. Swinfield mentions Gilbert only in passing, as "Gilbertus de Chyvenkngke, capellanus."[106] On 3 October 1287, Gilbert received his first benefice when he was appointed to Lyndney by the dean and chapter of Hereford cathedral.[107] Like many Hereford canons, Gilbert was Oxford educated: he left Lydney on 28 February 1289 to attend the university.[108] Gilbert was probably at Oxford until around 1291, when he again appears as "vicario ecclesie de Lyndeneye."[109] In

1289 he is listed simply as "domini Gilberti de Chiveninge," apparently having no other explicit title or attachment to any parish. By 1303, Gilbert had acquired (at least) his second benefice; it is not clear whether he abandoned Lyndney when the abbot and convent of Lyre assigned him to Much Markle on 6 February 1303.[110] Gilbert had also become a priest by this time, likely ordained sometime between 1291 and 1303. It is unclear exactly when Gilbert became a secular canon at Hereford. According to Ronald C. Finucane, Gilbert was the relic custodian for Thomas Cantilupe from 1287 until at least 1307,[111] though, as the record of his education suggests, Gilbert was not present at Hereford throughout this entire period. His periodic absence might explain why Hereford had multiple keepers ("custodes tumuli") (*AASS* 641).

The canonization of Thomas Cantilupe was crucial to the future of Hereford Cathedral, which – like Norwich – had no major saint or shrine. In the person of Gilbert, then, we can see that a relic custodian could take on significant authority in shaping the legend of a future saint. Patrick Daly explains the complex juridical procedures involved in such a canonization hearing, the importance of postulators to making the case for canonization at a local level, as well as the essential participation of the clerical and aristocratic elite in the petitions sent to Rome.[112] For a petition to be successful, bishops, religious communities, local nobility, and the monarch had to demonstrate support.[113] If the petitions to Rome were successful – and in Cantilupe's case, they obviously were – a papal delegation would travel to the saint's diocese to carry out a local inquiry, called a "processus informativus." The papal commissioners Clement V assigned were William Durand, bishop of the French diocese of Mende; Richard Baldock, bishop of London; and William de Testu, papal nuncio in England. Of these, only Durand was consistently present to hear local testimony.[114] Their job was to interview eyewitnesses, both of the putative saint's life and miracles. As a postulator (and shrine keeper), Gilbert of Chevening communicated some of this information to the papal representatives. And with his narrative, Gilbert participates in inventing both a saint and his miracle-working relics.

In one case, Gilbert narrates a miracle that he witnessed and sanctioned as Thomas Cantilupe's relic custodian ("ipos existente custode tumuli dicti domini Thomae" [*AASS* 622]). The cripple of whom Gilbert speaks, Juliana Kock, is not present to speak for herself. (In fact, there is no mention of her whereabouts in 1307.) The report allows only that she "lived for twelve years, as it was reported by many from the aforesaid parish of Eton, after the aforementioned miracle" (*AASS* 622).[115] It would appear that she died between 1299 and 1307 and that Gilbert testified for her because he witnessed her cure in 1287: "Dominus Gilbertus de Chevenigh presbyter, perpetuus vicarius ecclesiae de Magna Markele requisitus, ut narraret, si quid sciebat de miraculo, quod in personam Julianae Kock dicitur contigisse" (*AASS* 622). The text makes no mention of her death, however, and her voice is conspicuously absent from Gilbert's second-hand testimony. Gilbert presents her as the ideal and pitiable supplicant: as he would have it, Kock was extremely crippled ("alius contractus pedibus ... tibias plicatas & ... curva"). Moreover, her behaviour demonstrates her faith and devotion to the would-be saint; she does not merely hope for but "expects" a miracle at Hereford (*AASS* 622).[116] Gilbert derives this characterization from Juliana's behaviour, which he witnessed ("Videns ipsa Juliana") (*AASS* 622). Both Henry of St Alban's, who was "at that time the custodian, with that same witness, of the aforesaid tomb" ("custodi tunc cum ipso teste [scil. Gilbert] dicti tumuli"), and Roger of Sevenake, "tunc canonico Herefordiae, jam defunctis," ratify Gilbert's version of events (*AASS* 622). Their official eyewitness accounts function much like Jocelin of Brakelond's written description of Edmund of Bury's incorrupt body: in this case, the narrative constructs Cantilupe's body as a relic and assures the papal delegates, who did not witness the miracle, that Hereford is a holy place.

Gilbert similarly confirms another miracle, in which St Thomas cures two blind children.[117] In this case, though the mother of the boys, Margaret, is the witness, the narrative highlights Gilbert's role in selecting the miracle: "And lord Gilbert, custodian of the aforesaid tomb who produced witnesses of this miracle, responded that it was so" (*AASS* 638).[118] Gilbert's authority is unmistakable. He does not merely corroborate Margaret's testimony, but rather affirms its validity ("quod sic"). The narrative subordinates Margaret's description of the suffering and recovery of her children to Gilbert's declaration. We believe that the boys were initially healthy, as Margaret claims, partly because Gilbert authorizes her version of events: one boy suffers from blindness; Margaret's midwife injures the other (*AASS* 638). She brings her sons to St Thomas's tomb ("ad tumulum dicti S. Thomae"), where the putative saint cures them. Gilbert's intrusion at the end of Margaret's personal tale illustrates his narrative authority and central role in the canonization proceedings; the miracle happened because he says it did.

Like Gilbert, Thomas of Monmouth assumes a position of authority and special privilege in his *The Life and Miracles of St William of Norwich*, which he began in 1150 to invent a local cult for Norwich. The story of William of Norwich is a familiar one: William, a child martyr, was found brutally murdered in March 1144. Many blamed the local Jewish community; and by 1150, Thomas of Monmouth was actively campaigning for William's cult and advancing his own special place in it. Thomas is a unusual relic custodian in that he appoints himself William's exclusive mediator. He has a remarkable predilection for self-aggrandizement. His role is hence even more involved than that of Gilbert, who appears in several miracles but certainly makes no dominant claim over Cantilupe's remains or sanctity. By contrast, Thomas became the primary guardian of William's shrine during the 1150s and, as Benedicta Ward has suggested, aggressively sought to associate the shrine site not merely with William himself but with holy power (and, I would add, with saintly *praesentia*).[119]

Before little St William, Norwich – like Hereford, which had no principal saint until Cantilupe – was without a patron. In retelling his vision of Herbert, founder of Norwich, Thomas both foregrounds his own role at the centre of the would-be cult and emphasizes what Norwich lacks. Herbert instructs Thomas to translate the child martyr, and he entrusts Thomas with a message meant to convince the prior of Norwich of William's holiness:

> Let them remember that their wont was when I used to set out for the court of the King, to pray of me that I should endeavour to obtain from the king some venerable relics of the saints [uenerabiles sanctorum ... reliquias] ... But I used to say to them that I would seek for nothing of this sort then ... because the time would come when, by God's grace assisting them, they would have such great and worshipful relics as that by them the Church of Norwich would be greatly exalted and become celebrated through the whole of England ... These, I declare, are those relics which I have told you before would be bestowed upon you.[120]

Through Herbert, Thomas reminds his audience that Norwich had long been without any relics. Moreover, Herbert's message enables Thomas to present William as the answer not only to the desire of the Norwich community to possess holy bodies, but also as the realization of Herbert's prophecy: Herbert refrained from collecting any relics because he knew that another, greater relic awaited the community. With his narrative, Thomas places William – and himself – at the centre of Norwich's God-given destiny. As Thomas would have it, William's body is a divine gift to Norwich. By extension, Thomas is the mediator of God's command, William's self-appointed "private secretary" ("familiari secretario") (139).

Thomas predicates his narrative authority and reliability on a holy vision, thereby circumventing any argument against his version of events. As Simon Yarrow remarks, the visions certainly have "propaganda value."[121] In his account of William's first translation, Thomas highlights his own prestige as one of the six monks who undertakes the nighttime disinterment of William's body: "[A]t night after *Lauds* were finished, and when all the convent, except us six, had betaken themselves to the dormitory" (122),[122] they go to exhume the child martyr. Thomas himself is the only fearless monk present: he not only opens the casket but takes two teeth as souvenirs. He characterizes his theft as "pious" ("pio … furto," 122–3); his own narrative supports his assertion, as Herbert, the founder of Norwich, orders Thomas to translate William; and St William himself personally appoints Thomas his caretaker.

Not surprisingly, Thomas includes miracles in which William punishes those who do not respect William's (and/or Thomas's) instructions about how to treat the shrine. As in Harley 2278, to misbehave at the shrine is to offend the saint himself; but it is also to offend Thomas. In one such instance, Thomas insists that St William refused to heal Richard of Lynn, a fellow monk, because Richard failed to offer candles at William's tomb. Richard, exceedingly ill, spends the night at William's sepulcher, whereupon William himself appears to him in a vision, demanding why he should heal someone with no offering: "If I cure you, what reward will you give?" (138).[123] William then specifies that Richard should offer the candles he acquired dishonestly and planned to give to his sister-in-law. Understandably, Richard demurs from William's exacting (and rather precise) request. William will have none of it: "Bring those candles that I ask for, and hand them over to Dom Thomas my private secretary to be kept in his custody … For verily God so wills and bids this to be done" (139).[124] Thomas, the narrator of this exchange, implicitly claims access not merely to William's bones but to the saint's (and God's) direct commands.

The exchange invites us to imagine Thomas using St William as a mouthpiece to realize his own vision of how the shrine should look. In another instance, Thomas depicts William as objecting strongly to the removal of his carpet and lantern by Prior Elias. Richard's candles are to make up in part for Elias's oversight (139), and as far as Thomas is concerned, Richard "was ordered to hand [the candles] over to me"

(142). Thomas is not merely William's servant in this narrative, but an agent in some respects more powerful than the saint himself: Thomas determines what he will write; it even seems as though Thomas determines what William wants and says. Moreover, while lecturing Richard, St William warns that if Elias fails to return the carpet and lamp, if he "rebel[s] against the divine ordaining, let him hold it for certain that right soon he shall pay a heavy penalty" (139–40).[125] William goes on to threaten Richard, too; and sure enough, when both men perish (143–5, 165–7), Thomas uses the occasion to emphasize the importance of William – and of his own position as William's "private secretary." For, ultimately, both men die for disobeying Thomas's written version of what William wants.

Through his prose, Thomas creates a powerful saint. In a way, Thomas himself *is* William, insofar as William tends to want what will benefit Thomas in his position at Norwich. Thomas offers some possible ways in which the relic custodian might manipulate language – by presenting his own desires as those of the saint – in order to get what he wants (say, candles). While, unlike Thomas, Gilbert does not insert himself into the canonization proceedings, he nonetheless authorizes the testimony of those who, like Margaret, experienced Cantilupe's *praesentia* first hand. The character of the relic custodian is a unique commonplace, then, insofar as he is able to generate, rather than merely affirm, *praesentia*. Many of the other commonplaces of relic discourse render the shrine and relics intelligible, ensuring that all would understand the shrine site as the central location of saintly *praesentia*. As master puppeteer, the relic custodian can produce the very narrative that endows the relics with *praesentia* in the first place. In narratives that feature immoral relic custodians and/or questing supplicants, the custodian is frequently the character who most easily manipulates how others perceive his relics; and he usually has more intimate access to the relic than any other character. As the next two chapters will show, Malory and Chaucer use relic custodians to interrogate how the appointed elite create a relic's value and *praesentia*. Their custodians – Joseph of Arimathea, Galahad, the Pardoner, and Pandarus – illustrate how the meaning of relics depends closely upon what their keepers say and write about them.

PART TWO

The Trouble with Relic Discourse

Chapter Three

English Grail Legends and the Holy Blood

The Holy Grail may well be the most famous, and most mysterious, pseudo-blood relic in late medieval literature. But, oddly, critics have rarely considered its importance *as relic,* something that the English literature of the period, by contrast, emphasizes.[1] This chapter shows that several English narratives in the Grail tradition – the late fourteenth-century alliterative *Joseph of Arimathie*, Henry Lovelich's fifteenth-century *The History of the Holy Grail*, and Thomas Malory's late fifteenth-century *Le Morte d'Arthur* – use relic discourse to present Joseph of Arimathea as a globe-trotting relic custodian and the questing knights as supplicants.[2] The first part of this chapter takes up Joseph's role in transporting and keeping the Grail. These works tap into the medieval legend that presents Joseph as the first to bring Christianity – and blood relics – to England. They share much in common with blood-relic treatises by Robert Grosseteste, the monks at Hailes, and William Sudbury, which similarly depict Joseph as the first English relic custodian, in order to authenticate and popularize the blood relics at Hailes and Westminster.[3] Thus, while the alliterative *Joseph* author, Lovelich, and Malory all derived their narratives from the French tradition of the Grail, we should also think of these literary texts as indebted to English cults of the Holy Blood and the writings about them – and as indebted to relic discourse.[4] As Richard Barber has suggested, Malory himself may have been devoted to the Blood at Hailes; and certainly Malory attends to the Grail as object (rather than apparition) in a way the French romances do not.[5] It is thus unsurprising to find the Joseph strain of the Grail legends front and centre in Malory's narrative.[6] The second part of the chapter focuses on Malory's depiction of his Grail knights as supplicants. In his sympathetic portrayal of Lancelot's failure to access the

Grail fully – no matter how many times he confesses – Malory exposes purveyors of relic discourse as making promises (e.g., that any supplicant will be healed if he is penitent) they cannot keep. For no matter how carefully Lancelot follows their rules, he will never attain what he calls the "holy bloode."[7] And he ends the quest in defeat.

This chapter attempts to come to terms with the ways in which relic discourse informs Malory's Grail quest – without explaining away such characteristics as allegorical explorations of the Arthurian court or of chivalry in general. Sir Thomas Malory, born to a gentry family in the English Midlands around 1416, is famous for having been a "public nuisance" who was "in and out of gaol for 'attempted murder, rape, extortion, malicious damage and sacrilegious robbery' "[8] – to say nothing of escaping from jail several times. Briefly released in 1462, by 1468 Malory was in jail again, where he composed *Le Morte d'Arthur* between 1468 and 1470. Given his own legal imbroglios, it is no surprise that we have often followed Eugène Vinaver in interpreting Malory's Grail quest, an explicitly religious text, in secular terms – Malory's desire having been to "secularize the Grail theme as much as the story will allow."[9] From this perspective, the religious discourse of Malory's Grail quest helps us to see something about the court and about politics, not about late medieval religion.

But Malory's Grail quest also shows us something about the celestial values it explores – about relic discourse and about fifteenth-century religious culture in general. For Malory's translation draws our attention to how these celestial values are sometimes based on materiality, on things. As Dorsey Armstrong has pointed out, Malory adapted the quest from "a pursuit of understanding to a hunt for the physical object of the grail."[10] In focusing on the Grail as a physical object, Malory's text draws our attention to the religious objects that proliferated in fifteenth-century England, to their treatment, use, and to the religious discourses associated with these holy objects.[11] The fifteenth century saw an unprecedented increase in the production and circulation of religious images, statues, and personal devotional objects; it was a culture of what Gail Gibson has called the "incarnational aesthetic," one that emphasized touching and/or interacting with "concrete images."[12] This incarnational aesthetic dovetailed with affective piety, the practice of meditating on Christ's bodily suffering. Lay practices and vernacular theologies were thus central to the religious culture of the fifteenth century.[13] So, too, the gentry, whose ownership, commissioning, and use of many of these objects – books of hours, *arma Christi*, personal totems and relics – influenced as well as responded to clerical concerns of that era.[14] Growing up in a gentry family, Malory would have been enmeshed in the richly material religious culture of fifteenth-century England.

And yet, relic discourse and veneration do not always square with the idea of a fifteenth-century incarnational aesthetic.[15] Even the most prominent lay parishoner could not own a major cathedral relic or commission a new shrine for such a relic – these undertakings, under the purview of the clergy, would simply have been too expensive. Major cathedral shrines were distinct from the kinds of concrete images that layfolk endowed or touched. Malory's emphasis on the Grail's tactile nature in fact showcases this difference: the Grail, like many major relics, is accessible only to a few. The knights pursue a physical object that most of them cannot reach. Reading Malory's changes to his source text in the context of fifteenth-century piety in general, and relic discourse in particular, reveals the Grail quest of the *Morte* as deeply invested in how the culture of relics encourages, but does not necessarily reward, certain kinds of behaviour, and in how the relic is simultaneously an object but also – most clearly manifested by the Grail's ascension into heaven – not here at all, in heaven and beyond the reach of the living.

The Grail as Historical Blood Relic

Scholars have read the Grail in an almost bewildering variety of ways: as representative of a hermeneutic system, as a Eucharistic vessel or as the Eucharist itself,[16] as pagan and ritualistic, as a symbol of "doubt and high anxiety,"[17] or even as mimetic of the knightly body.[18] I have no wish to limit the Grail to one interpretation – as Sandra Ness Ihle has rightly pointed out, "the essence of the Grail in the [French] *Queste* is its mystery"[19]– nor to discount these interesting readings of its significance. However, Malory consistently describes the Grail using the technical terminology, metaphors, and commonplaces of relic discourse. When it appears, it is accompanied by "suche a savour as all the spycery of the worlde had bene there" (II 793, 798). Incorrupt saints' bodies were often said to smell not merely pleasant but of spices, and the lovely odor of holy bodies is a hagiographical commonplace.[20] What is more, Malory refers to the Grail as "the rychyst thynge that ony man hath lyvynge" (II 793). Conventionally, holy bodies are similarly said to be exceedingly valuable, even more valuable than gems and gold.[21]

And at the end of the quest, the Grail knights Galahad, Percival, and Bors build a lavish reliquary for the Grail, consisting of "a cheste of golde and of precious stonys that coverde the holy vessell" (II 1034).[22] So, too, the *Joseph* author explains that Joseph of Arimathea and his son, Josaphe, build a "luytel whucche" (a reliquary) for "þat ilke blod."[23]

Insofar as these characters all enshrine the Grail, they clearly treat it as a relic. So, too, when the Grail first appears at Camelot, it is completely invisible. Covered "with whyght samyte" (II 865), it calls to mind the relics of English cathedral feretories, similarly hidden from view by cathedral architecture and shrine canopies:[24]

> *Than entird into the halle the Holy Grayle coverde with whyght samyte, but there was none that myght se hit nother whom that bare hit*. And there was all the halle fulfylled with good odoures, and every knyght had such metis and drynkes as he beste loved in thys worlde.
>
> And whan the Holy Grayle had bene borne thorow the hall, than the holy vessell departed suddeynly, that they wyst nat where hit becam. Than had they all breth to speke. (II 865; emphasis added)

Malory's passage indicates both the tactile nature of the Grail, which he associates with food, and its evanescence: no one can see it, and it departs suddenly to an unspecified (or secret) location. The French *La Queste del Saint Graal*, by contrast, allows that when the Holy Grail "entered the room, covered with a white silk cloth … no one could see who carried it."[25] The passage suggests merely that the *bearer* of the Grail remained invisible, the resulting image being one of the Grail floating in the air. According to this account, the Grail itself is *not* invisible or difficult to see – or, alternatively, seeing it covered with a white cloth constitutes a kind of access, a kind of vision. Malory emphasizes, as the French source text does not, the Grail's own indeterminate appearance: "there was *none that myght se hit* nother whom that bare hit." In the *Morte*, that is, no knight can see the Grail at all. No other version of the Grail quest presents the Holy Blood itself as invisible.[26]

What is more, Gawain blames this lack of vision on the "whyte samyte" that covers the Grail:

> "But one thyng begyled us, *that we myght nat se the Holy Grayle: hit was so preciously coverde*. Wherefore I woll make here a vow that to-morne, withoute longer abydynge, I shall laboure in the queste of the Sankgreall, and that I shall holde me oute a twelve-month and a day or more if nede be,

> and never shall I returne unto the courte agayne *tylle I have sene hit more opynly than hit hath bene shewed here.*" (II 866; emphasis added)

In this passage, Gawain explicitly complains about the Grail's covering, identifying the silk covering as the reason the knights cannot view this object. The passive voice at the end of Gawain's speech similarly suggests that a force beyond the knights' control inhibits their view of the object – Gawain wishes to see it "more opynly than hit hath bene shewed." The French Gawain similarly motivates the quest for the Grail. And yet, he does not suggest that the Grail's covering is the root cause of the knights' failure to see:

> "But the observers there were so deceived that they couldn't see the Grail clearly; its true form remained hidden from them. For that reason, I now make this vow: that tomorrow morning I will undertake the Quest ... I will not return to court, no matter what happens, until I have seen the Grail more clearly than I did today, assuming that I can see it at all. If I cannot, I will come back."[27]

The Gawain of the French *Queste* takes an entirely different attitude, blaming the shortcomings of the "observers" for their inability to see the Grail and distancing these shortcomings from Arthur's court.[28] He makes no mention of the white silk covering. In Malory, none can see the Grail *because of* this covering. In the French version, it is irrelevant. The French Gawain allows the possibility that he will fail; but Malory's Gawain, having blamed the presentation and covering of the Grail, takes it as an affront that he could not see the Grail in the first place. This hidden or partially hidden quality of the Grail informs every subsequent appearance of the holy vessel in the *Morte* – except, that is, in its final appearance to Galahad.

Of course, Malory's Gawain is hardly an exemplary character, and we may understand his reaction to the Grail as foreshadowing an unwillingness to take responsibility for his shortcomings.[29] And yet, the changes in the passage highlight not the vices of the knights present, but the degree to which practical concerns (the precious covering) occlude this most holy of objects. The Grail is not, after all, merely any personal, small relic, nor is it a personal totem. Instead, the focal point of a religious quest, the Grail takes on and even surpasses the importance of the major cathedral shrines that contributed to the emergence of relic discourse.[30] Just as Malory presents the Grail using the technical terminology and metaphors of relic discourse, he renders the characters of the *Morte* according to the commonplaces of the virtuous supplicant, the depraved supplicant, and the relic custodian. Of the questing knights, only the pure, faithful, and penitent achieve success. And of the successful knights, Galahad – the last in a long line of relic custodians – has the most intimate contact with the Grail itself.

In fact, in many moments throughout the quest, Malory portrays the Grail as a historical blood relic of Christ. Nicholas Vincent has identified three kinds of medieval blood relic: effluvial, eucharistic, and historical. I assign the latter adjective to what Vincent calls "the literal blood of Christ"[31] – actual blood from Christ's human body that survives on earth. The other two types of blood relic are miraculous: effluvial relics were from a statue or image of Christ that began to bleed;[32] eucharistic blood relics usually consisted of a consecrated host that was miraculously transformed into flesh and blood.[33] Of these, historical relics were both the most important and the most controversial. As concrete reminders of Christ's presence on earth, their prestige was uncontested – but often enough, theologians discounted the possibility that, after the Ascension, anything of Jesus's body was left behind.[34] In any case, historical relics of the Holy Blood were the focus of popular cults in England, particularly at Glastonbury and Hailes. And Malory clearly presents the Grail, throughout the quest, as this kind of blood relic.

At the opening of the *Sankgreal*, Malory identifies the Grail as "the sygnyfycacion oof blyssed bloode off Oure Lorde Jesu Cryste, whyche was brought into thys londe by Joseph off Aramathye" (II 845–6). Here, Malory emphasizes Joseph's role in transporting the Grail to England. In doing so, he calls to mind the Joseph strain of the Grail story, which presents the Grail as a relic of Christ's Passion – and hence as a historical blood relic of Christ.[35] Moreover, Joseph of Arimathea often featured prominently in clerical legends of historical blood relics (and arguments for their historical veracity) – which were widespread in England from the twelfth through fifteenth centuries – many of which were still circulating when Malory was writing his *Morte*.[36] Such treatises include an account attributed to Robert Grosseteste, *c.* 1247, in which Grosseteste explains "the process by which Joseph of Arimathea" collected the blood from Christ's side and kept it in a vase.[37] In 1360, the monks at Hailes similarly employed the Grail legends and Joseph of Arimathea to help popularize their blood relic[38]; and William Sudbury, writing in the 1380s or 1390s, cites the legend that Joseph brought with him to England a miracle-working vase of Holy Blood from Christ's

Crucifixion. Nicholas Vincent suggests that Sudbury's source may well have been a version of the *Estoire del Saint Graal*.[39]

Even more tantalizingly, Grosseteste specifies that Joseph and his descendents passed the precious liquid from father to son. One has only to think of Galahad, the last living descendent of Joseph and the last Grail custodian, to connect Malory's account with other Grail narratives that feature Joseph as the central figure. Valerie Lagorio associates Joseph of Arimathea with the legend of a pious Jew who cared for blood relics of Christ at Hailes, thereby indicating Joseph's connection to the Holy Blood.[40] She also identifies Joseph as the "collector and preserver of the Precious Blood," explaining that as cults of the blood relics of Christ grew in popularity, so too did Joseph's fame as keeper of the Holy Blood.[41] Both the alliterative *Joseph* author and Lovelich highlight Joseph's role as relic custodian and the Grail as relic. If this all were not reason enough to consider the Grail as a relic of the holy blood, Ector explains to Percival that the Grail "is an holy vessell ... and therein ys a parte of the bloode of oure Lorde Jesu Cryste" (II 817); and Lancelot at one point actually refers to the Grail as "the holy bloode" (II 896) – typical nomenclature for the Eucharist, but also for historical blood relics of Christ.

Malory's treatment of the Grail as a tactile, inaccessible object differs substantially from his rendition of other blood miracles in the *Morte*, most importantly those of Percival's sister and of Sir Urré. Urré appears at the end of the book of Lancelot and Guenivere, and thus outside of the context of (and after) the Grail quest. The depiction and significance of blood in this miracle is nevertheless helpful in understanding Malory's construction of and additions to the Grail quest: the miracle of Urré is likely original to the *Morte* and thus represents, as clearly as possible, Malory's own interest in blood and in the miraculous. Urré, a knight of Hungary, sustains "seven grete woundis" in his fight with Sir Alpheus of Spain, injuries that "shulde one tyme fester and another tyme blede, so that he shulde never be hole untyll the beste knyght of the worlde had serched hys woundis" (III 1145). His mother seeks help in Arthur's court, where Arthur himself promises that all aristocratic men will "asay to handyll your sonne" (III 1146). Those present attempt to heal Sir Urré but only manage to intensify his suffering: "som of hys woundis renewed uppon bledynge" (III 1147). Arthur, desiring to identify the best knight (III 1149) – Galahad and Percival having both died in the Grail quest – exhausts the list of nobles who might help (III 1146–50). The 110 knights who attempt to heal Urré fail utterly, and Urré's blood continues to flow.

In this context, Urré's blood, the result of a curse, would seem to signify precisely the opposite of the life-giving blood of the Grail. But for Lancelot, who failed the Grail quest, blood in general is not exactly a promising sign. When Lancelot, waylaid by the Lady of the Lake, finally arrives, he thus demurs from helping Urré, lest it appear that he believes himself better than other knights (III 1151); but I think we might also consider how Lancelot's other adventures with blood, in addition to convention and even penitence, inform his reluctance. When Arthur insists, Lancelot prays over Urré, whose wounds at first "bled a lytyll" but then heal entirely (III 1152). Lancelot's success, in this instance, is remarkable. Presumably, Galahad having died during the Grail quest, Lancelot is once again the "beste knyght of the worlde" (III 1145) and is therefore able to help the afflicted Urré. Even so, blood is central to this miracle – and given his contested status as Grail Knight, central to Lancelot as well. And blood helps to explain, I think, Lancelot's response to his victory: "And ever sir Launcelote wepte, as he had bene a chylde that had bene beatyn!" (III 1152). Lancelot's tears have been understood as a sign of humility; of penitence and conversion; of recognition of what might have been; of foreshadowing the downfall of Camelot.[42] But it is also possible that Lancelot weeps in remembering the recent Grail quest and the holiest of blood he was unable to approach, let alone handle. This interpretation need not stand on its own, for tears are often polyvalent signs. Nevertheless, Lancelot's clear success in this instance demonstrates that Urré's blood is different in kind from that of the Grail. Malory's treatment of the Grail is precise and directly related to relic discourse in a way that Urré's blood is not – except insofar as it reminds us of what happens to Lancelot in earlier parts of the *Morte*.

The blood miracle of Percival's sister, by contrast, does occur within the Grail quest proper. But here, too, Malory's treatment of blood is markedly different from his treatment of the Grail, in spite of the fact that unlike Urré's blood – a punishment and curse – the blood of Percival's sister has healing properties. Indeed, as Donald Hoffman observes, "The woman known only as Perceval's sister who sacrifices her life to save another … presents the only character in all of Malory who comes near to achieving an *imitatio Christi*."[43] Martin Shichtman, arguing that her sacrifice symbolizes the loss of virginity, nevertheless allows that more traditional readings understand "the blood sacrifice made by Percival's sister in relation to the blood sacrifice made by Christ on the cross, and the eucharistic emphases of the Grail quest certainly require such a reading."[44] On the face of it, in other words, Percival's sister has a lot in common with the Grail, particularly if we focus on the Grail's eucharistic importance. After all, once she discovers the reason for "the custum of thys castell" – which is to "hylde thys dyshe full of bloode of hir ryght arme" (II 1000) – she does not hesitate to offer her blood to save the "jantillwoman" who suffers there (II 1002). Ultimately, this sacrifice causes her death, for "she had bled so muche that she myght nat lyve" (II 1003); but her blood saves the lady of the castle all the same (II 1004). Her actions square with those of virgin martyrs, and her suffering is also, clearly, analogous to Christ's similarly life-giving sacrifice.

Yet as I have suggested, Malory draws from contemporary, fifteenth-century religious culture and from relic discourse in depicting the Grail as the material vessel in which Joseph of Arimathea collected the blood of the suffering Christ – more as a relic than as a Eucharistic vessel, in other words. The Grail's inaccessibility alone differentiates it from the blood of Percival's sister, which heals even a woman whose moral standing is hardly clear. Lancelot's ability to approach her body is yet another indication of this difference: when he comes upon Percival's sister, dead and adrift in a "shippe withoute sayle other ore" (II 1011), Lancelot not only boards and views the body, but also reads the missive describing what happened and stays on the boat with Percival's sister for over a month. To be sure, this is Lancelot's most holy period, directly preceding Galahad's arrival and their sojorn together. All the same, Lancelot's ability to interact with Percival's sister and to heal Sir Urré suggests that these two characters, defined by blood, are nonetheless distinct from the Grail. What is more, there is no relic, per se, of Percival's sister. Her blood, collected in a dish, does not outlast her as a tactile symbol of her sanctity. Instead, the sufffering gentlewoman uses (and is healed by) it. The blood of the Grail, by contrast – and like the historical blood relics of Westminster and Hailes – lasts, until it is spirited away at the end of the quest. Its holiness cannot help just anyone.

A Family of Relic Custodians: Joseph of Arimathea and His Descendents

Understanding the Grail as a relic illuminates a dominant thread in the *Morte*, Lovelich, and the alliterative *Joseph*. Modern scholars often interpret Malory in particular as using religious discourse to reveal bodily experience (say, sex and violence) as inherently flawed and Arthur's court as bound to fail. But read through the lens of relic discourse, the quest for attaining and protecting the Grail emblematizes the difficulty of reconciling discourse with practice – without necessarily condemning those who fall short of perfection – and, as I suggested earlier, the difficulties of reconciling the cult of relics with fifteenth-century religious practices in general. Malory indicates that the virtuous supplicant of relic discourse is paradoxical: that, on the one hand, anyone who is penitent enough deserves access to the Grail or any relic; but on the other, that only those who are always already holy – who surpass any "Erthly Man," in Lovelich's terms[45]– will achieve it. In the *Tale of the Sankgreal*, the alliterative *Joseph*, and *The History of the Holy Grail*, this latter group comprises the descendents of Joseph of Arimathea. Their custodial legacy is to care for the Grail as no one else can. Moreover, the presence of Joseph and his descendents signifies the Grail's importance and helps to generate its mystique and meaning. This aspect of the English Grail tradition sheds light on the disparities between the fifteenth-century incarnational aesthetic and the shrines of major relics, which were, like the Grail (itself a major relic), often accessible only to relic custodians. Such shrines, at least sometimes, must have seemed distant from the supplicants who visited them, hardly commensurate with a tactile religious culture that could be at once intimate and deeply revelatory.[46]

In their emphasis on Joseph of Arimathea; his son, Joseph; and their eventual descendent, Galahad, both the fifteenth-century *History of the Holy Grail* and the fourteenth-century alliterative *Joseph* derive the Grail's special status in part from its keepers. The author of the alliterative *Joseph* portrays Joseph and his son, Josaphe, as the guardians of the Holy Blood. Composed sometime around 1350, this acephalous poem centers on the conversion of King Evelake and his brother-in-law Seraph and on their battle with King Tholomer.[47] The two Josephs are instrumental in the conversions of Evelake and Seraph; they debate with clerics and hold forth on points of faith and doctrine in order to teach the pagan kings. This religious authority stems in part from Joseph's and Josaphe's divinely appointed positions as relic keepers. Christ himself instructs them on how to care for this wondrous relic:

Þenne spekes a vois to Ioseph, was Ihesu Crist himselue:
"Iosep, marke on þe treo and make a luytel whucche
forte do in þat ilke blod þou berest aboute.
Whon þe lust speke with me lift þe lide sone:
Þou schalt fynde me redi riȝt bi þi syde.
And bote þou and þi sone me no mon touche."[48]

Christ establishes Joseph's and Josaphe's primary custodial duties. First, and most importantly, Christ asks that Joseph make a reliquary for the Grail, "forte do in þat ilke blod þou berest a-boute" (*Joseph* 40). Both David Lawton and Walter W. Skeat define "whucche," which also appears as "wȝucche," as "a hutch, ark, [or] large wooden box."[49] The word appears in the *Middle English Dictionary* (*MED*) as "whicch(e)," from the OE noun "hwicce" or "hwæcce," meaning "A storage container, bin, or locker; a chest; also, a coffin" (whicch(e) 1a). But the word can also denote a reliquary, "a structure devoted to a saint, sanctuary, shrine" (whicch(e) 3a).[50] Christ's instructions to the Josephs suggest a causal relationship between enshrining the Grail and communicating with God. Obviously, Christ speaks to them even before they build the reliquary box for the Grail. But Christ's promise is that, after they enshrine the Holy Blood, they need merely to "lift þe lide" of the shrine and Christ himself will be "riȝt bi þi syde." As Christ would have it, enshrinement yields direct and immediate contact with the saint. This configuration is not unlike Lydgate's assertion in the *Extra Miracles of St Edmund* that "To seyntes shryned or set in tabernacles, / God hath mervaylles wrought many moo than oon."[51] The *Joseph* poet portrays Christ as creating his own *praesentia* inside the reliquary. But the poet also renders this *praesentia* as both dependent on enshrinement and as something exclusive, something that only Joseph of Arimathea and his descendents can encounter intimately.

Indeed, Christ specifies that Joseph and Josaphe will be able to view the Grail whenever they choose to do so: "Whon þe lust speke with me lift þe lide sone: / Þou schalt fynde me redi riȝt bi þi syde." With this line, the poet imbues the relic with Christ's *praesentia* and elides the Grail with the second person of the Trinity: when they lift the lid, the Josephs will not find the Holy Blood; they will find "me" – that is, Christ himself. Joseph and Josaphe can thus view the Grail at their leisure and communicate with Christ at the spot of this relic. Christ's final words to Joseph on the subject cement Joseph's and Josaphe's privileged positions as relic custodians: "And, bote þou and þi sone me no mon touche." This intimate contact is reminiscent of Jocelin of Brakelond's description of St Edmund's early shrine at Bury, which featured a "hole in the coffin-lid through which the guardians of the feretory used of old to thrust their hands that they might touch the holy body."[52] The Josephs hold this privileged position; nobody but those who are charged with keeping it may touch the Grail. What is more, in rendering Christ as specifically restricting access to the Holy Blood, the poet implies that others will desire intimate contact with this holy relic. The Josephs are therefore to mediate contact with Christ himself and, by extension, given Christ's assertion that they will be able to "speke" with him, interpret his will for the supplicants who visit the "whucche" and its wondrous relic.

Joseph's and Josaphe's privileged status directly contrasts with the legendary fates of Seraphe (called Nasciens after his conversion), Evelake (called Mordrains after his conversion), and Lancelot, all of whom God punishes for presuming to approach the Grail (Malory II 907–9, 1026).[53] Unlike these ill-fated, would-be supplicants, Josaphe "to his whucche weendes," where "feole preiers he made" (*Joseph* 237–8). There, a voice confirms that Josaphe is "iugget clene" and "digne" (251–2). Acccording to Christ's promise, Josaphe "lifte[s] vp and þe lide [of the reliquary] warpes [opens]" (257). At this point, were Josaphe unworthy (not "digne"), like Lancelot, he would be instructed to leave or, like Evelake, he would be struck down by blindness. Instead, he has a vision of Christ on the cross surrounded by angels, each of whom bears a relic: the true cross, the nails, the crown of thorns, the lance, and the burial cloth (258–68). (That is, Josaphe has a vision of even more relics.) Josaphe at first "falles for fere forþwiþ þe wȝucche" (267), but he rises again. He is still staring into the reliquary when Joseph arrives: "þenne þei loken in atte wȝucche loueliche boþe" (281). At this point, Joseph and Josaphe have another vision: they see eleven more angels, two of which appear holding a silver basin, holy water, and incense (285–93). Once the "disch wiþ þe blode" is placed upon the altar, the nails and lance on the other end, and a "vessel of gold" in between (297–8), Christ himself consecrates Josaphe a bishop: "Ihesu made for to greiþe Iosaphe in þat geyn weede, / and sacrede him to bisschop wiþ boto his hondes, / and tolde him of his vestimens what þei signefyen" (299–301).[54] The *Joseph* poet thus associates relic keeping with not just clerical but episcopal status.

The unspoken corollary is that access to this relic is somehow predicated on clerical authority. Many of the keepers at major shrines, like Gilbert of Chevening, would have been clerics who were sometimes directly responsible for constructing a relic's meaning.[55] Their position was thus radically different from that of the average pilgrim, who encountered the shrine and frequently relied upon clerical narratives to interpret it. It is difficult not to associate the clerical celibacy and virtue of Joseph and his descendents with the practices of the clerics whose efforts birthed the Grail quest: the Cistercian monks whose piety and austerity are well known.[56]

In his version of Nasciens's punishment for attempting to see what is reserved for the Josephs, Henry Lovelich similarly juxtaposes Joseph with the nonclerical characters who attempt to approach the Holy Blood. Lovelich's fifteenth-century *The History of the Holy Grail*, like the alliterative *Joseph*, features Joseph of Arimathea, his son, and their involvement both in keeping the Holy Blood and converting two important pagans, Seraphe and Evelake.[57] (Once converted, these characters go by the names of Nasciens and Mordrains.) Lovelich refers to the Grail's container as an "Arch," which may refer to a kind of reliquary; certainly the cathedral feretories of late medieval England themselves resembled arks. Moreover, Joseph of Arimathea reveals the many relics "in the Arch" to Nasciens and Mordrains (Lovelich XVII 8); he is clearly in control of this moment, which includes the revelation of the vestments he wore when Christ consecrated him "Bisschop of [His] Owne hond" (XVII 11). These garments are bizarre evidence of Joseph's importance: he is living, but his clothes are already relics. Among these holy objects, Joseph shows Nasciens and Mordrains "the holy disch Anon, / Where-Inne that Sank Ryal was I-don" (XVII 17–18). Lovelich refers to the blood from Christ at the Crucifixion, contained in the cup from the Last Supper. In this instance, the cup is itself a kind of reliquary; and Nasciens's penalty is as a result of looking *inside* the dish: "Whanne with-Inne he gan to looke, / He him withdrowh, & for drede he qwooke" (XVII 51–2). Unlike Josaphe in the alliterative *Joseph*, however, Christ does not comfort Nasciens or affirm that he has behaved appropriately. Rather, Nasciens himself immediately understands that he has "offendid ȝit Goddis presens, / For that I have sein so moche be Owtraye / That non Erthly Man ne Owhte to have saye" (XVII 62–4). Nasciens, converted pagan and exemplary new Christian, admits that he is different in kind from those who are deserving of the Grail's secrets: he is not otherworldly. His statement implies that, because Joseph and his son may see the Grail openly, they are not earthly men, bound by imperfection and sin. In this paradigm, only those who do not need penance and confession may care for and view the Grail.

Even while, on the one hand, Lovelich steps back from this absolute dichotomy – after an angel heals Nasciens, Joseph explains that Nasciens will eventually have "knowleching / Of Sank Ryal" (XVII 169–70) – he nevertheless maintains Joseph's special position in relation to the Holy Blood. For, as Lagorio has pointed out, "[o]wing to his professed aim of achieving a faithful transcription of his French material, the significant deviations from the French text can only reflect Lovelich's interest in

St Joseph of Glastonbury."[58] In this particular moment, Lovelich endows Joseph with the understanding that, in the French text, only "li angeles" have.[59] Lovelich's Joseph does not need an angel's aid to explain the miraculous appearance of the lance (which restores Nasciens's sight): he interprets the symbol himself. And his own prophetic version of the Grail's future similarly emphasizes his elite status. While some may gain knowledge of the Holy Blood, Joseph is the only one ("I alone") who may see its secrets: "The Secretis of Seint Graal, / That Somme men it Clepin 'sanc Ryal,' / There may non dedlych Man there Se / But I alone" (XVII 171–4). Lovelich thereby maintains Joseph's unique position as custodian and mediator of the Grail's power and mysteries. Lovelich grants Joseph, and only Joseph, the power to create the Grail's meaning. This role emphasizes England's importance to the Grail story, as Lagorio has shown.[60] Likewise, the elite status of Joseph, Josephus (or Joseph, which is how Malory renders Josaphe), and Galahad subtends Malory's *Tale of the Sankgreal* and precludes anyone else, however well-intentioned, from fully succeeding in the Grail quest.

Malory never explicitly refers to Joseph as a relic custodian, feretrar, shrine keeper, or *custos*. He nonetheless renders both Joseph and his son, Joseph, as relic custodians who mediate the encounter between the Grail and even the most successful knights. Malory's Joseph translates the Grail from one continent to another: "Here folowyth the noble tale off the Sankegreall, whyche called ys the holy vessell and the sygnyfycacion of blyssed bloode off oure Lorde Jesu Cryste, whyche was brought into thys londe by Joseph off Aramathye" (Malory II 845–6). By opening the *Tale of the Sankgreall* with Joseph, Malory positions him at the heart of the narrative. An English quest for the Grail would be impossible without Joseph, who transports the holy object "into thys londe." In fact, Joseph and his descendents bookend the quest. At the culmination of the pursuit of the Grail, Joseph himself celebrates Mass and displays the holy vessel: "And than the bysshop [Joseph of Arimathea] ... put hit [the Eucharist] into the holy vessell agayne, and than he ded that longed to a preste to do masse" (II 1029). Once he consecrates the host (the "obley") and dips it into the Grail, Joseph vanishes (II 1030). Indicating the special status of the Grail knights, Christ himself administers communion. But even in this revelation, Christ specifies that these knights see only "*parte* of my secretes and of my hydde thynges" (II 1030; emphasis added). Divine ordination reserves the rest of these "hydde thynges" for Galahad, Joseph's direct descendent and the last custodian of the Grail.

Insofar as Malory emphasizes the familial relationship between Joseph of Arimathea, his son Joseph, and their descendent Galahad, he suggests that the virtuous supplicant is, indeed, a fictional creation. Virtuous supplicants obviously existed. But Malory showcases the degree to which those who achieve the Grail are destined to do so, rendering these knights as otherworldly and, as has become a critical commonplace in scholarly approaches to Galahad, almost superhuman. Malory introduces Galahad, for instance, as a member of an elite caste: "Sir, I brynge you here a yonge knyght the whyche ys of kynges lynage and of the kynrede of Joseph of Aramathy, whereby the mervayles of this courte and of stronge realmys shall be fully complevysshed" (II 859). In fact, Galahad is the last of Joseph's line (II 881). At the end of the *Sankgreall*, when Galahad is both king of Sarras and the Grail's primary keeper, Joseph, son of Joseph of Arimathea, appears to Galahad to explain their exclusive status:

> Galahad ... arose up erly and hys felowis, and cam to the paleyse, and saw tofore hem the holy vessell, and a man knelyng on his kneys in lyknesse of a bysshop ... And so he cam to the sakerynge, and anone made an ende. He called sir Galahad unto hym and seyde,
>
> "Com forthe, the servaunte of Jesu Cryste, and thou shalt se that thou has much desired to se" ... "Now wotist thou what I am?" seyde the good man. "Nay, sir," seyde sir Galahad.
>
> "I am Joseph, the sonne of Joseph or Aramathy,[61] which oure Lorde hath sente to the to bere the felyship. And wotyst thou wherefore He hathe sente me more than ony other? For thou hast resembled me in to thynges: that thou hast sene, that ys the mervayles of the Sankgreall, and for thou hast bene a clene mayde as I have be and am." (II 1034–5)

This passage foregrounds Joseph's episcopal role ("in lyknesse of a bysshop"), emphasizing, yet again, that keepers of the Grail are both celibate and clerical. Joseph explains that he and Galahad share not only common ancestry but special custodial access to their relic. For Joseph's words – "thou shalt se that thou has much desired to se" – reinforce Christ's assertion at Corbenic that up to this point, Galahad and the other Grail knights have experienced only a partial vision of the Holy Blood.

Galahad's privileged status as the holiest of the three Grail knights is thus beyond question, "plac[ing] Galahad in a position of unassailable privilege."[62] Unlike every other knight on the Grail quest, Galahad has no need for sacramental absolution. At the first hermitage, in fact, Galahad is not required to confess and is instructed to go on an adventure (II 982–3) – something that Gawain is told he cannot do because of his sin. Galahad is consistently described in saintly terms: he is "the holy knyght" (II 886); "he worchith all by myracle," according to the Queen of the Waste Land (II 906), and he is the only one of the three Grail knights to do so. He heals Evelake, for example, who has suffered blindness and torment for three hundred years because he dared approach the Grail too closely (II 908, 1031). By virtue of his purity, Galahad calms the boiling water of a well – the "hete myght nat abyde hys pure virginité" (II 1025). The newly calmed well is "takyn in the contrey for a miracle, and so ever afftir was hit called Galahaddis Welle" (II 1026). He relieves the pain of one of his ancestors, who suffers in a fiery tomb because he sinned against Joseph of Arimathea (II 1026), and he heals a cripple once he arrives in Sarras, simply by telling him to "aryse up and shew thy good wyll!" (II 1033). Galahad is even said to be able, like many saints in hagiography, to choose the time of his death. In this way, just as hagiographers present their saints as imitators of Christ, Malory presents Lancelot's bastard son as very similar to the holy body he seeks.[63] Galahad's holiness stems from his body's virginal state. His body is like that of Christ himself, and he shares ancestry with the Grail's original guardian. As a result, he can legitimately approach and view the Grail. His success has nothing at all to do with whether he manifests faith, humility, and penitence – for Galahad has no need to repent.

Depictions of these flawless relic keepers imply that the virtuous pilgrim exists only discursively, beyond the ability of most to attain in practical terms. Malory, the *Joseph* poet, and Lovelich do not argue that *anyone* can attain the holiness or exclusive position that God grants the Josephs. Instead, these writers associate holiness with the otherworldly – "And, bote þou and þi sone me no mon touche" (*Joseph* 43); or as Lovelich's Nasciens puts it, "non Erthly Man ne Owhte to" see the Grail (XVII 64). So, too, in depicting the Josephs as clerical, even episcopal, these authors suggest that privilege is the result of holding an ecclesiastical position. These writers thereby unsettle the commonplace in relic discourse that the penitent, faithful, and humble supplicant is deserving of the miraculous – for surely Evelake, converted pagan and Christian hero, meets those qualifications. So does Lancelot. Instead, as Joseph's initial reaction to Josaphe's openly gazing on the contents of the "whucche" suggests, even the most pious character takes a risk in approaching a relic.[64] Until Josaphe assures him that Christ has granted him "muche gostliche grace" (*Joseph* 280), Joseph chastizes his son, asking him " 'Whi lengest þou ... / and so stille liggest lokynde in þe whucche?' " (277–8). If Joseph is bemused at even the sight of his son – the only other relic custodian for the Grail, appointed by Christ himself – having intimate contact with this holy object, it follows that even the most holy supplicant would not be able to do so (and indeed, in the alliterative *Joseph*, nobody else does). As the next section argues, Lancelot's failure to achieve the Grail, in spite of his exemplary behaviour during the quest and his elevated status, reveals an inherent flaw in the tenets of relic discourse, which presuppose relics as accessible to anyone who behaves appropriately. In highlighting Lancelot's consistent attempts to live up to the fiction of the perfect supplicant – who is humble, devout, and contrite – Malory ascribes Lancelot's shortcomings to this commonplace of relic discourse. Malory's text thus presents relic discourse, rather than Lancelot's immorality, as the problem Lancelot cannot, in the end, overcome.

Exemplary Supplicants and the Trouble with Confession

It has been typical to regard Lancelot's failure to achieve the Grail as the result of his inability to stop loving Guenivere.[65] This interpretation depends largely on assuming the continuity of Malory's *Morte*, for Lancelot does not admit to having made a halfhearted confession and contrition until *after* the quest itself is over.[66] Throughout the *Sankgreal* itself, however, Lancelot manifests genuine repentance and, *pace* Karen Cherewatuk, expiates his sin in the context of the quest.[67] Claims about Malory's *Morte* as a whole are far beyond the purview of this book. But in the ideological context of relic discourse, which overlays Malory's *Sankgreal* but not the other books of the *Morte*, Lancelot appears as the mistreated supplicant who, in spite of his adherence to the commonplace of the exemplary supplicant, does not secure miraculous contact with the Grail.

By emphasizing the elite status of the custodians of the Holy Blood, the authors of *Le Morte d'Arthur*, the alliterative *Joseph*, and *The History of the Holy Grail* call attention to the inequality between the shrine keepers and supplicants of relic discourse. And by presenting his Grail, unlike that of the French *Queste*, as invisible, Malory highlights this disparity. In the *Sankgreal*, seeing the Grail serves as a litmus test for holiness: only those who somehow always already possess this quality – virgins, clerics, and, in Galahad's case, a virginal relic custodian – are able to view the relic. Correspondingly, one expects those who cannot see the Holy Blood to be morally deficient. When the Grail restores Percival and Ector, who have mortally wounded each other, to health, Ector suggests as much: "I woote ful well [that the Grail] is an holy vessell that is borne by a mayden, and therein ys a parte of the bloode of oure Lorde Jesu Cryste. But hit may nat be sene … but yff hit be by an holy man" (Malory II 817). Ector's assertion predicates the entire Grail quest on holiness and vision – if one cannot see the Grail, one must not be holy.[68] But Lancelot, neither depraved nor perfect, complicates this tidy premise. Confession is a paradoxical requirement in the Grail quest, then, one that is presented as paving the way for a knight's success, but one that does not necessarily result in attaining the Grail.

Malory presents Lancelot as the exemplary supplicant of relic discourse: he is humble, penitent, and faithful. According to the directions of the hermits to whom he confesses, Lancelot expiates his sin – wearing a hair shirt, avoiding meat, and renouncing his love for the queen (II 897, 927). And yet, Lancelot's behaviour does not ensure his success. I think it is too easy to assume that Lancelot fails because he is still invested in "incresyng of his shevalry [chivalry]" (II 931) or because, as Malory tells us at the beginning of *The Book of Sir Launcelot and Queen Guinevere*, "had nat sir Launcelot bene in his prevy thoughtes and in hys myndis so sette inwardly to the quene as he was in semynge outewarde to God, there had no knyght passed hym in the queste of the Sankgreall" (III 1045). In the *Sankgreal*, Malory never informs us that Lancelot's "prevy thoughts" bend towards the queen. Rather, in the context of the quest itself, the character of Lancelot provides a way to explore the difficulty of resolving the tenets of relic discourse – which predicate securing a miracle on penance and humility – with practice. When Nacien, one of the many hermits the Grail knights meet on the quest, explicates Gawain's vision of the black and white bulls, for example, he associates good behaviour, and achieving the Grail, with confession: "the blacke bullis whych seyde, 'go we hens,' they were tho whych … toke uppon hem to go in the queste of the Sankgreall withoute confession" (II 946).[69] The corollary is that, had they confessed, these knights would have succeeded. Nevertheless, only those knights whom Malory renders clerical finish the quest, suggesting that the relative success or failure of each knight is predetermined. It does not matter what the knights do (though it is certainly not shocking that a knight like Percival does not succumb to the devil's wiles). It only matters what or who they are.

Those knights, such as Gawain, who refuse or are incapable of true repentance, have no hope of completing the journey. Gawain, headstrong and perpetually bored, distills many of the qualities of the depraved supplicant. His inclination is to give up the quest at the first signs of failure. He repeatedly commits murder and refuses confession at every opportunity. And he has no interest in the Grail's heavenly mysteries: he is the one to complain that the Grail is "coverde" when it appears at Camelot, and he even identifies the Grail's occlusion as a moment of deception: "one thyng begyled us, that we myght nat se the Holy Grayle: hit was so preciously coverde" (II 866). Gawain is not satisfied with this encounter with the Grail, and his objection to its occlusion motivates the quest for the Sankgreal: "Wherefore I woll make here a vow that to-morne, withoute longer abydynge, I shall laboure in the queste of the Sankgreall ... and never shall I returne unto the courte agayne *tylle I have sene hit more opynly than hit hath bene shewed here*" (II 866; emphasis added). Gawain's motive is a curious one. Jill Mann argues that Gawain's desire to see the Grail reflects "the same impulse towards closeness that characterizes knightly engagement in adventure elsewhere."[70] It strikes me, however, that there is more than knightly convention at work in Gawain's sentiments. Mann's claim assumes the Grail to be the object of an ordinary quest – but as the Grail's otherworldly power,[71] Bors's wonder (II 799), and Arthur's dismay at the beginning of the quest indicate (II 866), the adventure of the Sankgreal is anything but ordinary. Gawain's desire underscores this extraordinariness: he does not seek to be healed, nor to fulfill a penitential vow, nor even to go on holiday. Instead, he claims only to want to *see* the Grail. We might even interpret Gawain's wish to see the Grail as a manifestation of curiosity – a trait not to be found in devout pilgrims.[72]

Gawain's subsequent failure to see the Holy Blood is proof positive of his sinful nature and indicts the other knights who follow his lead, most of whom are later identified in visions as "black" and riddled with their own sin.[73] If there were any doubt of Gawain's moral state, or the likelihood that he or any of the "black" knights will complete the quest, Malory presents a series of hermits and recluses, each of whose prophecies are gloomy and unpromising. These religious assure Gawain that Galahad "woll nat of youre felyship" because Gawain is "wycked and synfull, and [Galahad] ys full blyssed" (II 890). Gawain, naturally, responds by helping Gareth and Uwaine kill the seven knights of the Castle of Maidens. He refuses to repent when a hermit convicts him of murdering these knights and of having "lyved myschevously many wyntirs. And Sir Galahad ys a mayde and synned never, and that ys the cause he shall enchyve where he goth that ye nor none suche shall never attayne … for ye have used the moste untrewyst lyff that ever I herd knyght lyve" (II 891–2). Gawain briefly expresses remorse – "Sir, what penaunce shall I do?" (II 892) – but does not follow through, commenting, "I may do no penaunce, for we knyghtes adventures many tymes suffir grete woo and payne" (II 892). It would be difficult to miss Gawain's pride and sinfulness, or his casual dismissal of the hermit's advice. Gawain goes on to slay Uwaine, and he rejects other opportunities to be confessed, as well.

In one of these instances, Nacien the hermit explains that confession is a necessary prerequisite for completing the Grail quest: "And the blacke bullis whych seyde, 'go we hens,' they were tho whych at Pentecoste at the hyghe feste toke uppon hem to go in the queste of the Sankgreall withoute confession" (II 946). Here the old hermit explains the meaning of a dream vision in which Gawain sees 150 bulls in a meadow. Save three white (or mostly white) bulls – representing the Grail knights Galahad, Percival, and Bors – each and every bull is black. These black bulls, having tired of their surroundings, determine that they will "go … to seke bettir pasture!" (II 942). According to Nacien, these restless animals signify those knights who are both sinful and impenitent. They, like Gawain, cannot be bothered to complete the quest (II 941). The hermit could not be more clear: confession is an essential component of achieving the Grail, even the primary component. By extension, enacting this sacrament should, figuratively speaking, turn a black bull into a white bull. The white bulls of Gawain's vision represent, after all, those knights who will achieve the Grail. Nacien's interpretation of the dream thus implies that penance would have ensured the success of the many knights who fail. And yet Bors, it will be remembered, confesses – but he nevertheless appears as the only white bull with a black spot: "there [Gawain] saw a rake of bullis, an hundrith and fyffty, that were proude and black, save three of hem was all whyght, and one had a blacke spotte" (II 942). In spite of the hermit's interpretation, then, Gawain's dream illustrates that confession alone cannot transform the black bulls into white bulls. In fact, it seems clear that no regular knight (here represented by the homogenized black bulls) will ever be able to complete the quest.

Gawain's subsequent refusal to narrate his sins verbally is therefore simultaneously paramount and immaterial, and he becomes with each passing scene in the *Sankgreal* a kind of anti-pilgrim. Nacien describes him in the terms that are applied to knights who will fail the quest, as a "grete murtherar," an "untrew knyght," and a "synner" (II 948). Instead of being convicted of his shortcomings, Gawain makes more excuses: " 'Sir,' seyde sir Gawayne, 'and I had leyser I wolde speke with you, but my felow sir Ector ys gone and abithe me yondir bynethe the hylle' " (II 949). Nacien again emphasizes confession – " 'Well,' seyde the good man, 'thou were better to be counceyled' " (II 949) – but Gawain leaves, a failed pilgrim in every respect, and one who admits that he has tired of the pilgrimage itself: "Truly … I am ny wery of thys queste, and lothe I am to folow further in straunge contreyes" (II 941). Malory presents Gawain's weariness as the direct result of his sinfulness, which prevents him from encountering any adventures whatsoever. We might also understand his exhaustion as indicating his lack of perseverance – another feature that contrasts with those that define good pilgrims. However, Gawain's own vision indicates that, even if he were penitent and enterprising, his status as a black bull would prevent him from achieving the Grail.

So, too, Lancelot's failure to achieve the Grail, in spite of his penance, illustrates the impossibility of attaining Galahad's (or even Percival's or Bors's) status. As Malory attests, Lancelot does not have and will never possess the "power" to access the Grail.[74] Though he possesses the requisite characteristics of a successful pilgrim – faith and penance among them – Lancelot is never fully able to compensate for his worldly and fleshly sins. The inadequacy of Lancelot's penitence belies the clerical suggestion, throughout the quest, that confession is the single most important qualification to achieving the Grail. Only those knights who have been chosen, a priori, as the Grail knights are able to make confession count.[75] Before the adventure of the Holy Blood even begins – and, not coincidentally, immediately following two early apparitions of the Grail – Bors himself, having seen a vision of the Grail at Corbenic, follows King Pelles's advice and "wyth a good wyll … was confessed" (II 799). But once is not enough even for Bors, who professes his sins again after a hermit explains that "shall none attayne hit [the Sankgreal] but by clennes, that ys pure confession" (II 955). Bors, the most worldly of the three Grail knights, complies. He goes with the hermit to a chapel where "he was clene confessed"; he enacts his penance not to eat meat and to wear a "scarlet cote" (II 955). Even so, Bors does not achieve Galahad's elite status; and Bors alone of the Grail knights returns to Camelot.

Lancelot's inability to see the Grail can thus be seen to demonstrate that, in spite of Nacien's assertion, confession by itself is not enough. Celibacy in particular is the prerequisite for seeing the Sankgreal, even for those who are willing to repent.[76] As Cherewatuk has pointed out, Lancelot demonstrates contrition when, sleeping by a stone cross, he is so overcome by sin that he cannot wake when the holy vessel appears and heals a sick knight[77]: "Launcelot wyst nat where [the Grail] was becom; for he was overtakyn with synne, that he had no power to ryse agayne the holy vessell. Wherefore aftir that many men seyde hym shame, but he toke repentaunce aftir that" (II 894–5). While Malory acknowledges Lancelot's "sin" and "shame," he immediately defends Lancelot, who "toke repentaunce" in response to this episode. Indeed, rather than assessing Lancelot's condition as hopeless, the squire presents sacramental absolution as a way to earn God's grace: "'I dare well sey,' seyde the squyre, 'that he dwellith in som dedly synne whereof he was never confessed'" (II 895). In the context of relic discourse, the squire's statement makes perfect sense: the exemplary supplicant is frequently sinful but repentant. To wit, miracles of justice, in which the saint rescues a criminal (innocent *or* penitent), are common in the miracle collections of shrine sites.[78] There is no reason to imagine that Lancelot cannot avail himself of this systematic mercy, especially given that Lancelot identifies his problem: "My synne and my wyckednes hath brought me unto grete dishonoure!" (II 896).

Lancelot thus begins his quest with contrition. His behaviour thereby, as Cherewatuk has argued, broadly corresponds to the first requirement of confession.[79] What is more, Lancelot outwardly manifests his sorrow; before he confesses for the first time, he "wepte with hevy harte" (II 897). Chaucer's Parson explains that the theology of confession emphasizes frequent and *tearful* confession by mouth as the best outward sign of contrition.[80] Moreover, when Lancelot meets another "good man," who informs him that because of his "synne," he "shall have no power to se" the Grail, Lancelot's first response is "to wepe" (II 927). Reacting to Lancelot's assertion that he has already been confessed, this "good man" imposes penance on Lancelot: wearing a hair shirt, abstaining from meat and alcohol, and attending daily Mass (II 927). Lancelot thereby expiates his sin: "So he toke the hayre *and put hit uppon hym*" (II 927; emphasis added). This moment clearly demonstrates that, in the *Sankgreal*, Lancelot enacts satisfaction.[81] Whether he returns to sin after the *Sankgreal* is beside the point. And as the exemplary supplicant commonplace makes clear, the penitent supplicant has just as much right to expect a miracle as anybody.[82]

In spite of Lancelot's asceticism, a gentlewoman whom Lancelot meets is not much more encouraging about his chances of seeing the

Grail: " 'I wote what adventure ye seke, for ye were beforetyme nerar than ye be now, and yet shall ye se hit more opynly than ever ye dud' " (II 928). While this woman implicitly acknowledges the efficacy of Lancelot's penance, her prophecy nevertheless affirms that he will never achieve the status of Galahad, Percival, and Bors: he will see it "more opynly," which is not the same thing as seeing it openly or entirely. When, having seen only a "grete clerenesse" or light, Lancelot attempts to enter the chamber wherein he sees the Grail, he catches only a glimpse of it before he is struck down by "a breeth that hym thought hit was entromedled with fyre, which smote hym so sore in the vysayge that hym thought hit brente hys vysayge. And therewith he felle to the erthe and had no power to aryse" (II 1016). He loses his sight and hearing, and he is taken for dead. True, Lancelot is imperfect – but so are many of the supplicants of relic discourse. Witness Osgothus, whose disregard for St Edmund's shrine I discussed in chapter 2. Edmund punishes Osgothus's derisive attitude, but when Edward the Confessor (who is present for both the punishment and healing miracle) intervenes on Osgothus's behalf, Edmund heals this disrespectful pagan.[83] In the context of relic discourse, even Osgothus achieves a measure of contact with and respect for St Edmund's shrine. By contrast, Lancelot, imperfect but contrite and respectful in his attitude to the Grail, suffers defeat, dishonor, and infamy.

Lancelot's state emphasizes the difference between the penitential pilgrim and the relic custodian or member of the clerical elite, whose status as much as virtue enables him to interact with, and even serve as a mediator for, relics. Galahad is perfect; Percival nearly so; and Bors is virtuous but, as in Gawain's vision of the black and white bulls, in which Bors is the only white bull with a black spot, tainted by his sole sexual encounter with a woman. Nacien describes the benefits of Lancelot's physical penitence (wearing a hair shirt), but he makes it clear that the knights who fail are always already bad, "of pore fayth and of wycked beleve," lacking in "charité, abstinaunce and trouthe" (II 948). Nacien's list of characteristics corresponds to the depraved supplicant of relic discourse, whom hagiographers present God and the saints as punishing.[84] However, in emphasizing the Grail's material nature, implicitly contrasting it with the many accessible religious objects of the fifteenth century, Malory rejects the idea that every supplicant who conforms to ideal behaviour – penance, faithfulness, humility – attains his or her goal. Lancelot's failure to achieve the Grail, in spite of his penance, illustrates the impossibility of attaining Galahad's (or even Percival's or Bors's) status. Though he possesses the requisite characteristics of a successful pilgrim, Lancelot is never able fully to compensate for his worldly and fleshly sins.

In inculcating Gawain with the desire to see, Malory troubles the commonplaces of the virtuous and the depraved supplicant. Gawain, flawed to the core, cannot but want the wrong thing. And in contrast to the criminals and pagans for whom saints sometimes work miracles, Gawain has no hope for redemption. In the context of the *Sankgreal*, Gawain's absolute badness suggests that relic discourse assumes a flexibility – e.g., even pagans can benefit from the relic's power, if only they convert – that does not in fact exist. So, too, Lancelot's attempts to be good (and, I think, moving and genuine penitence) reveal the qualities of the exemplary supplicant as nothing but a fictional list. Even Lancelot, a fictional character, cannot avail himself of the promises of relic discourse. Instead, Malory, Lovelich, and the *Joseph* poet all emphasize the degree to which the relic custodian functions as both the creator and mediator of his relics. Malory in particular revises the implicit premise of relic discourse: that if a supplicant is only good enough, he or she will earn a miracle. Malory's *Sankgreal* suggests that none can live up to such discursive ideals. Malory even disregards the ideals themselves. To wit, in Galahad, Malory substitutes the dynastic relic custodian, the only one pure enough to attain the Holy Blood, for the ideal supplicant. And when Galahad dies, a hand spirits away the Grail, suggesting the degree of control a relic custodian might exercise over his object: without Galahad, the events of the text imply, the Grail ceases to exist. Indeed, "sythen," as Malory tells us, "was there never man so hardy to sey that he hade seyne the Sankgreal" (II 1035).

Chapter Four

Relic Discourse in the Pardoner's Prologue and Tale and *Troilus and Criseyde*

In a book about relics and relic discourse, it is impossible not to talk about the Pardoner. One of Chaucer's most frequently discussed characters, the Pardoner himself resembes a relic, exposed to the daylight for everyone to see. Students are riveted (in disgust, usually) by Chaucer-the-pilgrim's description of him: stringy hair, bulbous eyes, connoisseur (ahem) of fashion, and bringing up the rear of the company with his friend the Summoner, a man so vile he frightens children. At first glance, the Pardoner represents everything that is corrupt about religion and commerce: as he freely admits, he subverts his own motto (*Radix malorum est cupiditas*) all the time. But as a purveyor of false relics, the Pardoner showcases the discourse he so expertly deploys. In his more successful moments, the "fallible" Pardoner (to use Alastair Minnis's recent term) uses rhetoric and manipulates his fake relics to shape the response of his audiences – ultimately, to make money.[1] But on the Canterbury pilgrimage, the Pardoner reveals the workings of relic discourse, exposing the pratices at relic cults as constructed and revealing the commonplaces and terminology upon which these practices depend. Paradoxically, this exposure does not undermine the pilgrimage to Canterbury or ridicule all relics, but rather calls attention to the language surrounding pilgrimage and relic cults, to the deceptive possibilities of rhetoric, and to pilgrim behaviour (both of the pilgrim company en route to Canterbury and of the riotous pilgrims in the Pardoner's Tale).

The importance of Pandarus in the context of relic discourse is not so obvious. But as this chapter argues, in bringing to bear relic discourse as a hermeneutic tool on the Pardoner's Prologue and Tale and *Troilus and Criseyde*, we can and should understand both the Pardoner and

Pandarus as parodic relic custodians – and Criseyde herself as a kind of relic, with Troilus as the consummate pilgrim. Chaucer's depiction of these characters (as well as other, more unlikely moments in the *Troilus*, such as the description of Criseyde) raises questions about artifice, dissimulation, and the power and limitations of language, ultimately calling attention to the signifying power (or impotence) of shrines and to relic discourse *as discourse*. The Pardoner's Prologue and Tale, as well as *Troilus and Criseyde*, exhibit some of the same tensions within relic discourse as Malory's *Morte*, the status of pilgrims – and whether exemplary behaviour ensures a good outcome – being one of these anxieties.

These texts invite us to think about language and about devotional spectacle: in the Pardoner's performance; in Pandarus's slippery rhetoric; in Troilus's procession through the streets of Troy; in the celebration of the Palladium; in the rioters' reaction to the treasure they find. Scholars have long attended to Pandarus's careful (manipulative) orchestration of the liaison between Troilus and Criseyde.[2] Pandarus's use of the first-person plural pronoun aligns his own fate with that of Troilus and suggests that they might both benefit from Criseyde's favours. His words and intentions have sparked decades of debate: and we still do not entirely agree (or know) what Pandarus means or what precisely he intends to happen;[3] Barry Windeatt has characterized Pandarus as "protean, mobile, shifting."[4] Both Pandarus and the Pardoner disguise their intentions, and both freely exploit the word "entente" as they do so.[5] There is a sense, in other words, in which these characters deliberately craft an outside (through rhetoric) that hides what is inside (their intentions, whatever those might be). The Pardoner reveals his "entente" to the other Canterbury pilgrims ("to wynne, / And nothyng for correccioun of synne"), but he usually keeps this information to himself.[6] In *Troilus and Criseyde*, Criseyde, as well as Pandarus, keeps her own counsel: both the language the narrator ascribes to Criseyde's thought and the way the narrator describes her highlight the disconnect between meaning and intent, between the outside and inside. Criseyde hints at a radical split between inside and outside, between a public façade – her "estat" – and what she thinks, privately, in her closet. As she muses while navigating Pandarus's expression of Troilus's predicament, " 'I shal felen what he meneth, ywis,' " deciding to herself that "[i]t nedeth me ful sleighly for to pleie.' "[7] Criseyde thereby acknowledges the possibility that neither her nor Pandarus's behaviour and words necessarily correspond to their innermost thoughts.

The interplay between inside and outside, between action and intention, informs the rhetorical gymnastics of *Troilus and Criseyde* and shares a lot in common with the concerns of relic discourse, including the preoccupation with whether outward artifice (or a spectacular shrine) resembles inward intention (or, say, rotting saints' bones). Whether by accident or design, Chaucer draws liberally from these conventions in both poems, which he places squarely within the devotional contexts of late fourteenth-century England. The emphasis on the general slipperiness of words – and the depiction of Criseyde as relic, Troilus as pilgrim, and Pandarus and the Pardoner as relic custodians – has something to tell us about the dependence of pilgrimage and other ritual practices associated with the cult of relics on both words and appropriate behaviour. Both the Pardoner's Tale and *Troilus and Criseyde* configure the stakes of pilgrim behaviour in the highest possible terms: death for the pilgrims who follow, and who break, the rules. Death for Troilus; death for the Pardoner's rioters. These outcomes offer a grim assessment of the discourse surrounding the cult of relics, a discourse which precludes access and presents only those who have already attained holiness as deserving of a miracle. In this context, neither Troilus – who sins from the outset in his derision of the Religion of Love but quickly repents (*Troilus* I 183–210) – nor the sinful Canterbury pilgrims stand a chance. Their sympathetic portrayal suggests that Chaucer, like Malory, engages with the paradoxes of a discourse that demands, but does not necessarily reward, certain kinds of behaviour. Desire for the relic – for Criseyde, for the shrine of St Thomas – is not necessarily the problem. Rather, the discourse, to which the Canterbury pilgrims so vociferously object, emerges as inadequate.

This chapter begins by turning to the Pardoner's Prologue and Tale, arguing that the Pardoner is a parodic relic custodian in a long line of literary and historical pardoners and clerics who deal in fake relics, the analogues to Chaucer's Pardoner being no exception: Boccaccio's Brother Onion and Masuccio's Girolamo. These characters – in addition to those in Caesarius of Heisterbach, Jacques de Vitry, John Heywood, and Thomas More, to name only a few – position the Pardoner squarely within a rich literary tradition that drew from the discourse of relics. Understood in this context, the Pardoner's Tale might be understood as a parody of a pilgrimage.[8] The tensions within relic discourse – including, for instance, the tendency to recognize treasure for its own sake, rather than as representing the saint – illuminate the rioters' excitement at seeing the treasure, as well as their subsequent fate. There is a sense in which *any* pilgrim could mistake the shrine for the saint, and a sense in which the shrine is an unstable and even dangerous sign.

So, too, in *Troilus and Criseyde*, relic discourse can enrich our understanding of the poem's focus on issues of meditation and enclosure. The most influential critical responses to Criseyde have focused on her agency.[9] I extend this debate by pointing out that in the context of relic discourse, we can understand Criseyde as a kind of relic, and thus as simultaneously having and not having power. Criseyde as relic – as saint – possesses the authority vested in a saint and her body parts; but she, like a saint's relic, is nevertheless delimited by what is said and written about her (primarily by Pandarus). Her position as relic enables us to understand Troilus as a religious supplicant and Pandarus as a parodic relic custodian. Identifying what Pandarus has in common with some of the conventions of relic discourse is particularly important, as scholars have long debated the implications of Pandarus as go-between. Understanding Pandarus within the context of relic discourse illustrates that the saint's power is both created and circumscribed by his or her mediator.[10] The rhetorical dishonesty of the Pardoner and Pandarus ultimately suggests the troubling possibility that the reliquary might not honestly represent its contents; or that, as Troilus laments in front of Criseyde's house, the shrine might be empty: "And farwel shryne, of which the seynt is oute!" (*Troilus* V 553).

"Sothell theves":[11] (Immoral) Relic Custodians

Obviously, reading the Pardoner and Pandarus as parodic custodians requires another look at the role of historical relic custodians. A relic custodian's job was to care for the remains of the saints: he guarded, regulated, and controlled relics and the access to them.[12] Perhaps most crucially, a shrine keeper's job involved financial management and rhetorical dexterity – and like their literary counterparts in the Pardoner and Pandarus, they used language to confer value on their objects. Their presence was crucial to the devotional practices of relic cults.[13] We might think of relic custodians as privileged gatekeepers and expert rhetoricians, issues Chaucer, like Malory, finds to be of great interest.

It is not difficult to imagine that an immoral relic custodian might use the tricks of his trade to profit by unwitting supplicants. One particular sermon, "On Kinds of Theft," identifies rhetorical dishonesty and falsified relics as the means by which immoral relic custodians and/or pardoners – "sothell theves" – thrive[14]:

> Sothell theves beþ þe iij, þat slyly can robbe men with many queynt sotell wordes and with fals behestynges, and sum with fals letters and seeles, with crosses and reliques þat þei bere abowten þem, and sei þat þei be of seyntes bones or of holy mens cloþinge and behoteþ myche mede þat will offre to hem, and hire þe letters of pardon ichon of oþur … þe wiche þei sell all for þe penny and for no mans mede, with many fals lesyngges, as þe feend here maistur techeþ hem for to robbe þe pore pepull sotelly of þer goodes.[15]

The passage describes the person who, in the interests of making a profit, uses deceitful rhetoric to value his "letters of pardon" and fake relics. These pardoners employ "many queynt sotell wordes and with fals behestynges," and they lie about their worthless objects, which they "sei" are "seyntes bones." The author thus implies that "sotell wordes" and "fals lesyngges" are the means by which such people identify what they have as relics. Such a connection is surely obvious. But while many scholars have noted the literary and historical tradition of satirizing pardoners, none have yet commented on the degree to which satires of pardoners and/or relic custodians identify relic discourse as enabling this rhetorical subterfuge.[16] Immoral pardoners and relic custodians, with their dissembling rhetoric and outrageous relics, may well have been the perfect vehicle for probing how rhetoric and representative language (as well as representative objects, like shrines) can deceive. Chaucer's Pardoner is merely the most elaborate and famous example.

Relic custodians' abuses appear as a common criticism of relic cults throughout the Middle Ages. Guibert of Nogent remarks scathingly about such corruption:

> We repeatedly see [the cult of saints] trivialized through gossip and made an object of ridicule through the dragging around of reliquaries. Daily we see someone's pockets completely emptied by the lies of those whom Jerome called "rabble rousers" from their rabid style of speech.[17]

The Pardoner and his European analogues in Boccaccio and Masuccio are immoral relic custodians whose livelihood similarly depends upon – as Caesarius of Heisterbach observes of such characters – "carrying round the vessel of [a] holy relic, and extorting money by behaving dishonestly."[18] These analogues highlight the importance of the Pardoner's relics and of the Pardoner as relic custodian, since in these tales, fake relics, deceptive rhetoric, and immoral relic custodians (rather than pardoners in particular) are the central concern. Later satirists such as John Heywood picked up these details: Heywood's 1533 play *The Pardoner and the Frere* satirizes a corrupt pardoner who, like Chaucer's Pardoner, uses fake relics to make money.[19] Heywood, like Boccaccio, Masuccio, and Guibert, depicts greedy and rhetorically nimble relic custodians whose dissembling rhetoric is their most essential tool.

The author of the late fourteenth-century *Fasciculus morum* similarly frets about how language and rhetoric can manipulate and deceive. And while the author of "On Kinds of Theft" censures those who use language to confer value on fake relics, the author of the *Fasciculus* goes one step further, presenting enshrined fake relics as a metaphor for dishonest language:

> We should thus know that people who veil their sins in this fashion are like these false pardoners, who show their relics in some golden vessel that is decorated with precious gems, or else wrapped in cloths of gold and silk, so that they may look truly precious before the people. But as it often happens, when they open them up, you will find nothing but the bones from a farm animal that have been pulled out of a ditch, stinking and dried up and worthy of every abomination. In the same [w]ay, when such people ought to show their sins frankly and truthfully in confession, they put so many excuses around them like wrappers, as if they wanted to make of their sins relics to be worshipped, whereas in truth they stink horribly before God and his angels.[20]

In this text, fake (enshrined) relics distill a cluster of ideas associated with deceptive rhetoric: the prevaricating sinner, the immoral pardoner, as well as actual illegitimate saints' bones. This passage takes as a commonplace the idea that reliquaries, by identifying their contents as precious even while they hid those same contents, functioned both to classify and conceal the objects they contained. The *Fasciculus* author thereby compares the dissembling sinner specifically to immoral pardoners and relic custodians who use relic discourse to value fake or outrageous relics as genuine.[21] So, too, a reformist critique lambastes those who

> Assenten to pardoners disceyuynge þe peple in feiþ & charite ... for whanne þere comeþ a pardoner wiþ stollen bullis & false relekis, grauntynge mo ȝeris of pardon þan comen bifore domes day for ȝeuynge of worldly catel to riche placis where is no nede, he schal be sped & resceyued of curatis for to haue part of þat he getiþ.[22]

Though this author does not explicitly present enshrined relics as a metaphor for manipulative rhetoric, we are nonetheless given a dishonest pardoner who deceives people both with his "stollen bullis & false relekis" and by virtue of what he *says* about these objects: "þis pardoner schalle telle of more power þan euere crist grauntid to petir or poul or ony apostle, to drawe þe almes fro pore bedrede neiȝeboris."[23] (We may consider this text less Wycliffite than conventional – a "medieval cliché," as Peter Marshall says.)[24] Similarly, Langland associates pardoners with manipulative language. His pardoner, "raughte with his rageman rynges and broches," uses fake "bulles" "to deceyve the peple" and to "parten the silver / That the povere [peple] of the parissche sholde have if they ne were."[25] Both Langland and the Wycliffite author specify that the pardoner or relic custodian (or both) uses language in order to mislead ("deceyve," "disceyuynge") his audience. As is plain, Chaucer's Pardoner belongs in their company. Like the "sothell theves" from "On Kinds of Theft," he fools and deceives his audiences with his "hauteyn speche" (VI 330), seasoned with a few words of Latin (VI 344–5). And as in almost all of the aforementioned examples, fake relics comprise one of his most profitable props; he uses them in the service of what G. R. Owst aptly calls a "travelling peep-show."[26]

The Pardoner's Relics

When Chaucer the pilgrim introduces the Pardoner in the General Prologue to the *Canterbury Tales*, he makes it clear that we should pay special attention to the Pardoner's relics. The General Prologue portrait affiliates the Pardoner with relic cults and pilgrimages by the pilgrim souvenir he wears,[27] but even more so by the relics he carries:

> For in his male he hadde a pilwe-beer,
> Which that he seyde was Oure Lady veyl;
> He seyde he hadde a gobet of the seyl
> That Seint Peter hadde, whan that he wente
> Upon the see, til Jhesu Crist hym hente.
> He hadde a croys of latoun ful of stones,
> And in a glas he hadde pigges bones.
> But with thise relikes, whan that he fond
> A povre person dwellynge upon lond,
> Upon a day he gat hym moore moneye
> Than that the person gat in monthes tweye;

And thus, with feyned flaterye and japes,
He made the person and the peple his apes. (I 694–706)

Of the forty-five lines allocated to describing the Pardoner, four describe his singing, three his travelling companion and personal history, fourteen his physical appearance (including Chaucer's notorious speculation that he is "a geldyng or a mare" [I 691]), and six his ecclesiastical role and preaching. Chaucer devotes no fewer than eighteen lines to describing the Pardoner's relics, and in his own prologue, the Pardoner himself calls attention to his "sholder-boon / Which that was of an hooly Jewes sheep" (VI 350–1), among other relics. The amount of space allocated to relics clearly shows their importance to Chaucer's conception of the Pardoner and suggests that Chaucer conceived of this character as a part of the literature satirizing immoral pardoners and purveyors of fake relics.

Chaucer thus highlights the Pardoner's relics at the expense of some of his more preoccupying attributes, and readers from John Heywood to Thomas More attended to this emphasis in ways that many contemporary scholars have not.[28] Indeed, most scholarship on Chaucer's Pardoner has not taken account of the significance of relics within late medieval culture in general. Few studies have examined the Pardoner's relics (and the Pardoner's presentation of them) with reference to medieval devotional practices – and those that have done so frequently elide distinctions between various kinds of relics.[29] Siegfried Wenzel has sought to counter some inherited assumptions about relics in general (including the notion that pardoners were never associated with relics); Wenzel also debunked the idea that the Pardoner sells relics.[30] However, his work does not incorporate the conventions of relic cults into an interpretation of the Pardoner and does not examine the relics Chaucer's character claims to have. Nor does Seeta Chaganti explore the history of relics and their cults in her assessment of the Pardoner, focusing instead on how the Old Man in the Pardoner's Tale is a figure for metaphor itself,[31] and on how the Host's insult "embod[ies] the transformative and transitional act required in figurative expression."[32] In other words, when the Host wishes the Pardoner's balls were enshrined in "an hogges toord," he refers indirectly to the bodily digestive process that, like metaphor, turns one thing into something else. For Chaganti, the Pardoner's Tale thus provides a way to conceive of her book's argument: that what she calls the "poetics of enshrinement" provides a model for understanding the act of poetic creation as a moment of mental enshrinement.

Chaganti and Wenzel are exceptions to a critical discussion that foregrounds the Pardoner's gender identity and sexual proclivities,[33] his status as a preacher, his moral decrepitude, and the quality of his rhetoric.[34] These issues are vital to the Pardoner's character, and the Pardoner cannot be adequately understood without taking into account his physicality, morality, preaching, and even sexuality. But it is equally difficult to understand the Pardoner's character without taking into account his relics and how he handles them. By making Canterbury the destination of the pilgrimage, Chaucer identifies relics and relic shrines as the ostensible reason for his characters getting together in the first place.

And of these pilgrims, the Pardoner is the most explicitly associated with relics; in fact, he manipulates his relics (physically and rhetorically) in order to make a living. The Pardoner in some ways resembles a relic custodian: his occupation similarly requires him to control his relics and dictate the conditions of access to them. He can be thought of as a kind of private entrepreneur who tries to capitalize on a well-established system relating to the custody of relics. Though his relics are fake, his character still serves to satirize relic custodians, who similarly guarded and regulated contact with their (presumably real and supposedly holy) objects. More to the point, the Pardoner, his legitimate historical counterparts, and his European analogues in Boccaccio and Masuccio sought to occlude relics – whether by rhetoric, as in the Pardoner's case, or by means of elaborate shrines, as in the case of (for example) cathedral relic keepers. Chaucer's Pardoner hence occupies the liminal space between two worlds, that of the mainstream relic cult and that of the fake relic cult. He reveals what immoral pardoners have in common with orthodox relic keepers: they all deploy language (sometimes unscrupulously) to value their devotional objects. The primary difference is that our Pardoner, probably a layperson, uses relic discourse in ways unsanctioned by the clerics at popular shrines.[35]

In this vein, Boccaccio's Fra Cipolla (or Brother Onion) successfully presents a peacock feather as Saint Gabriel's feather – one wonders what he could have done with the Pardoner's pillowcase or sheep's shoulder bone. (One also thinks of the Host's *reductio ad absurdum*, when in a moment of anger he speculates that the Pardoner would try to pass off even his befouled underwear as a relic.[36]) In the European analogues to Chaucer's Pardoner, immoral relic custodians use relic discourse to portray common objects as relics, in effect hiding what these objects actually are by placing them in rhetorical reliquaries. These texts often satirize relic cults' corruption and relic keepers, but they also, by analogy, problematize material occlusion, which could misidentify the object contained in a shrine by hiding it from view.

From Material to Rhetorical Occlusion: The Pardoner's European Analogues

Both Boccaccio's *Decameron* and Masuccio Salernitano's mid-fifteenth-century *Novellino* present immoral relic custodians whose methods are remarkably like those of Chaucer's Pardoner. Boccaccio's Brother Onion and Masuccio's character, Girolamo, can be considered parodic relic custodians who dictate the conditions of access to the relics they carry. But they do not control access by physical or material occlusion. Instead, they use rhetorical occlusion or ornamentation in the place of ornamented and "elaborate reliquaries or containers."[37] They are thereby able to profess their artefacts to be valuable, and in so doing, they actually hide what their supposed relics really are (certainly not authentic relics!). These characters affirm Guibert of Nogent's objection that it is not difficult to profit via non-notable relics.[38] Guibert fretted that non-notable relics were falsely advertised and then exposed; so, too, these immoral characters physically expose their (non-notable, outrageous, and patently fake) relics, even as they rhetorically occlude what they have by telling a lie about it.

Brother Onion appears in Boccaccio's *Decameron*, in the tenth story of the sixth day. Onion's job, travelling to raise money for his order, takes him to Val d'Elsa, where the people are "stupid enough" to pay him for the privilege of seeing his alleged relics.[39] These include Onion's "most holy and beautiful relic" ("santissima e bella reliquia"), which is supposedly Saint Gabriel's feather;[40] a finger of the Holy Spirit; one of the ribs of the True-Word-Made-Flesh-at-the-Windows; vestments of the Holy Catholic faith; beams from the Star of Bethlehem; a phial of Saint Michael's sweat; Saint Lazarus's jaw bones; the sound of bells from Solomon's temple in a phial; the wooden shoe of Saint Gherardo da Villamagna; and finally, the charcoal used to roast Saint Lawrence.[41] His list could not be more ridiculous, and with it Boccaccio mocks the practice of venerating exceedingly implausible relics. But Boccaccio also focuses on Onion's method of displaying his relics. In fact, the plot of this story revolves around whether Onion can successfully present a piece of coal as a relic – whether he can rhetorically occlude the coal so that the audience will venerate it as a relic. This situation comes about when two of his friends decide to test his rhetorical skill by playing a joke on him. They steal his "most holy and beautiful relic," which is actually a peacock feather, and replace it with a lump of coal. Their challenge is blatant: Onion needs to be able to manipulate this object rhetorically in order to construct it as a relic, but also to conceal what it actually is (just a lump of coal courtesy of his friends).

Onion occludes his lump of coal, not by placing it in an opaque and locked container, but by narrating his method of obtaining it. His story, which includes a visit to Jerusalem and the description of many (implausible) relics, serves (like a reliquary, or like writing about relics) to identify his relics as precious and worthy of veneration. Once Onion has explained the provenance of the coal, he "opened the box, and displayed the charcoal. The foolish throng gazed upon it in reverent admiration."[42] Presumably the notable relics in cathedral reliquaries were often authentic relics, unlike those Onion claims to have. But this moment nevertheless suggests a parallel between physically concealed relics, however genuine, and fake relics concealed by rhetoric. A believer in Onion's audience may "see" a precious relic, but this is not, in fact, what Onion has – as the reader knows from the very outset. His rhetoric accomplishes what a physical reliquary might: it affirms that the "throng" has gathered for a purpose and that the object of their veneration is genuine and worthwhile. That is to say, here in the *Decameron*, rhetoric functions as a reliquary – figuratively, rather than literally, ornamenting and occluding an object of veneration.

Masuccio Salernitano's mid-fifteenth-century *Novellino*, published (probably posthumously) in 1476,[43] operates similarly, featuring an immoral relic custodian who occludes (and valorizes) an object by categorizing it as something else. Masuccio tells the tale of an "unscrupulous Franciscan friar" named Girolamo, who "deceives credulous people with a spurious relic and a fake miracle."[44] Girolamo is clearly identified as an immoral relic custodian. Masuccio rails against greedy and ambitious friars, who "by hook or by crook" win "for themselves a bellyful of florins, in spite of the fact that such traffic [of relics and indulgences] is expressly forbidden by the most sacred rules of their religion."[45] In this story, the money-hungry friar comes across the body of a knight,

> which either because it had been very well preserved, or peradventure on account of the temperate manner of life used by the knight while he was living, or for some other reason, was still in so sound and perfect a

> state, that not only was every bone thereof well settled in its right position ["che non solamente ogn'osso stava al suo debito seggio collocate"], but the skin was in so little degree fallen to decay ["ma la pelle in maniera immaculate"] that, by touching the head, the lower parts of the body would move themselves.[46]

In this body Girolamo sees a relic in the making. He decides to steal part of it "to be styled by him a sacred relic" ("sotto nome de reliquia") and thereby to "sweep into his purse hundreds and thousands of ducats."[47] Masuccio's criticism of Girolamo, an immoral relic custodian who profits by what "is expressly forbidden,"[48] is certainly a satire of clerical corruption in general, but it also satirizes the manipulation of access to relics in the service of power and revenue in particular. For Girolamo does not simply steal a body part and "style" it an anonymous, non-notable relic. Instead, Girolamo steals a large enough portion of the body to make the implicit claim that the relic he has and exposes is notable.

In order to do this, Girolamo (like the Pardoner, as the next section demonstrates) claims a relationship to institutional authority by professing that the relic has been passed along to him through a patriarch and a vicar. By extension, he insinuates that these powerful men approve of his enterprise. More importantly, Girolamo emphasizes the physical importance of his artefact:

> I am now minded to bring before your eyes a most marvelous relic ... This relic is nothing else than the arm and the entire right hand of that most excellent and glorious writer of the words and deeds of Christ Jesus our Redeemer, Saint Luke the Evangelist, which precious thing the Patriarch of Constantinople gave to our Father Vicar. Whereupon this latter despatched me into Calabria therewith, for the reasons aforesaid, forasmuch as there has never been in this province up to the present time either the body or the limb of any saint whatever. On this account, my friends here gathered together, let each one of you in devout fashion uncover his head before looking at this precious treasure which our great God, more through the working of a miracle than through any act of mine, has granted you leave to behold.[49]

Girolamo's claim is not as impressive as having Saint Luke's entire body (though it is eminently more practical). Nevertheless, it does seem as though Girolamo is suggesting that what he has is very powerful –

for surely the forearm that wrote the Gospel would have been considered a notable relic. Girolamo maintains that his body-part relic is not small; he is careful to say that he has "the arm and the *entire* right hand" ("cioè un braccio con la mano destra intera") that Saint Luke used to write the Gospel. This is no small claim for *any* relic. Finally, Girolamo reminds the audience that there has never been a notable relic (not "the body or the limb of any saint whatever") in their area of the country. This occasion is, therefore, according to the friar, a momentous one. If his claims were true, he would be right on more than one count: first, because such a relic had never before been there, and second, because such relics were not normally displayed openly. Moreover, his emphasis on sight in this passage ("monstrare" and "di vedere vi ha concesso") is especially tantalizing because he is promising to expose the very kind of relic that would typically have been most sequestered and most inaccessible.

The Pardoner as Relic Custodian

The Pardoner similarly uses rhetoric to conceal his counterfeit relics. He obfuscates what he has so carefully that, when he exhibits his relics to solicit money, he follows a specific procedure:

> First I pronounce whennes that I come,
> And thanne my bulles shewe I, alle and some.
> Oure lige lordes seel on my patente,
> That shewe I first, my body to warente,
> That no man be so boold, ne preest ne clerk,
> Me to destourbe of Cristes hooly werk.
> And after that thanne telle I forth my tales;
> Bulles of popes and of cardynales,
> Of patriarkes and bishopes I shewe,
> And in Latyn I speke a wordes fewe,
> To saffron with my predicacioun,
> And for to stire hem to devocioun.
> Thanne shewe I forth my longe cristal stones …
> Relikes been they, as wenen they echoon. (VI 335–47, 349)

Before he brings out his supposedly holy objects, he predisposes his audience, by his rhetorical strategies, to believe the relics he will show them are real. He is specific about the order in which he does this, explaining to the pilgrims that "*First* I pronounce whennes that I come"; "*thanne* my bulles shewe I"; and, before he brings out his relics, he shows his patent "*first*." These actions serve to establish his authority and to demonstrate his rhetorical skill (it seems he always performs these actions in the same order). He continues to detail the sequence of information he gives the pilgrims: after identifying himself, showing his bulls and patent, "*thanne* telle I forth my tales"; and finally, "*Thanne shewe I forth* my longe cristal stones / … / Relikes been they, as wenen they echoon." It is clear, based on the sequence here and the Pardoner's repeated use of the words "thanne" and "first," that he does not expose his relics until this point in his performance. Furthermore, his language – "shewe I" and "first" – indicates his (usually) careful control of the situation. The Pardoner shows forth his relics only once his audience has been adequately prepared to see them as such – only once, that is, he has placed them carefully within rhetorical reliquaries.

He has thus rhetorically primed his audience to "see" his relics – which, as Chaucer the pilgrim tells the reader, are the worst kind of fakes – as legitimate:

> Thanne shewe I forth my longe cristal stones,
> Ycrammed ful of cloutes and of bones –
> Relikes been they, as wenen they echoon.
> Thanne have I in latoun a sholder-boon
> Which that was of an hooly Jewes sheep. (VI 347–51)

The Pardoner goes on to claim that this sheep bone, if dipped "in any welle" (VI 353), will cure livestock. In addition, if the owner of these sheep and cattle drinks from the well, "His beestes and his stoor shal multiplie" (VI 365). The Pardoner then introduces the "miteyn eek, that ye may se" (VI 372), which multiplies grain. Already, the Pardoner has spent a considerable amount of time (forty-one of fifty-nine lines) delineating the miraculous powers of his relics. Like Onion, Girolamo, or Heywood's Pardoner, Chaucer's Pardoner carefully regulates the display and use of his relics. He furthermore exhibits these objects in a particular order – first his bulls, then one relic, then another. The Pardoner manifests here the attitude of the seasoned relic custodian, who orders and orchestrates his display of relics to garner the best profit possible.

By revealing his "entente" (VI 423) to the other pilgrims, the Pardoner also reveals his intimate understanding and expert deployment of relic discourse, as well as his expert rhetorical occlusion of his relics.

He is, by his own account, a very good relic custodian. Moreover, the Pardoner capitalizes on traditions of control and access in order to profit by his relics. He refers expressly to limiting access to his relics:

> Goode men and wommen, o thyng warne I yow:
> If any wight be in this chirche now
> That hath doon synne horrible, that he
> Dar nat, for shame, of it yshryven be,
> Or any womman, be she yong or old,
> That hath ymaked hir housbonde cokewold,
> Swich folk *shal have no power ne no grace*
> To offren to my relikes in this place. (VI 377–84; emphasis added)

The Pardoner does offer a remedy for this problem (he will absolve them of their sins). But by positioning himself as the pilgrims' intermediary, the Pardoner places himself between the pilgrims and his relics; they must pass by him if they are to "offren to my relikes." More than this, he demarcates the difference between those who, like him, have access to and control over relics and those who are dependent upon hierarchical power to access relics at all. Such people, if they do not follow the requirements of the church (like confession), "shal have no power ne no grace" to access relics. And regardless of whether the Pardoner is actually authorized to absolve sin, he knows very well that confession was typically presented as necessary to accessing relics.[50] The Pardoner, in this moment, articulates one of the key terms for relic custodians, supplicants, and indeed for relic discourse as well: "power." For the Pardoner, no matter his state of sin, always has the "power" to access his relics. The pilgrims, on the other hand, are at the mercy of a corrupt relic custodian whose conditions dictate whether they will have any "power" to access his relics at all.

This moment – in which the Pardoner offers the pilgrims his relics, even after he has explained that they are fakes – also reveals the limitations of relic discourse, which only works insofar as the audience is unaware of it as a discursive practice. The pilgrims are not angered or even dissuaded from their pilgrimage by the Pardoner's attempt to use the discourse he has just explained – but "al the peple" laugh at the Pardoner (VI 961). These characters may all be said to see, suddenly, that when the conventions of a discourse are exposed, the discourse itself becomes ridiculous. The kiss of peace – another social practice described and codified by language – thus brings the pilgrim company back into the very system they briefly recognized and ridiculed.

But even before the Knight's intervention, this laughter does not, as many readings of the Pardoner have suggested, threaten or undermine the pilgrimage to Canterbury. The Pardoner's relics are demonstrably different from those in Canterbury Cathedral, after all, not least because the Pardoner's are fakes. Moreover, the Pardoner, himself likely a layperson, would have not had any better access to the relics at the journey's end than his fellow pilgrims. With this character, then, Chaucer probes not only the limits of relic discourse, relic custodians, or even the role of pardoners. Instead, Chaucer also presents us with a kind of rebellious supplicant – one on a pilgrimage but with his own collection of (albeit fake and non-notable) relics. Put another way, the Pardoner – and perhaps many pardoners of the later Middle Ages – represents a radical kind of layperson, one who takes the power of relics into his or her own hands. As R.N. Swanson points out, it is not all that surprising that such a person made many church officials uneasy.[51] Chaucer's Pardoner, deviant, immoral, and fallible, is all too aware of his plebian status; of the insignificant status of the relics he carries; of the fact that, apart from his rhetorical expertise, he is in the end only like everybody else.

The Pardoner's Tale, Tresor, and the Literalized Metaphor

While the Pardoner's Prologue contains explicit references to relics and centers on a parodic relic custodian, the Pardoner's Tale seems at first glance to have little, if anything, to do with the cult of saints. But as this section will argue, the treasure of the Tale functions in part as a literalized metaphor for saints' relics (which were commonly described as treasure).[52] In this context, the rioters' excitement at seeing the treasure (and their subsequent fate) illustrates the moral danger in lavish reliquaries, which could too easily be appreciated only for their splendor and not for their saint.[53] Their excitement also illustrates the difficulties of figurative language, which could only too easily be manipulated or misunderstood. In the case of the shrine at Canterbury, descriptions of Becket's reliquary show how the literalized metaphor (the "tresor") might displace what it represented (the relics). One might even say that the shrine loomed so large that, upon their arrival at Canterbury, pilgrims simply forgot about Becket. In this, the physical appearance of the shrine corresponds to the literary elision of shrine and relic – a commonplace of relic discourse that pervades and informs the Pardoner's Tale. There, the substitution of shrine for saint challenges the idea that figurative signs are easy to interpret and foregrounds the shiftiness of signifying language in general.

Canterbury Cathedral was obviously central to the devotional culture of late medieval Europe, largely because of its famous martyr, Thomas Becket. Even before Becket's death in 1170, the splendor of Canterbury Cathedral would probably have been overwhelming: tombs of kings and saints, including St Alphege, St Dunstan, and St Anselm;[54] relics, including the arm of St George, patron saint of England; a thriving tourist industry, largely dependent on the pilgrims who made the visit to their city; and by 1220, St Thomas's shrine and the promise of healing and relief from any number of maladies. A testament to the history of Christianity in England, the cathedral provided a concrete reminder of St Augustine and St Gregory the Great, and by the mid-fifteenth century, of the Black Prince and Henry IV as well, whose monuments flanked St Thomas's elaborate, gem-encrusted shrine. Its splendour and importance are well known; but these facts bear repeating here primarily because Canterbury Cathedral is seldom factored into readings of the Pardoner.[55]

This material context lies in the background of the entire *Canterbury Tales*, but even more particularly of the Pardoner (and, by extension, of his Tale). Of course opaque cathedral feretories were not the only kind of reliquary, and notable relics were not the only kind of relic. But it cannot be overstated that these were the most splendid kinds of reliquaries and lucrative kinds of relics, regarded the most seriously by a spectrum of mainstream and reformist theologians.[56] Becket's body was housed in just such an opaque, gilded, and even gated shrine. It is difficult to imagine that Chaucer's contemporaries would not have been aware of what such shrine architecture looked like, any more than twenty-first-century audiences would be ignorant of what a skyscraper looks like. Erasmus's account testifies to the predominance of such opulent reliquaries at Canterbury Cathedral, where even he was not allowed the privilege of seeing Becket's bones:

> OGYGIUS: He opened for us the chest ["aperuit thecam"] in which the holy man's body is said to lie ["in qua reliquum sancti viri corpus quiescere dicitur"].
>
> MENEDEMUS: You saw the bones ["Vidisti ossa"]?
>
> OGYGIUS: No, that's not permitted, nor would it be possible without the use of ladders ["Id quidem fas non est, nec liceret nisi admotis scalis"]. But the wooden chest conceals a golden chest; when this is drawn up by ropes, it reveals inestimable treasure.[57]

Crucially, the "inestimable treasure" to which Ogygius here refers is *not* Becket's relics, but rather his lavish reliquary. This exchange highlights the degree to which relics' literal metaphors – their opulent shrines – gradually eclipsed, even effaced, their contents. Just what, one wonders, did pilgrims expect (or want) to see? In *The Annales of England*, John Stow describes Becket's shrine base as "builded about a mans height, all of stone," and so opulently decorated with gold and gems that these treasures "filled two great chestes, such as 6 or 8 strong men coulde doe no more, then conueie one of them at once out of the church."[58] Stow here emphasizes the sheer height, weight, and opulence of the shrine; since he is unlikely to have seen the reliquary himself, his account may record what he heard others say about this monument. Likewise, one Venetian pilgrim, writing around 1500, details carefully the "precious stones" he viewed on the shrine and, *not* mentioning Becket's relics, comments that "*everything* is far surpassed by a ruby" – known as the Regale of France – which was given by the King of France.[59] Earlier accounts similarly focused on the shrine, without articulating that the reliquary was merely meant to represent Thomas Becket's sanctity. Matthew Paris, for example, noted that Archbishop Langton "had prepared for the honourable reception of the body a shrine of the purest gold of Ophir and precious stones, and of workmanship even costlier than the material."[60] Even in this account, it seems that the gem-encrusted *feretrum* usurped the place of Thomas Becket. It is certainly possible that supplicants took the relics' existence as a given and saw no need to mention them. But one thing, at least, is clear: at Canterbury, most encounters would *not* have been with Becket's relics, but rather with his shrine, and if the contemporary accounts are accurate, probably not very close encounters.

So, too, in the Pardoner's Tale, the rioters' "tresor" overshadows the quest to kill death. The ubiquity and cultural importance of relic discourse mean that while the treasure of the Pardoner's has many figural meanings – greed being the most obvious – understanding this pursuit for worldly goods in the context of relic discourse illuminates what the rioters may have in common with all (not just depraved) pilgrims: the desire to overcome death, perhaps even the desire to come into closer contact with major relics than was typically possible. Without discounting the polysemy of "treasure," then, I will emphasize the figural meaning of the treasure as saints' relics, which were themselves regularly described as treasure, as "thesauri," or as more precious than gems or gold.[61] We should also understand this treasure as referring to saints' shrines, which were often made from actual treasure, from gold and gems. Hence, though saints' relics were often called "treasure," it is appropriate to understand this vehicle as having the potential to displace its tenor (that is, the relics themselves), such that "tresor" designates not relics but rather reliquaries – and such that "tresor" connotes the difficulties of figurative language in general.

In a twelfth-century account of Harold Godwinson's gift of relics to Waltham abbey,[62] the Waltham chronicler registers alarm at this possibility:

> I fear that, if these precious relics of the saints are entrusted to these reliquaries of gold and silver ["capsis istis aureis et argenteis"], something "far more valuable than gold or precious stones and sweeter than honey and the honeycomb" may, through the prevailing madness of wicked men, be stolen from the church, and in these man-made vessels these holy things may be alienated through the greed of evil men in later generations, and put to the use of sinners.[63]

Lydgate's account of attempted thefts at St Edmund's reliquary similarly implies that shrines could make viewers forget about saints.[64] He narrates that a man from Flanders

> Kam vndyr colour off oblacion,
> Kyssed the shryne lyk a slyh pilour [robber],
> And with his teth, the book makith mencion,
> Rauhte off a nowche ... (*EF* 3236–9)

The accompanying illumination depicts Edmund's punishment of the Flemish would-be thief, whose teeth Edmund cements to the shrine (fol. 109r).[65] Lydgate does not depict this "slyh pilour" as remotely concerned with Edmund himself. The next miracle story features eight "theuys" who break into the monastery "to bern away the gold with stonys bryhte" (*EF* 3259). Lydgate credits none of the thieves with a desire "to bern away" Edmund's *relics*. While Lydgate does not explicitly problematize the shrine's adornment, these miracles nonetheless provide instances in which the reliquary eclipses the relic as the central object. This fascination with Edmund's worldly adornment, rather than with Edmund's relics, epitomizes the kind of alienation the Waltham chronicler worried about.[66]

As these instances make clear, a sumptuous reliquary could overshadow the saint and his or her relics. Such is the case in the Pardoner's

Tale. While the rioters begin by seeking to "sleen this false traytour Deeth" (VI 699), they forget about their quest once they see treasure: "No lenger thanne after Deeth they soughte" (VI 772). As the Old Man cryptically suggests to the rioters, this treasure stands in for, replaces, and even serves as the location of death. So, too, relics comprise a place of death, in that major and notable relics are literally large parts of a dead saint's body. They also, however, serve as an important sign for the resurrection (and healing) of the body – as Melvin Storm comments, "[p]ilgrimage in the truest sense, after all, is … ultimately directed toward overcoming death."[67] Chaucer-the-pilgrim identifies Thomas of Canterbury as a saint to whom pilgrims give thanks because Becket "hem hath holpen whan that they were seeke" (I 18). St Thomas of Canterbury is thus credited with the power to defer death by healing illnesses that cause it. Such narratives were commonplace: a significant proportion of the stories depicted in miracle collections and stained glass involve both healing the sick and resurrecting the dead, and a significant number of pilgrims are depicted as travelling to a shrine in order to be so healed.[68] In their focus on defeating "a privee theef men clepeth Deeth, / That in this contree al the peple sleeth" (VI 675–6) – and thereby prolonging life – the three ne'er-do-wells of the Pardoner's Tale do not differ fundamentally in their intention from pilgrims who seek to circumvent mortality or sickness. And they, too, seek a particular physical location: they surely cannot kill Death if they cannot get close to it. So, too, pilgrimage depended on the notion that one physical space – and indeed, the remains of one physical body – was holier than another. Getting close to that space was often essential to achieve contact with the miraculous (or to give thanks for a miracle). Pilgrims to Canterbury certainly responded to the idea that travel to and praying at these sites was more effective than praying for healing at home.

The rioters' response to the treasure gives us an idea of one potential response pilgrims may have had to an ornate shrine. When the rioters find this treasure, they are captivated by its material beauty. They abandon their pursuit of Death, and the language quickly turns to vision and wealth:

> *No lenger thanne after Deeth they soughte,*
> But ech of hem so glad was of that sighte,
> For that the floryns been so faire and brighte,
> That doun they sette hem by this precious hoord. (VI 772–5; emphasis added)

Chaucer here makes a causal connection ("No lenger thanne") between seeing the treasure and forsaking the quest. What is more, Chaucer describes the treasure itself using the vocabulary associated with relic cults and employed by purveyors of relic discourse to confer value on shrines and saints. In this case, the rioters are sidetracked by the "sight" of what is "bright"; moreover, the florins are also "faire" and "precious." These are precisely the kinds of adjectives employed to describe saints, relics, and their shrines from the eleventh through early sixteenth centuries. These words obviously describe money, too – and clearly the Tale is invested in depicting the rioters' immoral greed. But accounting for the figural (as well as literal) meaning of words such as "bright" and "precious" illuminates the difficulty that any pilgrim might have in distinguishing between a beautiful shrine and what it signified. Moreover, the syntax of these and other lines renders these money/shrine words as crucial: "bright" appears once more, where its rhyme is "myght" (VI 840), a polyvalent word in this instance, meaning not only possibility but also power. These three words alone – "sight," "bright," and "might" – are reminiscent of how relic discourse constructed the appropriate experience at a shrine, where the brightness of the saint was, in a manner of speaking, concealed from sight and where, as the Pardoner himself comments earlier, very few are allowed the "power and grace" – one is tempted to say the "might" – to access the relics themselves.

One of the rioters does express a kind of anxiety – or at least awareness – that, according to the conventions of relic discourse and the clerical regulations of relic cults, they do not have the "power and grace" to claim this treasure. He advocates subterfuge:

But trewely, by daye it may nat bee.
Men wolde seyn that we were theves stronge,
And for oure owene tresor doon us honge.
This tresor moste ycaried be by nyghte
As wisely and as slyly as it myghte …
And two of us shul kepen subtilly
This tresor wel … (VI 788–92, 798–9)

This speech functions in at least two ways that evoke relic discourse. First, the rioter repeats the word "tresor," a word very conventionally associated with relics and reliquaries, as well as with purses and money. Second, this speech aligns this rioter's plan with relic translations, which were highly regulated and controlled ceremonies. In fact, at the opening of these ceremonies, clerics would traditionally exhume the corpse, a job often carried out at night.[69] Relic translation also occasioned a vigil on the eve of the translation ceremony, when clerics were appointed to keep watch over the relics. Here, the two remaining men are instructed to "kepen subtilly / This tresor wel." I think it is well within the realm of possibility that the Pardoner is here satirizing a *furta sacra*, or relic theft.[70]

Of course, these rioters are not officiants or clerics, and they do not have any legitimate claim (neither "power" nor "grace") over the gold they have found. Identifying the gold as "oure owene tresor" is thus not only risky, but in the context of relic discourse, threatening to the established order of relic cults in two ways. First, the rioters attempt to occupy a position that would have been reserved for the clergy. In this, they are like the Pardoner himself, who offers absolution and who preaches, knowing full well that these are clerical tasks. Second, in their intense desire for the treasure, the rioters expose the degree to which opulent shrines presented saints' relics as if they were earthly, man-made treasure. The rioters' extraordinarily immoral behaviour gestures towards the danger in lavish shrines, which could then be treated by the unscrupulous as a means to make a profit. The Pardoner certainly deploys relic discourse for explicitly financial ends. "Myn entente," he tells the pilgrims, "is nat but for to wynne, / And nothyng for correccioun of synne" (VI 403–4). In this instance, the Pardoner designates the meaning of relics as objects for turning a profit: the tenor of a reliquary is thus its treasure, not the relic, and certainly not heaven. In the Pardoner's paradigm, in other words, the rioters interpret the treasure perfectly adequately. While the Pardoner obviously knows but does not care that this interpretation is disordered (the rioters do, after all, meet with less-than-ideal ends), his attitude nevertheless reveals the pliability of relic discourse: given that its primary metaphor is derived from material goods, it is perhaps no surprise that this metaphor could be co-opted as an end in itself. Like the elision of shrine and saint, then, the Pardoner's Tale presents shrine (treasure) as significant in itself. The primary difference here, perhaps, is that the Pardoner's Tale foregrounds the problem of such a shifty metaphor, which could as easily result in death as healing.

In the Pardoner, Chaucer gives us a character who successfully uses relic discourse to present his fake relics as having spiritual value. His character thereby reveals one danger in this discourse: that it could be used as a way to sanctify just about *any* object (to wit, Brother Onion's lump of coal). What is more, the Pardoner depends upon the complicity of his audience: they must accept as genuine what he shows them. He does not think much of those to whom he preaches and takes a certain pride in duping them. The Pardoner's expert use of relic discourse indicates the constructedness of a saint's value, of a relic's value, so much so that language (or shrine) can be said to create the saint. In this way, the end of the Tale, Harry Bailley's anger, and the pilgrims' amusement can all be seen to stem from the Pardoner's own explanation of the metaphors he uses, that relics gesture towards material treasure rather than heavenly salvation. It is thus most fitting that the Host ends with a crude explanation of the function of metaphor:

> I wolde I hadde thy coillons in myn hond
> In stide of relikes or of seintuarie.
> Lat kutte hem of, I wol thee helpe hem carie;
> They shul be shryned in an hogges toord! (VI 952–5)

As Chaganti has pointed out, in his anger, the Host comments on the primary function of metaphor: to take one thing and turn it into something else.[71] But he also comments on the significatory function of reliquaries and relic discourse, implicitly acknowledging that the Pardoner's admission – of caring about financial gain – displaces the tenor, the relic, from its metaphor, the shrine. The Pardoner cares nothing about what the relic might represent. Instead, in eliding relic and shrine – in deriving the value of random objects from how he enshrines them, rhetorically – the Pardoner intimates the degree to which a relic custodian or writer could manipulate and construct the value and meaning of relics. The shrine is not a neutral signifying object, and it has the ability to remove the relic from sight and from thought. To some degree, this idea is the basis for Bailley's crude joke, for surely if anyone were to view his imaginary shrine, none would think of the Pardoner's "coillons" so much as the pig excrement. The Pardoner's Prologue and Tale, then, ultimately reveal the complexity of the relationship between signs and what they signify, and how quickly this relationship can collapse – both within the context of relic discourse, but also in the context of language more generally.

Translating Criseyde: The Absent Relic and the Fall of Troy(lus)

We might similarly think of language as creating the saint in *Troilus and Criseyde*: Criseyde herself. In his despair after Criseyde has left Troy,

Troilus laments his predicament in front of her empty house: "Yet syn I may no bet, fayn wolde I kisse / Thy colde dores, dorste I for this route; / And farwel shryne, of which the seynt is oute!" (V 551–3).[72] Alastair Minnis has rightly characterized this passage as one in which "Troilus, faced with the empty house of Criseyde, has the urge to kiss it as one might kiss a relic"; Minnis goes on to suggest that "the idea of a saint living in his shrine was suggested to Chaucer by the common late-medieval conception of pagan idols as the dwelling of demons."[73] D. W. Robertson analgously describes Troilus's affection for Criseyde as "idolatry."[74] V. A. Kolve concurs, associating Criseyde with Christian ideas of idolatry.[75] But I think it is more likely still that this idea was suggested to Chaucer by the proliferation of late medieval shrines and of relic discourse – which could inspire idolatry, to be sure, but which did not necessarily lead to idolatry. This possibility seems all the more attractive given that in the *Troilus*, Criseyde is closely associated with the Palladium, an object which Chaucer explicitly calls Troy's "relik" (I 153).[76] As John Fleming has rightly observed, "[t]here is a remarkable parallel between the Palladium and Criseyde, and one that astonishingly remains unremarked."[77] This object substantively changes how we might understand other liturgical moments in Chaucer's poem, moments which have rightly been understood to participate in the discourses of both courtly love – the Religion of Love in particular – and paganism.[78] But these moments are polyvalent, and they invoke relic discourse as well: Criseyde is both the metaphorical saint of courtly love and the religious saint of a pilgrimage to relics. Relic discourse in particular illuminates the poem's concerns with slippery rhetoric, shedding light on Chaucer's exploration of the disconnect between meaning and intent, between the outside and inside – of, in short, the difficulties and dangers of communication, one of the central issues he takes up in the *Troilus*.

In spite of the recent turn to religion,[79] *Troilus and Criseyde* is seldom considered in its religious contexts. Some have remarked on the interplay between pagan and Christan or Boethian elements of this work, focusing in particular on Troilus's apotheosis at the end of the poem.[80] It will be the argument of this section that instead, at least some of the religious discourse of this poem illuminates the importance of the tactile world. While this world (and the language that describes it) can be deceptive and unreliable, *Troilus and Criseyde* does not necessarily present it as completely superseded by ideas of Boethian happiness. In fact, in playing with the parardoxes inherent in relic discourse, which frequently insists on the always-already perfection of successful pilgrims, Chaucer's *Troilus* maintains a sympathetic attitude to Troilus's worldly suffering, emphasizing the importance of Criseyde's physical presence and the disastrous results of her absence. Troilus's death thus reveals the inadequacies of relic discourse, without necessarily discounting the discourse of relics or the importance of shrines (as a Boethian reading might seem to require). Instead, Troilus's fate – "Swich fin hath, lo, this Troilus for love" (V 1828), a line that strikes me as plaintive rather than as laden with "emphatic disgust"[81] – illustrates that exemplary pilgrim behaviour will not necessarily result in a miraculous cure; following the rules of an imperfect system might not ensure success.

There are two explicit references to relics in the poem, both of which ultimately have to do with Criseyde. In the one I cite at the beginning of this section, Troilus refers to Criseyde's house as a shrine. For this metaphor to make sense, we must understand Criseyde as a kind of relic: Troilus calls her the shrine's "saint" and implies that the reliquary is itself meaningless without its holy object. His comparison points to the similarity between shrines and rhetorical expression, both of which, like Criseyde's promises, might be empty. In the other instance, Chaucer expressly identifies the feast of the Palladium as the feast of Troy's "relik": "Thei hadde a relik, heet Palladion, / That was hire trist aboven everichon" (I 153–4). The term appears in none of the three main sources for the *Troilus* – neither in Boccaccio's *Il Filostrato*, nor Guido delle Colonne's or Benoît de Sainte-Maure's accounts of Troy's fall. Boccaccio refers to the object simply as "Pallas" and "Palladio fatale."[82] Benoît (Guido's source) calls the Palladium "Un signe fier e precios" (An awesome and precious sign); Antenor (whose importance to Criseyde I discuss in this chapter) explains simply that "Apelez est Palladion" (It is called the Palladium).[83] Guido follows suit, referring to the Palladium as a marvellous sign ("mirabile signum"), which Elizabeth Meek translates as "image."[84] When Antenor explains the importance of the Palladium, he again designates it a sign: "Huius autem signi nomen, pro eo quod a dea Pallade creditur esse datum, Palladium communiter appellatur." ("The name of this image is called Palladium by everyone, because it is believed to have been given by the goddess Pallas.")[85] Though Guido rails against greedy clerics,[86] neither he nor Benoît situate the Palladium within the medieval cult of relics, focusing instead on its role in Troy's fall.

Chaucer's brief use of the term "relik" thus inaugurates a literary tradition that depicts the Palladium as a relic at the centre of a devotional festival.[87] In *The Troy Book*, Lydgate refers to this object as a relic multiple times:

> And hider sent þoruȝ his puruyaunce [the Palladyoun]
> For a relik, only of his grace …
> In sustenynge and reuelacioun
> And sovereyn helpe eke of þis cite.
> Þe whiche neuer may distroyed be …
> Til þis relik stole be a-way.
> And ȝit, in soth, þer is no man þat may
> From þe place stere it nor remewe,
> But þe prest to whom it is dwe
> Only of offys to touche it with his hond.
> So myȝtely conseruyd is þe bond
> Þat who attempteth, in conclusioun,
> It to remewe of presumpcioun,
> At þe fyn, platly, he shal fayle:
> For force noon may him nat availle;
> For it in soth wil nat remeved be
> Excepte of hym to whom of duete
> It aparteneth, as ȝe han herde to-forn.[88]

This excerpt from *The Troy Book* employs some of the most essential tenets of relic discourse, including the affirmation of the relic custodian's privileged access to this object – "þe prest to whom it is dwe / Only of offys to touche it with his hond." Having heard about this protective relic, Ulysses complains that while it remains in Troy, the Greek campaign is "in ydel and in veyn."[89] Antenor responds by detailing how he will steal the relic: "þe prest, þe whiche hath þe gouernaunce / Of þis relyk … / … with gold & tresour shal be blent."[90] In this moment, Lydgate draws on the conventions of immoral and greedy relic custodians, situating the Palladium in relation to late medieval English devotional culture. What is more, he incorporates the crucial detail from Guido and Benoît to which Chaucer only alludes: that Antenor's theft of the Palladium, Troy's best and more prestigious relic, precipitates Troy's fall.

Chaucer, I believe, expects his readers to know the details of Antenor's crime.[91] Hence, when *Troilus and Criseyde* obliquely refers to Antenor's treachery in the middle of the parliamentary debate about what to do with Criseyde – a detail Chaucer interposes into the story, as C. S.

Lewis has pointed out – it is incumbent upon the reader to notice that Antenor is also, in a manner of speaking, stealing Criseyde.[92] This additional information renders Criseyde as analogous to the Palladium:

> "O kyng Priam," quod they, "thus sygge we,
> That al oure vois is to forgon Criseyde."
> And to deliveren Antenor they preyde.
> …
> This folk desiren now deliveraunce
> Of Antenor, that brought hem to meschaunce,
> For he was after traitour to the town
> Of Troye. Allas, they quytte hym out to rathe!…
> But Antenor, he shal com hom to towne,
> And she shal out; thus seyden here and howne.
> For which delibered was by parlement
> For Antenor to yelden out Criseyde … (IV 194–6, 202–5, 209–12)

This passage refers to Antenor's theft of the Palladium, which ultimately leads to Troy's destruction – the cataclysmic event described by the narrator as the citizens' "meschaunce." Chaucer includes this material in the middle of a debate about Criseyde's fate and frames it with the phrases "to forgon Criseyde" and "to yelden out Criseyde."[93] These phrases, grammatically speaking, present Antenor as the direct cause of Criseyde's inevitable absence from Troy. Chaucer thereby styles Criseyde a kind of saint, a relic – a devotional object to be worshipped. If, as it seems, relic discourse illuminates some of Chaucer's narrative choices in the poem, we cannot merely dismiss this move as consonant only with discourses of courtly love (or burlesques of religious discourse). Were this passage about Antenor drawing only from these discourses and presenting Criseyde as a saint of love, it would surely have been more economical to *call Criseyde a saint*. But in this passage, Chaucer goes to the trouble of adding to Boccaccio's text details that foreground Criseyde's relationship to Antenor and to the Palladium – details that, in Chaucer's text, associate Criseyde with a relic and the cult of relics.

The narrator enforces this depiction of Criseyde-as-relic in the opening exchange between Pandarus and Criseyde in Book II. There, when Pandarus and Criseyde exchange their initial pleasantries, Pandarus tries to lighten the mood: "Do wey youre barbe," he commands, "and shew youre face bare" (II 110). This line refers explicitly to the veil that is part of Criseyde's widow's garb. But it also emphasizes that, to some extent at least, Criseyde is hiding. Indirectly, Pandarus's demand recalls the earlier description of Criseyde at the feast of the Palladium, where she is said to be dressed "In widewes habit blak ... / ... / Nas nevere yet seyn thyng to ben preysed derre, / Nor under cloude blak so bright a sterre" (I 170, 174–5). In this passage, the narrator affirms that Criseyde stands "in beaute first" (I 172), and yet, the literal description does not make it clear whether the viewer could in fact see the entirety of Criseyde's face. She is, metaphorically speaking, "under cloude blak," and though it is clear that her beauty is visible enough to wound Troilus, that she is partly obscured aligns her person with the cult of major relics in late fourteenth-century England. Criseyde's response to Pandarus's imperative in Book II similarly suggests, first, that she is not so pliable as to obey his every command, but second, that she situates herself in the context of saints and hagiography: "It satte me wel bet ay in a cave / To bidde and rede *on holy seyntes lyves*; / Lat maydens gon to daunce, and yonge wyves" (II 117–19; emphasis added). Criseyde identifies herself with a particular kind of woman, and to be sure, her response befits a widow determined to perform according to the conventions of that role. But in juxtaposing the reading of hagiography with self-exposure, the narrator aligns hiding her face with the lives of saints. Criseyde's veil, like the feretory shrine, conceals its saint and, to some degree, enables Criseyde to construct her own identity through the kind of text (a saint's life) that best describes her virtue.

And yet, in his deft handling of this scene – to the point that the narrator tells us, "For nevere, sith the tyme that she was born, / To knowe thyng desired she so faste" (II 143–4) – Pandarus positions himself in the role of rhetorician and manipulator: he will assign meaning to Criseyde and to Troilus. In a manner of speaking, Pandarus jockeys for the role of relic custodian, bound and determined to fashion Criseyde as the centre of his (and Troilus's) cult. He configures even Criseyde's letter to Troilus as a sort of talisman or contact relic, instructing Troilus to " 'arise and see / A charme that was sent right now to the, / The which kan helen the of thyn accesse' " (II 1313–15). In attributing healing powers to this object and emphasizing Troilus's illness, Pandarus suggests that this letter, by virtue of its association with Criseyde (the relic), has taken on the thaumaturgic powers of a *brandea*, a non-notable contact relic.

Insofar as Pandarus highlights Troilus's virtue, then, we might think of him as constructing the perfect, virtuous supplicant. Troilus is, according to Pandarus, he "In whom that alle vertu list habounde, / As alle trouthe and alle gentilesse, / Wisdom, honour, fredom, and worthinesse" (II 159–61). The list of repetitive (but desirable) qualities intimates that Troilus will behave as the exemplary pilgrim, a point Pandarus emphasizes in confirming that Troilus and Hector are "voide of vices" (II 173) and that Troilus, in addition to being a fearsome warrior, is the "frendlieste man / Of gret estat" (II 204–5). During this section of text, Pandarus creates the character of Troilus, almost as if he were a cleric pleading for a miracle from his devotional object. The private conversation that follows (II 215–19) – to which neither we nor the characters in the poem are privy – underscores Pandarus's exclusive access to Criseyde and his self-created role as the mediator between her and the one who, being ill, needs her grace for his cure. At the end of this exchange, ostensibly about Criseyde's "estat" and "governaunce" (II 219), Pandarus again insists that she remove her widow's habit: "Cast youre widewes habit to mischaunce! / What list yow thus youreself to disfigure?" (II 222–3). He refers to Troilus's coming suit, of course; but nevertheless, in orchestrating this exposure, Pandarus reveals both his own control over the situation – and Criseyde's position as saintly object of devotion, hitherto occluded. Though her initial letter to Troilus is guarded ("[a]l covered she tho wordes under sheld" [II 1327]), Pandarus ensures that this "sheld" does not remain in place for long.

In a manner of speaking, Pandarus facilitates her exhumation, her rejoining the world of supplicant and love object, of prayer and worship. As a widow, she has remained buried up to this point, almost as if in viewing her at the temple of Pallas, Troilus set in motion a string of events not unlike those in the invention of a saint: the rediscovery of the body; the light that affirms the sanctity of the object (Criseyde's brightness, in this case); the cleric who, like Pandarus, away from the sight and hearing of all others, privately disinters the body to affirm its state. I would suggest that we might read Pandarus's address to Criseyde – "Ye ben the womman in this world lyvynge / … / That I best love, and lothest am to greve" (II 235, 237) – as a kind of prayer, the overture to a patron saint that reflects the very fear of retribution that writers like Jocelin of Brakelond and Simeon of Durham articulate.[94] Pandarus's careful rhetoric inspires in Criseyde the promise of special attention: "I am to no man holden, trewely, / So muche as yow, and have so litel quyt" (II 241–2); she invites him to be frank and intimate with her, to leave off his "fremde manere speche" (II 248). The exchange is bizarre, to be sure, but I think we might also read this special relationship in terms of devotional object and/or relic and custodian, the caregiver who decides which pilgrims are to approach most closely and upon whose care and attention the saint's reputation depends.

In this context, Pandarus's accusatory speech describes not the woman who withholds love, but the impotent relic: "Wo worth the faire gemme vertulees! / Wo worth that herbe also that dooth no boote!" (II 344–5). These metaphors draw on the tradition of courtly love, envisioning the lady as the medicine for her suffering lover. However, these metaphors stem from the discourse of saints and relics, as well, which were also frequently envisioned as "gems" (of chastity, for instance, or in describing the saint as reliquary) and imagined as the cure for sickness. Whatever his claims to the contrary, Pandarus is not only the "baude" (II 353), but also the relic custodian, carefully presenting Criseyde *to herself* as saint, object of devotion, able to cure a supplicant and remiss if she fails to do so. In preemptively assuaging Criseyde's concern for her reputation, Pandarus underscores this possibility: "What, who wol demen, though he se a man / To temple go, that he th'ymages eteth?" (II 372–3). The comparison aligns Criseyde with images of devotion – shrines, say, or relics. This moment is also the first configuration of Criseyde's house as a place of worship, a comparison Troilus mines and makes even more specific after Criseyde's departure for the Greek camp, referring to her house as a "shryne" (V 553). In reassuring Criseyde that Troilus is no heathen, Pandarus adds to his depiction of Troilus as virtuous (or, at least, not depraved!) supplicant. To consume the image or relic, after all, would be the ultimate blasphemy, to deface or destroy the very object that drew a pilgrim to a pilgrimage site in the first place. In any case, the comparison very clearly renders Criseyde as the devotional totem, the image or relic, and Troilus as the supplicant in need of help.[95] Insofar as Pandarus orchestrates this comparison, he further emphasizes his position as the creator and mediator of a successful cult. It is perhaps no surprise that Pandarus ends this exchange with Criseyde by claiming ownership of her promise to show Troilus good cheer: keep your promise "unto me" (II 493), he says, clearly demarcating his role in constructing both Troilus's virtue and her sanctity.

Indeed, throughout this section, Pandarus draws from religious discourse, both in describing Troilus's suffering and in facilitating Troilus's first pilgrimage, as it were, to Criseyde. He describes his own antics from Book I, when he goes to great lengths to wrest the truth from Troilus, as "prech[ing]" (II 569); he styles Criseyde as Troilus's "leche" (II

571, 1582); and he later addresses Criseyde with what he calls a "long sermoun" (II 1115, 1299). He identifies his long speech to Criseyde herself as a confession – "Now have I plat to yow myn herte shryven" (II 579) – and Criseyde herself, taking on the role of saintly intercessor, asks that Pandarus tell her "youre joly wo and youre penaunce" (II 1105). So, too, in explaining her song about lovers, Antigone comments to Criseyde that "Men moste axe at seyntes if it is / Aught fair in hevene ..." (II 894–5). Taken together with the explicit references to Criseyde as relic, as Palladium, and her house as a temple or shrine, it seems clear that relic discourse pervades these moments of the poem, emphasizing Criseyde's role as healing physician, object of a cult, even the totemic protector of Troy(lus).

Other well-documented commonplaces relating to the cult of relics lie in the background of the *Troilus*, as well. One such topos is the beneficent saint from legends of *furta sacra*. Criseyde allows Pandarus to act as her emissary – even, in a manner of speaking, to enshrine her in his house:

> Criseyde, which that koude as muche good
> As half a world, *took hede of his preiere* ...
> "I wol," quod she, "myn uncle lief and deere;
> Syn that yow list, it skile is to be so.
> I am right glad with yow to dwellen here;
> I seyde but a-game I wolde go." (III 638–48; emphasis added)

Patrick Geary has shown that one convention of *furta sacra* is the insistence on a saint's willingness to allow his or her body or body parts – his or her relics, that is – to be translated from one shrine to another.[96] We may read this moment in *Troilus* as one in which Criseyde, woman, saint, *and* relic, grants her abductor (and future custodian) permission to guard her body "in my litel closet yonder" (III 663). Indeed, in the context of relic discourse, Pandarus's behaviour is consonant with that of a relic custodian: in bringing Criseyde to his house – and indeed in keeping her there – Pandarus situates himself as the mediator of a holy object, who facilitates and guards his relic in a "litel closet." Moreover, the sleeping arrangements resemble a shrine and its environs: Pandarus is "wardein" (III 665) and sleeps in the outer circle; Criseyde's women are in the "myddel chamber" (III 666); and Criseyde is "in my litel closet yonder" (III 663).[97] While he cannot entirely control the nature of their tryst, Pandarus does serve as Criseyde's gatekeeper, orchestrating Troilus's liaison with her. In this paradigm, Criseyde's granting of Pandarus's "priere" and capitulating to Pandarus's desire – "syn that yow list" – parody the benign saint, whose supposed desire to accompany his or her thief in fact serves the interests of the religious community responsible for stealing the relics. Pandarus's response to Criseyde works to establish that, in fact, *his* desire is really *her* desire: "Now am I glad," he says, "syn that *yow [Criseyde] list* to dwelle" (III 651; emphasis added). Pandarus thus projects his wishes – for Criseyde agrees to stay "syn that yow [Pandarus] list" – onto Criseyde, much as those who wrote accounts of *furta sacra* projected the needs of their communities onto the saint whose body they had taken. This rhetorical move presumably sought to inspire confidence in pilgrims that the saint wanted to be there and would grant their prayers.

Troilus the Pilgrim, Pandarus the Custodian

Troilus similarly needs assurance about Criseyde's volition and affection for him: "But Troilus, that thoughte his herte bledde / For wo, *til that he herde som tydynge*" (II 950–1; emphasis added). Moreover, it is obvious that Troilus is presented as a penitent pilgrim. The narrator refers to Troilus as a lover whose manner of "com[ing] to his lady grace" (II 32) is like a pilgrimage to Rome: "For every wight which that to Rome went / Halt nat o path, or alwey o manere" (II 36–7). So, too, once Criseyde leaves Troy, Troilus's desire to visit her in the Greek camp resembles a pilgrimage: "And ofte tyme he was in purpos grete / Hymselven lik a pilgrym to desgise / To seen hire" (V 1576–8).[98] The text employs the term "pilgrym" flexibly, referring both to the metaphorical pilgrimage of the lover and to the religious pilgrimage of the supplicant to a shrine. For, just as purveyors of relic discourse promise that any pilgrim will be healed if he first confesses, at several moments in the text, Pandarus occupies the role of Troilus's confessor and claims that if Troilus tells him "al thi wo," he will be Troilus's "boote" (I 830, 832). So, too, Pandarus refers to himself as Troilus's physician: "For whoso list have helyng of his leche, / To hym byhoveth first unwre his wownde" (I 857–8). In substituting his healing for Criseyde's – who, as saint, is the more logical heavenly physician – Pandarus emphasizes his own role as Troilus's mediator (and even suggests by implication that he can absolve Troilus's sins). Certainly we may recognize Pandarus as the consummate "go-between," as Gretchen Mieszkowski has recently put it.[99] But his role as Troilus's confessor makes it clear that his position is more powerful still than a mere "ordinary idealized go-between"[100]: he is the cleric, the relic custodian, who manages access to the saint.

As custodian, Pandarus has immediate and unmediated access to (and perhaps even control over) Criseyde. And just as the Pardoner demands that the pilgrims confess before they "offren to [his] relics" (VI 384), Pandarus insists that he hear Troilus's confession before arranging a private audience with Criseyde. His attitude shares much in common with the late medieval theology of confession, which, as Chaucer's Parson outlines, presents "confessioun of mouth" (*Canterbury Tales* X 107, 958) as a "signe of contricioun" (X 316).[101] As if Pandarus himself were present to hear the Parson explicate that being "ful of teeris" (X 993) is a component of true confession, Pandarus turns lachrymose as he recounts for Criseyde Troilus's (and ostensibly his own) suffering (II 326). (So, too, Troilus bathes his letter to Criseyde "with his salte teris" [*Troilus* II 1086].) What is more, he twice refers to his narrative as a confession: "here I me shryve" (II 440), and "Now have I plat to yow myn herte shryven" (II 579). Chaucer adds these details to Boccaccio's text, which highlights not the theology but the rhetorical cunning of this moment. *Troilus and Criseyde* obviously emphasizes both. Criseyde's initial response – she complains of his "paynted proces" (II 424) – perhaps hints that Pandarus is unlike the truly penitent, who "shalt *nat* eek peynte thy confessioun by faire subtile wordes, to covere the moore thy synne" (*Canterbury Tales* X 1021; emphasis added). When Pandarus attributes to Troilus language consonant with the medieval theology of confession, he is more successful: "My lowe confessioun / Accepte in gree, and sende me swich penaunce / As liketh the" (*Troilus* II 528–30). In this poem, to confess according to the dictates of orthodoxy – and according to conventions of relic discourse – is to placate the god of love and win the saint's support. Criseyde's decisions to communicate with Troilus (Book I), visit Troilus's sickbed (Book II), stay with Pandarus (Book III), even, ultimately, leave for the Greek camp (Book IV), thus reveal the degree to which Pandarus's "preiere," even his use of relic discourse, works – until, that is, convention requires Criseyde to cater to a new supplicant (Diomede).

In presenting Criseyde as approximating a relic, Chaucer's poem suggests by extension the possibility that a saint's agency – to intercede on behalf of supplicants, to endorse her body's removal from one place to another, or to approve of its enshrinement – is in fact circumscribed by discourse and convention. Criseyde has little say about how Pandarus and Troilus construct her as an object of devotion. Neither does the saint at the centre of a popular cult influence what happens to her relics, what clerics write, the orthodox and demotic practices at a shrine. (Though indeed, written accounts of miraculous intervention construct the saint as having agency and involvement at the site of her relics.) The saint, governed by the discourses used to describe and value her, has no more will than is frequently attributed to Criseyde.

In a critical landscape that until recently had often passed over religious elements in Chaucer's works,[102] it is important to recognize that we can regard Chaucer both as religious and as skeptical, his texts in dialogue with religious discourses (rather than merely replicating these discourses). The two collections *Chaucer's Religious Tales* and *Chaucer and Religion* very rightly point out that we should take Chaucer's religious culture seriously;[103] I would add simply that taking medieval religion – and belief, and faith – seriously need not preclude examining the construction of religious discourses, particularly in the case of an author as widely known for his satire as Chaucer.[104] I have often thought that the most beautiful moments in Chaucer's poetry occur precisely when a character acknowledges the inadequacy of discourse to explain human (and religious) experience: the narrator's assessment of Troilus's suffering ("Swich fin hath, lo, this Troilus for love" [V 1828]) or Arcite's own shocked exclamation, having lived up to the courtly ideals governing Athens: "What is this world? What asketh men to have?" (*Canterbury Tales* I 2777).[105] I see in the breakdown of religious discourse a subtle presentation of the material world as something that matters every bit as much as transcendent ideals – not, somehow, a rejection of these ideals altogether.

As the demise of Troilus and the rioters shows, a danger of relic discourse was that pilgrims would value the wrong thing and even sacrifice themselves for it: for treasure, for gold. The rioters do not die because they fail to venerate ephemeral things: they die because they do not understand a sign (treasure) and, as importantly, because they do not attend to and care for each other; they murder each other instead. In the *Troilus*, the eponymous hero gives his life not for a saint but rather for the figure constructed by Pandarus and, perhaps most crucially of all, by Troilus. His downfall reflects discursive failures – of courtly and of relic discourse – not necessarily absolute shortcomings of the material world. Troilus's response to Criseyde's empty house suggests that in fact, without the saint, the shrine (and Pandarus's words as well, as it turns out) is beautiful but meaningless. But such a moment does not strip the saint of value – in a way, it presents the saint's body as terribly valuable, the thing that gave discourse power in the first place. This is precisely the problem that many Wycliffite writers take up: that shrines distract pilgrims from what is important (the saint, the poor); that, as Wyclif put it, lavish shrines in fact get things backwards, for they enable immoderate clerics to fashion saints of "pars persona empte" – just about any body parts, provided they are bought and paid for. As we shall see, these texts share in common with the rioters' dismal ends a call to remember that "Hyt is not al gold that glareth."[106]

Chapter Five

Wycliffite Texts and the Problem of Enshrinement

But It apperyd that she lafft soom of hyr dyscyplys behynd hyr, ffor the nygth ffolowyng the more part of the asshys of that ffyre that she was brent In, were hadd awaye, and kepyd ffor a precious Relyk, In an erthyn pott.

– Describing disciples of Joan Boughton, who was executed for heresy in 1494[1]

Saints' relics, that is to say the flesh and bones of dead men, should not be venerated by the people, nor exhumed [and translated] from their stinking graves.

– William White, from Thomas Netter's *Fasciculi Zizaniorum*[2]

When dissenter Joan Boughton was being executed in 1494, she appealed to the Virgin Mary for help. After she was dead, adherents to her way of thinking gathered up her ashes and deposited them in a simple reliquary – an "erthen pott." These and other Wycliffites were clearly not troubled by relics, provided that they were appropriately housed in a simple and unadorned shrine.[3] By contrast, William White and his disciples held that relics were not to be venerated, regardless of how simple and unadorned their containers. This chapter will take, as its central images, Boughton's "erthyn pott" and White's stinking body parts, in order to show how Wycliffite responses to pilgrimage and shrines call attention to the disparity between opulent reliquaries and their decomposing relics. In so doing, these authors identify the trouble with clerics who, in defending the practices at relic cults, insist that a literalized metaphor – a shrine – better represents the saint than his or her own body. Wycliffite writers point out that in using such metaphors to valorize the saint, proponents of relic discourse morally endanger supplicants who, like the Pardoner's three hapless rioters, may focus so intently on the shrine and its "tresor" that they forget about the saint. As this chapter shows, many Wycliffite authors never suggest that saints' bones have no value – only that lavish shrines encourage people to regard relics as disproportionately valuable. They hence voice concern with lavish enshrinement, but very rarely with relics or saints per se.

This chapter begins with the premise that not all Wycliffites reviled saints' relics and that in fact, some Wycliffites (Boughton's disciples, for example) even venerated saints' bones and ashes. I will argue that condemning relics' presentation in opulent shrines and images, and not necessarily the relics themselves, was a key component of Wycliffite polemic. (If, as we usually assume, all Wycliffites hated relics, they would hardly have bothered to envision more acceptable ways to present them.) These authors believe that opulent shrines are not essential to the veneration of saints; and they reject the convention of relic discourse that gold and jewels signify better than bodies or body parts. The chapter then turns to questions of representation and poverty: if Wycliffites found shrines to be troublesome metaphors for sanctity, what sorts of metaphors would be considered appropriate? Both the *Lanterne of Liȝt* and *Pierce the Plowman's Crede* present the bodies of the poor – and not lavish reliquaries – as analogous to saints' relics: both serve as reminders of the transience of life's pleasures, the dust and decay to which we will all return, and the hope of redemption.

The Trouble with Shrines

Though Wycliffites seldom refer explicitly to relics, scholars have frequently assumed that Wycliffite polemic against images and pilgrimage refers, by extension, to the veneration of saints' relics – and that to criticize opulent shrines is to criticize relics.[4] Citing the *Twelve Conclusions*, Roger Dymmok, and Reginald Pecock, for instance, John F. Davis presents "the most characteristic and enduring tenets of later Lollardy" as "those denouncing pilgrimages to the relics of the saints and the veneration of images."[5] But in fact, these sources make clear distinctions between the problem of images (or shrines) and the acceptability of relics: in their defenses of orthodox practice, Dymmock and Pecock both strongly suggest that they respond not to criticisms of relics, but to the practices surrounding their veneration. So, too, W. R. Jones, citing Pecock, claims that "Lollard opposition to images was associated with an aversion to pilgrimages and intercessory prayers to saints, for which image and relic cults provided the motivation and the opportunity."[6] But no Wycliffite treatise identifies relic cults themselves as the absolute problem; Wyclif himself allows the possibility of acceptable cults.[7] Again, the trappings and the discourse are the issue. The conflation of relics and images is sometimes even more pronounced in work that does not focus expressly on Wycliffism or heterodoxy: Hans Belting observes merely that "[i]n medieval imagination, images and relics *were never two distinct realities*."[8] Caroline Walker Bynum similarly notes that in the Middle Ages, relics and images "were conflated, with no sense of incongruity."[9] But *pace* Belting and Bynum, the texts I examine here suggest the opposite: that medieval writers frequently understood relics as distinct from images and that objections to one do not necessarily imply objections to the other.

It seems to me that if relics necessarily occasioned Wycliffite opposition to pilgrimage, saints' bones might have featured more habitually or explicitly in dissenting literature and heretical belief.[10] Surprisingly, they did not. As Christina von Nolcken and others have noted, "criticism of abuses connected with relics is expressed much more extremely in many orthodox [rather than in reformist] works ... It is not a subject frequently treated by the Wycliffites, despite their dislike of outward forms of religion."[11] The early fifteenth-century *Lanterne of Liȝt* criticizes some of the social practices surrounding the cult of relics, such as the commodification of devotional rituals in general and sumptuous enshrinement in particular. But the *Lanterne* author does *not* similarly censure relics, which were often at the centre of the pilgrim activity he deplores.[12] So, too, in the 1428 Norwich heresy trials, pilgrimage and images feature thirty-four and thirty-seven times, respectively, but relics only twice.[13] And in the 1486 and 1511–12 Coventry trials, the defendants and witnesses are credited with stock phrases about local images: Richard Hegham very conventionally (by Wycliffite standards) avers that "to adore or venerate images of Blessed Mary of the Tower of the said city, or of other saints, is foolish because they are but wood and stones."[14] Relics are only mentioned once: one Roger Brown evidently "preached, taught, held, asserted, and instructed that people should not adore the image of Blessed Mary of Walsingham nor the blood of Christ at Hailes."[15] Though many other Wycliffites complain about the image of Mary of Walsingham,[16] nothing more is said about the blood at Hailes – an extremely lucrative historical blood relic of Christ.[17] That Brown reviles a passion relic is important: as will become evident, many Wycliffites were remarkably consistent in their attitude to devotional objects, holding (like many mainstream and reformist thinkers) that some relics (like passion relics) were more dubious than others.[18] Of course, we must regard with skepticism any evidence from heresy trials such as these, depending as they did on questionnaires to solicit information from witnesses.[19] All the same, the general absence of objections to body-part relics is striking.

In fact, there is evidence for Wycliffite body-part relic cults: witness Joan Boughton's disciples who, after her execution for heresy in 1494, gathered "the more part of the asshys of that ffyre that she was brent In" and kept them "ffor a precious Relyk, In an erthyn pott."[20] Boughton was not the only popularly venerated Wycliffite saint: the place of Richard Wyche's June 1440 execution quickly became a pilgrimage site where, according to John Foxe, followers "upreared a great heap of stones, and set up a wooden cross there by night."[21] By 15 July 1440, pilgrimages to "the place of Wyche's burial" were forbidden; and as John Thomson points out, on the day Wyche was burnt, "John Copyn, probably the executioner, [was questioned] about the burning of the heart of the heretic recently burnt, an action which," Thomson continues, "suggests Wyche's followers may have been trying to procure relics of him."[22] One chronicler gives the following account of the activity following Wyche's execution:

> Meny menne and wommen wente be nyghte to the place where he was brend, and offrid there money and ymageȝ of wax, and made thair praiers knelyng as thay wolde haue don to a saynt, and kiste the ground and baar away with thaym the asshis of his body as for reliqueȝ.[23]

As Thomson suggests, this behaviour does seem "paradoxical" coming from Wycliffites.[24] At the same time, however, it is worth thinking about whether such practices would have been deemed inappropriate by all Lollards, many of whom criticized opulent shrines but, as in the *Lanterne*, not the "holi seyntis" for whom the shrines were built (*Lanterne of Liȝt* 43). In his February 1505 abjuration in Hereford, for example, John Croft admitted, "Also I have redde and taughte agayn the veneration and worshipyng of images standyng in churchis … and agayn the shrynyng of seyntis bonys in goold and sylver, and hangyng aboute thaym the same."[25] Nowhere in his abjuration does Croft indicate that he criticized relics; he rather rescinds having read and taught against their lavish enshrinement. Wycliffite treatment of relics in fact reveals a complex regard for the holy dead – a regard that, in its disdain for ostentatious display, unnecessary expenditure, and misleading verbiage, has affiliations with many contemporary and mainstream commentaries and satires that ridicule bawdy laypeople, greedy clerics, and immoral relic custodians, Chaucer's Pardoner being merely the most frequently cited example.

We hence cannot and should not assume that every Wycliffite objection to the social practices surrounding relics implies, by necessary extension, a criticism of relics; and we can and should question more carefully whether those Wycliffites who clearly venerated relics were behaving, as John Thomson has suggested of Richard Wyche's devotees, paradoxically. The treatment of relics is yet another reminder that we must consider Wycliffite affinities with, as well as scorn for, the mainstream religious practices and literary traditions of the late fourteenth and fifteenth centuries. Here, I wish to suggest that to have a "Wycliffite" attitude to relics is not as easily discernible from many "orthodox" attitudes to relics as we might imagine. Often enough, both aggressively questioned the lavish material surroundings of the cult; and, as I will discuss in this chapter, both tap into a tradition, going back to late antiquity, that contrasts relics' lavish surroundings with the lay poor.

Fake and Stinking Relics

As is well known, dissenters frequently objected to images because, unlike the living poor, who are "quick images of God," images are but dead wood. In fact, pointing out that lavish images of various kinds (statues, church buildings, reliquaries) divert resources from the poor is a Wycliffite commonplace.[26] Such a critique obviously contrasts living flesh with lumber – what God animates with what the artisan carves. It would seem to follow that dissenting belief must reject saints' bones, but there are very few explicit critiques of relics themselves. Instead, as I will demonstrate in what follows, the most crushing rhetoric is reserved for lavish shrines. This is not to say that no Wycliffite censured relics. Though little evidence has survived that relics were subjected to the same kind of diatribes as pilgrimage or images, there are several brief instances of critiques that are directly leveled at saints' bones. I address four of these here.[27] However, three of these work with and depend upon literary tradition (and even orthodox satire); they should therefore be understood in their literary (as well as historical and theological) contexts. And though the fourth instance does offer a no-holds-barred condemnation of relics, in the end, its concern is as much with reliquaries as with relics. Taken in these contexts, we can see that criticizing relics (fake or otherwise) is not necessarily a hallmark only of Wycliffites. When writers excoriate relics, that is, they frequently work from within mainstream traditions that feature many of the same complaints. Such criticisms are not only uncommon in Wycliffite thought, then – they also have a lot in common with mainstream attitudes to the cult of saints.

The first three examples all advance a very common (and even conservative) objection that saints' bones could be fakes. In the first instance, the author of the Wycliffite text *How the Office of Curates Is Ordained of God* rails against "pardoner[s] wiþ stollen bullis & false relekis."[28] Both mainstream and reformist thinkers would have agreed with such a statement; as R.N. Swanson and Siegfried Wenzel have shown, associating pardoners with fake relics was a commonplace in a wide spectrum of literature and theology.[29] (As one late medieval sermon author puts it, such pardoners come "with fals letters and seeles, with crosses and reliques þat þei bere abowten þem, and sei þat þei be of seyntes bones or of holy mens cloþinge and behoteþ myche mede þat will offre to hem.")[30] In the second example, William Wynch similarly draws from literary satire in his 1507 censure of fake relics. In what sounds like a direct allusion to Chaucer's Pardoner, Wynch protests that "among the reliques that be worshipped in churches is many a shippes [sheep's] bone."[31] The degree to which such texts work within a satirical tradition diffuses, to some extent, the reformist critique they offer – for, as my reading of the Pardoner made clear, few such critiques have as their aim dispensing with saints' relics altogether and were commonplace in the late Middle Ages.[32] In the third instance, the author of the early fifteenth-century eucharistic tract *De oblacione iugis sacrificii*, or Titus Tract, similarly inveighs against "worme-eten bonys" and "þinggis þat ben callid images, reliquiis, þe wiche in comparson of God or of man ben but uerri trifelis."[33] Here, too, though the distaste for relics is more strongly expressed, the author seems to be concerned at least partly with fake relics: these devotional objects are only "callid" images and relics, the implication being that they are in reality something else, perhaps fakes. Obviously these writers take the threat of illegitimate relics very seriously. That said, the terms of these critiques were conventional in orthodox quarters as well and circulated freely in orthodox sermons and popular poetry. They should not necessarily be read as emblematic of Wycliffite polemic.

The fourth instance comes from William White and the testimony of three 1428 Norwich witnesses. Bishop Alnwick began prosecutions in these trials in September of that year after having arrested White, the "revered teacher of the Norfolk Lollards."[34] Their objections to relics – more totalizing than the three earlier examples, very much in line with the views of White – are nevertheless "unusual," as Margaret Aston has pointed out.[35] (One wonders whether it is White's devotees, and not Wyche's, who act "paradoxically.") White, a Wycliffite itinerant preacher of the early fifteenth century, disparages relics as putrid, oozing, disgusting, and not worthy of any veneration. All the same, the text links idolatry more closely to material translation than to relics per se:

> Next we say to you, we object and we articulate, that after and against your aforesaid abjuration, you held, affirmed, wrote and taught that saints' relics, *that is to say the flesh and bones of dead men*, should not be venerated by the people, *nor exhumed [and translated] from their stinking graves*, nor placed in a gold and silver repository; because men doing thusly do not honor God and the saints, but commit idolatry.
>
> (Item tibi dicimus, objicimus et articulamur, quod post et contra tuam praedictam abjurationem, tu tenuisti, affirmasti, scripsisti et docuisti, quod reliquiae sanctorum, *scilicet carnes et ossa hominis mortui*, non debent a populo venerari, *nec de monumento foetido extrahi*, nec in capsa aurea vel argentea reponi; quia homines sic facientes non honorant Deum et sanctos ejus, sed committunt idolatriam.)[36]

In the records of the Norwich trials, Robert Cavell, John Skylly, and Margaret Baxter are credited (almost verbatim) with having held the same beliefs about relics as White.[37] All the same, the order of information in this passage (first exhumation, then translation) suggests that the relics' enshrinement "in a gold and silver repository" is a more immediate cause of idolatry than the relics alone, as the bones themselves would not have held the same appeal. Even in this instance, then, though White's disciples clearly speak against relics themselves, they – like many of their Wycliffite counterparts – rest at least part of their objection on the unstated premise that reliquaries, and not relics, are the primary cause of saints' cults' idolatry.

Wyclif on Sumptuous Barbarism and Luxurious Shrines

Wyclif, who does not expressly condemn relics themselves, is similarly appalled by the immoderate display of many saints' cults:

> In many countries greed often causes churches to buy parts of a human being so that he may be canonized as a confessor or martyr and [may be] more honored by pilgrimages, by sumptuous offerings and by the ornamentation of his tomb with gold and precious stones than the body of the mother of God herself, or [the bodies] of the apostles Peter and Paul or of other famous saints.[38]

> (Unde in multis patriis cupido pecunie facit in multis ecclesiis quod pars persone empte, ut canonizetur pro confessore vel martire, plus honoretur peregrinacione, sumptuosa oblacione et sepulcri ornacione auro et lapidibus preciosis quam corpus matris Dei, apostolorum Petri et Pauli vel alterius notorie beati.)[39]

In this passage from his *Tractatus de Ecclesia*, Wyclif criticizes the practice of canonizing and enshrining "pars persona empte" (body parts, and evidently random ones, that have been purchased) in order to profit by a saint's cult. His problem is not with relics but with clerical avarice, which is presented as the root cause ("cupido pecunie *facit*") of a disordered cult. Wyclif's critique illustrates the degree to which relics had become associated with (or indeed eclipsed by) their opulent containers. As Thomas Netter observes, "Wyclif did not speak much against the makers and cults of images, *but rather impugns clerics for their immoderation*." ("Wicleffus non multa est locutus contra factores et cultores imaginum, *sed tantum in illis immoderationem clericis imputavit*.")[40] Wyclif in fact goes one step further, presenting clerics who create saints to make money not as simply immoderate, but greedy. They also fail to practice what they preach: that *shrines* are made for *saints*, not the other way around. It is clear that Wyclif shares with his more moderate predecessors a distaste for lavish expenditure and gem-encrusted shrines.

But Wyclif does not evince the same distaste for relics in general. In fact, he indirectly condones venerating legitimate and prestigious relics, suggesting that the problem is in presenting "pars persone empte" as if they were more valuable than relics Wyclif identifies as legitimate and notable: of Mary, the apostles, and other traditional saints.[41] By lambasting the means by which churches acquire their relics and contrasting their obscurity with the relics of these "famous saints," Wyclif makes clear both his regard for acceptable saints – even, one may surmise, acceptable saints' relics – and also that his primary objection is to profiting by making new saints and not to relics per se. The unstated corollary is that one may venerate saints (and, perhaps, their relics, too), provided that one is somber, restrained, and fiscally responsible.

Moreover, as he makes clear in *De Eucharistia*, Wyclif believes that relics can be treated appropriately as long as God, and not the material thing, is worshipped: "It is conceded, therefore, that relics, images, and the sacraments must be adored with prudence" ("Conceditur ergo quod reliquie, ymagines et sacramenta sunt cum prudencia adoranda").[42] Mainstream theologians, too, were concerned with how to express prudent adoration, as discussions of *latria*, *dulia*, and *hyperdulia* indicate; the topic of appropriate veneration would be addressed in the vernacular in *Dives and Pauper*.[43] Nor is Wyclif alone in his concern about enthusiastic pilgrims who miss the point of a shrine. In one of his sermons, Wyclif observes, "Nor ought we to be excessive in our pilgrimages nor the sumptuous honors we bestow on dead relics in the ground, but rather we should adore the blessed spirits of the dead with moderation" ("Nec in peregrinacionibus nec in sumptuosis honoracionibus reliquiarum mortuorum in terris excedere, sed beatos spiritus mortuorum cum prudencia adorare").[44] As in *Tractatus de Ecclesia*, Wyclif emphasizes that neither matter nor money should be the focal points of adoration. Other contemporary theologians advanced this very argument in *defence* of relics. In his late fourteenth-century reply to the Wycliffite *Twelve Conclusions*, for example, Roger Dymmok argues that "We do not honor the insensible relics of the saints on account of the relics themselves, [but rather] we honor the saints themselves, whose relics these are." ("non veneramur reliquias sanctorum insensibiles propter ipsas reliquias in se … sanctos ipsos honoramus, quorum sunt reliquie.")[45]

The problem – for Wyclif and implicitly for orthodox apologists like Dymmok – is that lavish shrines and money-making pilgrimage sites make it very difficult, if not impossible, for supplicants to venerate saints prudently. To wit, in the same sermon in which Wyclif advocates an appropriate kind of (spiritual) adoration, he also observes, "it would be to the honor of saints and the advantage of the church were the jewels with which the sepulchres of saints have been foolishly and uselessly adorned, to be distributed to the poor." ("Unde ad honorem foret sanctorum et utilitatem ecclesie quod distributa forent pauperibus iocalia sepulcrorum, quibus stulte ac eciam inaniter sunt ornata.")[46] It is possible that Wyclif was dismissing relics out of hand, but it seems more likely that he worried over shrines that, as in Erasmus's sixteenth-century description of Canterbury, "shone and dazzled with rare and surpassingly large jewels" ("gemmis raris ac praegrandibus collucebant, nitebant ac fulgurabant").[47] Put another way, excessive wealth precipitates idolatry. As Wyclif writes in *De Eucharistia* – where, it should be remembered, he allows that relics might be venerated prudently – "in such idolatry we who call ourselves Christians often sin more than barbarians in adoring the images of saints, relics, and the sacrament of the altar." ("In ista ydolatria nos vocati christiani peccamus sepe plus barbaris adorando sanctorum ymagines, reliquias et sacramentum altaris.")[48] It is clear that Wyclif does not unequivocally approve of the cult of saints; but it is equally clear that his disapproval focuses on money and greed: when he refers to idolatry, or sumptuous barbarism, that is, he is probably thinking of opulent shrines and prodigal offerings. Wyclif, focusing as he does on relics' containers and not on saints' bones, offers us a sense of how lay supplicants might have experienced pilgrimage: as an encounter with a dazzling casket, rather than as an opportunity to adore, prudently, the "blessed spirits" of the holy dead.

Wycliffites on Sumptuous Barbarism and Luxurious Shrines

Many later fourteenth- and fifteenth-century reformers similarly directed their vitriol not against relics but rather against reliquaries, which, as in the eighth conclusion of the Wycliffite *Twelve Conclusions*, encouraged greed and diverted attention away from "þe pore almes hous."[49] While the author of the *Conclusions* offers a satirical take on passion relics, the eighth conclusion is far more invested in censuring shrines than relics:

> Þe viii conclusiun nedful to telle to þe puple begylid is [þat] þe pilgrimage, preyeris, and offringis made to blynde rodys and to deue ymages of tre and of ston, ben ner of kin to ydolatrie and fer fro almesse dede … Þis conclusiun God opinly schewith, comanding to don almesse dede to men þat ben nedy, for þei ben þe ymage of God in a more liknesse þan þe stok or þe ston … But we preye þe, pilgrym, us to telle qwan þu offrist to seyntis bonis enschrinid in ony place, qweþir releuis þu þe seynt þat is in blisse, or þe pore almes hous þat is so wel enduwid.[50]

This passage does not vindicate relics, and it might even seem to repudiate offerings to any saints' bones at all. But it is worth splitting hairs in this case, for the author specifies that these bones are "enschrinid," thereby describing a very particular kind of saint's relic (one enclosed in an opulent reliquary, perhaps) and eschews the financial transaction occasioned by enshrinement. It is certainly possible that this author detested relics as well – but importantly, that is not what he objects to in the eighth conclusion.

A vernacular treatise, "Images and Pilgrimages," likewise distinguishes between saints' relics and their containers – and yet again, its author censures enshrining relics, not necessarily relics per se.[51] The basic criticism is that, in common practice, relics are only understood to be precious insofar as their shrines are lavish and offerings are plentiful. But reliquaries, buildings, and other containers should not be understood as more valuable than (nor as conferring value on) what they contain:

> For oure lord God dwellis by grace in gode mennus soulis, and wiþoute comparesoun bettere þan all ymagis made of man in erþe, and better þan alle bodies of seyntis, be þe bones of hem neuer so gloriously shreynyd in gold.
>
> Also men erren myche in offrynge to þes ymagis. For to þe gayest and most rychely arayed ymage raþeest wil þe puple offur, and nouȝt to no pore ymage stondyng in a symple kirk or chapel, but ȝif it stonde ryaly tabernaclid wiþ keruyng and peyntid wiþ gold and precious iewelis.[52]

Immoral attention to beautiful images, in this account, results in the maltreatment and neglect of the poor. Elsewhere, the author laments those who "waste her godis in syche *riche* ymagis, for, where is *most richessis aboute a stok, þere wil þe blynd puple most offur*."[53] The author goes on in terms reminiscent of Wyclif's *De Eucharistia*, as well as *Dives and Pauper*: "And so it semes þat þe puple worschipis þe gaye peyntyng of þe rotun stok and nouȝt þe seynt in whos name it is seett þere."[54] The criticism here is pointed: people notice and offer more to images that are "rychely arayed" than to those that are not. Such images and shrines detract from the true value of the living poor, whose bodies are "better þan alle bodies of seyntis"; make prudent adoration impossible because supplicants pay homage to "þe gaye peyntyng of þe rotun stok" rather than "þe seynt in whos name it is seett þere"; and crucially, are not the same as relics. As the author makes abundantly clear, people do not offer to saints' bones; they offer to saints' *shrines*, which confer too much value on one kind of (dead and holy) body over another (living and impoverished) one. Relics, by extension, are not themselves the primary problem. Their shrines, on the other hand, misdirect attention away from the common fate that relics share with supplicants' bodies: death, decay, and resurrection as well.

The Middle English translation of the *Rosarium Theologie* similarly distinguishes between relics and reliquaries. There, the author cites mainstream authorities whose concern for the poor anticipates his own.[55] The entry under "reliquariam" explains, "of reliques bene 3. kyndez"; the first of these, of "þe bodiez of sentis," concerns us here.[56] This section focuses on the social injustice occasioned by the opulent milieux of many saint's cults, and it does so by emphasizing the arguments of theologians who targeted the financial disorder that too often accompanied a successful cult. Having cited Augustine's and Jerome's defenses of relics, thc author moves on to say,

> Bot for þer bene many errours and abusions sprongen or risen in þe puple about relikez Innocent þe 3. seiþ þus ... "Prelatez forsoþ suffer noȝt þam þat comeþ to þer chirchez because of worschiping for to be deceyued by diuerse feynyngs & false techings, as it is wont to be done in many placez *for occasion of lucre*."[57]

Throughout this entry, the author compiles views on relics that emphasize how relic cults, and not the relics themselves, become an "occasion of lucre":

> Item Bernardus in Floribus, "O how mich abusion, how mich wickednes, is it *þat þe bones of seyntes ben putte out to lucre*, þat wiche quicke forsoke al monye now ded bene compelled for to begge." Item Crisostomus, Omelia 42, "Forsoþe martirez ioyeþ noȝt wen þei bene honored of þe monez for wiche pore men wepeþ."[58]

Lucre, money, the poor, and begging constitute the focal points of this entry, which, in spite of its opening by defining a certain kind of relic (saints' bones), does not include a discussion of the relics themselves at all. The concern here expressed is very obviously with relics' containers: The phrase "ben putte out to lucre" seems almost certainly to describe opulent reliquaries. It is as if those who translate these bones away from their original graves do a disservice both to the poor *and* to the saint. The surprising corollary is that we might not need to read all Wycliffite relic cults as "paradoxical." Some, like the cults of Boughton and Wyche, rather than putting out their relics "to lucre," place them in simple and unadorned reliquaries. These simple signs offer a coherent alternative to the sumptuous barbarism and "clerical immoderation" perceived at many relic shrines.[59]

Such objections to reliquaries had practical as well as theological ramifications. As is already evident, the argument usually ran that a cult's "lucre" would be better spent on the poor. A vernacular sermon addressing financial abuses, "Of Poor Preaching Priests," similarly identifies the injustice in diverting almes "fro pore nedy men bouȝt wiþ cristis precious blood," but it also suggests that "þe wast tresour hanged on stockis & stones be wisly spendid in defence of þe rewme."[60] This sentence identifies what, at a pilgrim site, had economic worth: in this case, the "tresour," which presumably refers to pilgrim offerings. These offerings, and not the "stockis & stones," are valuable and might be used for military defence. So, too, written accounts of both the Oldcastle rebellion of 1414 and William Perkins's attempted rebellion of 1431 suggest that these groups identified relics' accoutrements (and not relics per se) as having economic and political worth. The Perkins rebels, in language nearly identical to that attributed to the Oldcastle cohort, threaten "to despoil both churches and religious houses of relics and other goods and chattels found in them."[61] The close association between relics and "other ecclesiastical goods" or "other goods and chattels" suggests that the rebels were thinking of reliquaries and not of the relics themselves. The very word "other," after all, includes relics in the list of valuable ecclesiastical goods – goods that could have been better used elsewhere, presumably. It would seem that in the case of both rebellions, gilded and gem-encrusted shrines formed the chief cause of concern; it seems hardly likely that the rebels intended to heap up saints' bones in their pile of loot.

Reginald Pecock's *c.* 1449 *The Repressor of Overmuch Blaming of the Clergy* distinguishes between saints' bones and shrines, too – though he, perhaps unsurprisingly, argues in favour of enshrinement and against leaving bones left out in the "baar feeld."[62] Pecock's approach supports my suggestion that reformist thinkers objected primarily to profligate spending at relic cults, worrying that translation and sumptuous enshrinement disenfranchise the poor. In chapter 8, Supposition 3, part of his section on pilgrimage, Pecock associates "rememoratijf visible signes" with reliquaries, rather than relics. Though Pecock considers both relics and images as tactile reminders of the spiritual world, his emphasis on translation, enshrinement, and even adornment highlights these objects' differences at the expense of their similarities, thereby suggesting that perhaps dissenters were responding to one object (i.e., shrines) more vociferously than another (i.e., relics):

> Sithen the bodi or the bonis or othere relikis of eny persoon is a ful nyȝ rememoratijf signe of the same persoon, it is ful resonable and ful worthi that where the bodi or bonis or eny releef or relik of a Seint mai be had, that it be sett up in a comoun place to which peple may haue her deuout neiȝing and accesse, forto haue her deuout biholding ther upon forto make the seid therbi remembraunce. And ferther, sithen it is not resonable and conuenient that suche bodies or bonis or relikis be left withoute in the baar feeld, (and that bothe for it were aȝens the eese of the peple whiche schulde come therto in reyny and wyndi wedris, and for that thei myȝten thanne be take awey bi wickid men not dreding God), therfore it is ful resonable and worthi forto bilde ouer tho bodies and bonis and othere relikis chapellis or chirchis; ȝhe, and forto bilde bisidis hem auter and queris, that the office of preising God and of preiyng to God and to Seintis be in the better forme doon.[63]

Like Wyclif himself and like the author of the *Twelve Conclusions*, Pecock here associates reliquaries with images, and he distinguishes between relics and these other devotional objects. Interestingly, he does not here claim that the "lay folk" of whom he speaks object to bones left – like those of Richard Wyche, perhaps – in the "baar feeld," but rather implies, by his extended justification for translation and enshrinement, that he is responding to protest at these bones' enshrinement in feretory chapels and churches. Though Pecock on the one hand identifies relics as "rememoratijf signe[s]," on the other, he very clearly describes how the clergy have erected, "ouer tho bodies and bonis … relikis chappelis or chirchis; ȝhe, and forto bilde bisidis hem auter and queris." Pecock thus accentuates relics' translation from the "baar feeld" to the inner sancta of churches and cathedrals, where many of them were contained within elaborate, gilded, gem-encrusted, and expensive shrines.[64] Moreover, though Pecock advocates broad access, his own discussion, emphasizing as it does "relikis chappelis or chirchis" and "auter and queris," suggests that he speaks of access to shrines, not necessarily to the relics themselves. In defending relics, that is, Pecock never assumes that his opponents wish to abolish relic cults completely. Rather, he emphasizes the social practices surrounding relic cults, implying that reformist thinkers objected to these practices without dismissing the cults (or the relics, for that matter) out of hand.[65]

Getting Things Right: Wycliffite Relics and Simple Shrines

In this context, Wycliffite relics and even reformist shrines are hardly surprising. Wyche and Boughton were both executed for their adherence to, for example, the idea that live bodies were more valuable than dead ones. Yet I think it would be a mistake to assume that, because her disciples carted away her ashes for preservation, they were somehow not Wycliffite enough. On the contrary, as I have shown thus far, Wycliffites usually objected to the demotic practices of relic cults: immoderate spending, lavish enshrinement, and so on. They very seldom objected to *relics*, and we need to revise our assumption that Wycliffites never venerated them, for clearly they sometimes did. The followers of Boughton and Wyche presented their relics in what one might even consider a reformist way: the shrines they constructed or used were hardly opulent. In fact, descriptions of them emphasize the shrines' modesty: Boughton's relics are to be placed in an "erthyn pott"; Wyche's so-called shrine is made of stones and plain (unpainted, ungilded) wood; and his disciples visit the "place" where he was buried rather than a feretory chapel. The simplicity of these reformist cults brings into sharp relief how lavish (and perhaps prodigal) many popular cults of the fourteenth and fifteenth centuries had become, and we should not necessarily read these unadorned shrines as evidence that some Wycliffites "got things wrong," because "the pressures of popular piety were strong."[66] It strikes me that the reaction here is far more radical: the disciples of Boughton and Wyche were actually trying to get things right by offering a coherent alternative to the sumptuous barbarism they perceived at many medieval relic shrines.

Hence, we must revisit Thomson's suggestion that the Wycliffites who made pilgrimages to the site of Richard Wyche's execution were behaving "paradoxically." For body-part relics – comprising as they do the sanctified flesh of saints, whose promised resurrection will reanimate the dead corpse – are markedly different from their containers, made by "mannes crafte."[67] These relics are more like living flesh than dead wood. That some Wycliffites might criticize opulent reliquaries but still venerate body-part relics thus affirms that they value the body, alive *and* dead, more than any manufactured object. Seen in this light,

Wycliffite relic cults are hardly paradoxical. Instead, they are perfectly commensurate with the espoused belief that what God makes has inherent value, even if "mannes crafte" does not.

The Value of the Body and the Problem of the Poor

These dissenting responses make it clear that shrines were frequently perceived as being no different than other prodigal images (such as the "Lefdy of Falsyngham")[68] that similarly distracted Christians from freely giving to their fellow humans in need. In suggesting that these shrines were inadequate metaphors for saints' relics, these writers take a basic commonplace of relic discourse to task: that a lavish shrine best represented the saint's holiness. They hence, like the authors of the *Lanterne of Liȝt* and *Pierce the Plowman's Crede,* turn the discourse on its head. The *Lanterne* and the *Crede* both offer the human body as more valuable than any material treasure, and, even more explicitly than the works discussed thus far, they present the bodies of the suffering poor, as epitomized by Peres, and not shrines or even relics, as the best possible metaphors for salvific grace.

In the *Lanterne of Liȝt*, the author privileges bodies over other kinds of material treasure by contrasting human bodies with ornate buildings: "Þe place halowiþ not þe man, but þe man halowiþ þe place. Alas what woodnes is þis, to boost of hooli placis, & we oure silf to be suche viciouse foolis" (36). These disordered "hooli placis" are those "vndirputten [with] schynyng marbel stoones"; their beams "glistiren al in gold," and the "auters ben dyuerseli araied wiþ preciouse stoones" (37). (By contrast, the acceptable monument is built simply, with readily available materials: "of lyme of tymbre & of stoon wiþ oþir necessarijs þat longen þerto" [36].) The attendant danger is that, as the *Lanterne* author calls them, "viciouse foolis" will see these deficient signs and mistakenly assume that the building derives its value from gold and gems, rather than from the people who worship in it (36, 37). As the *Lanterne* author recounts, even Christ's disciples make this mistake: they show Jesus "þe *curiouse werk in stoones* [of the temple] wenyng þus to plese her maistir" (42). The narrator presents Christ's response as emphasizing the disciples' error. Because of their foolishness, Jesus leaves them

> wiþ doulful chere ... *for mannes bilding stood ful strong, but bodi & soule þat he made to be his owene dwelling place* were fallen from keping of his lawe in

> to þe sowel of stinking synne. But scribis & pharisees weren in cause of þis greet mischef. (42; emphasis added)

This passage explicitly contrasts the value of bodies with the insignificance of "curiouse bilding[s]" (37). Such buildings "iape [the apostles'] iȝen" (37), so that they do not see the value of the "bodi & soule," which, as Christ specifies, "he made." The *Lanterne* author hence predicates the difference between a "curiouse" building and the human "bodi & soule" on the difference between what God creates and what humans make; obviously, what God creates is more precious. By extension, Christ refers not only to the bodies of his misguided apostles, but also to *all* bodies, which are *all* created by God, regretting the tendency to cherish only what has economic value.

We should take note of the lexical similarity between these "curiouse" buildings and shrines, which the *Lanterne* author conventionally refers to as being adorned with "preciouse stoones" and "gold" (37). Like church buildings, a shrine might be considered a kind of container that distracts from, rather than *represents*, what has true value (the saint's body or body parts inside). The *Lanterne* makes this point in its urgent and timely critique of execution[69]:

> Wherto make ȝe schrynes to seyntis & ȝit ȝe drawen, hangen & brennen hem þat holden þe weie of Crist and wandren aftir hise holi seyntis & þouȝ þis schewe not in ȝoure outwarde dede ȝe don þis slawȝtir in worde and wille[?] (43)

This passage immediately follows Christ's distinction between the "curiouse" temple and the human "bodi and soule," suggesting that here, too, the *Lanterne* author criticizes undervaluing the human body. In this instance, the author points out the hypocrisy in enshrining some saints while persecuting others. The text does not employ a blanket criticism of enshrining saints' relics, but rather juxtaposes that act with a monstrous one: the drawing, hanging, and burning of those who *follow* Christ's "holi seyntis." For the *Lanterne* author, the bodies of these faithful Christians are every bit as valuable as the enshrined relics. The scandal is that these living saints are treated differently and that enshrinement thereby becomes a vehicle for masking inner vice.

In other words, though the passage does not condemn enshrinement outright, its logic presents enshrinement as a form of meaningless display *when contrasted with* the maltreatment (and murder) of persecuted

Christians. The *Lanterne* author draws out this criticism by comparing current practice with that of the pharisees, who "weren in cause" of the temple's "curiouse werk in stoones" but were not inwardly righteous: "Crist seiþ, woo to ȝou, scribis & pharises ... ȝe bilden þe toumbes of holi prophetis, & wondirfulli honouren her graues, but ȝe swen ȝoure fadris steppis in purswyng of riȝtwise blood & þise sectis don þe same, but wiþ more malice in worde & dede" (42–3). The primary concern is hence not with the relic, the saints, or the prophets so enshrined, but rather with dissembling clerics whose behaviour is diametrically opposed to their moral state: such people "clensen clene al þat is outward but certis wiþynne [they] ben replete wiþ miche raveyn & vnclennes" (43). Shrines and ostentatious buildings hence function as metaphors for hypocrisy. The elaborate shrine represents not only clerical profligacy and corruption, but even more generally, any discord between what is outside (an opulent shrine) and what is inside (a Christian body which, for the *Lanterne* author, is like any other). The *Lanterne* author thereby problematizes the treasure metaphor of relic discourse by showing that rather than signifying the heavenly promise of resurrection, reliquaries could be signs of moral deficiency.

The *Lanterne* author, in presenting the act of enshrinement as a model for how all Christian bodies – prophets, saints, and heretics – are to be treated, amplifies the Wycliffite dictum that reliquaries be simple. (It is no surprise that the acceptable church – built "of lyme of tymbre & of stoon wiþ oþir necessarijs þat longen þerto" [36] – sounds a lot like the unassuming reliquaries of Boughton and Wyche.) The basic premise is clear: "Þe place halowiþ not þe man, but þe man halowiþ the place. Alas what woodnes is þis, to boost of hooli placis, & we oure silf to be suche viciouse foolis" (36). For the *Lanterne* author, the clerics who enshrine some saints while persecuting others to the death violate this basic principle and harm the bodies of the poor in the process: "Þan as miche woden drem þe chirche schynneþ in wowis & sche nediþ in þe pore; sche wlappiþ hir stoones in gold, & hir owene sones sche forsakiþ nakid; of þe spensis of nedi is mad a veyn seruise, to riche mennes iȝen" (38). This passage employs parallelism to compare a lavish church "wlappi[d]" in gold with a naked body, which is obviously wrapped in nothing. Those who build lavish buildings and shrines while neglecting these people have forgotten not only that bodies matter, but that bodies are vessels for the Holy Spirit and hence matter the most. Such an idea undermines defences of enshrinement, which almost always assert as a basic premise that jewels signify better than bodies – and that in some sense, jewels are perceived as more precious than saints' bodies. Wycliffite texts like the *Lanterne* suggest instead that all Christian bodies are precious: fallen, subject to decay, and yet beautiful and valuable, both in themselves and in what they signify.

Pierce the Plowman's Crede, an alliterative poem in the tradition of Langland's *Piers Plowman* and dated within ten years of 1393, portrays a man's quest to learn the tenets of his faith from friars, all of whom are revealed to be greedy hypocrites.[70] Like the *Lanterne*, the *Crede* presents a human body – that of Peres – as a better signifier than shrines or tombs.[71] Indeed, by juxtaposing Peres's body with the lavish splendour of the Dominican church and its tombs, the *Crede* author debunks the treasure metaphor of relic discourse:

> Tombes *opon tabernacles* tyld opon lofte,
> Housed in hirnes harde set abouten,
> Of armede alabaustre [alfor] for the nones,
> [Made vpon marbel in many maner wyse,
> Knyghtes in her conisantes (emblems) clad for the nones,]
> *All it semed seyntes y-sacred opon erthe.* (181–6; emphasis added)

These tombs are so resplendent that they completely misrepresent their contents, which because of their containers, the narrator observes, "semed seyntes y-sacred opon erthe." Moreover, in describing these tombs, this passage employs architectural terminology ("tabernacles") often associated with shrines and images. In this respect, the *Crede* is not unlike a portion of "Images and Pilgrimages," the early fifteenth-century treatise on images I discussed earlier in this chapter. Both texts employ the word "tabernacles" or "tabernaclid":

> For oure lord God dwellis by grace in gode mennus soulis, and wiþoute comparesoun bettere þan all ymagis made of man in erþe, and better þan alle bodies of seyntis, be þe bones of hem neuer so gloriously shreynyd in gold.
>
> Also men erren myche in offrynge to þes ymagis. For to þe gayest and most rychely arayed ymage raþeest wil þe puple offur, and nouȝt to no pore ymage stondyng in a symple kirk or chapel, but *ȝif it stonde ryaly tabernaclid* wiþ keruyng and peyntid wiþ gold and precious iewelis.[72]

As Anne Hudson explains, "ryaly tabernaclid" refers "to the habit of placing the image of the saint in a decorated archway or shrine."[73]

I would push Hudson's observation even further: as the definition in the *Middle English Dictionary* makes clear, the words "tabernacles" and "tabernaclid" are associated not just with images, but also with the cult of relics:

> (a) An ornate canopied tomb, a canopied shrine ... (d) a canopied niche or recess in a wall, pillar, etc. designed to contain an image; (e) an ornamental representation of a canopied niche painted or embroidered on fabric; ... (g) *fig*. a shrine.[74]

The phrase "an ornate canopied tomb, a canopied shrine" designates a specific *kind* of shrine (one covered with a canopy).[75] Generally speaking, only the most important shrines at major cult centers would have had canopies. Made of wood, gilded and in some cases decorated with expensive gems, these objects were suspended above the *feretrum* (often on a pulley system, as at Winchester and Canterbury); they covered the shrine itself but at intervals were raised to display the reliquary.[76] (The canopy at Thomas Becket's shrine is probably the most famous example.) The poet's language thus suggests that the tombs in the Dominican church look like shrines. The *Crede* author may well have been thinking of the misleading nature of shrines in describing these tombs – and he may well have employed the term "tabernacles" in order to make the comparison stick.

The bodies contained within these shrine-like tombs are obviously not relics, and this is exactly the point: an opulent container can make it seem as if, as Wyclif points out in *Tractatus de Ecclesia*, "pars persona empte" are celebrated saints – "seyntes y-sacred opon erthe," as the *Crede* author puts it. Opulent shrines might therefore confer value on the wrong body and, in their expense, harm the poor:

> [And] a curious cros craftly entayled,
> With tabernacles y-tight to toten all abouten.
> The pris of a plough-lond of peynes so rounde
> To aparaile that pyler were pure lytel. (167–70)

These lines explicitly articulate the cost to the poor of elaborately decorated cathedrals, indicting, as Bruce Holsinger has suggested, spending that would exceed the "pris of a plough-lond."[77] But this passage also prepares us for understanding the Dominican tombs as representative of what Holsinger has called the "frozen cruelty in ekphrastic writing, a refusal of empathy."[78] By contrasting close-fitting tabernacles – again, a word that may refer to shrines as well as to images or church decoration in general – with a ploughman's suffering, it seems clear that the *Crede* author is setting up a deliberate comparison between this ekphrastic cruelty and a different image: that of Peres's body.[79]

Peres, unlike the tombs, appears to be what he in fact is. He therefore epitomizes the Wycliffite alternative to sumptuous reliquaries. The description of his body recalls the description of the Dominican tombs, reminding the reader that some containers (bodies, even clothing) are more valuable – and signify more accurately – than others:

> His cote was of a cloute that cary was y-called,
> His hod was full of holes and his heer oute, ...
> His ton toteden out as he the londe treddede,
> His hosen ouerhongen his hokschynes on eueriche a side. (422–3, 425–6)

Unlike the alabaster tombs,[80] "Housed in hirnes harde set abouten," Peres's clothing is made from rags ("cloute"), and this covering is replete with holes: he has no corner or niche in which to hide from the cold, and his covering is so poor that even his toes stick out of his shoes. In fact, Peres's body is the very opposite of the Dominican tombs: they fit perfectly into their niches, which are "harde set abouten," and they are "tyld opon lofte." They thus elevate their bodies away from the ground – away from the dirt and dust to which all shall return. The tombs, that is to say, misdirect attention away from not only the bodies they contain – which only *seem* to be saints because of their wondrous containers – but also from the common fate that all bodies share: death, decay, burial in the earth, and the hope of resurrection. Peres, by contrast, "the londe treddede"; his feet are firmly planted on the cold, hard ground – ground so cold and hard it causes his wife's feet to crack and bleed (436). He is the very image of the suffering, postlapsarian laborer. We are able to see and thus read Peres's body in a way that we cannot see or read saints' bodies (or here, the bodies in the Dominican tombs, which seem like saints precisely because they are not visible). This heroic ploughman is thus presented as the *better image*.

By emphasizing how different the Dominican tombs are from the bodies they contain, the *Crede* author gestures towards the profound difference between reliquaries and the bodies *they* contain. Some proponents of relic discourse, by contrast, elide the difference between the relic and reliquary, claiming that in encountering the shrine, supplicants encounter the saint: the reliquary better represents the saint in heaven than the relics themselves. This line of argumentation enabled many clerics to justify occluding the most prestigious relics in expensive shrines. The *Crede*, by contrast, offers us Peres's body as a signifier for holiness. In Peres we have the most simple and precious relic of all: the human body, visible through Peres's tattered rags, which comprise the most simple, fitting, and precious reliquary. Moreover, in presenting the failure of the Dominican tombs accurately to represent what they enclose, the poem implies that relic discourse could function to justify social practices that were flawed, and fundamentally so. Rather than figuring forth the saint, lavish containers in fact circumscribe the worth of a saint's body (and indeed all other bodies). In this paradigm, reliquaries, crafted by humans and valued for their economic worth, are in some sense the *opposite* of bodies and body parts.

William White similarly presents the relationship between relics and shrines as oxymoronic:

> Next we say to you, we object and we articulate, that after and against your aforesaid abjuration, you held, affirmed, wrote and taught that saints' relics, *that is to say the flesh and bones of dead men*, should not be venerated by the people, *nor exhumed [and translated] from their stinking graves*, nor placed in a gold and silver repository; because men doing thusly do not honor God and the saints, but commit idolatry.
>
> (Item tibi dicimus, objicimus et articulamur, quod post et contra tuam praedictam abjurationem, tu tenuisti, affirmasti, scripsisti et docuisti, quod reliquiae sanctorum, *scilicet carnes et ossa hominis mortui*, non debent a populo venerari, *nec de monumento foetido extrahi*, nec in capsa aurea vel argentea reponi; quia homines sic facientes non honorant Deum et sanctos ejus, sed committunt idolatriam.)[81]

Reliquaries made of gold and silver can hardly be seen to represent the "flesh and bones of dead men." For White, both the insignificance of the relic and also the mis-signification of the reliquary suggest that clerics who use relic discourse insist on what cannot be true (that the relic is a locus of intercession; that the shrine is the best means of signifying the saint's holiness; that the saint's body is fundamentally different from a pilgrim's body). His critique of enshrining stinking bones indicates that mainstream uses of relic discourse depend upon presenting contradictions – the reliquary and the relic – as commensurate.

Unlike an opulent shrine or tomb, the "poor man" and saints' bones comprise the same matter. Both are bodies. Shannon Gayk has shown that many Wycliffite writers argued for the usefulness of signs that emanate from God's creation: dirt, mud – and, I would add, bodies and body parts, perhaps even the rotting bodies of saints.[82] One might go so far as to suggest that by substituting one metaphor (the poor) for another (the shrine), relic discourse becomes, in the hands of Wycliffite authors, a way to advocate for the sanctity of the poor.[83] For while Wycliffite critiques of enshrinement identify a contradictory premise of relic discourse (that shrines are like saints), they do not dismiss the discourse altogether. Instead, as I have sought to demonstrate in this chapter, Wycliffites modify conventions of relic discourse in order to show how the social practices of relic cults indirectly harmed members of the very community the relic and its cult were supposed to help: the poor and the sick. Wycliffite writings about relics and shrines thus construct the relic – and relic discourse – as a potential force for social change. In doing so, these texts indicate that, while relic discourse could serve the interests of those who wished to reinforce hierarchical values and make money, in different hands it could also remind viewers of inequality, suffering, the imperfection of the body, and the transience of life.

Coda: The Cultural Work of Relic Discourse

The number of recent scholarly and popular studies about relics attests to the continuing importance of these devotional objects and their cults.[1] Contrary to what we might expect, these objects are not vestiges of a more superstitious past, but, as Peter Manseau suggests, at the very centre of some of the most controversial news stories of the twenty-first century:

> In the news every night we hear of the difficulty of finding peace in the Middle East and Central Asia, regions both at war with outside forces and bitterly divided between Shia and Sunni Muslims. Broadly speaking, the Shiites revere relics; the Sunnis despise them. In Saudi Arabia, the Wahhabi government of fundamentalist Sunnis has bulldozed relic-containing mosques and shrines they see as examples of idolatry.[2]

Questions of Muslim belief aside, Manseau wants to illustrate the degree to which many civilizations, across space and time, both understand bodies as somehow sanctified and struggle with how to express this sanctity appropriately. This problem is at the heart of relic discourse, too: a discourse devoted to negotiating and challenging distinctions between life and death, between holy and regular bodies, between heaven and earth. In some sense, relics are at the very centre of discussions of human existence, distilling as they do essential human experiences: how to live, how to die, how to interpret death. Relics – whether we venerate them or regard them with suspicion and derision – continue to tell us something about who we are.

Whence the importance of relic discourse, the very language we still employ in our attempts to understand what relics mean, what they do, and how they matter. The travelling exhibit *Treasures of Heaven*, which I visited in London, UK, draws much of its terminology from relic discourse and from medieval practices. This is no surprise: the reliquaries on display are all medieval. Nonetheless, I was both intrigued and taken aback by the description of the discovery of St Cuthbert's body, for instance, which presented medieval hagiography as fact, suggesting that in the Middle Ages, Cuthbert's body *was* whole – as opposed to emphasizing that this wholeness, whether factual or not, is a key component of Cuthbert's discursive history. Caroline Walker Bynum rightly cautions, "[w]e cannot take stories of miraculous matter literally … [These] stories were often constructed – usually by clergy – to stereotype certain groups"; such stories suggest "that authorities feared anticlerical or anti-Christian reactions."[3] The exhibit thus illustrates our ongoing need to imagine the possibility that dead bodies might remain incorrupt, whether or not this belief squares with widely accepted interpretations of science and the natural world. Bodies matter; but bodies, living and dead, decay. Relic discourse affords some flexibility, in that its basic tenets eschew fear and insist on the possibility of static (if, simultaneously, as Sarah Stanbury has so convincingly suggested, animated) matter.[4]

The ultimate purpose of this book has thus been to draw attention to the constructed nature of relics' meaning, to how some of the most common narratives about medieval practices – that "fragmentation … paradoxically increased the power of the relic,"[5] that all reliquaries became more accessible – are, while not incorrect, at the least incomplete. Addressing such lacunae reveals much about late medieval cultural practices, how the most secular writers (Malory, for instance) might be informed by the religious practices they encountered, and reminds us that too frequently, we repeat inherited wisdom without asking ourselves whether it represents the entire story. If we only take into account, as Eamon Duffy remarks in his review of Bynum's *Christian Materiality*, that opaque reliquaries

> increasingly gave way to crystal monstrances, designed to expose the relic to view, and to "speaking reliquaries," containers often grotesquely fashioned in the shape of a body part … and often with a crystal window, designed to "flaunt the fragments of bone" that they contained' "[6] –

then we miss how the *increasing* occlusion of major relics, in England at least, affected the reception and understanding of such objects. What is more, at least some reliquary windows were added much later: a window in one "speaking reliquary" from the *Treasures of Heaven* exhibit, for instance, was added in the eighteenth century. It is tricky to assume that the object we see appears exactly as it did in the Middle Ages, and by extension to derive our thinking about the medieval theology of relics only from what we can now see.

None of this is to claim that I am somehow inured from assumptions about these objects, or that everything in this book is absolutely correct. In some sense, instead, the point I wish to make is that relics and relic discourse are interesting precisely because they draw our attention to falsehood, artifice – to assumption, to what remains unsaid. It is with this point I will end. In the Introduction, I quoted from the *Fasciculus morum*, where the author compares enshrined fake relics to euphemized sin. That passage shares with Wycliffite approaches to relics – indeed, with many of the texts this study considers – an underlying concern that a container might not accurately represent its contents. This concern is a concomitant of anxieties surrounding the representation of holiness by human bodies and body parts, and whether or not the shrines and the language associated with those bodies can convey appropriately that representation. Clearly, then, relic discourse performs the cultural work of distilling questions about the value of the body and how to represent it. But, as the Wycliffite texts of chapter 5 indicate, relic discourse also, insofar as it invites questions about the relationship between a shrine's appearance and that of its relics, provides a means for considering both the function of religious images in particular and, more generally, of sincerity and duplicity. The *Lanterne* author, for instance, employs reliquaries in his critique of those who enshrine some saints but persecute others.[7] These Christian leaders are like the "scribis & pharises" who "clensen clene al þat is outward" – building "toumbes of holi prophetis, & wondirfulli honouren her graues" – but who are, "wiþynne, … replete wiþ miche raveyn & vnclennes."[8] For the *Lanterne* author, shrines themselves can function as metaphors for hypocrisy, signalling disjuncture between outward behaviour and inner "vnclennes."

This Wycliffite attention to the disjuncture between sign and signified indicates a widespread recognition of the limits of representative language. Indeed, as Shannon Gayk and others have pointed out, this recognition is not particular to Wycliffites, who were not themselves averse to using powerful figurative imagery and alliterative verse form in conveying an argument.[9] As Part II of this study has demonstrated, relic discourse enabled the exploration of pilgrim behaviour:

did virtuous action guarantee results? Frequently enough, the answer is no. So, too, relic discourse afforded, for some writers at least, an avenue for exploring the tenuous relationship between a metaphorical vehicle and its tenor – and the degree to which the vehicle might obscure, rather than illuminate, the tenor. The rhetorical construction of Criseyde, in which Criseyde, Pandarus, and Troilus all collude, does not perhaps correspond to the actual Criseyde, to the woman whom the conventional blazon – she is the "bright … sterre" (I 175), for instance – is supposed to describe. Bringing relic discourse to bear on our reading of Criseyde suggests the difficulty of communication and highlights the degree to which, in substituting one thing for something else, metaphorical description displaces the tenor. Just who or what is Criseyde? The descriptions of her in Book I of the *Troilus* do not necessarily make that clear.

Like the descriptions of the shrine in the texts I considered in chapter 2, the metaphor stands in for its referent to the point that it becomes, in Orwell's phrase, "dead" – it refers to itself, even simply to convention, rather than to actual things, people, and events. In this way, the Wycliffite approach to relic discourse indicates the impotence, to some degree, of that discourse. Insofar as shrines are so opulent that they cannot successfully express holiness; insofar as the dominant figurative language of relic discourse centers on lavish and rich images (of treasure, gems, shining light), it supplants what, for many of the Wycliffite authors mentioned in chapter 5, is the primary point, the primary tenor: the poor, the decaying body, the transience of the life we lead here. Ultimately, then, from the technical terminology, metaphors, and commonplaces of relic discourse to its various manifestations in the texts of Part II of this book, it seems clear that relic discourse transforms discussions about the relationship between the sign and what it signifies. The answer, in many cases, is that what mainstream authors champion as perfect signifiers of the saint's holiness (the shrine, the virtuous supplicant, etc.) fails in some way to convey God's grace accurately. The shrine distracts viewers from the poor. The virtuous supplicant in Malory's text is always already virtuous, closing off the possibility for most to attain this status. The hierarchy of the discourse, in other words, emphasizes inaccessibility and wealth, to the point that Wycliffite revisions of relic discourse foreground the very object that some mainstream writers such as Lydgate or Bradshaw seem to want us to forget: the decaying body of the saint, the actual relic itself.

In using the images of a shrine and relic to explore the discord between actual and perceived intention, Lydgate's "The Pain and Sorrow of Evil Marriage" illustrates the relevance of relic discourse to the exploration of hypocrisy and dissembling language.[10] In narrating his relief at having narrowly escaped "the yoke and bondis of mariage" (7), the poet identifies the guile of brides as the root cause of what married life actually offers (from the poet's perspective, "thylke perelis of Hell" [35]). Lydgate illustrates the duplicity of wives – and the corresponding inability of any husband to see that "[v]nder suche falsenes," women merely "feyneth [hem] to be triewe" (61) – by describing their behaviour at the site of a relic cult:

> Of ther nature they gretly hem delite,
> With holy fface fayned for the nones,
> In seyntuaries ther ffrendes to visite,
> More than for relikkes or any seyntis bones,
> Though they be closed vnder precious stones;
> To gete hem pardoun, like there olde vsages,
> To kys no shrynes, but lusty yong images. (106–12)

This stanza presents the wifely attitude at a relic site as the pinnacle of chicanery: these women care only for show, not for saints' relics. Part of their display is for the benefit of their friends and the young men they hope to seduce: they have substituted the bodies of their potential conquests, which are "lusty yong images," for religious artefacts.[11] But by contrasting their pious expressions, "fayned" for the occasion, with their behaviour and desires, Lydgate sets up a contrast between their outward appearance and their inner moral vacuity. The perceived intention of these wives (that, based on their "holy fface," they are actually there to venerate relics) does not accord with their actual intentions (to gossip and fornicate). It is inevitable that women – who are, as the poem tells us, "gladly variable" (42), "Dyvers of hert, full of duplicite, / Right mastirfull, hasty and eke proude, / Crabbed of langage when þei lust cry lowde" (47–9) – disregard what is *inside* the shrine and treat "seyntuaries" as spaces for social performance. But the stanza also implies the similarity between these wives and the relics, which are (like the true intentions of these women, metaphorically speaking) enclosed "vnder precious stones," a sort of "holy fface fayned for the nones," if you will.

Neither the wives' outward demeanor nor the shrine's "precious stones" represent the true significance of what is inside. Lydgate depicts the wives as socialites whose posturing merely confirms their superficiality. By contrast, he clearly regards the relics as having great value. And yet, in this exploration of inner worth and how to convey it, Lydgate deploys one of the most common metaphors of relic discourse and relic sites – treasure, "precious stones" – and contrasts it with what lies inside (literally, relics – figuratively, in this case, the depraved indifference of the wives to anything holy). No sane reader would expect Lydgate suddenly to compliment these wives; it is no surprise that, in the presence of a lavish shrine, they forget about the saint. But relic discourse informs and enriches how we understand Lydgate's exploration of artifice and dishonesty in this poem. As Lydgate's diatribe indicates, neither language nor social performance, both flawed, can always communicate what is on the inside. Indeed, Lydgate draws on relic discourse to reveal the limitations of both language and appearances in communicating intent.

I end with this point because in many respects, understanding relic discourse makes possible the recognition that, just as text always played a vital role in creating the meaning of, and sometimes serving as a substitute for, the physical remains of saints, so, too, saints' relics contributed to late medieval understandings of how representative language functioned in general. Both a shrine and language had the ability – even the propensity – to deceive. What is said does not always accord with the speaker's intentions; and if relics were fake, the beauty of a shrine could be entirely out of keeping with its contents. Outward appearances were not always to be trusted. This study thus offers one answer to Brian Stock's question about "the status of a physical object having religious associations during an age of increasing literacy … [D]oes it now derive its meaning from being interpreted through a text?"[12] As I have sought to demonstrate in this book, in respect of the role relics played in the literary and religious culture of late medieval England, the answer to Stock's question is yes. But with a caveat. The preponderance of relic discourse, and the increasing importance of descriptions of relics as we move through the period from 1100 to 1538, indicate that, as shrine monuments grew in size (and perhaps, as literacy increased as well), the meaning of relics came to depend more and more on being interpreted through writing.

But as metaphors for understanding the difficulties of communication, shrines themselves came to represent duplicity – of the inability of either the holy object itself *or of language* to convey the meaning and status of a relic. In drawing on the discord between relics and shrines in his tirade against women, Lydgate's poem reminds us that, insofar as the wives enshrine their duplicity, masking it behind a "holy fface," language and behaviour were, like shrines, fraught with the potential to misrepresent. Relic discourse illustrates that relics derived meaning through text – but also that the text itself was potentially flawed.

Notes

Introduction: Relic Discourse

1 For the report of this crime and the quotations in this section, see Jennifer Medina, "Relic of Saint Disappears from Its Case Inside Church," *New York Times* (14 June 2011), http://www.nytimes.com/2011/06/15/us/15relic.html?_r=0, accessed 15 June 2011.

2 Jennifer Medina, "California: Woman Arrested in Relic's Disappearance," *New York Times* (17 June 2011, http://www.nytimes.com/2011/06/18/us/18brfs-California.html, accessed 20 June 2011.

3 "Facilisque accessus his et illis, ac fortasse minus dignis quam expediret." See *Miracula S. Oswaldi*, in *Eadmer of Canterbury: Lives and Miracles of Saints Oda, Dunstan, and Oswald*, ed. and trans. Bernard J. Muir and Andrew J. Turner (Oxford: Oxford University Press, 2006), 300–1.

4 "Ac in loco saecularium personarum frequentia uacuo irreuerentique accessu remoto collocaret." See *Miracula S. Oswaldi*, 298–301.

5 Dudley Althaus, "Vial of Pope John Paul II's Blood Tours Mexico," *Houston Chronicle* (29 August 2011), http://www.chron.com/news/article/Vial-of-Pope-John-Paul-II-s-blood-tours-Mexico-2141982.php, accessed 21 September 2011.

6 See for instance the British Museum's page for the *Treasures of Heaven* exhibit, which identifies "the relics of Christ and the saints – objects associated with them, such as body parts or possessions – continue to provide a bridge between heaven and earth today." http://www.britishmuseum.org/whats_on/exhibitions/treasures_of_heaven/introduction.aspx, accessed 16 September 2011. But see also Cynthia Hahn's work on how reliquaries in particular signify, most recently "What Do Reliquaries Do for Relics?" *Numen* 57 (2010): 284–316. At 289, Hahn remarks that "the

reliquary works hard to 'represent' the relic as powerful, holy, and sacred, part of the larger institution of the Church."

7 Hahn entitled a paper on the tomb of Ambrose, given at the 1996 Dumbarton Oaks Symposium, "The Discourse of Relics: Saints, Stories and the Sacred." This talk was published as "Narrative on the Golden Altar of Sant'Ambrogio in Milan: Presentation and Reception," Dumbarton Oaks Papers 53 (1999): 167–87. Though Hahn does not discuss relic discourse in the terms I outline in this study, she does posit both the metaphorical relationship between the shrine and relic and the subsequent difficulty of understanding a relic's importance merely by looking at the shrine. See also "The Voices of the Saints: Speaking Reliquaries," *Gesta* 36 (1997): 20–31. Unfortunately, Hahn's latest study, *Strange Beauty: Origins and Issues in the Making of Medieval Reliquaries 400–circa 1204* (University Park: Pennsylvania State University Press, 2012), was not yet available when my book went to press.

8 Siegfried Wenzel, ed. and trans., *Fasciculus morum: A Fourteenth-Century Preacher's Handbook* (University Park: Pennsylvania State University Press, 1989), 477.

9 For a related discussion of the term "translation," see "Introduction," in *Medieval and Early Modern Devotional Objects in Global Perspective: Translations of the Sacred*, ed. Elizabeth Robertson and Jennifer Jahner (New York: Palgrave, 2010), 2.

10 Geoffrey of Vinsauf, *Poetria nova*, trans. Margaret Nims (Toronto: PIMS, 1967), 43, 52. Carolyn Dinshaw, to whose discussion of *translatio* my approach is indebted, points out that translation is the "mechanism of rhetorical trope in general," citing Quintilian's *Institutio oratoria* and Donatus's *Ars grammatica* (*Chaucer's Sexual Poetics* [Madison: University of Wisconsin Press, 1989], 249 n. 16). The notion that "transference" and "substitution" were rhetorical concepts was a commonplace. For a discussion of translation theory, metaphor, and metonymy, see Rita Copeland, *Rhetoric, Hermeneutics, and Translation in the Middle Ages: Academic Traditions and Vernacular Texts* (Cambridge: Cambridge University Press, 1991), 27–30, 42–5. See also J.J. Murphy, "The Arts of Poetry and Prose," in *The Cambridge History of Literary Criticism:* Vol. 2, *The Middle Ages*, ed. Alastair Minnis and Ian Johnson (Cambridge: Cambridge University Press, 2005), 42–67.

11 Dinshaw, *Chaucer's Sexual Poetics*, 133, 134.

12 Hahn, "What Do Reliquaries Do for Relics?" 307.

13 For a theorized consideration of enshrinement, metaphor, and semiotic theory, see Seeta Chaganti, *The Medieval Poetics of the Reliquary: Enshrinement, Inscription, Performance* (New York: Palgrave, 2008), 14–15, 137–50; on *translatio* and metaphor, see Dinshaw, *Chaucer's Sexual Poetics*, 137–41.

14 Paul de Man, *Allegories of Reading: Figural Language in Rousseau, Nietzsche, Rilke, and Proust* (New Haven, CT: Yale University Press, 1979), 15, 62–72.
15 Hahn, "What Do Reliquaries Do for Relics?" 291, 301.
16 For a discussion of Wycliffite testimony as possibly formulaic, see Anne Hudson, *The Premature Reformation: Wycliffite Texts and Lollard History* (Oxford: Oxford University Press, 1988), 33–9.
17 Rachel Koopmans, *Wonderful to Relate: Miracle Stories and Miracle Collecting in High Medieval England* (Philadelphia: University of Pennsylvania Press, 2011), 5.
18 Obviously, oral narrative would have been a crucial way for shrine keepers to explain the meaning of relics to visiting pilgrims – we know such preaching took place at Canterbury, for instance. All the same, the written record reveals cultural habits both in what it emphasizes, conceals, and changes. But on the importance of oral culture in the circulation of miracles, in the twelfth and thirteenth centuries in particular, see Koopmans, *Wonderful to Relate*.
19 See http://thewalters.org/eventscalendar/eventdetails.aspx?e=1568, accessed 25 January 2011. Some of the so-called speaking reliquaries in this exhibit – reliquaries designed in the shape of body parts – feature windows that were not added until the eighteenth and nineteenth centuries. I discuss this exhibit in more detail in the Coda; on speaking reliquaries, see also chapter 1, n. 14.
20 Chaganti, *The Medieval Poetics of the Reliquary*, 26.
21 I speak here not of small phylacteries or personal relics and souvenirs, but rather of the cathedral shrine monuments of England's major saints. On the distinct developments of English shrines, see John Crook, *English Medieval Shrines* (Woodbridge, Suffolk: Boydell Press, 2011), 212, 257, and passim. See also Christopher Wilson, *The Shrines of St William of York* (York: Yorkshire Museum, 1977), 20. For a detailed discussion of the English shrine base and feretory shrines in England, see chapter 1.
22 In *Die Reliquiare des christlichen Kultus und ihre Entwicklung* (Freiburg-im-Breisgau: Herder, 1940), 100, Joseph Braun notes that, before the thirteenth century, crystal reliquaries were rare. Too often, however, contemporary scholars take such commentary as proof positive that *all* reliquaries employed such viewing techniques. It is important to keep in mind the wide variety of reliquaries in the Middle Ages and that while some kinds of reliquaries became gradually more visible as time went on, this trend is not true of cathedral feretories.
23 Some late medieval cults seem to have grown out of a common regard for a saint as friend (the unsanctioned cult of Richard Scrope may be a

good example of this phenomenon, as suggested by an illumination in the Bolton Hours, York Minster MS Add 2, fol. 100v). On Scrope's cult, see especially J.W. McKenna, "Popular Canonization as Political Propaganda: The Cult of Archbishop Scrope," *Speculum* 45 (1970): 608–23. Writings about other cults manifest what Christopher A. Jones, speaking of Anglo-Saxon relic cults, has called the "impersonal sanctity" that could result from the concealment of relics. Early medieval reliquaries and their attendant lexicon have led Jones to suggest that "most early medieval people experienced relics not as anything suggestive of a person or even a body, but as a closed box or stone slab." See "Old English Words for Relics of Saints," *Florilegium* 26 (2009): 90. I thank Drew for sharing an earlier draft with me. Jones builds in particular upon the work of Cynthia Hahn, who has long challenged assumptions about easy access to relics and complicated the relationship between reliquary and relic. See especially Hahn, "Metaphor and Meaning in Early Medieval Reliquaries," in *Seeing the Invisible in Late Antiquity and the Early Middle Ages*, ed. Giselle de Nie, Karl F. Morrison, and Marco Mostert (Turnhout: Brepols, 2005), 239–64; "The Voices of the Saints"; and "Narrative on the Golden Altar of Sant'Ambrogio in Milan."

24 John Blair, "St Frideswide's," *Oxoniensia* 53 (1988): 247.

25 See the discussion in chapter 1.

26 In fact, since 1905 there have been only six book-length studies on relics in England. These are rarely cited; one is unpublished (Islwyn Geoffrey Thomas's very fine dissertation); and only three go past 1200, at which point the environment at cathedral shrines radically changed. None offers an extended literary consideration of the historical and discursive function of relics in late medieval England. See Ben Nilson, *Cathedral Shrines of Medieval England* (Woodbridge, Suffolk: Boydell and Brewer, 1998); David Rollason, *Saints and Relics in Anglo-Saxon England* (Cambridge, MA: Basil Blackwell, 1989); Islwyn Geoffrey Thomas, "The Cult of Saints' Relics in Medieval England" (PhD diss., University of London, 1974); J. Charles Wall, *Shrines of British Saints* (London: Methuen, 1905); Chaganti, *The Medieval Poetics of the Reliquary*; and, most recently, Crook's *English Medieval Shrines*. Other studies of individual cults are indispensible but do not focus on the cult of relics more broadly construed. Two recent examples include Virginia Blanton's *Signs of Devotion: The Cult of St Æthelthryth in Medieval England, 695–1615* (University Park: Pennsylvania State University Press, 2007); and Gerald Bonner, David Rollason, and Clare Stancliffe, ed., *St Cuthbert, His Cult and His Community to AD 1200* (Woodbridge, Suffolk: Boydell Press, 1989).

27 Chaganti, *The Medieval Poetics of the Reliquary*, passim.
28 By contrast, studies of cults of relics on the continent, where substantially more such artefacts survive, have proliferated. These groundbreaking works include Caroline Walker Bynum's *The Resurrection of the Body* (New York: Columbia University Press, 1995), as well as her recent *Wonderful Blood* (Philadelphia: University of Pennsylvania Press, 2007); Patrick Geary's *Furta Sacra: Thefts of Relics in the Central Middle Ages*, 2nd ed (Princeton, NJ: Princeton University Press, 1990); Peter Brown's *The Cult of the Saints: Its Rise and Function in Latin Christianity* (Chicago: University of Chicago Press, 1981). Of these studies, only one – Caroline Walker Bynum's *Wonderful Blood* – ventures past the thirteenth century; none centres on England.
29 Dinshaw, *Chaucer's Sexual Poetics*, 159–68. On 163, Dinshaw characterizes relics as "sacred fragments" in which " 'grace survives undivided.' " The idea of the fragment is central to the title of Dinshaw's chapter, "Eunuch Hermeneutics."
30 To be sure, much of the interest has been in the theological, rather than cultural, significance of relics. As Dinshaw explains of her "brief discussion" of relics, she cites "sources from the early through the late Middle Ages; veneration of relics varied through the age, *but the essential theological idea of relics remained fairly consistent*" (*Chaucer's Sexual Poetics*, 264–5 n. 21; emphasis added). Nevertheless, as Hahn rightly points out, "It was practice not theology that determined the shape of the cult of relics" ("What Do Reliquaries Do for Relics?" 294).
31 Sarah Beckwith, *Christ's Body: Identity, Culture and Society in Late Medieval Writings* (London: Routledge, 1993), 2.
32 David Aers and Lynn Staley, *The Powers of the Holy: Religion, Politics, and Gender in Late Mediveal English Culture* (University Park: Pennsylvania State University Press, 1996); Margaret Aston, *England's Iconoclasts.* Vol. 1, *Laws against Images* (Oxford: Oxford University Press, 1988); Sarah Beckwith, *Christ's Body*, and *Signifying God: Social Relation and Symbolic Act in the York Corpus Christi Plays* (Chicago: University of Chicago Press, 2001); Eamon Duffy, *The Stripping of the Altars: Traditional Religion in England, c. 1400–1580* (New Haven, CT: Yale University Press, 1992, rev. 2005); Gail McMurray Gibson, *The Theater of Devotion: East Anglian Drama and Society in the Late Middle Ages* (Chicago: University of Chicago Press, 1989); Miri Rubin, *Corpus Christi: The Eucharist in Late Medieval Culture* (Cambridge: Cambridge University Press, 1991); and James Simpson, *Reform and Cultural Revolution* (Oxford: Oxford University Press, 2002).

33 See David Aers, *Faith, Ethics and Church: Writing in England, 1360–1409* (Cambridge: D.S. Brewer, 2000), 1–15; Beckwith, especially *Signifying God*; and Gibson, *The Theater of Devotion*.

34 For the most influential studies in this area, see Aers and Staley, *The Powers of the Holy*; Beckwith, *Christ's Body*; and Rubin, *Corpus Christi*.

35 Beckwith, *Christ's Body*; and Rubin, *Corpus Christi*.

36 Beckwith, *Christ's Body*, 3–4.

37 See Victricius of Rouen's fourth-century *De laude sanctorum*, ed. I. Mulders and R. Demeulenaere, CCSL 64 (Turnhout: Brepols, 1985). And see "In Praise of the Saints," ed. and trans. Phillipe Buc, in *Medieval Hagiography: An Anthology*, ed. Thomas Head (New York: Routledge, 2001), 31–51.

38 For the typical interpretation of Victricius, see Crook, who comments of Victricius's "reception of the Milanese saints" that "a fragment of a saintly body, or even a contact relic, *was considered just as powerful as the whole body, and worthy of the same veneration*" (*English Medieval Shrines*, 11; emphasis added).

39 Aers and Staley, *The Powers of the Holy*, 9.

40 Rubin, *Corpus Christi*, 9. Rubin is speaking of eucharistic language in particular. On the symbolic in general, Beckwith similarly comments, *Christ's Body*, 2, "symbolic forms sometimes mobilize meaning in the service of power … symbols, in other words, have an ideological dimension."

41 Aers criticizes the tendency of scholars, until the influential studies of Beckwith and Rubin – and, it should be noted, of Gail Gibson, as well – to reproduce rather than interrogate late medieval " 'devotion to the humanity of Jesus' " (*The Powers of the Holy*, 17). For a recent study that takes this kind of interrogative approach, see Sarah Stanbury, *The Visual Object of Desire in Late Medieval England* (Philadelphia: University of Pennsylvania Press, 2008).

42 Eamon Duffy, "Preface to the Second Edition," *Stripping of the Altars*, xix. In this preface, Duffy rejects the idea of a monolithic religious culture, and he uses the phrase "I quote" ironically, as an example of what he is *not* arguing.

43 For studies that have examined the politicized nature of hagiography, see Kathleen Ashley and Pamela Sheingorn, *Writing Faith: Text, Sign, and History in the Miracles of Sainte Foy* (Chicago: University of Chicago Press, 1999); and *A Companion to Middle English Hagiography*, ed. Sarah Salih (Cambridge: D.S. Brewer, 2006).

44 Bynum, *The Resurrection of the Body*; Brown, *The Cult of the Saints*; and Geary, *Furta Sacra*.

45 Lee Patterson, "Chaucer's Pardoner on the Couch," *Speculum* 76 (2001): 675–6; emphasis in original.
46 Dinshaw, *Chaucer's Sexual Poetics*, 163.
47 Sarah Salih, "Saints, Cults and Lives in Late Medieval England," in *A Companion to Middle English Hagiography*, ed. Sarah Salih (Cambridge: D.S. Brewer, 2006), 1. Some historians have made similar claims. Carole Rawcliffe observes that, when pilgrims arrived at a shrine, they were "at the very boundary where the sacred and the temporal met." See "Curing Bodies and Healing Souls: Pilgrimage and the Sick in Medieval East Anglia," in *Pilgrimage: The English Experience from Becket to Bunyan*, ed. Colin Morris and Peter Roberts (Cambridge: Cambridge University Press, 2002), 120. And for Simon Yarrow, miracles of ritual healing constitute a performance of "a sequence of symbolic actions and gestures that linked their everyday life with the divine as represented by the presence of a saint's relics." See *Saints and Their Communities* (Oxford: Clarendon Press, 2006), 18.
48 For the sections on relics that have most influenced literary scholars, see Bynum, *The Resurrection of the Body*, 59–114, 200–3.
49 On prodigies and sacramentals, see Caroline Walker Bynum, *Christian Materiality* (New York: Zone, 2011), 148–9, 159–62.
50 This is *not* to say that medieval theology did not understand Christ and Mary as embodied, but rather that their divine status was distinct from other saints, as medieval discussions of *latria*, *dulia*, and *hyperdulia* make clear. On *latria* and *dulia*, see Kathleen Kamerick, *Popular Piety and Art in the Late Middle Ages: Image Worship and Idolatry in England, 1350–1500* (New York: Palgrave, 2002), 32–4. Christ was divine as well as human; Mary was born without sin and, according to the doctrine of her assumption, ascended bodily into heaven. Pilgrims certainly share with Christ and Mary the possession of a body, but unlike Christ and Mary, other saints could not claim the same kind of divine status, and in that way, their relics have more in common with pilgrims than relics of Christ and Mary.
51 When the dreamer sees a knight who resembles both a knight and Piers Plowman, Faith explains to him that this knight is Jesus, who "wol juste in Piers armes, / In his helm and in his haubergeon, *humana natura* / In Piers paltok [jacket] the Plowman this prikiere shal ryde." See William Langland, *The Vision of Piers Plowman: A Critical Edition of the B-Text*, ed. A.V.C. Schmidt (London: Everyman, 1978; rpt. 2001), XVIII.22–3, 25. Christ similarly tells Satan that he is "in liknesse of a leode, that Lord am of hevene" (XVIII.357).
52 See Gibson, *The Theater of Devotion*, 1–18.
53 Michael Camille, *The Gothic Idol: Ideology and Image-Making in Medieval Art* (Cambridge: Cambridge University Press, 1989), 219.

54 Leslie Watkiss and Marjorie Chibnall, ed. and trans., *The Waltham Chronicle* (Oxford: Clarendon Press, 1994), 37. See the discussion in this chapter of Godwinson's donation.

55 Koopmans convincingly suggests that the cults themselves often responded to lay preference and that "[t]he powers inherent in moving miracle stories, some of the most forceful narratives people make, were multidimensional and directional" (*Wonderful to Relate*, 27). Maintaining and shaping the material surroundings of major cults is a slightly different matter, however, because it requires a large capital outlay – something that even the church or cathedral in question could not always afford. See, for instance, Kathy Lavezzo's discussion of the "great financier Aaron of Lincoln," who in 1183 loaned the monks at St Alban money to build a new shrine: "jactitabat se feretrum Beato Albano nostro fecisse, et ipsi, dehospitato, hospitium de pecunia sua praeparasse" ("The Minster and the Privy: Rereading the Prioress's Tale," *PMLA* 126 [2011]: 363). Lavezzo translates this line as follows: "Aaron 'boasted that it was he who had made the *window* for our Saint Alban and that from his own money he had prepared a home for the homeless saint' " (363; emphasis added). But it is clear that the "feretrum" in Walsingham's passage refers not to a window but to a cathedral feretory – a shrine. See Thomas Walsingham, *Gesta abbatum monasterii sancti Albani*, ed. H.T. Riley, 3 vols. (London: Longman, 1867), I, 193–4. It is important to note, too – as Lavezzo discusses throughout her article – that Aaron of Lincoln is a Jewish lender. His financial underwriting of the shrine-building is thus not based on his own devotional preferences.

56 On English miracle collections in the High Middle Ages, see Koopmans, *Wonderful to Relate*.

57 Bynum, *Christian Materiality*, 105.

58 Stanbury, *The Visual Object of Desire*, 5–7, 12–14, 19, 23–9.

59 For more on the *arma Christi*, see Lisa H. Cooper and Andrea Denny Brown, eds., *The Arma Christi in Medieval and Early Modern Material Culture: Objects, Representation, and Devotional Practice* (Burlington, VT: Ashgate, 2013); and see Anthony Bale, *The Jew in the Medieval Book: English Antisemitisms 1350–1500* (Cambridge: Cambridge University Press, 2006), 145–68, 175–81.

60 I owe this point to Alastair Minnis.

61 See, for instance, Ashley and Sheingorn, *Writing Faith*; and Thomas Head, *Hagiography and the Cult of Saints: The Diocese of Orléans, 800–1200* (Cambridge: Cambridge University Press, 1990).

62 For a recent discussion of this issue, see Shannon Gayk, *Image, Text, and Religious Reform in Fifteenth-Century England* (Cambridge: Cambridge University Press, 2010), 1–10.

63 On the differences between English and continental shrines, see Crook, *English Medieval Shrines*, 212, 257, and passim.

64 Indeed, as Hahn points out, Thiofrid's is the "only medieval treatise focused on the meaning of relics and specifically discusses reliquaries." "What Do Reliquaries Do for Relics?" 294.

65 *On the Relics of Saints* survives in one extant manuscript, probably in Guibert's hand: Paris BnF *lat.* 2900. It very likely did not circulate beyond Guibert's own monastery. See Jay Rubenstein, "Introduction," in *Monodies and On the Relics of Saints: The Autobiography and a Manifesto of a French Monk from the Time of the Crusades*, ed. and trans. Joseph McAlhany and Jay Rubenstein (New York: Penguin, 2011), vii–viii.

66 On the skeptical tradition of the early twelfth century and its relationship to the cult of relics, see E. Gordon Whatley, *The Saint of London: The Life and Miracles of St. Erkenwald* (Binghamton, NY: MRTS, 1989), 48, 41–56; and see the discussion in chapter 1.

67 Quoted in Whatley, *The Saint of London*, 48; emphasis added.

68 Michele Camillo Ferrari, who has worked more on Thiofrid of Echternach than any other contemporary scholar, suggests that Thiofrid was concerned to record conventional attitudes to relic cults. See Ferrari, "Lemmata sanctorum: Thiofrid d'Echternach et le discours sur les reliques au XIIe siècle," *Cahiers de civilisation médiévale* 38 (1995): 219. Arnold Angenendt has characterized *Flores epytaphii sanctorum* as "the most comprehensive interpretation" of the holiness and power of saints' relics. See "Relics and Their Veneration," in *Treasures of Heaven: Saints, Relics, and Devotion in Medieval Europe*, ed. Martina Bagnoli, Holger A. Klein, C. Griffith Mann, and James Robinson (New Haven, CT: Yale University Press, 2011), 22.

69 These ideas have become a commonplace among literary scholars and historians alike. See, for example, Dinshaw, *Chaucer's Sexual Poetics*, 163; Lee Patterson, "Chaucer's Pardoner on the Couch," 675–6; for other instances, see this chapter, n. 47.

70 Jones, "Old English Words for Relics of the Saints," 89–90.

71 Kathleen Ashley and Pamela Sheingorn indicate the importance of narrative to perceptions of holiness: "All authors of hagiographic texts 'write faith' in the sense that they construct and reconstruct saints' lives and miracles for believers." See *Writing Faith*, 1.

72 On Earl Harold's gifts of relics to Waltham priory, see Mary Frances Smith, Robin Fleming, and Patricia Halpin, "Court and Piety in Late Anglo-Saxon England," *Catholic Historical Review* 87 (2001): 587.

73 Watkiss and Chibnall, *The Waltham Chronicle*, 37.

74 See the discussion in chapter 4.

75 As Thomas explains in "The Cult of Saints' Relics," 110–11, the author of this list includes "great detail on the ornamentation of all the reliquaries it names, and its arrangement reveals no concern with the types of saint or of relics. Pride of place is accorded to St Osborne (Osburgh) because of the value of her shrine and the separate head-reliquary."
76 G.H. Martin, ed. and trans., *Knighton's Chronicle 1337–1396* (Oxford: Clarendon Press, 1995), 190–1.
77 On the conventions of *furta sacra*, see Geary, *Furta Sacra*, 108–28. And see the discussion of unsanctioned relic thefts in chapter 4.
78 Martin, *Knighton's Chronicle*, 190–3. On the head shrine of Hugh of Lincoln, see David A. Stocker, "The Mystery of the Shrines of St Hugh," in *St Hugh of Lincoln*, ed. H. Mayr-Harting (Oxford: Clarendon Press, 1987), 91.
79 On the political and ideological importance of *St Edmund and St Fremund*, see Fiona Somerset, " 'Hard is with seyntis forto make affray,' " in *John Lydgate*, ed. Larry Scanlon and James Simpson (Notre Dame, IN: Notre Dame University Press, 2006), 258–78.
80 Anthony Bale and A.S.G. Edwards, ed., *John Lydgate's* Lives of Ss Edmund and Fremund *and the* Extra Miracles of St Edmund (Heidelberg: Winter 2009), *EM*, 313–20. All subsequent citations are from this edition and will refer to *EF* (*Ss Edmund and Fremund*) and *EM* (*Extra Miracles*) and line number.
81 See for example André Wilmart, ed., "Edmeri Cantuariensis cantoris nova opuscula de sanctorum veneratione et obsecratione," *Revue des sciences religieuses* 15 (1935): 184–219, 354–79; and see the discussion in chapter 1.
82 "When he was at the celebrated monastery of Fécamp, [St Hugh of Lincoln] extracted by biting two small fragments of the bone of the arm of the most blessed lover of Christ, Mary Magdalen" ("Apud Fiscamni quoque insigne monasterium, de osse brachii beatissime Christi dilectricis Marie Magdalene duo mordicitus excussit frustra"). See Adam of Eynsham, *Magna Vita Sancti Hugonis*, ed. and trans. Decima L. Douie and Dom Hugh Farmer, 2 vols. (New York: Thomas Nelson and Sons, 1961), II, 168–9.
83 On Chaucer's Pardoner and the "power" and "grace" necessary to access relics, see chapter 4; on Lancelot's lack of "power" to access the Grail, see chapter 3.

1. Representing Relics

1 See Wulfstan, *Narratio metrica de S. Swithuno*, in *The Cult of St Swithun*, ed., trans., and comp. Michael Lapidge (Oxford: Oxford University Press,

2003), 335–552. It is likely that the establishment of Swithun's cult in 971 was motivated in part by the late tenth-century Benedictine reform in England – Æthelwold of Winchester was one of the most involved reformers, and Winchester, like many reformed abbeys, had a vested interest in relic cults. See David Rollason, *Saints and Relics in Anglo-Saxon England* (Cambridge, MA: Basil Blackwell, 1989), 174–86. I discuss some of these miracles in "Miracles of Justice," *Encyclopedia of Medieval Pilgrimage*, ed. Larissa J. Taylor et al. (Leiden: Brill, 2010), 438–40.

2 See R.W. Southern, *Medieval Humanism* (New York: Harper and Row, 1970), 158–80; Benedicta Ward, *Miracles and the Medieval Mind: Theory, Record and Event, 1000–1215* (Philadelphia: University of Pennsylvania Press, 1987), 4–9; and E. Gordon Whatley, *The Saint of London: The Life and Miracles of St. Erkenwald* (Binghamton, NY: MRTS, 1989), 41–56.

3 Rachel Koopmans, *Wonderful to Relate: Miracle Stories and Miracle Collecting in High Medieval England* (Philadelphia: University of Pennsylvania Press, 2011), 3–4.

4 See Eric W. Kemp, *Canonization and Authority in the Western Church* (Oxford: Oxford University Press, 1948), 97–106; and see André Vauchez, *Sainthood in the Later Middle Ages*, trans. Jean Birrell (Cambridge: Cambridge University Press, 1997), 22–32.

5 Quoted in Whatley, *The Saint of London*, 50.

6 William Langland, *Piers Plowman: A New Annotated Edition of the C-Text*, ed. Derek Pearsall (Exeter: University of Exeter Press, 1978; rpt. 2008), Prologue, 96–102.

7 The lines refer to images as well; as Pearsall notes, "Langland suggests that the miraculous relics and images for which offerings were enjoined were commonly false." See Langland, *Piers Plowman*, 48 n. 96–9. On votive offerings, see John Crook, *Medieval English Shrines* (Woodbridge, Suffolk: Boydell Press, 2011), 20–3.

8 This fifteenth-century proclamation is from the Sarum *Processionale* (Salisbury Cathedral MS. 148) and printed in C. Wordsworth, ed., *Ceremonies and Processions of the Cathedral Church of Salisbury* (Cambridge: Cambridge University Press, 1901), 33–42. As Wordsworth (42) explains, "the rubrick for the Feast of Relicks, in the month of July ... mentions the public reading on that festival": "Si tantum restat iter, fiat statio in ecclesia, ibique leguntur Nomina Reliquiarum in lingua materna" ("If some resist the journey, they shall remain in the church, where the Names of the Relics are read in the mother tongue"). The list opens with the following: "Right worshipfull maystres, ye shall vnderstande that in this church of sar' be of olde tyme of the zifte and bryngynge hyder of olde frendys and trewe

cristen men thes Relykes that folwith" (33). We might even understand the "lingua materna" as, metaphorically, "bryngynge hyder … thes relykes."

9 On the importance of Guibert's writings more generally and on Guibert's life, see Jay Rubenstein, *Guibert of Nogent: Portrait of a Medieval Mind* (New York: Routledge, 2002). Rubenstein argues that Guibert's discomfort with the cult of relics in general, rather than distaste for the physical body in particular, informed *On the Relics of Saints;* he discusses this relic treatise at 124–38.

10 As Hahn observes, "At the turn of the twelfth century, Thiofridus of Echternach writes *the only medieval treatise focused on the meaning of relics* and specifically discusses reliquaries … in effect, it was practice not theology that determined the shape of the cult of relics" ("What Do Reliquaries Do for Relics?" *Numen* 57 [2010]: 294; emphasis added).

11 Leslie Watkiss and Marjorie Chibnall, ed. and trans., *The Waltham Chronicle* (Oxford: Clarendon Press, 1994), 37.

12 See Eadmer of Canterbury's twelfth-century account of Oswald's translation, in which he advocates keeping Oswald's body away from those who are "less worthy than was suitable" ("minus dignis"). *Miracula S. Oswaldi,* in *Eadmer of Canterbury: Lives and Miracles of Saints Oda, Dunstan, and Oswald,* ed. and trans. Bernard J. Muir and Andrew J. Turner (Oxford: Oxford University Press, 2006), 300–1. I discuss this passage in more detail in the Introduction.

13 See Tim Tatton-Brown's discussion of the pilgrim's route at Canterbury, "Canterbury and the Architecture of Pilgrimage Shrines in England," in *Pilgrimage: The English Experience from Becket to Bunyan,* ed. Colin Morris and Peter Roberts (Cambridge: Cambridge University Press, 2002), 99–107; and see my discussion of shrine architecture in this chapter. Ben Nilson suggests a slightly different route. See "The Medieval Experience at the Shrine," in *Pilgrimage Explored,* ed. J. Stopford (York: York Medieval Press, 1999), 96, 101–2.

14 The so-called "speaking" reliquary was a shaped or body-part reliquary to which German scholars referred as "redende Reliquiare." Hahn queries whether a "speaking" reliquary (what she prefers to call a "shaped" reliquary) really " 'assumed the shape of its relic … feet, fingers, hands, legs, and heads' " (20). She argues, instead, that this type of reliquary very often misleads viewers about the kind of relic it contained. See "The Voices of the Saints: Speaking Reliquaries," *Gesta* 36 (1997): 20. Hahn makes a persuasive case for the *lack* of correspondence between these so-called speaking reliquaries and their contents.

15 Hahn, "The Voices of the Saints," 20.

16 Hahn, "The Voices of the Saints," 20.
17 Ellen M. Shortell, "Dismembering Saint Quentin: Gothic Architecture and the Display of Relics," *Gesta* 36 (1997): 32; emphasis added. Shortell refers to thirteenth-century Saint Quentin, but her comment about Gothic architecture applies to many English cathedrals as well, where relics were similarly translated to the eastern end of the building, behind the high altar.
18 Two manuscript illuminations of Edward the Confessor's tomb shrine, from the thirteenth-century *Estoire de Seint Aedward le rei* (Cambridge Library MS Ee. 3.59), depict a reliquary on top of Edward's portholed tomb shrine. John Crook identifies this reliquary as the feretory into which Edward's body was translated in 1241 – the illuminations are unlikely to resemble the tomb shrine as it would have appeared before this date. See "The Typology of Early Medieval Shrines," *Antiquaries Journal* 70 (1990): 52. On tomb shrines in general, see Crook, *English Medieval Shrines*, 191–204; Crook, "The Typology of Early Medieval Shrines," 50–2; Crook, *The Architectural Setting of the Cult of Saints in the Early Christian West, c.300–c.1200* (Oxford: Oxford University Press, 2000), 258–67; and Stephen Lamia, "The Cross and the Crown," in *Decorations for the Holy Dead*, ed. Stephen Lamia and Elizabeth Valdez del Álamo (Turnhout: Brepols, 2002), 50–1.
19 See Benedict of Peterborough's account in James C. Robertson, ed., *Materials for the History of Thomas Becket*, 7 vols. (London: Longman, 1875–85), II, 81.
20 Crook, *The Architectural Setting*, 254–5.
21 On Edward's early tomb shrine, see Lamia, "The Cross and the Crown," 42–8.
22 The location of some tomb shrines is nevertheless uncertain, as most of these monuments do not survive. Of those we do know about, St Swithun's original grave site was probably adjacent to the New Minster, accessible through the north door of the nave at Winchester (Nilson, "Medieval Experience," 97); by 1226, St Osmund's tomb shrine lay in the southwest side of the Trinity Chapel at Salisbury Cathedral, pending Osmund's official canonization in 1457. Before 1226, the shrine was possibly in the eastern end of the nave. See Crook, *English Medieval Shrines*, 197–204; Tatton-Brown, "The Burial Places of St Osmund," *Spire* 69 (1999): 20–1; and on Osmund's various monuments, see Daphne Stroud, "The Cult and Tombs of St Osmund at Salisbury," *Wiltshire Archaeological and Natural History Magazine* 78 (1984): 50–4. The relics of St Thomas Cantilupe were originally translated to a tomb shrine in the north transept of Hereford Cathedral in 1287 (Nicola Coldstream, "The Medieval Tombs and the

Shrine of Saint Thomas Cantilupe," in *Hereford Cathedral: A History*, ed. Gerald Aylmer and John Tiller [London: Hambledon Press, 2000], 323). In "The Mystery of the Shrines of St Hugh," in *St Hugh of Lincoln*, ed. H. Mayr-Harting (Oxford: Clarendon Press, 1987), 110, 123, David A. Stocker suggests that the early tomb shrine of St Hugh of Lincoln was in the northernmost chapel of the eastern transept.

23 R. Willis, *The Architectural History of York Cathedral* (London: Office of the Archaeological Institute, 1848), 51. On William of York's early tomb shrine, see also Christopher Wilson, *The Shrines of St William of York* (York: Yorkshire Museum, 1977), 2, 8–9, 12–17.

24 On these miracles, see Christopher Norton, *Saint William of York* (York: University of York Medieval Press, 2006), 150–69. For other tomb shrine cures – and some of the differences between cures "ad tumulum" and "ad feretrum" – see John Blair, "St Frideswide's," *Oxoniensia* 53 (1988): 248–9. Blair suggests that the "normal *locus* for invalids spending long-term vigils in the church was the grave, whereas the main liturgical focus of the cult was the feretory" (249).

25 Blair, "St Frideswide's," 247. This development is also outlined in Nicola Coldstream, "English Decorated Shrine Bases," *Journal of the British Archaeological Association* 129 (1976): 15–34; Crook, "The Typology of Early Medieval Shrines"; Ben Nilson, *Cathedral Shrines of Medieval England* (Woodbridge, Suffolk: Boydell Press, 1998), 45–6; and Tatton-Brown, "The Burial Places of St Osmund."

26 The tomb shrine of St Osmund of Salisbury is a notable exception, though here we might credit the survival of his tomb shrine with his late and drawn-out canonization. See especially Tatton-Brown, "The Burial Places of St Osmund."

27 Coldstream, "English Decorated Shrine Bases," 24–8. On Edward the Confessor's feretory shrine, see also J. G. O'Neilly and L. E. Tanner, "The Shrine of St Edward the Confessor," *Archaeologia* 100 (1966): 129–54. Though Edward's body was likely translated into the feretory in 1241 (see this chapter, n. 18), the reliquary was not moved to its location in the east end of the cathedral until 1269.

28 Vance uses these illuminations as the basis for his argument that the Pardoner's relics threaten the pilgrimage. See Eugene Vance, "Chaucer's Pardoner: Relics, Discourse, and Frames of Propriety," *New Literary History* 20 (1989): 739–40. On Edward the Confessor's tomb shrine, see Crook, *English Medieval Shrines*, 187–94.

29 Coldstream, "English Decorated Shrine Bases," 17; on the later popularity of niche bases over pillar bases, see Nilson, *Cathedral Shrines*, 45–6.

30 On niches and portholes, see especially Coldstream, "English Decorated Shrine Bases," 16; Crook, *The Architectural Setting*, 259, 266; Lamia, "The Cross and the Crown," 49–50; Nilson, *Cathedral Shrines*, 44–5; and Tatton-Brown, "Canterbury and Pilgrimage Shrine Architecture," 94.

31 Nilson, *Cathedral Shrines*, 46–54; and J. Charles Wall, *Shrines of British Saints* (London: Methuen, 1905), 19–25.

32 Nilson, *Cathedral Shrines*, 46.

33 I am grateful to Louise Hampson and to Andrew Morrison, curator of archaeology at the Yorkshire Museum, who in 2007 facilitated my visit to see this shrine base, which unfortunately was not on display. On shrine bases, see especially Coldstream, "English Decorated Shrine Bases"; see also Blair, "St Frideswide's," 246–54; Nilson, *Cathedral Shrines*, 34–46; and Wall, 1–34.

34 My sincere thanks to Dr John Crook, who in July 2007 took me on a tour of Winchester Cathdral, showing me the architectural history of St Swithun (and his various resting places).

35 David A. Stocker, "The Tomb and Shrine of Bishop Grosseteste in Lincoln Cathedral," in *England in the Thirteenth Century: Proceedings of the 1984 Harlaxton Symposium*, ed. W. M. Ormrod (Woodbridge, Suffolk: Boydell and Brewer, 1985), 146.

36 Tatton-Brown, "Canterbury and Pilgrimage Shrine Architecture," 101.

37 Nilson, *Cathedral Shrines*, 34–91. Nilson refutes earlier ideas that "shrines were intended to be visible from afar" and convincingly explains how various barriers (rood and quire screens, reredoses, and even shrine canopies and curtains) would have made visibility from the nave difficult if not impossible (81). See also Tatton-Brown, "Canterbury and Pilgrimage Shrine Architecture," 99–103.

38 See O'Neilly and Tanner, "The Shrine of St Edward the Confessor," 131, 150–4.

39 See Jocelin of Brakelond's account of Edmund's early thirteenth-century translation (possibly to the shrine depicted in British Library MS Harley 2278). H.E. Butler, ed. and trans., *The Chronicle of Jocelin of Brakelond* (London: Thomas Nelson and Sons, 1949), 106–16.

40 Coldstream, "English Decorated Shrine Bases," 22.

41 Often, watching chambers were built, and the shrines were kept locked whenever the relic custodians were not present. See Nilson, *Cathedral Shrines*, 52–3, 142; and Diana Webb, *Pilgrimage in Medieval England* (London: Hambledon and London, 2000), 85.

42 See Wall, 13–16, 19–24, 148–75.

43 Ogygius: He opened for us the reliquary ["aperuit thecam"] in which the holy man's body is said to lie ["in qua reliquum sancti viri corpus quiescere dicitur"].

MENEDEMUS: You saw the bones ["Vidisti ossa"]?
OGYGIUS: No, that's not permitted, nor would it be possible without the use of ladders ["Id quidem fas non est, nec liceret nisi admotis scalis"]. But the wooden chest conceals a golden chest; when this is drawn up by ropes, it reveals inestimable treasure.

(Desiderius Erasmus, *Peregrinatio religionis ergo*, in *Opera omnia Desiderii Erasmi Roterodami*, ed. L.-E. Halkin, F. Bierlaire, and R. Hoven, 20 vols. [Amsterdam: North Holland, 1969–92], Vol. I, Pt. 3, 490. The English translation is taken from Craig R. Thompson, trans., *Colloquies*, vols. 39–40 of *Collected Works of Erasmus*, 84 vols. [Toronto: University of Toronto Press, 1997], XL, 645, which I have modified slightly, rendering "thecam" as reliquary, rather than chest. Erasmus refers to the canopy that covered Becket's shrine – Becket's relics were hence contained in a "chest within a chest" [671].)

44 The *Customary of the Shrine of St Thomas* describes some of the Canterbury custodial duties, including ringing the bell to announce the opening of the shrine; keeping pilgrims out of the shrine area during lunch, reopening the shrine after lunch; and ensuring that pilgrims behave appropriately. See British Library MS Add. 59616, fols.1–4; and see Nilson, *Cathedral Shrines*, 128–34.
45 As Tatton-Brown suggests, "Canterbury and Pilgrimage Shrine Architecture," 101, the new surroundings of late medieval feretories accommodated a greater influx of pilgrims – but we might ask whether accommodating more pilgrims always resulted in greater lay access to the shrines, a problem Tatton-Brown's discussion of royal tombs and screens in fact indicates.
46 Frederick J. Furnivall and Walter G. Stone, ed., *The Tale of Beryn, with a Prologue of the Merry Adventure of the Pardoner with a Tapster at Canterbury*, EETS e.s. 105 (London: Kegan Paul, Trench, Trübner & Co., 1909), 6. The evidence suggests that pilgrims probably venerated feretories, floors, or even the massive stone shrine bases. Even Benedict of Peterborough is explicit that pilgrims kissed the tomb ("ad osculum sarcophagi"), not Becket's bones (*Materials for the History of Thomas Becket*, II, 81). For the unlikelihood that relics themselves were kissed, see Crook, *The Architectural Setting*, 31–2.
47 On notable and non-notable relics, see the following discussion in this chapter. The less important non-notable relics that Erasmus was allowed to see at Canterbury are in stark contrast to Canterbury's notable relics: "We were shown a *pallium*, silk to be sure, but coarse, without gold or jewels,

and there was a face-cloth ['sudarium'], soiled by sweat from his neck and preserving obvious spots of blood. These memorials of the plain living of olden times we gladly kissed" (*Peregrinatio religionis ergo*, 487–8; trans. Thompson, *Collected Works of Erasmus*, 642–3).

48 For pictures of these kinds of reliquaries, see especially Henk van Os; see also Bynum, who contrasts "so-called 'speaking reliquaries' … and crystal monstrances" with "house- or casket-shaped containers that more effectively masked precise contents." *Wonderful Blood: Theology and Practice in Late Medieval Northern Germany and Beyond* (Philadelphia: University of Pennsylvania Press, 2007), 13; on "speaking" reliquaries, see this chapter, n. 14. The Virgin's milk at Walsingham and the Holy Blood at Westminster are two more famous examples of relics of the Holy Family, both of which were displayed in smaller, glass reliquaries. On Walsingham, see J.C. Dickinson, *The Shrine of Our Lady of Walsingham* (Cambridge: Cambridge Univeristy Press, 1956). On the Holy Blood and its various pilgrimage sites and monstrance-like reliquaries, see especially Nicolas Vincent, *The Holy Blood* (Cambridge: Cambridge University Press, 2001), 137–85. On other occasions, notable relics were exposed: in the tenth century, St Cuthbert's body was revealed to the select few, for example (Rollason, *Saints and Relics*, 106); and Henry II was able to look at Petroc's relics (Karen Jankulak, *The Medieval Cult of St Petroc* [Woodbridge, Suffolk: Boydell and Brewer, 2000], 30).

49 Public showings ("ostensiones") were infrequent, and it is not clear whether these involved exposing the relics themselves or merely displaying the reliquaries. Scott Montgomery suggests that at most ostensiones, relics would have been displayed in their containers. See "Exposure of Relics," in *The Encyclopedia of Medieval Pilgrimage* (Leiden: Brill, 2010), 205.

50 John Wickham Legg and W.H. St John Hope, ed., *Inventories of Christchurch Canterbury* (Westminster: Archibald Constable & Co., 1902), 34.

51 On the evidence for a medieval hierarchy of relics, see especially Mark Spurrell, "The Promotion and Demotion of Whole Relics," *Antiquaries Journal* 80 (2000): 67–85. See also Crook, "Enshrinement of Local Saints in Francia and England," in *Local Saints and Local Churches in the Early Medieval West*, ed. Alan Thacker and Richard Sharpe (New York: Oxford University Press, 2002), 198, and *The Architectural Setting*, 31; Nicole Hermann-Mascard, *Les reliques des saints* (Paris: Éditions Klincksieck, 1975), 45ff (esp. 70); Nilson, *Cathedral Shrines*, 3–5; and Islwyn Geoffrey Thomas, "The Cult of Saints' Relics in Medieval England" (PhD diss., University of London, 1974), 22, 29ff. Thomas seems to take the existence of greater and lesser relics as a given; he does not, like Spurrell, define these extensively but rather uses the terms throughout, referring to St Edmund's hair and

nail-clipping, for example, as "lesser relics" (161) and noting that in many cases, chronicles do not attend to "smaller relics," instead, as at Evesham, "illustrat[ing] abundantly the veneration paid to the remains of the major saints of the abbey" (163–4).

52 Spurrell, "The Promotion and Demotion of Whole Relics," 67.

53 See the Introduction.

54 See Melvin Storm, "The Pardoner's Invitation: Quaestor's Bag or Becket's Shrine?" *PMLA* 97 (1982): 810–18. See also Vance, "Chaucer's Pardoner," 739–41; Daniel Knapp, "The Relyk of a Seint: A Gloss on Chaucer's Pilgrimage," *English Literary History* 39 (1972): 1–26; and William Kamowski, " 'Coillons,' Relics, Skepticism and Faith on Chaucer's Road to Canterbury: An Observation on the Pardoner's and the Host's Confrontation," *English Language Notes* 28 (1991): 1–8. And see my discussion in chapter 4.

55 See Victricius of Rouen, *De laude sanctorum*, ed. I. Mulders and R. Demeulenaere, CCSL 64 (Turnhout: Brepols, 1985), 84–6. The line translates literally to "wherever it is anything, it is whole." See Gillian Clark, "Victricius of Rouen: Praising the Saints," *Journal of Early Christian Studies* 7 (1999): 392. For a discussion of Victricius, see Clark, "Victricius," 365–76, and "Translating Relics: Victricius of Rouen and Fourth-Century Debate," *Early Medieval Europe* 10 (2001): 161–76; see also Alan Thacker, "Loca Sanctorum: The Significance of Place in the Study of the Saints." In Local Saints and Local Churches in the Early Medieval West, edited by Alan Thacker and Richard Sharpe, 1–43. New York: Oxford University Press, 2002. Carolyn Dinshaw cites Victricius's passage in her discussion of relics; see *Chaucer's Sexual Poetics* (Madison: University of Wisconsin Press, 1989), 163.

56 Dinshaw, *Chaucer's Sexual Poetics*, 162–3. Dinshaw importantly points out the superiority of body-part relics to contact relics, but she does not note the vast difference between, say, a finger relic and an entire body (or even a leg), emphasizing instead the potency of any fragment.

57 Dinshaw, *Chaucer's Sexual Poetics*, 162.

58 Crook, *Medieval English Shrines*, 259.

59 Christopher A. Jones, "Old English Words for Relics of Saints," *Forilegium* 26 (2009), explains that the term "*corpus* could designate not only an intact body but also a fragment of one." In the Canterbury list, however, it seems clear that the attempt is explicitly to render Swithun's relic as more impressive than what they have. "Corpus" relics comprise the first category of this list; tellingly, "caput" relics are listed afterwards – and Swithun's head is not among them. Including Swithun's head in the "corpus" category, then – when a "caput" category was available – suggests, as Jones allows, that "[r]elic-seekers in a position to know the difference may have preferred whole to partial bodies and corporeal to contact relics" (87).

60 On this point, see especially Cynthia Hahn, "The Voices of the Saints."
61 See Eugene A. Dooley, *Church Law on Sacred Relics* (Washington, DC: Catholic University of America Press, 1931), 4–5.
62 For Pecock's biography, see Wendy Scase, "Reginald Pecock," in *Authors of the Middle Ages*, ed. M.C. Seymour (Aldershot: Variorum, 1996), VIII, 1–146.
63 Kirsty Campbell, *The Call to Read: Reginald Pecock's Books and Textual Communities* (Notre Dame, IN: University of Notre Dame Press, 2010), 3–6, 8.
64 Reginald Pecock, *Repressor of Overmuch Blaming of the Clergy*, ed. C. Babington, 2 vols. (London: Longman, Green, Longman, and Roberts, 1860; rpt. Elibrion Classics, 2005). Hereafter, I will cite this text parenthetically by volume and page number. For Pecock's defense of images in this text, see Margaret Aston, *England's Iconoclasts.* Vol. 1, *Laws against Images* (Oxford: Oxford University Press, 1988), 147–54; and for a discussion of Pecock's attitude to shrines (and what this tells us about Wycliffite thought), see chapter 5.
65 For a discussion of this term, see Jones, "Old English Words for Relics of Saints," 86–8.
66 See J. Armitage Robinson, ed., *Flete's History of Westminster Abbey* (Cambridge: Cambridge University Press, 1909), 68–73. Some theologians, Guibert of Nogent and Thiofrid of Ecternach among them, argued strenuously against body-part relics of Christ (such as the Holy Blood) because such relics undermined the real presence in the Eucharist. On the Holy Blood and its various pilgrimage sites and reliquaries, see especially Bynum, *Wonderful Blood*, 76–81; Nicholas Vincent, *The Holy Blood*, 137–85; and see the discussion in chapter 3.
67 On the Anglo-Saxon treatment of types of relic, see Jones, "Old English Words for Relics of Saints."
68 See J. Raine, ed., *Historia Dunelmensis Scriptores Tres*, Surtees Society 9 (London: Published for the Surtees Society by J.B. Nichols and Son, 1839), ccccxxvi–ccccxxx.
69 Raine, *Historia Dunelmensis Scriptores Tres*, ccccxxvi.
70 Raine, *Historia Dunelmensis Scriptores Tres*, ccccxxvi.
71 Legg and Hope, *Inventories of Christchurch Canterbury*, 80. For a brief discussion of this list, see Crook, *English Medieval Shrines*, 258–9. "Corpus" functions similarly in other instances. In his twelfth-century chronicle of Glastonbury abbey, Dominic of Evesham describes Egwin's relics as "reliquias, scilicet corpus sancti Ecgwini" (qtd. in Thomas, "The Cult of Saints' Relics," 165). In an account of the translation of Boltoph, the body is described as "major pars corporis sancti Botulphi abbatis" (qtd. in Thomas,

"The Cult of Saints' Relics," 296). On the term "corpus" in early medieval England, see Jones, "Old English Words for Relics of Saints."

72 On the other relics designated "corpus" that were not in fact whole bodies, see Legg and Hope, *Inventories of Christchurch Canterbury*, 35–6.

73 Jones has understood this decision, rightly I think, as indicating that people may have preferred full-body to contact relics. See "Old English Words for Relics of Saints," 87; on Wilfrid's role in designing the crypt at Ripon, see Crook, "Enshrinement," 207.

74 See for example Durham Cathedral's 1383 list, printed in Joseph T. Fowler, ed., *Extracts from the Account Rolls of the Abbey of Durham Cathedral*, 3 vols., Surtees Society 100 (Durham: Published for the Surtees Society by Andrews & Co, 1899), II, 425–40. See also Legg and Hope, *Inventories of Christchurch Canterbury*, 29–43, 79–94.

75 Legg and Hope, *Inventories of Christchurch Canterbury*, 79.

76 Legg and Hope, *Inventories of Christchurch Canterbury*, 80.

77 Legg and Hope, *Inventories of Christchurch Canterbury*, 82.

78 Legg and Hope, *Inventories of Christchurch Canterbury*, 83.

79 See Legg and Hope, *Inventories of Christchurch Canterbury*, 33; Nilson, *Cathedral Shrines*, 57–62; and Wall, *Shrines of British Saints*, 19–25. *Pace* Seeta Chaganti, then, it seems unlikely that pilgrims would commonly have seen head (or bust) reliquaries; see *The Medieval Poetics of the Reliquary: Enshrinement, Inscription, Performance* (New York: Palgrave, 2008), 105.

80 See Fowler, *Extracts from the Account Rolls*, II, 425–40. See also Legg and Hope, *Inventories of Christchurch Canterbury*, 29–43, 79–94.

81 See George Oliver, ed., *Lives of the Bishops of Exeter* (Exeter: William Roberts, Broadgate: 1861), 320–76. Denis Bethell does point out that "the mention of an 'arm' or a 'head' in a relic list means a metal 'arm' or 'head' often containing a small bone only." See "The Making of a Twelfth-Century Relic Collection," in *Popular Belief and Practice*, ed. G.J. Cuming and Derek Baker (Cambridge: Cambridge University Press, 1972), 71; and see Hahn, "The Voices of the Saints."

82 Fowler, *Extracts from the Account Rolls*, II, 426

83 Fowler, *Extracts from the Account Rolls*, II, 427, 430, 431, 433, 439.

84 See especially Robert W. Barrett Jr, *Against All England: Regional Identity and Cheshire Writing, 1195–1656* (Notre Dame, IN: University of Notre Dame Press, 2009), 51–8; and Cynthia Turner Camp, "Inventing the Past in Henry Bradshaw's *Life of St Werburge*," *Exemplaria* 23 (2011): 244–67.

85 Camp, "Inventing the Past," 258.

86 Camp is absolutely right to observe that "the shrine, rather than the relics, comes to do the work of Werburgh's absent body" ("Inventing the Past,"

261), but I believe that in the context of Werburge's cult and Bradshaw's poem, both the shrine and language had already accomplished this representative work – *even before the body disintegrated*.

87 Carl Horstmann, ed., *The Life of Saint Werburge of Chester*, EETS o.s. 88 (Woodbridge, Suffolk: Boydell and Brewer; rpt. 2002), 1.3378–91. All citations are from this edition and will be cited parenthetically by book and line number.

88 Joseph T. Fowler, ed., *The Life of St Cuthbert in English Verse, c. A.D. 1450*, Surtees Society 87 (Durham: Published for the Surtees Society by Andrews & Co, 1891), ll. 3894, 3896–8. All quotations are from this edition and will be cited parenthetically by line number.

89 Carl Horstmann, ed., *Vita S. Etheldredae Eliensis*, in *Altenglische Legenden* (Heilbronn: Gebr. Henninger, 1881), 282–307. All quotations are from this edition and will be cited parenthetically by line number. For a discussion of this text, see Virginia Blanton, *Signs of Devotion: The Cult of St. Æthelthryth in Medieval England, 695–1615* (Philadelphia: University of Pennsylvania Press, 2007), 249–57.

90 E.O. Blake, ed., *Liber Eliensis* (London: Offices of the Royal Historical Society, 1962), 229, 228–31. Blanton, *Signs of Devotion*, 122–9, suggests that Æthelthryth's body may have decayed even before the 1106 translation.

91 These are not the only alterations to the source text. In fact, the *Etheldreda* poet seems to have conflated two miracles from the *Liber Eliensis* (Book I, Miracles 41 and 49). In Miracle 41, a maurading Viking is blinded and killed for attempting to see the saint (Blake, *Liber Eliensis*, 56); in Miracle 49, an unlucky priest ("presbiter infelix"), having returned to Ely with his evil compatriots, uses this hole first to determine whether Æthelthryth is incorrupt and then to ascertain the state of her clothing. He, his family, and two of his conspirators die as a result (*Liber Eliensis*, 60–1).

92 This is true in both of the miracles that were probably the *Etheldreda* poet's sources: the greedy and curious Dane of Miracle 41, "his eyes having been plucked out from his head by divine power, ended his unholy life right then and there" ("oculis ab eius capite divinitus avulsis, sacrilegam inibi vitam finivit") (Blake, *Liber Eliensis*, 56). The author later comments of this Dane that "immediately, as he made the tiny hole [in the sarcophagus], he parted with his eyes and his very life" ("confestim ut exiguam fecit fenestrellam oculos amisit et vitam") (*Liber Eliensis*, 60). The "presbiter infelix" of Miracle 49 similarly dies ("morte") (*Liber Eliensis*, 61) as a result of his crime ("scelus") (*Liber Eliensis*, 60).

93 See Blake, *Liber Eliensis*, 56, 60.

94 The account in the *Vita*, which emphasizes Cerdyke's inappropriate desire to peek at the saint's body, seems almost lascivious and is perhaps commensurate with an emphasis on the superiority of Benedictine monks over secular canons. It is likely that the poet is emphasizing the superiority of Benedictine monks over the secular canons who preceded them before the tenth-century reform. For this reading (as it applies to the *Liber Eliensis*, where both the offending cleric and his wife and family suffer death), see Rollason, *Saints and Relics*, 181–2.

95 For useful summaries of Guibert's general argument, see Thomas Head, *Hagiography: An Anthology* (New York: Routledge, 2001), 399–403; Jay Rubenstein, *Guibert of Nogent* (New York: Routledge, 2002), 124–31; 138–52, 158–72; Rubenstein, "Introduction," in *Monodies and On the Relics of Saints*, ed. and trans. Joseph McAlhany and Jay Rubenstein (New York: Penguin, 2011), xvi–xxvi; and Brian Stock, *The Implications of Literacy: Written Language and Models of Interpretation in the Eleventh and Twelfth Centuries* (Princeton, NJ: Princeton University Press, 1983), 244–52.

96 Rubenstein, "Introduction," in *Monodies and On the Relics of Saints*, xvii.

97 Guibert of Nogent, *De sanctis et eorum pigneribus*, ed. R.B.C. Huygens, Corpus Christianorum Continuatio Mediaevalis 127 (Turnholt: Brepols, 1993), I, 607–35. All quotations are from this edition and will be cited parenthetically by book and line number. The translation is from Thomas Head, *Medieval Hagiography: An Anthology* (New York: Garland, 2000), 419, which I will also cite parenthetically by page number.

98 Iohannis Wyclif, *Tractatus de Ecclesia*, ed. Iohann Loserth and F.D. Matthew (London: Trübner, 1886), 465. And see the discussion of Wyclif in chapter 5.

99 Translation Stock, *The Implications of Literacy*, 250.

100 Stock, *The Implications of Literacy*, 244.

101 For this argument as it pertains to Guibert, see especially Lisa Robeson, "Writing as Relic," *Oral Tradition* 14 (1999): 437–9.

102 Stock, *The Implications of Literacy*, 249.

103 Steven Kruger, *The Spectral Jew: Conversion and Embodiment in Medieval Europe* (Minneapolis: University of Minnesota Press, 2006), 41.

104 For Guibert as critical of clerical abuses and the corruption of popular religious practices, see Colin Morris, "A Critique of Popular Religion," in *Popular Belief and Practice*, ed. G.J. Cuming and Derek Baker (Cambridge: Cambridge University Press, 1972), 55–60.

105 On this treatise, see especially Michele Camillo Ferrari, "Lemmata sanctorum: Thiofrid d'Echternach et le discours sur les reliques au XIIe siècle," *Cahiers de civilisation médiévale* 38 (1995): 215–25; and see Ferrari,

"Gold und Asche: Reliquie und Reliquiare als Medien in Thiofrid von Echternachs *Flores epytaphii sanctorum*," in *Reliquiare im Mittelalter*, ed. Bruno Reudenbach and Gia Toussaint (Berlin: Akademie Verlag, 2005), 61–74. See also Gernot R. Wieland, "The Hermeneutic Style of Thiofrid of Echternach," in *Anglo-Latin and Its Heritage: Essays in Honour of A.G. Rigg on His 64th Birthday*, ed. Siân Echard and Gernot R. Wieland (Turnhout: Brepols, 2001), 27–47.

106 Thiofrid of Ecternach, *Flores Epytaphii Sanctorum*, ed. Michele Camillo Ferrari, *Corpus Christianorum Continuatio Mediaevalis* CXXXIII (Turnholt: Brepols, 1996). All quotations are from this edition and will be cited parenthetically by book number, chapter number, and line numbers. I gratefully acknowledge Drew Jones for his help in translating this text; any errors that remain are my own.

107 See especially *liber* II, chapters two and three. In II 3, Thiofrid describes relics as "sic preciosi pulueris thesaurus" (13). See also Albert Blaise, *Lexicon latinitatis Medii Aevi* (Turnhout: Brepols, 1975), s.v. "thesaurus." Blaise identifies "thesaurus" as "trésor," but also as "reliques, corps saint," or as the "trésor d'une église."

108 See also Ferrari, "Lemmata sanctorum," 220.

109 For a recent discussion of the late medieval image debate, see Shannon Gayk, *Image, Text, and Religious Reform in Fifteenth-Century England* (Cambridge: Cambridge University Press, 2010), 1–14.

110 Witness, for instance, Henry Knighton's account of the destruction of a statue of St Catherine. This image is said to be "carved and painted in honour of St Catherine"; the heretics who disfigure and burn it, Richard the chaplain and William Smith, refer to the image as Catherine herself. See G. H. Martin, ed. and trans., *Knighton's Chronicle* (Oxford: Clarendon Press, 1995), 296–97. The close relationship between saint and image resulted in anxieties "that simple people would confuse an image with its prototype" (Kathleen Kamerick, *Popular Piety and Art in the Late Middle Ages: Image Worship and Idolatry in Enland, 1350–1500* [New York: Palgrave, 2002], 119). On the lifelike quality of some images, see Sarah Stanbury, *The Visual Object of Desire in Late Medieval England* (Philadelphia: University of Pennsylvania Press, 2008), 25–7.

111 Kamerick, *Popular Piety and Art*, 1.

112 While some smaller shrines illustrate the life and death of a saint – the many limoges reliquaries of Thomas Becket are cases in point, examples of which survive at the Louvre and at the Victoria and Albert Museum, among many others – feretories tended not to include that kind of narrative detail, though they did sometimes include images or figurative

sculpture, even (apparently) obscene and secular images. See Crook, *English Medieval Shrines*, 260, 276, and 282.

113 On translation, metaphor, and clothing, see Dinshaw, *Chaucer's Sexual Poetics*, 137–41.

2. The Commonplaces of Relic Discourse

1 On the dating and authorship of the *Extra Miracles*, see Anthony Bale and A.S.G. Edwards, ed., *John Lydgate's* Lives of Ss Edmund and Fremund *and the* Extra Miracles of St Edmund (Heidelberg: Winter 2009), 25–8; see also Bale, "St Edmund in Fifteenth-Century London," in *St Edmund, King and Martyr: Changing Images of a Medieval Saint*, ed. Anthony Bale (York: York Medieval Press, 2009), 147–9.

2 All parenthetical citations refer to Bale and Edwards, *John Lydgate's* Lives of Ss Edmund and Fremund. *EF* denotes the *Lives*; *EM* the *Extra Miracles*.

3 For Lydgate's support of the Lancastrian regime, see Karen A. Winstead, *John Capgrave's Fifteenth Century* (Philadelphia: University of Pennsylvania Press, 2007), 116–38.

4 Cynthia Hahn, "Seeing and Believing: The Construction of Sanctity in Early-Medieval Saints' Shrines," *Speculum* 72 (1997): 1087.

5 This is not to say that *only* these sorts of documents affirm the saint's presence at his or her shrine. As Rachel Koopmans points out, miracle stories often have a "particularized flavor. Dunstan was here. Dunstan helped me … Saints might not always be seen or sensed, but they live out posthumous lives in which they continue to care about the people on earth." See Koopmans, *Wonderful to Relate: Telling and Collecting Miracle Stories in High Medieval England* (Philadelphia: University of Pennsylvania Press, 2011), 23. These oral and, as Koopmans suggests, personal stories – which are beyond the purview of this study – also contribute to the perception of a saint as present ("Dunstan helped me") and powerful.

6 For a detailed discussion of development of English shrine architecture, see chapter 1.

7 On the increase in production of hagiography and miracle collections in the twelfth century, see Koopmans, *Wonderful to Relate*, 92–138; and Simon Yarrow, *Saints and Their Communities* (Oxford: Oxford University Press, 2006), 7–10. There are many reasons for this increase; Yarrow cites in particular the 1091 translation of six abbots of St Augustine's, Canterbury, to new shrines at the east end of the abbey; and the famous martyrdom of Thomas Becket in 1170 and his subsequent translation in 1220 (7–8).

It seems likely that the increasing importance of papal canonization also played a role in the hagiographic production of this period; see chapter 1.

8 In "The Alleged Incorruption of the Body of St Edmund," Antonia Gransden is interested in the actual preservation of Edmund's and Cuthbert's bodies, which is not my concern here. Nevertheless, her observation that Jocelin's and Simeon's accounts "have such realistic details that they would seem to be authentic" squares with my own reading of these narratives as representing an immediate, emotional, and unprecedented event. At his 1095 translation, for instance, Edmund's coffin "was publicly displayed open at Bury." Clearly, then, Jocelin and his fellow monks were reasonable in expecting to view the body. What is more, Gransden suggests that Baldwin displayed the body openly because the written authority of Abbo Fleury "proved inadequate; Abbo's authority needed to be underpinned by visual proof." See Gransden, "The Alleged Incorruption of the Body of St Edmund, King and Martyr," *Antiquaries Journal* 74 (1994): 135, 143, 149.

9 One wonders whether the widespread practice of enshrinement (and the elision of shrine and saint) by the fourteenth century contributed to how few relic treatises were composed in the later period. This hypothesis is untestable but nonetheless attractive, given that in the absence of controversy, fewer justifications or arguments for or against enshrinement may have been necessary. On earlier arguments, see the discussion of Guibert of Nogent and Thiofrid of Echternach in chapter 1, and see the discussion of thirteenth-century blood relic treatises – a very controversial topic in that period – in chapter 3.

10 Gransden, "The Alleged Incorruption of the Body of St Edmund," 135.

11 For a detailed discussion of the methodology of Part I of this book, see the Introduction and the opening of chapter 1.

12 On exhuming the saint's body at night as a common practice, see Ben Nilson, *Cathedral Shrines of Medieval England* (Woodbridge, Suffolk: Boydell and Brewer, 1998), 26–30. For St Frideswide's nighttime translation on 12 February 1180, see Benedicta Ward, *Miracles and the Medieval Mind: Theory, Record, and Event, 1000–1215* (Philadelphia: University of Pennsylvania Press, 1987), 83. On William of Norwich, see Thomas of Monmouth, *The Life and Miracles of St William of Norwich*, ed. and trans. A. Jessopp and M. R. James (Cambridge: Cambridge University Press, 1896), 122.

13 Richard Hamer and Vida Russel, ed., *Supplementary Lives in Some Manuscripts of the Gilte Legende*, EETS o.s. 315 (Oxford: Oxford University Press, 2000), 318; emphasis added.

14 John Mirk, *Festial*, ed. Susan Powell, 2 vols., EETS o.s. 334 (London: Oxford University Press, 2009), I, 180–1.

15 From *Annales Paulini*, qtd. in E. Gordon Whatley, ed. and trans., *The Saint of London: The Life and Miracles of St Erkenwald* (Binghamton, NY: Medieval & Renaissance Texts & Studies, 1989), 204; trans. 66–7.

16 The practice of exhuming the body in secret is in contrast to Patrick Geary's description of the earlier period on the continent, where, Geary explains, "at a *public* ceremony, they open the tomb with reverence and remove the body." See *Furta Sacra: Thefts of Relics in the Central Middle Ages* (Princeton, NJ: Princeton University Press, 1990), 12; emphasis added.

17 On Cuthbert, see Dominic Marner, *St Cuthbert: His Life and Cult in Medieval Durham* (Toronto: University of Toronto Press, 2000).

18 Simeon of Durham, *Symeonis monachi Opera omnia: Histoira ecclesiae dunhelmensis*, ed. Thomas Arnold, 2 vols. (London: Longman, 1882), I, 249. All citations are from this edition and will be cited parenthetically by page number.

19 Danish invaders killed Edmund, king of East Anglia, on 20 November 869. He was regarded as a martyr and defender of England from pagan Danes. See Bale, "Introduction," in *St Edmund, King and Martyr*, 1–4. For the history of Edmund's cult at Bury, see Yarrow, *Saints and Their Communities*, 24–62; and see Bale, "Introduction," 1–25. Yarrow dates Jocelin's account to 1204 (29). For an examination of how Jocelin describes the body itself, see Gransden, "The Alleged Incorruption of the Body of St Edmund," 153–5.

20 "Abbas autem predixit conuentui, ut se prepararent ad transferendum corpus nocte." H.E. Butler, ed., *The Chronicle of Jocelin of Brakelond* (London: Thomas Nelson and Sons, 1949), 112. All citations are from this edition and will be cited parenthetically by page number.

21 "loculum cum corpore … inclusus est loculus in feretro" (113).

22 "Putabamus omnes, quod abbas uellet loculum ostendere populo in octauis festi et reportare sanctum corpus coram omnibus; set male seducti sumus."

23 John James Munro, ed., *John Capgrave's Lives of St Augustine and St Gilbert of Sempringham, and a Sermon*, EETS o.s. 140 (London: Kegan Paul, Trench, Trübner & Co., 1910; rpt. 1971). All citations are from this edition and will be cited parenthetically by page number. Capgrave translated this prose *vita* in 1451 at the behest of Nicholas Reysby of Sempringham, then head of the English Gilbertines. This work has received little attention. For a recent overview, focusing on virgnity in the text, see Winstead, *John Capgrave's Fifteenth Century*, 100–3.

24 Winstead, *John Capgrave's Fifteenth Century*, 5. Winstead, 1–17, discusses Capgrave's life, education, and political affiliations (or lack thereof).
25 Winstead, *John Capgrave's Fifteenth Century*, 10–11.
26 See Gail McMurray Gibson, *The Theater of Devotion: East Anglian Drama and Society in the Late Middle Ages* (Chicago: University of Chicago Press, 1989), 18, 19–46.
27 Gibson, *The Theater of Devotion*, 18.
28 Some have argued that Capgrave's source for his *Life of St Gilbert* is *The Book of Saint Gilbert*, which survives in two manuscripts dating from the early and mid-thirteenth century. Assuming this to be the case, in his version of the translation ceremony, Capgrave closely follows his source text; see Raymonde Foreville and Gillian Keir, ed. and trans., *The Book of Saint Gilbert* (Oxford: Oxford University Press, 1987), 188–95. But for the argument that, in fact, Capgrave followed a fourteenth-century Gilbertine compilation throughout his rendition, see Jane C. Fredeman, "John Capgrave's Life of St. Gilbert of Sempringham," *Bulletin of the John Rylands University Library of Manchester* 55 (1972): 114–23. Fredeman suggests that many of the changes to the thirteenth-century redactions were the work of Capgrave's fourteenth-century predecessor (123), though the version of the translation in the fourteenth-century redaction is still very close to what Capgrave wrote.
29 That within the confines of this narrative, documentary evidence is sufficient proof of the state of Gilbert's body may stem in part from the growing importance of papal canonization. *The Book of Saint Gilbert*, for instance, comprises in part a collection of the miracles sent as a dossier to Rome, where papal delegates would not have had the opportunity to interact with or view the relics.
30 Joseph T. Fowler, ed., *Extracts from the Account Rolls of the Abbey of Durham Cathedral*, 3 vols., Surtees Society 100 (Durham: Published for the Surtees Society by Andrews & Co, 1899), II, 425–40 (427, 430, 431, 433, 434).
31 On the occlusion of many notable relics, see the discussion in chapter 1.
32 On the dating and authorship of the *Extra Miracles*, see this chapter, n. 1. *Extra Miracles* is itself a modern, editorial title.
33 Carl Horstmann, ed., *The Lives of St. Edmund and St. Fremund*, in *Altenglische Legenden* (Heilbronn: Gebr. Henninger, 1881), 376–440 (4.167–8).
34 All parenthetical citations refer to Bale and Edwards, *John Lydgate's* Lives of Ss Edmund and Fremund *and the* Extra Miracles of St Edmund. See this chapter, nn. 1–2.
35 For a discussion of Wycliffite responses to shrines and to relic discourse, see chapter 5.

36 See Bale and Edwards, "Introduction," in *John Lydgate's* Lives of Ss Edmund and Fremund, 19–20.

37 From a talk Nolan gave at the Thirteenth Biennial Congress of the New Chaucer Society. Qtd. in Larry Scanlon and James Simpson, ed., *John Lydgate* (Notre Dame, IN: University of Notre Dame Press, 2006), 4.

38 Derek Pearsall, *John Lydgate* (London: Kegan Paul, 1970), 1.

39 For a more complete list of Lydgate's influential patrons, see Robert J. Meyer-Lee, *Poets and Power from Chaucer to Wyatt* (Cambridge: Cambridge University Press, 2007), 50–4. Meyer-Lee also suggests that, *pace* Seth Lerer, Lydgate probably did not venture beyond the cloister very often (51).

40 On the Lancastrian regime and orthodoxy, see Paul Strohm, *England's Empty Throne Usurpation and Textual Legitimation, 1399–1422* (New Haven, CT: Yale University Press, 1998); both Scott-Morgan Straker and Maura Nolan sound cautionary notes about Lydgate as a propagandist: "Lydgate was capable of adopting a wide array of attitudes toward his patrons and of making complex statements to and about them. The familiar notion of the Lancastrian Lydgate imposes a false uniformity and simplicity onto those statements, preventing us from correctly assessing Lydgate's importance as a political writer" (Straker, "Propaganda, Intentionality, and the Lancastrian Lydgate," in *John Lydgate*, eds. Larry Scanlon and James Simpson [Notre Dame, IN: University of Notre Dame Press, 2006], 98). However, as the following discussion will make clear, I am not interested in the political or propagandistic importance of *Edmund and Fremund*, but rather, specifically, in Lydgate's depiction of Edmund's shrine and conflation of this monument with the saint's relics.

41 Maura Nolan, *John Lydgate and the Making of Public Culture* (Cambridge: Cambridge University Press, 2005), 3.

42 See A.S.G. Edwards, ed. and intro., *The Life of St Edmund, King and Martyr: A Facsimile* (London: British Library, 2004). On the dating and production of this manuscript, see Pearsall, *John Lydgate*, 26–7, 280–3. See also A.S.G. Edwards, "John Lydgate's *Lives of SS Edmund and Fremund*: Politics, Hagiography and Literature," in *St Edmund, King and Martyr: Changing Images of a Medieval Saint*, ed. Anthony Bale (York: York Medieval Press, 2009), 133–4; Edwards, "Introduction," in *The Life of St Edmund*, 8–15; Kathleen L. Scott, *Later Gothic Manuscripts, 1390–1490*, 2 vols (London: H. Miller, 1996), II, 225–9; and Bale and Edwards, *John Lydgate's* Lives of Ss Edmund and Fremund, 12.

43 Jennifer Sisk, "Lydgate's Problematic Commission: A Legend of St Edmund for Henry VI," *Journal of English and Germanic Philology* 109 (2010): 351. For an overview of recent approaches to Lydgate, see Anthony Bale,

"Twenty-First Century Lydgate," *Modern Philology* 105 (2008): 698–704; see also Bale, "Introduction," 18–25.

44 See Fiona Somerset, " 'Hard is with seyntis forto make affray,' " in *John Lydgate*, ed. Larry Scanlon and James Simpson (Notre Dame, IN: University of Notre Dame Press, 2006), 258–78. Somerset gives us a deft reading of St Edmund as an exemplar for Henry VI. See also Katherine J. Lewis, "Edmund of East Anglia, Henry VI and Ideals of Kingly Masculinity," in *Holiness and Masculinity in the Middle Ages*, ed. Patricia H. Cullum and Katherine J. Lewis (Cardiff: University of Wales Press, 2004), 158–73.

45 John Ganim, "Lydgate, Location, and the Poetics of Exemption," in *Lydgate Matters: Poetry and Material Culture in the Fifteenth Century*, ed. Lisa H. Cooper and Andrea Denny-Brown (New York: Palgrave, 2008), 167.

46 Sisk, "Lydgate's Problematic Commission," 352.

47 Jocelin's account hence records the change in practice in the twelfth century. See Gransden, "The Alleged Incorruption of the Body of St Edmund," 143–50.

48 There has been some disagreement about the dating of Bradshaw's poem. The general consensus is that the work dates to between 1506 and 1513, but Catherine Sanok has argued for dating Bradshaw's text somewhat earlier, *ca.* 1485–93. See *Her Life Historical: Exemplarity and Female Saints' Lives in Late Medieval England* (Philadelphia: University of Pennsylvania Press, 2007), 204 n. 1. For an explanation of the early sixteenth-century dates, see Robert W. Barrett Jr, *Against All England: Regional Identity and Cheshire Writing, 1195–1656* (Notre Dame, IN: Notre Dame University Press, 2009), 230 n. 34.

49 This interpretation extends into contemporary scholarship; in his excellent work on Bradshaw, for instance, Barrett remarks that "For Bradshaw's townsfolk, the social power of *the holy body* remains intact [after a fire], if not heightened: 'For it is well knowen, by olde antiquite / Sith *the holy shryne* came to their presence, / It hath ben their comfort and gladnes, truly' " (Barrett, *Against All England*, 44, emphasis added). Literally, the passage Barrett cites conveys the information that the townsfolk still venerate the shrine, which metaphorically represents the body.

50 Carl Horstmann, ed., *The Life of Saint Werburge of Chester*, EETS o.s. 88 (Woodbridge, Suffolk: Boydell and Brewer; rpt. 2002), 1.127–33. All citations are from this edition and will be cited parenthetically by book and line number. On the relationship between these sources and Bradshaw's poem, see Carl Horstmann, "Introduction," *The Life of Saint Werburge of Chester*, xvi–xxvi. Horstmann emphasizes Bradshaw's skill as a compiler and claims that it would be "unjust" to consider him a "mere translator" (xxvi).

51 See Horstmann, "Introduction," *The Life of Saint Werburge of Chester*, xxvi.

52 George Orwell, "Politics and the English Language," http://mla.stanford.edu/Politics_&_English_language.pdf, 2–3, accessed 10 January 2011.

53 Orwell, "Politics and the English Language," 3.

54 For a similar reading of this line, see Cynthia Turner Camp, "Inventing the Past in Henry Bradshaw's *Life of St Werburge*," *Exemplaria* 23 (2011): 260.

55 On Werburge's cult and regional identity creation, see Barrett, *Against All England*, 27–58; and on this cult and national identity formation, see Sanok, *Her Life Historical*, 89–105.

56 For a discussion of Wycliffite texts that present ostentatious shrines rather than saints as troublesome, see chapter 5.

57 On Saracens in medieval art, and on the importance of the turban, or "tortil," in identifying them, see Kathy Cawsey, "Disorienting Orientalism: Finding Saracens in Strange Places in Late Medieval English Manuscripts," *Exemplaria* 21 (2009): 382–4. Cawsey does not discuss the many illuminations of Edmund's shrine and its miracles. These illustrations frequently depict misbehaving Christians or Danes as Saracen, underscoring Cawsey's point that the text's originary narrative focuses on religion rather than on race or geography.

58 For a discussion of the attempted thefts in Harley 2278, which include a would-be thief who attempts to bite off a piece of Edmund's shrine, see chapter 4.

59 See Shannon Gayk, *Image, Text, and Religious Reform in Fifteenth-Century England* (Cambridge: Cambridge University Press, 2010), 1–14. On Lollard responses to images in particular, see Aston, *England's Iconoclasts.* Vol. 1, *Laws against Images* (Oxford: Oxford University Press, 1988), 96–159; and see the discussion in chapter 5.

60 Many orthodox reformers were committed to exploring the representative function of images, and some were invested in the significance of shrines as well. Reginald Pecock is one such example, on whose discussion of images and shrines, see chapter 5. For the growing discussion of vernacular theology and the late medieval image debate, see Kirsty Campbell, *The Call to Read: Reginald Pecock's Books and Textual Communities* (Notre Dame, IN: University of Notre Dame Press, 2010). See also Vincent Gillespie, "Vernacular Theology," in *Middle English*, ed. Paul Strohm (Oxford: Oxford University Press, 2007), 401–20; *Wycliffite Controversies*, ed. Mishtooni Bose and J. Patrick Hornbeck II (Turnhout: Brepols, 2011); and *After Arundel*, ed. Vincent Gillespie and Kantik Ghosh (Turnhout: Brepols, 2012).

61 On Erkenwald's cult, see Whatley, *The Saint of London*; Frank Grady, *Representing Righteous Heathens in Late Medieval England* (New York: Palgrave,

2005), 40–1; and Ruth Morse, "Introduction," in *Saint Erkenwald*, ed. Ruth Morse (Cambridge: D.S. Brewer, 1975), 13–15.

62 On the dating and authorship of this text, see Whatley, *The Saint of London*, 36–40.

63 On the changing religious climate in the twelfth century, see chapter 1.

64 Whatley, *The Saint of London*, 60–5, argues that Arcoid may well have undertaken the entire project in order to raise money for the construction of the reliquary.

65 *Miracula Sancti Erkenwaldi*, in Whatley, *The Saint of London*, 100–65 (132–3). All quotations are from this edition and will be cited parenthetically by page number.

66 This section represents another of Bradshaw's original creations. See Horstmann, "Introduction," *The Life of Saint Werburge of Chester*, xxvi.

67 On sanctuary, see David Hall, "The Sanctuary of St Cuthbert," in *St Cuthbert, His Cult and His Community to AD 1200*, ed. Gerald Bonner, David Rollason, and Clare Stancliffe (Woodbridge, Suffolk: Boydell and Brewer, 1989), 425–36.

68 On the relationship between Edmund's cult and maintaining Bury's liberty (or "banleuca"), see Anthony Bale, "Introduction," 7–8.

69 "Seyntuarye" is somewhat ambiguous in this case, as it could refer both to the area surrounding Edmund's shrine and to the right of sanctuary *at* a saint's shrine. I am taking "seyntuarye" to refer to the right of sanctuary. However, were we to understand "shrine" or "shrine area" here, we could take Lydgate as eliding, yet again, the shrine and the saint.

70 "lacrimabili gemitu, corde contrito et humiliato uultu."

71 For the importance of faith, see Victricius of Rouen, "In Praise of the Saints," ed. and trans. Philippe Buc, in *Medieval Hagiography: An Anthology*, ed. Thomas Head (New York: Routledge, 2001), 31–51 (43–5); Gregory of Tours, *Glory of the Martyrs*, ed. and trans. Raymond Van Dam (Liverpool: Liverpool University Press, 1988), 27, 44; and Guibert of Nogent, trans. Head, 410–12. Victricius specifies that "faith spurns arguments" and that "these things are to be seen *and not questioned*" (45; emphasis added). The *Gilte Legende* similarly characterizes seven blind men who are said to have been healed by Edward the Confessor. These men travel to Edward's "tombe," where they pray "hertely," and the people who take pity on them "knelid downe fulle devoutely and praied for them to God and to the holy seynte" (28). So, too, Gerald of Wales specifies that "whoever goes to the holy man's tomb, cleansed by penance and confession, will, whatever their illness, recover the joy of health" ("quicunque tumbam viri sancti in eadem ecclesia, vera poenitentia et confessione purgatus ac devotus

adierit, quacunque obsessus aegritudine, sanitatis guadia recuperabit"). See Gerald of Wales, "Vita Remigii," in *Giraldi Cambrensis Opera*, 8 vols., ed. J.S. Brewer et al., Rolls Series 21 (London: Longman, Green, Longman, and Roberts, 1861–91), VII, 28. For the translation, see Robert Bartlett, "The Hagiography of Angevin England," in *Thirteenth Century England V: Proceedings of the Newcastle upon Tyne Conference 1993*, ed. P.R. Cross and S.D. Lloyd (Woodbridge, Suffolk: Boydell Press, 1995), 41.

72 Mary S. Serjeantson, ed., *Bokenham's Legendys of Hooly Wummen*, EETS o.s. 206 (London: Oxford University Press, 1938), l. 155.

73 Walter W. Skeat, ed., *Joseph of Arimathie: The Romance of the Seint Graal, or Holy Grail* (Felinfach: Llanerch, 1992), "The Lyfe of Ioseph of Armathia," ll. 353–6.

74 André Wilmart, ed., "Edmeri Cantuariensis cantoris nova opuscula de sanctorum veneratione et obsecratione," *Revue des sciences religieuses* 15 (1935): 184–219, 354–79. Eadmer's homily, *Sententia de memoria sanctorum quos veneraris*, survives in a single manuscript (Christ Church Canterbury MS 371) which dates from the early twelfth century, sometime between 1124 and 1141 (Wilmart, "Edmeri Cantuariensis cantoris," 185). Jay Rubenstein divides the *Sententia* into three sections: 1) Saints can help in time of need; 2) Saints are advocates for everyday commemoration and continual supplication "before the particular relics that a community possesses"; 3) The saints remember those who supplicate before them. See "Liturgy against History: The Competing Visions of Lanfranc and Eadmer of Canterbury," *Speculum* 74 (1999): 30–3.

75 "Cum enim isti diebus ac noctibus insistunt laudibus dei pro gloria eorum, profecto credendum est illos per singula momenta offerre deo preces pro salute istorum." Eadmer, *Sententia*, ll. 23–5.

76 "Totis corporibus ante eorum reliquias prosternuntur, flexis genibus in humum usque deiciuntur, pronis uultibus incuruantur supplices eorum: – et ipsi ante deum ad haec rigidi starent, auditum auerterent, horum aliquid non curarent? – Quis hoc dixerit? Itaque supplicum deuotio non erit inutilis, non erit uana, non erit a gratia uacua." Eadmer, *Sententia*, ll. 25–30. Trans. Whatley, *The Saint of London*, 45–6.

77 Eadmer, *Sententia*, l. 31.

78 "Fides igitur qua credatur eos sibi posse subuenire firma existat; spes qua de bonitate illorum ut subuenire uelint praesumatur non deficiat; caritas in dilectionem ac deuotionem gaudii ac laudis ipsorum non tepescat." Eadmer, *Sententia*, ll. 36–9.

79 *De sanctis et eorum pigneribus*, ed. R.B.C. Huygens, Corpus Christianorum Continuatio Mediaevalis CXXVII (Turnholt: Brepols, 1993), I, 259. All

quotations are from this edition and will be cited parenthetically by book and line number. Translations are from Thomas Head, *Medieval Hagiography: An Anthology* (New York: Garland, 2000), 411, which I will also cite parenthetically by page number.

80 See my "Shrine Keepers," in *The Encyclopedia of Medieval Pilgrimage*, ed. Larissa J. Taylor et al. (Leiden: Brill, 2010), 595–7; and Eric W. Kemp, *Canonization and Authority in the Western Church* (London: Oxford University Press, 1948), 120. See also Nilson, *Cathedral Shrines*, 115–34, 147–54; and John Hewitt, "The 'Keeper of Saint Chad's Head' in Litchfield Cathedral, and Other Matters Concerning that Minster in the Fifteenth Century," *Archaeological Journal* 33 (1876): 73 and passim. Illtud Barrett explains that the custodial duties at Hereford continued even after the Reformation; William Ely was relic custodian of Cantilupe's relics after the shrine's destruction in 1538. See "Relics of St Thomas Cantilupe," in *St Thomas Cantilupe, Bishop of Hereford: Essays in His Honour*, ed. Meryl Jancey (Hereford: Friends of Hereford Cathedral, 1982), 181–5. Nilson discusses many of the shrine sites with surviving documentation of relic custodians, including that of Edward the Confessor and Cuthbert (*Cathedral Shrines*, 131–3), Etheldreda's shrine at Ely (115), and, of course, Thomas at Canterbury (96, 129). David Rollason argues that at Durham, Cuthbert's relic custodians – whom he calls "porters" – were integral in establishing the continuity of Durham's communal history. See *Saints and Relics in Anglo-Saxon England* (Cambridge, MA: Basil Blackwell, 1989), 199–200. See also Pierre André Sigal, *L'Homme et le miracle dans la France médiévale (XIe–XIIe siècle)* (Paris: Les Éditions du Cerf, 1985), 123–6.

81 Jonathan Hughes, *Pastors and Visionaries: Religion and Secular Life in Late Medieval Yorkshire* (Woodbridge, Suffolk: Boydell and Brewer, 1988), 306, 314.

82 In his description of the stripping of this monument, Sir William Bassett writes to Cromwell that he gave "the kepers of bothe placis admonicion and charge thatt no more offeryng schulld be made in those placis." Thomas Wright, ed., *Three Chapters of Letters Relating to the Suppression of the Monasteries* (London: Camden Society xxvi, 1843), 143.

83 Richard Marks, *Image and Devotion in Late Medieval England* (Stroud, Gloucestershire: Sutton, 2004), 197, 207–8.

84 Fowler, *Extracts from the Account Rolls*, II, 425–40.

85 A venerable priest questions the "clericum, igitur, sui sacratissimi corporis custodem … Elfredum dominum suum" ("the cleric, that is, Elfred, the custodian of the most holy body"). Reginald of Durham, *Libellus de Admirandis Beati Cuthberti Virtutibus*, ed. James Raine, Surtees Society 1 (London: J.B. Nichols and Son, 1835), 59.

86 Islwyn Geoffrey Thomas, "The Cult of Saints' Relics in Medieval England" (PhD diss., University of London, 1974), 161.
87 "erat foramen in operculo, ubi antiqui custodes martiris solebant manus inponere ad tangendum sanctum corpus."
88 "nouos substituens et leges eis proponens, ut sanctuaria honestius et diligentius custodirent."
89 Qtd. and trans. in Nilson, *Cathedral Shrines*, 134.
90 "Qualiter Sanctus Cuthbertus cuidam Sacristae suo in visu apparuit; et candelam, ne vestimenta sua comburerentur, extingui praecepit." In Reginald, *Libellus de Admirandis Beati Cuthberti Virtutibus*, 78.
91 Reginald, *Libellus de Admirandis Beati Cuthberti Virtutibus*, 78–81, 106–8.
92 See the discussion, earlier in this chapter, of Edmund's translation; and see chapter 1, nn. 18, 27.
93 British Library MS Add. 59616, fols. 1–4; and see Nilson, *Cathedral Shrines*, 128–34.
94 Observatory booths, two examples of which survive today at Oxford Christ Church (St Frideswide) and St Albans, sometimes aided in supervising pilgrims. See Sidney Heath, *Pilgrim Life in the Middle Ages* (London: Unwin, 1912), 280; and Nilson, *Cathedral Shrines*, 53.
95 Nilson, *Cathedral Shrines*, 136. Shrine keeers were (like the sacristans) often in charge of the pyx-boxes, or offertory boxes. Some have suggested that relic custodians may have exerted pressure on pilgrims to pay at the shrine. See Ben Nilson, "The Medieval Experience at the Shrine," in *Pilgrimage Explored*, ed. J. Stopford (Woodbridge, Suffolk: Boydell and Brewer, 1999), 108–12; and Nilson, *Cathedral Shrines*, 105–10.
96 On this kind of early shrine, see chapter 1. See *The Life of King Edward the Confessor*, Cambridge University Library MS Ee.3.59, fol. 33r. [Figure 1]
97 Thomas, 45. One such list is the 1316 Canterbury relic list, composed by one of the sacristans at Canterbury Cathedral. See Thomas, 57.
98 J. Wickham Legg and W.H. St John Hope, *Inventories of Christchurch Canterbury* (Westminster: Archibald Constable & Co, 1902), 80.
99 For a detailed discussion of such immoral relic custodians, see chapter 4.
100 On Benedict of Peterborough, see Ward, *Miracles and the Medieval Mind*, 89–94; see also Koopmans, *Wonderful to Relate*, 159–80.
101 On Thomas's role in popularizing St William of Norwich's cult, see Ward, *Miracles and the Medieval Mind*, 69, 71.
102 See Nilson, *Cathedral Shrines*, 132; and Ronald C. Finucane, "Cantilupe as Thaumatuge: Pilgrims and Their Miracles," in *St. Thomas Cantilupe, Bishop of Hereford: Essays in His Honour*, ed. Meryl Jancey (Hereford: Friends of Hereford Cathedral, 1982), 138–9, 142. A.B. Emden also

mentions Gilbert: "Gilbert de Chyveninge (Chiveninge, Chyvenigke). Vicar of Lydney, Gloucs., adm. 3 Oct. 1287; allowed 8 marks a year from the income of the benefice while studying at Oxford 28 Feb. 1289; still vicar in 1291 … rector of Much Marcele, Herefs., pr., adm. 6 Feb. 1303." See Emden, *A Biographical Register of the University of Oxford to A.D. 1500.* Vol. I, *A–E* (Oxford: Clarendon, 1957), 422. See also William W. Capes, ed., *Registrum Ricardi de Swinfield, Episcopi Herefordensis, A.D. 1283–1317* (Hereford: Wilson and Phillips, 1909), 15, 212, 227, 256, 526.

103 J. van Bolland et al., eds., "Miracula ex processu canonizationis," *Acta sanctorum,* Octobris I, 631, 622 (610–705),http://acta.chadwyck.com. All quotations are from this edition and will be cited parenthetically by page number; *AASS* is the abbreviation for *Acta sanctorum.*

104 On the importance of procurators to canonization proceedings, see André Vauchez, *Sainthood in the Later Middle Ages*, trans. Jean Birrell (Cambridge, UK: Cambridge University Press, 1997), 46. The role of the *procuratores,* whom Michael Richter calls the "main partner[s]" in Hereford of the delegates in Rome, was to present the case for the saint. "Collecting Miracles along the Anglo-Welsh Border in the Early Fourteenth Century," in *Multilingualism in Later Medieval Britain*, ed. D.A. Trotter (Cambridge, UK: D.S. Brewer, 2000), 53. While both Michael Richter and Patrick Daly have identified only one postulator, whom Daly identifies as Henry de Schorne, canon of Hereford cathedral and doctor of canon law ("Patrick H. Daly, "The Process of Canonization in the Thirteenth and Early Fourteenth Centuries," in *St Thomas Cantilupe, Bishop of Hereford: Essays in His Honour*, ed. Meryl Jancey [Hereford: Friends of Hereford Cathedral, 1982], 130), the text presents multiple postulators or procurators: "Nobilis vir Adamus le Schirreve … productus a *procuratoribus* capituli Herefordensis" (*AASS* 610; emphasis added). As Vauchez explains, by the middle of the thirteenth century, procurators were sometimes distinguished from postulators (*Sainthood in the Later Middle Ages*, 46 n. 55). Because other scholars sometimes use the titles interchangeably, however, I will not make a distinction between these terms here. My primary concern is with Chevening, who is most properly called a procurator.

105 However, as Robert N. Swanson and David Lepine write, "though we know relatively little about [the] social origins [of Hereford canons], it is clear that the chapter was mainly drawn from the upper, landowning levels of medieval society." It is thus possible that Gilbert also came from this class. See "The Later Middle Ages, 1268–1535," in *Hereford Cathedral: A History*, ed. Gerald Aylmer and John Tiller (London: Hambledon Press, 2000), 57.

106 Capes, *Registrum Ricardi de Swinfield*, 15.
107 Capes, *Registrum Ricardi de Swinfield*, 526.
108 Emden, *A Biographical Register*, 422. See Swanson and Lepine, "The Later Middle Ages," who explain that by 1450, more than two-thirds of Hereford canons had a university degree, usually from Oxford (59). Also like Gilbert, many Hereford canons tended to acquire "several" benefices (60).
109 Capes, *Registrum Ricardi de Swinfield*, 256.
110 Capes, *Registrum Ricardi de Swinfield*, 534.
111 Finucane, "Cantilupe as Thaumaturge," 138.
112 See Daly, "The Process of Canonization," 125–35.
113 Cantilupe's case can be seen to follow the formulaic pattern for canonization petitions, which by this point required a written *vita* and *miracula*, as well as witness testimony overseen by papal legates, who could not canonize without a papal mandate (Kemp, *Canonization and Authority in the Western Church*, 57–93, passim). See also Ronald C. Finucane, *Miracles and Pilgrims: Popular Beliefs in Medieval England* (Totowa, NJ: Rowman and Littlefield, 1977), 177–8; Michael Goodich, *Violence and Miracle in the Fourteenth Century: Private Grief and Public Salvation* (Chicago: University of Chicago Press, 1995), 6–8; and Vauchez, *Sainthood in the Later Middle Ages*, 540–54. In Cantilupe's case, Richard Swinfield, Cantilupe's episcopal successor; Edward I; archbishops of York; fifteen bishops; seven abbots; eleven counts; and other barons and nobles sent letters to Rome. See Daly, "The Process of Canonization," 127.
114 See Finucane, *Miracles and Pilgrims*, 176.
115 "Supervixit per duodecim annos, ut audivit referri a pluribus de parochia praedicta de Eton, post miraculum antedictum."
116 "Expectans ibi miraculose meritis dicti S. Thomae beneficium recipere sanitatis."
117 Elsewhere, Gilbert is responsible for corroborating a witness' testimony (*AASS* 641).
118 "Et dominus Gilbertus, qui produxit testes super hoc miraculo, tunc custos dicti tumuli … respondit, quod sic."
119 See Ward, *Miracles and the Medieval Mind*, 69, 71. Simon Yarrow's discussion focuses on the audience and context of Thomas's composition. See *Saints and Their Communities: Miracle Stories in Twelfth-Century England* (Oxford: Oxford University Press, 2006), 125–40.
120 Thomas of Monmouth, *The Life and Miracles of St William Norwich*, ed. and trans. A. Jessopp and M.R. James, 117. All quotations are from this edition and will be cited parenthetically by page number. See this chapter, n. 12.

121 Yarrow, *Saints and Their Communities*, 133.
122 "Nocte, nocturnis completis laudibus, cum preter nos sex totus se dormitorio contulisset conuentus."
123 I have modernized this translation from Jessopp and James.
124 "Quaesitas affer candelas, et domno Thome familiari secretario meo trade custodiendas … Deus utique uult, et ita fieri iubet."
125 "Verum si nullo adquieuerit pacto, immo et iussionem nostram paruipendere atque diuine dispensationi proterua presumpserit fronte contraire, non incertum habeat quod in proximo grauiter luat."

3. English Grail Legends and the Holy Blood

1 Two important exceptions are P.J.C. Field and Richard Barber. Field points out that "the effects that the Grail produces are very much what the late Middle Ages expected from relics," though he does not expand upon this assertion. See "Malory and the Grail," in *The Grail, the Quest, and the World of Arthur*, ed. Norris J. Lacy (Cambridge: D.S. Brewer, 2008), 150. See also Barber, "Sir Thomas Malory and the Holy Blood of Hailes," in *The Medieval Book and a Modern Collector*, ed. Takami Matsuda et al. (Cambridge: D.S. Brewer, 2004), 283–4; and Barber, *The Holy Grail: Imagination and Belief* (Cambridge, MA: Harvard University Press, 2004), 213–21.
2 Two other vernacular narratives highlight Joseph's apostolic importance to Glastonbury rather than his role as relic custodian. These are the late fourteenth-century *Titus and Vespasian or Destruction of Jerusalem*, ed. John Alexander Herbert (London: Roxburghe Club, 1905), and Henry Ellis, ed., *The Chronicle of John Hardyng* (London: F.C. and J. Rivington, 1812), which Hardyng completed in 1465. On *Titus and Vespasian*, see Valerie M. Lagorio, "The Evolving Legend of St Joseph of Glastonbury," *Speculum* 46 (1971): 218, 225. Edward Donald Kennedy has argued that Hardyng makes use of the Grail legend to advance an anti-Scottish agenda. See Kennedy, "John Hardyng and the Holy Grail," in *Glastonbury Abbey and the Arthurian Tradition*, ed. James P. Carley (Cambridge: D.S. Brewer, 2001), 249–68. Felicity Riddy suggests that this "chivalric nationalism" may explain why, in one version of his *Chronicle*, Hardyng distills the Grail quest to four lines, and in the other version, omits it from the narrative altogether. See Riddy, "Glastonbury, Joseph of Arimathea and the Grail," in *Glastonbury Abbey and the Arthurian Tradition*, 283.
3 See Nicholas Vincent, *The Holy Blood: King Henry III and the Westminster Blood Relic* (Cambridge: Cambridge University Press, 2001), 87–92, 99–100, 123–53. See also Lagorio, "The Evolving Legend of St Joseph of

Glastonbury," 218–20; and Valerie M. Lagorio, "Joseph of Arimathea: Vita of a Grail Saint," *Zeitschrift für Romanische Philologie* 91 (1975): 61–4.

4 On the relationship between the alliterative *Joseph* and its sources – the Vulgate *Queste del Saint Graal* and *Estoire del Saint Graal* – see W.R.J. Barron, "*Joseph of Arimathie* and the *Estoire del Saint Graal*," *Medium Ævum* 33 (1964): 184–94; and David A. Lawton, "Introduction," *Joseph of Arimathea: A Critical Edition*, ed. David A. Lawton (New York: Garland Publishing, 1983), xxix–xxxviii. Lawton suggests that *Joseph* was not influenced by what he calls "Glastonbury propaganda" (xxxix), showing that the poem evinces no "interest in, or knowledge of, the Glastonbury account" (xl). This lacuna does not preclude the *Joseph* poet from having presented – as I believe he clearly does – the Holy Blood as relic and the Josephs as its keepers. On Lovelich's *History*, which is similarly derived from the *Queste* and *Estoire*, see Lagorio, "The Evolving Legend of St Joseph of Glastonbury," 225–7. On Malory's treatment of his sources, see Dorsey Armstrong, *Gender and the Chivalric Community in Malory's* Morte d'Arthur (Gainesville: University Press of Florida, 2003), 144–72; and Dhira B. Mahoney, "The Truest and Holiest Tale: Malory's Transformation of *La Queste del saint Graal*," in *The Grail: A Casebook*, ed. Dhira B. Mahoney (New York: Garland, 2000), 379–96. See also Anne Marie D'Arcy, *Wisdom and the Grail: The Image of the Vessel in the* Queste del Saint Graal *and Malory's* Tale of the Sankgreal (Dublin: Four Courts Press, 2000), 22–8; Sandra Ness Ihle, *Malory's Grail Quest: Invention and Adaptation in Medieval Prose Romance* (Madison: University of Wisconsin Press, 1983), 31–53; and Roger Sherman Loomis, "The Origin of the Grail Legends," in *Arthurian Literature in the Middle Ages: A Collaborative History*, ed. Roger Sherman Loomis (Oxford: Clarendon Press, 1959), 274–94. Much of this work has to do with whether Malory foregrounded the chivalric romance or the religious quest in his translation of the French text.

5 As Field argues in "Malory and the Grail," Malory's Grail "has a physical existence"; a young woman "needs to use both hands to carry it" (148). See also Barber, *The Holy Grail*, 214.

6 I am inclined to agree with Phillip C. Boardman, who suggests that Malory derives his explanations of the Grail from the Joseph tradition. See Boardman, "Grail and Quest in the Medieval English World of Arthur," in *The Grail, the Quest, and the World of Arthur*, ed. Norris J. Lacy (Cambridge: D.S. Brewer, 2008), 126–40 (127).

7 Eugène Vinaver, ed., P.J.C. Field, rev., *The Works of Sir Thomas Malory*, 3 vols. (Oxford: Clarendon Press, 1990), II, 896. All subsequent citations are parenthetical and will refer to this edition by volume and page number.

8 Anne F. Sutton, "Malory in Newgate: A New Document," *The Library* 1 (2000): 243–62 [256, 244].
9 Vinaver, *Works of Sir Thomas Malory*, III, 1575.
10 Armstrong, *Gender and the Chivalric Community in Malory's* Morte d'Arthur, 150.
11 And as Mahoney has suggested, Malory "belongs firmly in the fifteenth century"; his Grail quest is "characteristic of the religious temper of fifteenth-century England, where secular and spiritual pursuits could be considered complementary rather than competitive elements of a knightly life." So, too, Mahoney rightly points out that common phrases in Malory's translation – "wrecched world," "worlde unstable," and "thys unsyker worlde" – "ring of the homiletic [and Boethian] tradition which surfaces so often in late medieval English literature." See "The Truest and Holiest Tale," 380, 391.
12 Gail McMurray Gibson, *The Theater of Devotion: East Anglian Drama and Society in the Late Middle Ages* (Chicago: University of Chicago Press, 1989), 5, 12, and see 1–18. On the popularity of religious images in the fifteenth century in particular, see recently Shannon Gayk, *Image, Text, and Religious Reform in Fifteenth-Century England* (Cambridge: Cambridge University Press, 2010), 1–14; and Sarah Stanbury, *The Visual Object of Desire in Late Medieval England* (Philadelphia: University of Pennsylvania Press, 2008), 1–32.
13 On vernacular theologies, see Vincent Gillespie, "Vernacular Theology," in *Oxford Twenty-First Century Approaches to Literature: Middle English*, ed. Paul Strohm (Oxford: Oxford University Press, 2007), 401–20; and see the cluster of articles in the journal *English Language Notes* by Elizabeth Robertson, Daniel Donoghue, Linda Georgianna, Kate Crassons, C. David Benson, Katherine C. Little, Lynn Staley, James Simpson, and Nicholas Watson ("Vernacular Theology and Medieval Studies," Bruce Holsinger and Elizabeth Robertson, ed., in *Literary History and the Religious Turn*, Bruce Holsinger, ed., *English Language Notes* 44 [2006]: 77–137).
14 On Malory and the fifteenth-century gentry, see most recently Raluca Radulescu, *The Gentry Context for Malory's* Morte Darthur (Woodbridge, Suffolk: Boydell and Brewer, 2003).
15 See the discussion in the Introduction.
16 Scholars such as Dhira Mahoney, Felicity Riddy, Miri Rubin, and Alison Stones have treated the Grail as Eucharistic vessel, or as somehow connected to the sacrament of the Mass. See for example D'Arcy, *Wisdom and the Grail*, 173, 322–31; Ihle, *Malory's Grail Quest*, 41, 43; and Jill Mann, "Malory and the Grail Legend," in *A Companion to Malory*, ed. Elizabeth Archibald and A.S.G. Edwards (Cambridge: D.S. Brewer, 1996), 206. For

the Grail as the Eucharist itself, see E. Anitchkof, "Le Saint Graal et les rites eucharistiques," *Romania* 55 (1929): 174–94; Albert Pauphilet, *Études sur la Queste del Saint Graal attribuée à Gautier Map* (Paris: E. Champion, 1921), 21–2; and Miri Rubin, *Corpus Christi: The Eucharist in Late Medieval Culture* (Cambridge: Cambridge University Press, 1991), 139–42.

17 Ben Ramm, *Discourse for the Holy Grail in Old French Romance* (Cambridge: D.S. Brewer, 2007), 4.

18 On the desire (and failure) to see as representative of a hermeneutic system, see Kenneth J. Tiller, " 'So precyously coverde': Malory's Hermeneutic Quest of the Sankgreal," *Arthuriana* 13 (2003): 83–97. Other readings of the Grail have focused on Malory's recuperation of Lancelot over the French version (see Charles W. Whitworth, "The Sacred and Secular in Malory's *Tale of the Senkgreal*," *Yearbook of English Studies* 5 [1975]: 19–29); as mimetic (see Mann, "Malory and the Grail Legend," 208); and as pagan and ritualistic (see Jessie L. Weston, *From Ritual to Romance* [New York: Doubleday, 1957]).

19 Ihle, *Malory's Grail Quest*, 40. Elsewhere, Ihle remarks, "In [Malory's] work the meaning of the Grail is known from the beginning: it is the Eucharistic vessel" (*Malory's Grail Quest*, 110).

20 On the holy odor of saints' bodies, see Caroline Walker Bynum, "Bodily Miracles and the Resurrection of the Body in the High Middle Ages," in *Belief in History: Innovative Approaches to European and American Religion*, ed. Thomas Kselman (Notre Dame, IN: Notre Dame University Press, 1991), 70.

21 For a discussion of the treasure metaphor, see chapter 1. See also Ben Nilson, *Cathedral Shrines of Medieval England* (Woodbridge, Suffolk: Boydell and Brewer, 1998), 17–18.

22 Galahad, Percival, and Bors pray at the Grail reliquary "every day" (II, 1034).

23 *Joseph of Arimathea: A Critical Edition*, ed. David A. Lawton (New York: Garland Publishing, 1983), ll. 39–40.

24 Nilson, *Cathedral Shrines*, 40–1, 51.

25 Norris J. Lacy, ed., *Lancelot-Grail: The Old French Arthurian Vulgate and Post-Vulgate in Translation*, 5 vols. (New York, Garland: 1993), IV, 7.

26 See D'Arcy, *Wisdom and the Grail*, 320–1.

27 Lacy, *Lancelot-Grail*, IV, 8.

28 Though Gawain is addressing the crowd at Camelot, the "observers" to whom he most directly refers are those at the Maimed King's court. On the Grail's appearance at Corbenic, the Maimed King's court, see Lacy, *Lancelot-Grail*, IV, 8.

29 See the following discussion of Gawain.
30 See the discussion in the Introduction, chapter 1, and chapter 2.
31 Vincent, *The Holy Blood*, 51.
32 Vincent, *The Holy Blood*, 45–9
33 Vincent, *The Holy Blood*, 49–51.
34 St Thomas Aquinas, Guibert of Nogent, Thiofrid of Echternach, and Reginald Pecock all argued *against* the possibility of body-part relics of Christ (including his blood). On Pecock, see my discussion in chapter 1, and on Aquinas, see Caroline Walker Bynum, *Christian Materiality* (New York: Zone, 2011), 151–6. For a similar observation, see Vincent, *The Holy Blood*, 63–4; and on the scholastic debate over blood relics, see Vincent, *The Holy Blood*, 81–117.
35 See Mahoney, "Introduction," *The Grail: A Casebook*, 2–5.
36 See Vincent, *The Holy Blood*, 82–136.
37 Vincent, 88. On Grosseteste's blood relic treatise, see also Caroline Walker Bynum, *Wonderful Blood: Theology and Practice in Late Medieval Northern Germany and Beyond* (Philadelphia: University of Pennsylvania Press, 2007), 98–101.
38 Vincent, *The Holy Blood*, 91.
39 The sole surviving manuscript copy of Sudbury's work dates from the 1460s or 1470s (Vincent, *The Holy Blood*, 132). Vincent suggests that Grosseteste may also have been influenced by mid-twelfth-century accounts of the Holy Grail (89–91, 108).
40 Lagorio, "The Evolving Legend of St Joseph of Glastonbury," 218.
41 Lagorio, "Joseph of Arimathea: The Vita of a Grail Saint," 61–4. See also Lagorio, "The Evolving Legend of St Joseph of Glastonbury," 218–20; and Roger Sherman Loomis, *The Grail: From Celtic Myth to Christian Symbol* (Princeton, NJ: Princeton University Press, 1963), 224–30, 260–1. In fact, there was a relic custodian for the blood relic at Hailes (Nilson, *Cathedral Shrines*, 130), as well as at Bruges (Vincent, *The Holy Blood*, 131).
42 On Lancelot's tears, see, for instance, Earl R. Anderson, " 'Ein Kind wird geschlagen': The Meaning of Malory's Tale of the Healing of Sir Urry," *Literature and Psychology* 49 (2003): 45–74 [45–6]; E.M. Bradstock, "The Juxtaposition of the 'Knight of the Cart' and 'The Healing of Sir Urry,' " *Journal of the Australasian Universities Modern Language Association* 50 (1978): 208–23 [212–13]; Beverly Kennedy, "Malory's Lancelot: 'Trewest Lover, of Synful Man,' " *Viator* 12 (1981): 409–56; P.E. Tucker, "A Source for the Healing of Sir Urry," *Modern Language Review* 50 (1955): 490–2; and Muriel Whitaker, *Arthur's Kingdom of Adventure* (Cambridge: D.S. Brewer, 1984), 50.
43 Donald Hoffman, "Perceval's Sister: Malory's 'Rejected' Masculinities," *Arthuriana* 6 (1996): 72–83 [73].

44 Martin B. Shichtman, "Percival's Sister: Genealogy, Virginity, and Blood," *Arthuriana* 9 (1999): 11–20 [18].
45 Henry Lovelich, *The History of the Holy Grail*, ed. Frederick J. Furnivall, EETS e.s. 20, 24, 28, 30, and 95; rpt. 4 vols. (London, UK: N. Trübner & Co., 1874–1905), XVII, 64. All subsequent citations are parenthetical and will refer to this edition by chapter and line number.
46 See the discussion of shrine architecture in chapters 1 and 2 and of relic custodians in chapter 2.
47 The alliterative *Joseph* is extant only in the Vernon manuscript, which has been dated to around 1400, fols. 403r–404v. One leaf, fol. 402, is missing. For a description of the manuscript and of *Joseph* in its manuscript contexts, see Lawton, *Joseph of Arimathea: A Critical Edition*, xiii–xxix.
48 Lawton, *Joseph of Arimathea: A Critical Edition*, ll. 38–43. Subsequent citations are parenthetical and will refer to this edition by the work's title and by line number.
49 Lawton, *Joseph of Arimathea*, 71; Walter W. Skeat, ed., *Joseph of Arimathie: The Romance of the Seint Graal, or Holy Grail*, EETS o.s. 44 (London: Trübner & Co, 1871; rpt. Felinfach: Llanerch, 1992), 92.
50 I owe this point to Drew Jones. For definition 3a), the *MED* cites the *South English Legendary*: "Þo men founden þis holie ȝwuchche In a fair place stonde with þis holie bodi a-boue þe se al on druye londe" http://quod.lib.umich.edu/m/med/, accessed 13 February 2013.
51 Anthony Bale and A.S.G. Edwards, ed., *John Lydgate's* Lives of Ss Edmund and Fremund *and the* Extra Miracles of St Edmund (Heidelberg: Winter, 2009), *Extra Miracles* ll. 167–8.
52 "Erat foramen in operculo, ubi antiqui custodes martiris solebant manus inponere ad tangendum sanctum corpus." H.E. Butler, ed., *The Chronicle of Jocelin of Brakelond* (London: Thomas Nelson and Sons, 1949), 112. See the discussion of Jocelin in chapter 2.
53 In Malory, a cleric explains Evelake's condition to Percival: "Ever he was bysy to be thereas the Sankgreall was. And on a tyme he nyghed hit so nyghe that Oure Lorde was displeased with hym, but ever he folowed hit more and more tyll God stroke hym allmoste blynde" (II 908).
54 Interestingly, this vision corresponds to images of the *arma Christi*. I thank Shannon Gayk for drawing this comparison to my attention. On the *arma Christi*, see the Introduction, n. 59.
55 On Gilbert of Chevening, see the discussion in chapter 2.
56 Cistercian houses are intimately connected to the Grail quest and to blood relics. On the Cistercian role in composing the *Queste del Saint Graal*, see Fanni Bogdanow, "An Interpretation of the Meaning and Purpose of the

Vulgate *Queste del Saint Graal* in the Light of the Mystical Theology of St Bernard," in *The Changing Face of Arthurian Romance*, ed. Alison Adams et al. (Woodbridge, Suffolk: Boydell Press, 1986), 23–46; D'Arcy, *Wisdom and the Grail*, 27–9, 75–164; and Pauphilet, *Études sur la Queste del Saint Graal*, 75–83. On Cistercian blood cults, see Bynum, *Wonderful Blood*, 52–68. The monks at Hailes were themselves Cistercians (Vincent, *The Holy Blood*, 77, 139–43). On the evidence for Cistercian authorship of the *Queste*, see Norris J. Lacy, "The Evolution and Legacy of French Prose Romance," in *The Cambridge Companion to Medieval Romance*, ed. Roberta L. Krueger (Cambridge: Cambridge University Press, 2000), 171.

57 On Lovelich's adaptation of his source material, see Lagorio, "The Evolving Legend of St Joseph of Glastonbury," 226.

58 Lagorio, "The Evolving Legend of St Joseph of Glastonbury," 226.

59 Lovelich, *The History of the Holy Grail*, I–II, 219.

60 Lagorio, "The Evolving Legend of St Joseph of Glastonbury," 218–20.

61 The Caxton version identifies this "bysshop" as Joseph of Aramathie, not Joseph's son. See Vinaver, *The Works of Sir Thomas Malory*, II, 781–2.

62 Shichtman, "Percival's Sister," 13.

63 For a very general discussion of hagiographical conventions in Malory, see Alfred Robert Kraemer, *Malory's Grail Seekers and Fifteenth-Century English Hagiography* (New York: Peter Lang, 1999). See also Lagorio, "Joseph of Arimathea: The Vita of a Grail Saint."

64 For a discussion of this danger as it appears in narratives of disinterment, see chapter 2.

65 See for example Stephen C.B. Atkinson, "Malory's Lancelot and the Quest of the Grail," in *Studies in Malory*, ed. James W. Spisak (Kalamazoo, MI: Medieval Institute Publications, 1985), 149. Atkinson bases his reading on the Caxton Malory, where some differences with the Winchester manuscript – the omission of Nacien's instruction that the knights need to be confessed, for instance (Atkinson, 151 n. 16) – directly inform Atkinson's reading of Malory's adaptation of his source material.

66 Vinaver, *The Works of Sir Thomas Malory*, III, 1045.

67 Karen Cherewatuk, "Malory's Launcelot and the Language of Sin and Confession," *Arthuriana* 16 (2006): 69–70. See the following discussion.

68 Field has also argued that Malory emphasizes holiness in the *Tale of the Sankgreal*. See "Malory and the Grail," 149.

69 As I discuss in chapter 2 (see n. 71), penitence is a characteristic of the exemplary supplicant. We may think of confession as falling under this rubric, though it is not always explicitly required. For the importance of confession to being granted an indulgence for visiting a shrine, see

Nilson, "The Medieval Experience at the Shrine," in *Pilgrimage Explored*, ed. J. Stopford (Woodbridge, Suffolk: York Medieval Press, 1999), 114; and Nicholas Vincent, "Some Pardoners' Tales: The Earliest English Indulgences," *Transactions of the Royal Historical Society* 12 (2002): 27–32, passim. Roger of Wendover, a thirteenth-century English chronicler, affirms that supplicants must see a priest who will "hear their confessions and grant absolution *before* they approached the shrine, 'it sometimes happening that some, their sins … being the cause, are unable perfectly to look upon the said piece, thereby sometimes incurring infirmities of divers sorts.' " Qtd. in Carole Rawcliffe, "Curing Bodies and Healing Souls: Pilgrimage and the Sick in Medieval East Anglia," in *Pilgrimage: The English Experience from Becket to Bunyan*, ed. Colin Morris and Peter Roberts (Cambridge: Cambridge University Press, 2002), 123. Nacien's assertion here runs contrary to Atkinson's claim that Malory "stresses the importance of the individual decision to repent" (138) and "omits from Nacien's speech the requirement that the knights confess before setting out" (151 n. 16).

70 Mann, "Malory and the Grail Legend," 211.

71 Vinaver, *The Works of Sir Thomas Malory*, I, 85; II, 816–17, 824, 828.

72 On curiosity and pilgrimage, see Diana Webb, *Medieval European Pilgrimage c.700–c.1500* (New York: Palgrave, 2002), 45; and Christian Zacher, *Curiosity and Pilgrimage: The Literature of Discovery in Fourteenth-Century England* (Baltimore, MD: Johns Hopkins University Press, 1976), especially 21–2. As Zacher explains, Augustine of Hippo associated curiosity specifically with the "lust of the eyes" or "*concupiscentia oculorum*" (22). Moreover, Augustine associates this visual lust with pilgrimage to relics, explaining that supplicants ought to celebrate the martyr's relics inwardly, rejecting the "love of the world," particularly "the lust of the flesh … and the lust of the eyes." Qtd. in Patricia Cox Miller, "Relics, Rhetoric and Mental Spectacles in Late Ancient Christianity," in *Seeing the Invisible in Late Antiquity and the Early Middle Ages*, ed. Giselle de Nie, Karl F. Morrison, and Marco Mostert (Turnhout: Brepols, 2005), 29.

73 See Vinaver, *The Works of Sir Thomas Malory*, II, 933–5, 942–3, 945–9.

74 Vinaver, *The Works of Sir Thomas Malory*, II, 894–5, 927, 1016.

75 This is not to say that Malory is presenting a criticism (or endorsement) of the theology of predestination. The point, rather, is that these knights achieve the Grail because of qualities they are born with, rather than because they follow the dicta of relic discourse.

76 When Percival is healed by the Sankgreal, and before the onset of the quest, he has a "glemerynge of the vessell and of the mayden that bare hit, for he was a parfyte mayden" (II 816). Ector, who is with Percival at the

time, does not see the Grail at all. Moreover, of the three who achieve the Grail, Galahad, Percival, and Bors, Merlin prophesied that "the two sholde be maydyns and the thirde sholde be chaste" (906). See also 933–5, 945–9.

77 Cherewatuk, "Malory's Launcelot," 69.

78 See my "Miracles of Justice," in *The Encyclopedia of Medieval Pilgrimage*, ed. Larissa J. Taylor et al. (Leiden: Brill, 2010), 438–40.

79 Cherewatuk, "Malory's Lancelot," 68–9. For a more detailed outline of mainstream and reformist attitudes to confession, see Katherine C. Little, *Confession and Resistance: Defining the Self in Late Medieval England* (Notre Dame, IN: University of Notre Dame Press, 2006), 49–77; Vincent, "Some Pardoners' Tales," 27–31, 49–50; and my discussion of Pandarus and confession in chapter 4.

80 Larry D. Benson, ed., *The Riverside Chaucer* (Boston: Houghton Mifflin, 1987), X, 316.

81 *Pace* Cherewatuk, who mistakenly observes that in Malory's *Sankgreal*, "we witness no specific … acts of fleshly denial. In contrast, in Malory's more morally stringent source, *La Quest de Saint Graal*, the hermit … gives him a hairshirt and denies him meat and wine" (69–70). Cherewatuck must simply have missed this moment in Malory (II 927), which undercuts her argument that Lancelot does not perform satisfaction until *The Tale of Lancelot and Guinevere*. Clearly, he performs satisfaction in the *Tale of the Sankgreal*.

82 Malo, "Miracles of Justice"; see also the discussion in chapter 2.

83 Bale and Edwards, *John Lydgate's* Lives of Ss Edmund and Fremund *and the* Extra Miracles of St Edmund, *EF* 3333–60.

84 On virtuous and depraved supplicants, see the discussion in chapter 2.

4. Relic Discourse in The Pardoner's Prologue and Tale and *Troilus and Criseyde*

1 See Alastair Minnis, *Fallible Authors: Chaucer's Pardoner and the Wife of Bath* (Philadelphia: University of Pennsylvania Press, 2008), 98–131.

2 As E. Talbot Donaldson has famously argued, the Pardoner, Pandarus, and Chaucer all "create fiction in order to shape reality" ("Chaucer's Three Ps: Pardoner, Pandarus, and Poet," *Michigan Literary Quarterly* 14 [1975]: 292); and see John M. Fyler, "The Fabrications of Pandarus," *Modern Language Quarterly* (1980): 115–30. For a recent version of the argument that Pandarus is "linked to the narrative nexus of the poem," see Michael Modarelli, "Pandarus's 'Grete Emprise': Narration and Subjectivity in Chaucer's *Troilus and Criseyde*," *English Studies* 89 (2008): 404.

3 See Gretchen Mieszkowski, " 'The Least Innocent of All Innocent-Sounding Lines': The Legacy of Donaldson's Troilus Criticism," *Chaucer Review* 41 (2007): 299–310.

4 Barry Windeatt, *Oxford Guides to Chaucer: Troilus and Criseyde* (New York: Oxford University Press, 1992), 290.

5 On "entente," see Rosemary P. McGerr, *Chaucer's Open Books: Resistance to Closure in Medieval Discourse* (Gainesville: University of Florida Press, 1998), 96–118. The word "entente" occurs thirty-five times in *Troilus and Criseyde*: (http://www.umm.maine.edu/faculty/necastro/chaucer/concordance/tr/tr.txt.WebConcordance/framconc.htm); and as Modarelli points out, this count does not include other terms for "entente," such as "entencioun," "entende," "purpose," and "emprise" ("Pandarus's 'Grete Emprise,' " 413 n. 48).

6 *The Canterbury Tales*, in *The Riverside Chaucer*, ed. Larry D. Benson (Boston: Houghton Mifflin, 1987), Fragment VI, lines 403–4. Subsequent citations from the *Canterbury Tales* are parenthetical and will refer to this edition by fragment and line number.

7 *Troilus and Criseyde*, in The *Riverside Chaucer*, ed. Larry D. Benson (Boston: Houghton Mifflin, 1987), Book II, lines 387, 462. Subsequent citations from *Troilus and Criseyde* are parenthetical and will refer to this edition by book and line number.

8 In "The Pardoner's Invitation: Quaestor's Bag or Becket's Shrine?," *PMLA* 97 (1982): 810–18, Melvin Storm also reads the rioters as on a kind of pilgrimage or quest. However, Storm's focus on what the rioters have in common with Chaucer's Canterbury pilgrims – the failure to achieve, as they might have done had they undertaken their journey "aright," "an admirable spiritual quest" (814) – and the Pardoner's role in ensuring this failure, differs substantially from my own approach. In my view, Storm misreads Chaucer's exploration of how the material elements of pilgrimage, such as relics, represent otherworldly sanctity. Hence, I disagree with Storm's rhetorical question: "Does Chaucer, perhaps, intend the rioters' initial misconception as a subtle reminder that any pilgrim is similarly in error who conceives of his goal as physical relics rather than spiritual values and perceives his reward as temporal rather than eternal?" (814). The answer, I believe, is emphatically no. As this book seeks to demonstrate, the signifying value of relics and shrines cannot be so simply reduced to a binary between temporal gain and eternal rewards.

9 For an overview of some of the most influential studies on Criseyde, see Lorraine Kochanske Stock, " 'Slydynge' Critics: Changing Critical Constructions of Chaucer's Criseyde in the Past Century," in *New Perspectives*

on Criseyde, ed. Cindy L. Vitto and Marcia Smith Marzec (Asheville, NC: Pegasus, 2004), 11–36. See also David Aers, *Chaucer, Langland and the Creative Imagination* (London: Routledge, 1980), 117–42; Laura L. Howes, "Chaucer's Criseyde: The Betrayer Betrayed," in *Reading Medieval Culture: Essays in Honor of Robert W. Hanning*, ed. Robert M. Stein and Sandra Pierson Prior (Notre Dame, IN: University of Notre Dame Press, 2005), 324–43; and Jennifer Summit, "Troilus and Criseyde," in *The Yale Companion to Chaucer*, ed. Seth Lerer (New Haven, CT: Yale University Press, 2006), 213–42. On *Troilus* and rhetoric, see Rita Copeland, "Chaucer and Rhetoric," in *The Yale Companion to Chaucer*, 132–4.

10 See for example Gretchen Mieszkowski, *Medieval Go-Betweens and Chaucer's Pandarus* (New York: Palgrave, 2006). Pandarus has recently been regarded as a voyeur, a perpetrator of incest, and even as having homoerotic desire for Troilus. See Sarah Stanbury, "The Voyeur and the Private Life in Troilus and Criseyde," *Studies in the Age of Chaucer* 13 (1991): 141–58; Mieszkowski, " 'The Least Innocent of All Innocent-Sounding Lines,' " 299–310; Richard W. Fehrenbacher, " 'Al that which chargeth nought to seye,' " *Exemplaria* 9 (1997): 341–69; Tison Pugh, "Queer Pandarus? Silence and Sexual Ambiguity in Chaucer's *Troilus and Criseyde*," *Philological Quarterly* 80.1 (2001): 17–35; and Richard Ziekowitz, "Sutured Looks and Homoeroticism: Reading Troilus and Pandarus Cinematically," in *Men and Masculinities in Chaucer's Troilus and Criseyde*, ed. Tison Pugh and Marcia Smith Marzec (Cambridge: D.S. Brewer, 2008), 148–60.

11 See Woodburn O. Ross, ed., *Middle English Sermons*, EETS o.s. 209 (London: Oxford University Press, 1940), 125.

12 See the discussion in chapter 2.

13 See chapter 2 on Thomas Monmouth's role in popularizing St William of Norwich's cult and on Gilbert of Chevening's role not only in popularizing Thomas Cantilupe's cult but also securing his canonization.

14 This sermon appears in Ross's EETS edition of the sermons from British Library MS Royal 18 B.xxiii. The manuscript has been dated to the middle of the fifteenth century. See Ross, *Middle English Sermons*, xxxix.

15 Ross, *Middle English Sermons*, 125.

16 For more on the literary and historical tradition of criticizing and satirizing pardoners, see Alastair Minnis, *Fallible Authors*, 101–12; R.N. Swanson, *Indulgences in Late Medieval England: Passports to Paradise?* (Cambridge: Cambridge University Press, 2007), 182–98; and Islwyn Geoffrey Thomas, "The Cult of Saints' Relics in Medieval England" (PhD diss., University of London, 1974), 14–22. See also Jill Mann, *Chaucer and Medieval Estates Satire* (Cambridge: Cambridge University Press, 1973), 150–2; Peter Marshall,

Religious Identities in Henry VII's England (New York: Ashgate, 2006), 134; G.R. Owst, *Preaching in Medieval England: An Introduction to Sermon Manuscripts of the Period c. 1350–1450* (Cambridge: Cambridge University Press, 1926), 99–110, 349–51. *Pace* Alfred L. Kellogg and Louis A. Haselmayer, "Chaucer's Satire of the Pardoner," *PMLA* 66 (1951): 251–77, it seems clear that the satire directed against the Pardoner is indeed directed against false pardoners in particular (rather than institutional decay in general).

17 "Crebro teri perspicimus ista susurro et facta feretrorum circumlatione ridicula et eorum, quos a rabie declamandi rabulos Ieronimus vocat, mendaciis cotidie cernimus alieni marsupii profunda nudari" (Guibert of Nogent, *De Sanctis et eorum Pigneribus*, ed. R.B.C. Huygens, *Corpus Christianorum Continuatio Mediaevalis* CXXVII [Turnhout: Brepols, 1993], I, ll. 395–8). English translations are taken from Thomas Head, ed. and trans., "On Saints and Their Relics," in *Medieval Hagiography: An Anthology* (New York: Garland, 2000), 414.

18 Caesarius of Heisterbach, *The Dialogue on Miracles*, trans. H. von E. Scott and C.C. Swinton Bland, 2 vols (London: George Routledge, 1929), II, 70. For a similar fourteenth-century complaint, see Richard FitzRalph's 1356 sermon against Our Lady of Walsingham (among other shrines), British Library MS Lansdowne 393, fols. 105v–106, discussed in G.R. Owst, *Literature and Pulpit in Medieval England* (Cambridge: Cambridge University Press, 1933), 141. The Pardoner's occupation also resembles that of relic questers (Thomas, "The Cult of Saints' Relics," 17–18). These quests were criticized in the thirteenth century because of the abuses – such as extorting money from the poor or imprudent by displaying fake relics – associated with "des quêteurs" (Nicole Herrmann-Mascard, *Les reliques des saints: formation coutumière d'un droit* [Paris: Éditions Klincksieck, 1975], 306). See also Simon Yarrow, *Saints and Their Communities* (Oxford: Clarendon Press, 2006), 63–99; Pierre Héliot and Marie-Laure Chastang, "Quêtes et voyages de reliques au profit des églises françaises du Moyen Âge," *Revue d'historie ecclésiastique* 59 (1964): 789–822; R. Kaiser, "Quêtes itinérantes avec des reliques pour financer la construction des églises (XIe–XIIe siècles)," *Le Moyen Âge* 101 (1995): 205–25; and Pierre André Sigal, "Les voyages de reliques aux onzième et douzième siècles," in *Voyage, quête, pèlerinage dans la littérature et la civilisation médiévales* (Paris: Edition CUER, 1976), 73–104.

19 John Heywood, *The Pardoner and the Frere*, in *The Plays of John Heywood*, ed. R. Axton and P. Happé (Cambridge: D.S. Brewer, 1991), 93–109. Heywood lifts from Chaucer phrases such as "Here is a mytten eke, as ye may se" (97; compare *CT*, VI, 372) and "I shewe ye of a holy Jewes shepe / A bone"

(96), and he augments the General Prologue's eighteen lines on relics to eighty-one. Relics are paramount even in Heywood's stage directions: "In the meane whyle entreth the Pardoner with all his relyques, to declare what eche of them ben, and the hole power and vertu thereof" (95).

20 Siegfried Wenzel, ed. and trans., *Fasciculus morum* (University Park: Pennsylvania State University Press, 1989), 477.

21 Siegfried Wenzel first noted the relevance of this sermon to Chaucer's Pardoner. See "Chaucer's Pardoner and His Relics," *Studies in the Age of Chaucer* (1989): 39.

22 F.D. Matthew, ed., *The English Works of Wyclif hitherto Unprinted*, EETS o.s. 74 (London: Kegan Paul, 1880; rev. 1902), 154. I discuss Wycliffite critiques of pardoners, which are largely derived from these mainstream complaints, in the next chapter.

23 Matthew, *The English Works of Wyclif*, 154.

24 Marshall, *Religious Identities in Henry VII's England*, 134.

25 A.V.C. Schmidt, ed., *The Vision of Piers Plowman: A Critical Edition of the B-Text* (London: Everyman, 1978; rpt. 2001), Prologue, II, 73, 75, 79, 81–2.

26 Owst, *Preaching*, 100.

27 This souvenir or badge is a "vernycle … sowed upon his cappe" (I 685).

28 In More's 1529 *Dialogue against Heresy* – a work that, unlike Heywood's play, defends relics and their appropriate veneration – the Messenger, a character who questions the More-persona on matters of orthodoxy and faith, dismisses relics by observing that people often venerate "some olde rotten bone that was heppely some tyme *as Chaucer sayth* a bone of some holy Iewes shepe." Thomas More, *A Dialogue Concerning Heresies*, in *The Yale Edition of the Complete Works of St. Thomas More*, ed. Thomas M.C. Lawler, Germain Marc'hadour, and Richard C. Marius, 15 vols. (New Haven, CT: Yale University Press, 1963–97), VI, 98; emphasis added.

29 Such approaches often assume that the Pardoner's fake, non-notable relics could have had the same value as the legitimate, notable, and famous relics at Canterbury, or that a joke about relics necessarily devalued the relics at Canterbury. See Storm, "The Pardoner's Invitation." See also Eugene Vance, "Chaucer's Pardoner: Relics, Discourse, and Frames of Propriety," *New Literary History* 20 (1989): 723–45; Daniel Knapp, "The Relyk of a Seint: A Gloss on Chaucer's Pilgrimage," *English Literary History* 39 (1972): 1–26; and William Kamowski, " 'Coillons,' Relics, Skepticism and Faith on Chaucer's Road to Canterbury: An Observation on the Pardoner's and the Host's Confrontation," *English Language Notes* 28 (1991): 1–8. For the Pardoner's relics as inferior and unthreatening to the Canterbury pilgrimage, see Thomas, "The Cult of Saints' Relics," 15–18.

30 See Wenzel, "Chaucer's Pardoner," 38. For a more recent examination of pardoners and relics, see Nicholas Vincent, "Some Pardoners' Tales: The Earliest English Indulgences," *Transactions of the Royal Historical Society* 12 (2002): 53–5.
31 See Seeta Chaganti, *The Medieval Poetics of the Reliquary: Enshrinement, Inscription, Performance* (New York: Palgrave, 2008), 131–53.
32 Chaganti, *The Medieval Poetics of the Reliquary*, 147.
33 See, most recently, Glenn Burger, *Chaucer's Queer Nation* (Minneapolis: University of Minnesota Press, 2003), 119–31, 140–59; Richard Firth Green, "Further Evidence for Chaucer's Representation of the Pardoner as a Womanizer," *Medium Ævum* 71 (2002): 307–9; and Alastair Minnis, "Chaucer and the Queering Eunuch," *New Medieval Literatures* 6 (2003): 107–28. Carolyn Dinshaw's seminal work on the Pardoner, his sexuality, and his relics nevertheless does not contextualize relics in relation to late medieval England; see *Chaucer's Sexual Poetics* (Madison: University of Wisconsin Press, 1989), 156–84.
34 See Minnis, *Fallible Authors*, 98–169; and Minnis, "Chaucer's Pardoner and the 'Office of Preacher,' " in Piero Boitani and Anna Torti, eds., *Intellectuals and Writers in Fourteenth Century Europe: The J.A.W. Bennett Memorial Lectures* (Tübingen: Gunter Narr Verlag, 1986), 88–119.
35 On the Pardoner's non-clerical status, see Minnis, *Fallible Authors*, 112–18 and Swanson, *Indulgences*, 181–3.
36 "Thou woldest make me kisse thyn olde breech, / And swere it were a relyk of a seint, / Though it were with thy fundement depeint!" (VI 948–50).
37 Patrick Geary, "Sacred Commodities: The Circulation of Medieval Relics," in *The Social Life of Things: Commodities in Cultural Perspective*, ed. Arjun Appadurai (Cambridge: Cambridge University Press, 1986), 174.
38 Non-notable or lesser relics include the smaller or less important body parts of saints, as well as the material objects associated with the saints. On medieval classifications of relics, see the discussion in chapter 1.
39 Giovanni Boccaccio, *Decameron*, ed. Vittore Branca (Firenze: Le Monnier, 1951–2), 760. English translations are taken from Giovanni Boccaccio, *Decameron*, ed. and trans. Mark Musa and Peter E. Bondanella (New York: Norton, 1977), 109.
40 Boccaccio, *Decameron*, ed. Branca, 762; trans. Musa and Bondanella, 110.
41 See Boccaccio, *Decameron*, ed. Branca, 771; trans. Musa and Bondanella, 114.
42 Boccaccio, *Decameron*, ed. Branca, 773–4; trans. Musa and Bondanella, 115.
43 Masuccio Salernitano, born Tommaso Guardati, vanished from public record in 1474; his date of death is uncertain.

44 Alastair Minnis, "The Construction of Chaucer's Pardoner," in *Promissory Notes on the Treasury of Merits: Indulgences in Late Medieval Europe*, ed. R. N. Swanson (Leiden: Brill, 2006), 170.

45 Masuccio, *Il Novellino*, ed. Alfredo Mauro (Bari: Guis. Laterza & Figli, 1940), 43. English translations are taken from Masuccio, *The Novellino*, trans. W. G. Waters (London: Lawrence and Bullen, 1905), 65. Canon 62 of the Fourth Lateran Council, reflecting the opinion of earlier theologians such as Augustine, expressly forbade the selling of relics. See Eric W. Kemp, *Canonization and Authority in the Western Church* (London: Oxford University Press, 1948), 105–6.

46 Masuccio, *Il Novellino*, ed. Mauro, 42; trans. Waters, 64.

47 Masuccio, *Il Novellino*, ed. Mauro, 43; trans. Waters, 64. For a detailed study of shrine accounts and offerings, which explains the financial importance of shrines to their cathedrals and relic custodians, see Ben Nilson, *Cathedral Shrines of Medieval England* (Woodbridge, Suffolk: Boydell and Brewer, 1998), 144–67, 182–90; and see the discussion of relic custodians in chapter 2.

48 Caesarius of Heisterbach, *The Dialogue on Miracles*, 70. This reference is presumably to the illegitimate trafficking in relics, but also to their unlawful use, both of which were forbidden in Canon 62 of the Fourth Lateran Council.

49 Masuccio, *Il Novellino*, ed. Mauro, 45; trans. Waters, 68.

50 See the discussion of the exemplary pilgrim, confession, and penance in chapter 2, especially n. 71; see also chapter 3, n. 69. Before Onion exhibits his relics, he "fatta prima con grande solennità la confessione" (first had the congregation recite the Confiteor) (see Boccaccio, *Decameron*, ed. Branca, 768; trans. Musa and Bondanella, 113). Girolamo, for his part, promises remission of sins ("remissioni di peccati") for those who give alms (Masuccio, *Il Novellino*, ed. Mauro, 46; trans. Waters, 69). For confession as integral to obtaining an indulgence at a shrine, see Ben Nilson, "The Medieval Experience at the Shrine," in *Pilgrimage Explored*, ed. J. Stopford (Woodbridge, Suffolk: York Medieval Press, 1999), 114. On the connection between confession, indulgences, and relics, see Vincent, "Some Pardoners' Tales," 23–58; Anne F. Harris, "Pilgrimage, Performance, and Stained Glass at Canterbury Cathedral," in *Art and Architecture of Late Medieval Pilgrimage in Northern Europe and the British Isles*, ed. Sarah Blick and Rita Tekippe (Leiden: Brill, 2005), 274–9. Swanson, *Indulgences*, 52–3, 116–17, outlines the interdependence of indulgences, confession, and relic translation ceremonies in particular.

51 Swanson observes that over time, pardoners "became increasingly laicised" and suggests that in fact, this "extra-clerical status" may have been

perceived as especially threatening to the established hierarchy (*Indulgences*, 181–3).

52 On the treasure metaphor, see chapter 1.

53 On the elision of shrine and saint, see the discussion in chapter 2.

54 For a comprehensive outline of Canterbury's many shrines and relics, see Thomas, "The Cult of Saints' Relics," 56–71; and J. Wickham Legg and W.H. St John Hope, ed., *Inventories of Christchurch Canterbury* (Westminster: Archibald Constable & Co, 1902). See also Patrick Collinson, Nigel Ramsay, and Margaret Sparks, ed., *A History of Canterbury Cathedral* (New York: Oxford University Press, 1995); Benedicta Ward, *Miracles and the Medieval Mind: Theory, Record, and Event, 1000–1215* (Philadelphia: University of Pennsylvania Press, 1987), 89–109; and Arthur Penrhyn Stanley, *Historical Memorials of Canterbury* (New York: E.P. Dutton, 1911), 187–214.

55 One notable exception is Daniel Knapp's "The Relyk of a Seint," which contextualizes the Pardoner in terms of the hair-shirt and hair-breeches relics at Canterbury Cathedral. Knapp's ultimate conclusion – that Chaucer holds "relics up to ridicule" (11) or that he cannot have intended the pilgrims to arrive at Canterbury (25–6), the Pardoner so threatens the pilgrimage – is not borne out by the evidence we now have about satiric pardoners and cathedral shrines. His article is nevertheless an important contribution to thinking about how attitudes to relics might have affected and shaped late medieval literature.

56 On the preponderance of this kind of reliquary at Canterbury, see Thomas, "The Cult of Saints' Relics," 56–71; see also J. Charles Wall, *Shrines of British Saints* (London: Methuen, 1905), 13–16, 19–24, 148–75; and Ben Nilson, *Cathedral Shrines*, 57–62.

57 Desiderius Erasmus, *Peregrinatio religionis ergo*, in *Opera omnia Desiderii Erasmi Roterodami*, ed. L.-E. Halkin, F. Bierlaire, and R. Hoven, 20 vols. (Amsterdam: North Holland, 1969–92), Vol. I, Pt. 3, 490. The English translation is taken from Craig R. Thompson, trans., *Colloquies*, vols. 39–40 of *Collected Works of Erasmus*, 84 vols. (Toronto: University of Toronto Press, 1997), XL, 645.

58 John Stow, *The Annales of England to 1605* (London, 1605, STC 23337), 970. The surviving illustration in British Library MS Cotton Tiberius E., fol. 269 supports this description, depicting as it does the shrine covered by the gilded wooden canopy, both of which are seated on a large stone shrine base with its niches (designed for kneeling pilgrims). See Wall, *Shrines of British Saints*, 162; and Stephen Lamia, "The Cross and the Crown, the Tomb and the Shrine: Decoration and Accommodation for England's Premier Saints," in *Decorations for the Holy Dead: Visual Embellishments*

on Tombs and Shrines of Saints, ed. Stephen Lamia and Elizabeth Valdez del Álamo (Turnhout: Brepols), 2002, 41. For other renditions of Becket's shrine, see Sarah Blick, "Reconstructing the Shrine of St Thomas Becket, Canterbury Cathedral," in *Art and Architecture of Late Medieval Pilgrimage in Northern Europe and the British Isles*, ed. Sarah Blick and Rita Tekippe (Leiden: Brill, 2005), 405–41. Blick reconstructs Becket's shrine based on surviving pilgrimage badges. See also John Crook, *English Medieval Shrines* (Woodbridge, Suffolk: Boydell Press, 2011), 213–19; and Tim Tatton-Brown, "Canterbury and the Architecture of Pilgrimage Shrines in England," in *Pilgrimage: The English Experience from Becket to Bunyan*, ed. Colin Morris and Peter Roberts (Cambridge: Cambridge University Press, 2002), 90–107.

59 Wall, *Shrines of British Saints*, 160; emphasis added.

60 "Preparaverat autem thecam ad corpus honorifice collocandum, de auro obrizo purissimo et gemmis pretiosissimis, artificio materiam superante." Frederic Madden, ed., *Matthaei Parisiensis, monachi Sancti Albani, Historia Anglorum*, 3 vols. (London: Longmans, Green, Reader, and Dyer, 1866), II, 241–2. Trans. Arthur Mason, *What Became of the Bones of St Thomas?* (Cambridge, Cambridge University Press, 1920), 79. For other medieval accounts, including those by Friar Simon Fitzsimmons and Aeneas Sylvius (who was to become Pope Pius II), see Blick, "Reconstructing the Shrine of St. Thomas Becket," 408–12; see also Wall, *Shrines of British Saints*, 159.

61 See the discussion of the commonplaces of relic discourse in chapter 2.

62 Earl Harold gave eighty-five relics to Waltham priory, of which he had collected fifty-nine. See Mary Frances Smith, Robin Fleming, and Patricia Halpin, "Court and Piety in Late Anglo-Saxon England," *Catholic Historical Review* 87 (2001): 587.

63 Leslie Watkiss and Marjorie Chibnall, ed. and trans., *The Waltham Chronicle* (Oxford: Clarendon Press, 1994), 37.

64 Anthony Bale and A.S.G. Edwards, eds., *John Lydgate's* Lives of Ss Edmund and Fremund *and the* Extra Miracles of St Edmund (Heidelberg: Winter 2009). All subsequent citations are from this edition and will refer to *EF* (*Ss Edmund and Fremund*) and *EM* (*Extra Miracles*) and line number.

65 A.S.G. Edwards, ed., *The Life of St Edmund, King and Martyr: A Facsimile of British Library MS Harley 2278* (London: British Library, 2004).

66 Other instances relevant to this discussion include Knighton's account of a fourteenth-century theft (of St Hugh's head), on which see the Introduction, and the fifteenth-century report of the theft of offerings at St Cuthbert's shrine. See Joseph T. Fowler, ed., *The Life of St Cuthbert in English Verse, c. A.D. 1450*, Surtees Society 87 (Durham: Published for the Surtees Society by Andrews & Co, 1891), ll. 6335–88.

67 Storm, "The Pardoner's Invitation," 813. For an overview of Storm's argument about the Tale, see this chapter, n. 8.
68 On the healing miracles of St Thomas of Canterbury in particular, see Ward, *Miracles and the Medieval Mind*, 90–6. On pilgrimage and the sick, see Ronald Finucane, *Miracles and Pilgrims: Popular Beliefs in Medieval England* (Totowa, NJ: Rowman and Littlefield, 1977), 39–55; and Carole Rawcliffe, "Curing Bodies and Healing Souls: Pilgrimage and the Sick in Medieval East Anglia," in *Pilgrimage:The English Experience from Becket to Bunyan*, ed. Colin Morris and Peter Roberts (Cambridge: Cambridge University Press, 2002), 108–40.
69 See the discussion of nighttime exhumation and translation in chapter 2.
70 Patrick Geary, *Furta Sacra: Thefts of Relics in the Central Middle Ages*, 2nd ed. (Princeton, NJ: Princeton University Press, 1990), 108–28, was the first to identify such thefts as a literary commonplace.
71 Chaganti, *The Medieval Poetics of the Reliquary*, 147.
72 On this quotation as evidence for parallels between profane and divine love, see John Leyerle, "The Heart and the Chain," in *The Learned and the Lewed, Harvard English Studies* 5, ed. Larry D. Benson (1974): 117.
73 Alastair Minnis, *Chaucer and Pagan Antiquity* (Woodbridge, Suffolk: Boydell and Brewer, 1982), 87.
74 D.W. Robertson, *A Preface to Chaucer: Studies in Medieval Perspectives* (Princeton, NJ: Princeton University Press, 1962), 499; on idolatry in general, see 99, 112–13, and 401.
75 V.A. Kolve, *Telling Images: Chaucer and the Imagery of Narrative II* (Stanford, CA: Stanford University Press, 2009), 244. See also John Fleming, *Classical Imitation and Interpretation in Chaucer's Troilus* (Lincoln: University of Nebrasks Press, 1990), 72–154. Fleming argues that the "poem's eroticism is inseparable, thematically and philosophically, from the idea of idolatry" (73).
76 Here I disagree with Kolve's reading of Criseyde's association with the Palladium: "At the conceptual center of his poem an identification is made between Criseyde … and a statue of the goddess Pallas Athena – a religious idol called the Palladion – whose continued presence (and worship) in Troy guarantees the safety of the city … By this means … Judeo-Christian ideas of idolatry interpenetrate the pagan ethos of the poem" (*Telling Images*, 244).
77 Fleming, *Classical Imitation*, 127. Fleming is one of the few who have noted this parallel between Criseyde and the Palladium. But he associates this parallel with idolatry: "The loss of Criseyde heralds Troilus' destruction, just as the loss of the Palladium will herald Troy's," calling Criseyde and

the Palladium "the parallel idolatries of great and little Troy" (*Classical Imitation*, 127). However, that Chaucer expressly calls the Palladium a relic – as none of his source texts do – complicates interpreting Criseyde and/or the Palladium as suggesting *only* idolatry. Rather, it seems clear that relic discourse – rather than "images of idolatry," as Kolve suggests (*Telling Images*, 245) – is a key component of the poem's religious moments.

78 On courtly love as a discourse rather than an actual practice, see David Burnley, *Courtliness and Literature in Medieval England* (New York: Addison-Wesley-Longman, 1998), esp. 99–121. On *Troilus and Criseyde* and the religion of love, see Alcuin Blamires, "The 'Religion of Love' in Chaucer's *Troilus and Criseyde* and Medieval Visual Art," in *Word and Visual Imagination: Studies in the Interaction of English Literature and the Visual Arts* (Erlangen: Universitätsbund Erlangen-Nürnberg, 1988), 11–31; and see Barry Windeatt's discussion in *Troilus and Criseyde* (Oxford: Oxford University Press, 1992), 231–4. C.S. Lewis is still one of the most frequently cited critics on this topic. See *The Allegory of Love* (Oxford: Clarendon Press, 1936). On idolatry and paganism in *Troilus and Criseyde*, see Robertson, *A Preface to Chaucer*, 499–503; Minnis, *Chaucer and Pagan Antiquity*, 83–6; and Frank Grady, *Representing Righteous Heathens* (New York: Palgrave, 2005), 103–9.

79 On the "Religious turn," see James Simpson, "Confessing Literature," *English Language Notes* 44 (2006): 122; and Nicholas Watson, "Desire for the Past," *Studies in the Age of Chaucer* 21 (1999): 59–97.

80 See Martin Camargo, "The Consolation of Pandarus," *Chaucer Review* 25 (1991): 214–28; E. Talbot Donaldson, "The Ending of *Troilus*," in *Speaking of Chaucer* (New York: Norton, 1970), 84–101; Jill Mann, "Chance and Destiny in *Troilus and Criseyde* and the *Knight's Tale*," in *The Cambridge Companion to Chaucer*, 2nd ed., ed. Piero Boitani and Jill Mann (Cambridge: Cambridge University Press, 2004), 93–111; Monica McAlpine, *The Genre of Troilus and Criseyde* (Ithaca, NY: Cornell University Press, 1978), 148–217; and V.A. Kolve, who remarks that in the final stanzas of the poem, "*Il Filostrato* is overwritten by Dante's *Divine Comedy* … First Troilus as a pagan, and then Chaucer as a Christian, will show us what it is like to look directly at the sun" (*Telling Images*, 15, 16–27, 253–6). Kolve continues his discussion of the pagan and Christian intersections in the final chapter to his volume, "God-Denying Fools," *Telling Images*, 223–56.

81 Donaldson, "The Ending of *Troilus*," 97.

82 *Troilus and Criseyde*, ed. Stephen Barney (New York: Norton, 2006), 16.

83 Benoît de Saint-Maure, *Le roman de Troie*, ed. Léopold Constans, Société des Anciens Textes Français, 6 vols. (Paris: Firmin-Didot et Cie., 1904–12), IV, ll. 25387, 25403.

84 Guido delle Colonne, *Historia destructionis Troiae*, ed. Nathaniel Edward Griffin (Cambridge, MA: Medieval Academy of America, 1936), 227; trans. Elizabeth Meek, *Historia Destructionis Troiae* (Bloomington: Indiana University Press, 1974), 29.350.

85 Guido, *Historia destructionis Troiae*, 227; trans. Meek, 29.364–5.

86 See Guido, *Historia destructionis Troiae*, 229; trans. Meek, 30.41–2.

87 On Chaucer's influence on *The Troy Book*, see C. David Benson, *The History of Troy in Middle English Literature* (Woodbridge, Suffolk: D.S. Brewer, 1980), 99–101; and Robert R. Edwards, "Introduction," in *Troy Book: Selections*, ed. Robert R. Edwards (Kalamazoo, MI: Medieval Institute Publications, 1998), 11–12. Other accounts to pick up on this lexicon include *The Laud Troy Book*, which has been dated to *c.* 1400 and gives the following account of the theft of the Palladium: "Antenor come thenne on a nyght, / And that prest, that wicked wyght, / ȝaff him that relike that was so riche" (J. Ernst Wülfing, ed., *The Laud Troy Book*, EETS o.s. 121, 122 [London: Kegan Paul, Trench, Trübner & Co., 1902, 1903], ll. 17947–49). See also line 18090. On the dating of *The Laud Troy Book*, see Benson, *The History of Troy*, 158.

88 Henry Bergen, ed., *Lydgate's Troy Book*, EETS e.s. 97, 103, 106, 126, 4 vols. (London, Kegan Paul, Trench, Trübner & Co., 1935), III, Bk. IV, 5596–7, 5604–6, 5611–23.

89 Lydgate, *Troy Book*, Vol. III, Bk. IV, 5659.

90 Lydgate, *Troy Book*, Vol. III, Bk. IV, 5672–3, 5676.

91 Benson makes a similar claim; see *The History of Troy*, 134.

92 See C.S. Lewis, "What Chaucer Really Did to *Il Filostrato*," *Essays and Studies* 17 (1932): 56–75. Reprinted in *Troilus and Criseyde*, ed. Stephen A. Barney (New York: Norton, 2006), 453–4, 456.

93 On the repetition of the phrase "for Antenor Criseyde" at IV 149, 177, 212, 347, and 378, see Michael Delahoyde, " 'Heryng th'effect' of the Names in *Troilus and Criseyde*," *Chaucer Review* 34.4 (2000): 364.

94 For a discussion of Jocelin's and Simeon's descriptions of the exhumation of St Edmund and St Cuthbert, see chapter 2.

95 Pandarus further effects this comparison in his invented account of overhearing Troilus's lament and confession to the God of Love (II 507–44).

96 On the complicity of the saint as one of the topoi in accounts of relic thefts, see Geary, *Furta Sacra*, 113–17.

97 On the layout of Pandarus's house, see Saul N. Brody, "Making a Play for Criseyde: The Staging of Pandarus's House in Chaucer's *Troilus and Criseyde*," *Speculum* 73 (1998): 115–40. Kolve suggests that "[r]hetorically speaking, the religious temple of Chaucer's Book I and the 'stewe' of

Book III are thus alternative versions of the same erotically charged space" (*Telling Images*, 251). In my reading, the similarity of these spaces suggests not only the "sacralization of erotic love" (Kolve, *Telling Images*, 250), but also the presentation of Criseyde's room as a kind of shrine.

98 These lines are directly translated from Boccaccio. Chaucer emphasizes the idea of Troilus as pilgrim, however, adding material such as II 32: "How Troilus com to his lady grace."

99 See Mieszkowski, *Medieval Go-Betweens*, 3.

100 Mieszkowski, *Medieval Go-Betweens*, 3.

101 Again, I think it appropriate to read these moments as engaging with multiple discourses, including those of courtly love *and also* relics. For an outline of mainstream and reformist attitudes to confession, see Katherine C. Little, *Confession and Resistance: Defining the Self in Late Medieval England* (Notre Dame, IN: University of Notre Dame Press, 2006), 49–77.

102 On this lacuna, see David Aers, "Faith, Ethics, and Community: Reflections on Late Medieval English Writing," *Journal of Medieval and Early Modern Studies* 28 (1998): 341–69.

103 C. David Benson and Elizabeth Robertson, eds., *Chaucer's Religious Tales* (Cambridge: D.S. Brewer, 1990); and Helen Phillips, ed., *Chaucer and Religion* (Cambridge: D.S. Brewer, 2010). For discussions of the way modern belief inflects our interpretations of medieval religion, see Kolve, *Telling Images*, 223–5; Jill Mann, "Chaucer and Atheism," *Studies in the Age of Chaucer* 17 (1995): 5–19; and Charles Muscatine, "Chaucer's Religion and the Chaucer Religion," in *Chaucer Traditions: Studies in Honour of Derek Brewer*, ed. Ruth Morse and Barry Windeatt (Cambridge: Cambridge University Press, 1990), 249–62.

104 See Nicholas Watson, "Chaucer's Public Christianity," *Religion and Literature* 37 (2005): 110–12.

105 For a reading of this moment as central to the Knight's Tale, see Aers, *Chaucer, Langland and the Creative Imagination*, 174–95.

106 *The House of Fame*, in *The Riverside Chaucer*, ed. Larry D. Benson (Boston: Houghton Mifflin, 1987), I 272.

5. Wycliffite Texts and the Problem of Enshrinement

1 A.H. Thomas and I.O. Thornley, ed., *Great Chronicle of London* (London: George W. Jones, 1938; rpt. Gloucester: Alan Sutton, 1983), 252.

2 "Reliquiae sanctorum, scilicet carnes et ossa hominis mortui, non debent a populo venerari, nec de monumento foetido extrahi." W.W. Shirley, ed., *Fasciculi Zizaniorum Magistri Johannis Wyclif cum tritico*, Rolls Series

(London: Longman, Brown, Green, Longmans, and Roberts 1858; rpt. London: Kraus, 1965), 429. Cited hereafter as *Fasciculi*. I discuss this passage in more detail later on in this chapter.

3 In using the term "Wycliffite" rather than "Lollard," I follow Andrew Cole, who challenges our use of "the very word used to harass Wycliffites in medieval England but still employed transparently by modern scholars as if it had little ideological, much less theological, significance: lollard." See *Literature and Heresy in the Age of Chaucer* (Cambridge: Cambridge University Press, 2008), xii, 72–4. But see also Anne Hudson's discussion of the term "lollere" in "Langland and Lollardy?" *Yearbook of Langland Studies* 17 (2003): 94–100.

4 See Anne Hudson, *The Premature Reformation: Wycliffite Texts and Lollard History* (Oxford: Oxford University Press, 1988), 305–7. There, Hudson includes William Wynch's comments criticizing inauthentic relics in her general overview of images, idolatry, and lay instruction. Though she includes this example as evidence that "[r]elics and even miracles at the shrines of saints may be faked," the antecedent for "relics" nevertheless seems to be "ornamented image" – and indeed, the reference to relics is sandwiched between a discussion of images as books for the laity and the dangers of "man's artistry" and pilgrimage. This kind of overview is helpful on the one hand, but I believe that, on the other, it has encouraged scholars to elide the distinction between relics and images. Sarah Stanbury, for instance, observes that "[i]n Lollard polemic images and relics are often folded together, as in the Twelve Conclusions" (*The Visual Object of Desire in Late Medieval England* [Philadelphia: University of Pennsylvania Press, 2008], 222 n. 47). Kathleen Kamerick similarly suggests that Dymmok "conflates 'relics and images,' reflecting widely held views about their similar natures, and allowing images to share in the sacral quality that inhered in the bones" (*Popular Piety and Art in the Late Middle Ages: Image Worship and Idolatry in England, 1350–1500* [New York: Palgrave, 2002], 33). But *pace* Stanbury and Kamerick, both the *Twelve Conclusions* and Dymmok's response to them clearly distinguish between images and relics. See the discussion of relics and images in this chapter.

5 John F. Davis, "Lollards, Reformers, and St. Thomas of Canterbury," *University of Birmingham Historical Journal*, 9 (1963–4): 2.

6 W.R. Jones, "Lollards and Images: The Defense of Religious Art in Later Medieval England," *Journal of the History of Ideas*, 34 (1973): 35.

7 See the discussion in the following section of this chapter, "Wyclif on Sumptuous Barbarism and Luxurious Shrines."

8 Hans Belting, *Likeness and Presence: A History of the Image before the Era of Art* (Chicago: University of Chicago Press, 1994), 301. Belting goes on to

point out that "images and relics both confirmed the experience of the living saint" (302), but it does not follow that the medieval devout conflated these objects.

9 Caroline Walker Bynum, *Christian Materiality: An Essay on Religion in Late Medieval Europe* (New York: Zone Books, 2011), 126–7.

10 Portions of the following discussion of Wycliffite attitudes to shrines and relics appeared in *Wycliffite Controversies*, ed. Mishtooni Bose and Patrick Hornbeck II (Turnhout: Brepols, 2011), 193–210. I am grateful for permission to reprint this material, in revised form, here.

11 Christina von Nolcken, "An Edition of Selected Parts of the Middle English Translation of the 'Rosarium Theologie' " (PhD diss., Oxford University, 1976), 569. See also von Nolcken, *Middle English Translation of the Rosarium Theologie: A Selection ed. from Cbr., Gonville and Caius Coll. MS 354/581* (Heidelberg: Carl Winter, 1979). The section on relics does not appear in von Nolcken's published edition of the *Rosarium*. I am grateful for Dr von Nolcken's generosity in sharing her unpublished work with me and to Shannon Gayk for drawing my attention to von Nolcken's contribution to this subject. Von Nolcken was one of the first to take up the issue of Wycliffites and saints, in "Another Kind of Saint: A Lollard Perception of John Wyclif," in *From Ockham to Wyclif*, ed. Anne Hudson and Michael Wilks, Studies in Church History, Subsidia 5 (Oxford: Basil Blackwell, 1987), 429–43.

12 Lillian Swinburn, ed., *Lanterne of Liȝt*, EETS o.s. 151 (London: Kegan Paul, Trench, Trübner & Co., 1917), 37. All quotations are from this edition and will be cited parenthetically. In the sections on pilgrimage (35–43), where one might expect to find a discussion of relics, the author argues, instead, that clerical greed causes "lewid" lay folk to divest themselves of their goods. The explicit contrast is between those whose outer display accords with their inner state and those the text considers to be hypocrites. Given that the *Lanterne* does not criticize the veneration of saints, it seems possible that it does not envision relics as inherently harmful, either.

13 Norman P. Tanner, ed., *Heresy Trials in the Diocese of Norwich, 1428–31*, Camden Society Fourth Series (London: Royal Historical Society, 1977), 11.

14 Shannon McSheffrey and Norman Tanner, ed. and trans., *Lollards of Coventry 1486–1522*, Camden Society Fifth Series (London: Cambridge University Press, 2003), 66. For general overviews of Wycliffite attitudes to images, see Margaret Aston, *Lollards and Reformers: Images and Literacy in Late Medieval Religion* (London: Hambledon Press, 1984), 135–92; Jones, "Lollards and Images," 31–5; Anne Hudson, *Selections from English*

Wycliffite Writings (Cambridge: Cambridge University Press, 1978), 179–81, cited in the following as *SEWW*; and Kamerick, *Popular Piety*, 13–34.

15 McSheffrey and Tanner, *Lollards of Coventry*, 69.

16 McSheffrey and Tanner, *Lollards of Coventry*, 17, 65, 299, 305.

17 On the blood at Hailes, see especially Nicholas Vincent, *The Holy Blood: King Henry III and the Westminster Blood Relic* (Cambridge: Cambridge University Press, 2001), 137–54. See also Caroline Walker Bynum, *Wonderful Blood: Theology and Practice in Late Medieval Northern Germany and Beyond* (Philadelphia: University of Pennsylvania Press, 2007), 143–4. On historical blood relics, see the discussion in chapter 3.

18 Though this chapter will focus primarily on Wycliffite texts, the term "reformist" is nevertheless important. In using this term – which includes but is not limited to Wycliffites – I wish to emphasize what Wycliffite thought shares in common with many longstanding critiques of mainstream practices and theology. In this particular case, a broad range of mainstream and reformist thinkers, including Wycliffites, regarded passion relics with skepticism. Passion relics were considered to be different in kind from body-part relics, and many conservative theologians and apologists (including Guibert of Nogent, Thiofrid of Ecternach, and Reginald Pecock) doubted whether any passion relic could be genuine. For Pecock on relics of Christ and Mary, see Reginald Pecock, *The Repressor of Overmuch Blaming of the Clergy*, ed. C. Babington, 2 vols. (London: Longman, Green, Longman, and Roberts, 1860; rpt. Elibrion Books, 2005), I, 183.

19 For a discussion of Wycliffite testimony as possibly formulaic, see Hudson, *The Premature Reformation*, 33–9.

20 Thomas and Thornley, *Great Chronicle of London*, 252.

21 Quoted in von Nolcken, "Another Kind of Saint," 437.

22 John Thomson, *The Later Lollards, 1414–1520* (London: Oxford University Press, 1965), 150.

23 John S. Davies, ed., *An English Chronicle of the Reigns of Richard II, Henry IV, Henry V, and Henry VI Written before the Year 1471*, Camden Society First Series (London: Royal Society, 1856), 56.

24 Thomson, *The Later Lollards*, 150.

25 A.T. Bannister, ed., *Register of Richard Mayew* (Hereford: Cantilupe Society Publications, 1919), 66–7.

26 One Wycliffite sermon, for example, laments that "riche men cloþen dede stockis & stonys wiþ precious cloþis, wiþ gold & siluer & perlis & gaynesse to þe world, & suffren pore men goo sore a cole & at moche meschefe." See F.D. Matthew, ed., *The English Works of Wyclif hitherto Unprinted*, 2nd ed., EETS o.s. 74 (Woodbridge, Suffolk: Boydell and Brewer;

rpt. 1998), 210. For a discussion of this "hallmark of the Lollards," see Margaret Aston, *England's Iconoclasts.* Vol. 1, *Laws against Images* (Oxford: Oxford University Press, 1988), 115, 124–6.

27 For another, similar objection, see Hudson, *The Premature Reformation*, 305. In one other instance, as von Nolcken describes in "An Edition," 569, a treatise discusses "the evils of exposing the bones of saints for money." Such a moment is, as von Nolcken suggests, "exceptional"; but it seems likely that the author of that treatise is tapping into orthodox criticisms going back to Canon 62 of the Fourth Lateran Council, which (reflecting the opinion of earlier theologians such as Augustine) expressly forbade profiting by relics. See Eric W. Kemp, *Canonization and Authority in the Western Church* (London: Oxford University Press, 1948), 105.

28 Matthew, *The English Works of Wyclif*, 154.

29 See Swanson, *Indulgences in Late Medieval England: Passports to Paradise?* (Cambridge: Cambridge University Press, 2007), 182–98, and Siegfried Wenzel, "Chaucer's Pardoner and His Relics," *Studies in the Age of Chaucer* 11 (1989): 37–41; and for a more extended discussion of pardoners and fake relics, see chapter 4.

30 Woodburn O. Ross, ed., *Middle English Sermons*, EETS o.s. 209 (London: Oxford University Press, 1940), 125. See the discussion of this passage in chapter 4.

31 Quoted in Hudson, *The Premature Reformation*, 305. Chaucer's Pardoner admits in his Prologue that one of his relics is merely the "sholder-boon" of "an hooly Jewes sheep" (VI 350–1).

32 See also Peter Marshall, who labels concern with fake relics a "medieval" – rather than specifically Wycliffite – "cliché." *Religious Identities in Henry VIII's England* (Burlington, VT: Ashgate, 2006), 134.

33 See Anne Hudson, ed., *The Works of a Lollard Preacher*, EETS o.s. 317 (Oxford: Oxford University Press, 2001), 231.

34 Steven Justice, "Inquisition, Speech, and Writing: A Case from Late Medieval Norwich," in *Criticism and Dissent in the Middle Ages*, ed. Rita Copeland (Cambridge: Cambridge University Press, 1996), 293.

35 Aston, *Lollards and Reformers*, 88; on White and relics, see 84–90.

36 Shirley, *Fasciculi*, 429, emphasis added.

37 Tanner, *Heresy Trials in the Diocese of Norwich*, 95. It must be noted that as this testimony mimics almost exactly the records we have of White's beliefs on the subject, it might not necessarily represent individual belief.

38 Mary-Ann Stouck, ed. and trans., "A Reformer's View of the Cult of the Saints," in *Medieval Saints: A Reader*, ed. Mary-Ann Stouck (Orchard Park, NY: Broadview Press, 1999), 597.

39 Iohannis Wyclif, *Tractatus de Ecclesia*, ed. Iohann Loserth and F. D. Matthew (London: Trübner, 1886), 465.
40 As Thomas Netter allowed, Wyclif does not seem to have had much to say about images or relics in general. See Netter, *Doctrinale antiquitatum fidei ecclesiae catholicae*, ed. B. Blanciotti, 3 vols. (Venice: Antonio Bassanese, 1757–9; rpt. Farnborough: Gregg, 1967), III, col. 902; emphasis added. On Netter, see Hudson, *The Premature Reformation*, 50–5. Hudson similarly observes, 302, that Wyclif's views on images were "not extreme." See also Aston, *England's Iconoclasts*, 143–4.
41 For a nearly identical objection, see Guibert of Nogent, *De Sanctis et Eorum Pigneribus*, ed. R.B.C. Huygens (Turnholt: Brepols, 1993), I, 596–8, discussed in chapter 1.
42 Wyclif, *De Eucharistia tractatus maior: Accedit tractatus de eucharistia et poenitentia sive de confessione*, ed. Johann Loserth(London: Trübner, 1892), 318.
43 Priscilla Heath Barnum, ed., *Dives and Pauper*, EETS o.s. 275, 280, 2 vols. (London: Oxford University Press, 1976, 1980), I, 101–9. There, Pauper explains that *latria* constitutes worship "þat longyȝt only to God"; *dulia* is that reverence "comoun to God and to creature resonable and intellectuel, þat is to seyne, to man, womman and aungel" (102). On *latria* and *dulia*, see Kamerick, *Popular Piety*, 32–4.
44 Johann Loserth and F.D. Matthew, ed., *Iohannis Wyclif Sermones*, 2 vols. (London: Trübner, 1888), II, 165. See also Aston, *England's Iconoclasts*, 103–4.
45 Roger Dymmok, *Liber Contra Duodecim Errores et Hereses Lollardorum*, ed. H.S. Cronin (London: Trübner, 1922), 192. Dymmok's rhetoric here is conventional. For other instances, see Aston, *England's Iconoclasts*, 23–5. See also Barnum, *Dives and Pauper*, where Pauper explains that God is to be worshipped above all things; one, therefore, kneels and worships "aforn þe ymage nought to þe ymage ... For ȝyf þu doo it for þe ymage or to þe ymage þu doist ydolatrye" (85).
46 Loserth and Matthew, *Johannis Wyclif Sermones*, II, 165; trans. Aston, *England's Iconoclasts*, 103–4.
47 Desiderius Erasmus, *Peregrinatio religionis ergo* in *Colloquia* in *Opera omnia Desiderii Erasmi Roterodami*, ed. L.-E. Halkin, F. Bierlaire, and R. Hoven, 20 vols. (Amsterdam: North Holland, 1969–92), Vol I, Pt. 3, 490. The English translation is taken from Craig R. Thompson, trans., *Colloquies*, vols. 39–40 of *Collected Works of Erasmus*, 84 vols. (Toronto: University of Toronto Press, 1997), XL, 645.
48 Wyclif, *De Eucharistia*, 317.
49 The *Conclusions* have been dated to 1395, when, according to Walsingham, they were posted on the doors at Westminster. See H.T. Riley, ed.,

Thomae Walsingham, quondam monachi S. Albani, Historia anglicana, 2 vols., Rolls Series 28 (London: Longman, Green, Longman, Roberts, and Green, 1863–4), II, 216. See also Hudson, *SEWW*, 150; and most recently, Wendy Scase, "The Audience and Framers of the Twelve Conclusions of the Lollards," in *Text and Controversy from Wyclif to Bale: Essays in Honor of Anne Hudson*, ed. Helen Barr and Ann M. Hutchison (Turnhout: Brepols, 2005), 283–301. Scase responds in part to Fiona Somerset (*Clerical Discourse and Lay Audience in Late Medieval England* [Cambridge: Cambridge University Press, 1998], 103–34) and revisits the question of the *Conclusions* and the vernacular (299–300).

50 Hudson, *SEWW*, 27. The section on passion relics runs as follows: "if þe rode tre, naylis, and þe spere and þe coroune of God schulde ben so holiche worchipid, þanne were Iudas lippis, qwoso mythte hem gete, a wondir gret relyk." Hudson, *SEWW*, 27. In this commentary on Judas's lips, it is clear that the writer is making a kind of obscene joke about a very particular kind of relic – a joke well within the bounds of a literary and theological tradition that held neither with many contact relics (as Judas's lips would be), nor with bodily relics of Christ. See also this chapter, n. 17.

51 The treatise survives in an early fifteenth-century manuscript. See Hudson, *SEWW*, 83–8, 179. Here, I disagree with Jones, "Lollards and Images," 35, who cites "Images and Pilgrimage" as evidence for Wycliffite distaste for pilgrimages, images, and relics in general.

52 Hudson, *SEWW*, 84.

53 Hudson, *SEWW*, 85; emphasis added.

54 Hudson, *SEWW*, 85.

55 Von Nolcken, "An Edition," 178–9. See this chapter, n. 10.

56 Von Nolcken, "An Edition," 178. The author's approach offers further evidence that passion and other contact relics were not thought of in the same terms as saints' bodies and other body-part relics. For a discussion of different kinds of relics, see chapter 1.

57 Von Nolcken, "An Edition," 178–9; emphasis added.

58 Von Nolcken, "An Edition," 179; emphasis added.

59 Netter, *Doctrinale antiquitatum fidei ecclesiae catholicae*, III, col. 902.

60 This sermon survives in one manuscript copy, Corpus Christi College Cambridge MS 296, dated to the late fourteenth or early fifteenth century. See Matthew, *The English Works of Wyclif*, 279. But on the difficulty of dating anonymous Wycliffite texts, see Hudson, *The Premature Reformation*, 11. Though this sermon does not discuss relics specifically, we might understand these adorned images as referring to shrines that contained relics.

61 Quoted in Aston, *Lollards and Reformers*, 34.

62 Pecock, *The Repressor of Overmuch Blaming of the Clergy*, I, 182. On the term "reformist," see this chapter, n. 18. On Pecock's rhetoric, see Mishtooni Bose, "Reginald Pecock's Vernacular Voice," in *Lollards and Their Influence in Late Medieval England*, ed. Fiona Somerset, Jill C. Havens, and Derrick G. Pitard (Woodbridge, Suffolk: Boydell Press, 2003), 221. Bose ultimately argues that Pecock was able to "plunder" Wycliffite rhetoric while distancing himself from his opponents' positions (228). See also Hudson, *The Premature Reformation*, 55–8.

63 Pecock, *The Repressor of Overmuch Blaming of the Clergy*, I, 182–3.

64 On the development of late medieval shrine architecture and the occlusion of major relics, see the discussion in chapter 1.

65 It seems to me that Pecock is also attempting to align English practice with the Roman tradition of constructing buildings *over* saints' graves. In the late antique period, churches grew up over the graves of popularly venerated saints. According to this line of thinking, shrines are not incidental but an essential component of the church building. Pecock hence conveys the idea that shrines are *more* essential to churches than if he presented them simply as metaphorical representations of the saints they contained. On late antique saints' cults, see John Crook, *English Medieval Shrines* (Woodbridge, Suffolk: Boydell Press, 2011), 3–24; and see Peter Brown's magesterial study, *The Cult of the Saints* (Chicago: University of Chicago Press, 1981).

66 Von Nolcken, "Another Kind of Saint," 436.

67 Hudson, *SEWW*, 116.

68 Tanner, *Heresy Trials in the Diocese of Norwich*, 148.

69 John Claydon was executed on 7 September 1415, largely for having owned the *Lanterne of Liȝt* and, as Nicholas Watson comments, having been so excited by the text "that he could not stop talking about it" ("Vernacular Apocalyptic: on the *Lanterne of Liȝt*," *Revista Canaria de Estudios Ingleses*, 47 [2003]: 116). On John Claydon, see Hudson, *The Premature Reformation*, 13, 211–13; see also David Wilkins, ed., *Concilia Magnae Britanniae et Hiberniae, AD 466–1718*, 4 vols. (London: R. Gosling, F. Gyles, T. Woodward, and C. Davis, 1737), III, 375. On the dating of the *Lanterne* to between 1409 and 1411, see Swinburn, "Introduction," *Lanterne of Liȝt*, viii–xiii.

70 On the poem's dating, see Hudson, *The Premature Reformation*, 13.

71 *Pierce the Plowman's Crede*, in *The Piers Plowman Tradition*, ed. Helen Barr (New York: Everyman, 1993). All quotations are from this text and will be cited parenthetically by line number. For a description of the poem, see Barr, "Introduction," *The Piers Plowman Tradition*, 8–14.

72 Hudson, *SEWW*, 84; emphasis added.

73 Hudson, *SEWW*, 181. On image tabernacles, see also Richard Marks, *Image and Devotion in Late Medieval England* (Stroud, Gloucestershire: Sutton, 2004), 240–3, and Thomas Wright, ed., *Three Chapters of Letters Relating to the Suppression of the Monasteries*, Camden Society xxvi (London: John Bowyer Nichols and Son, 1843), 143.

74 *Middle English Dictionary*, s.v. "tabernacles" (n) and "tabernaclid" (adj), http://quod.lib.umich.edu/m/med/, accessed 12 February 2013. In fact, one instance of the figurative use of "tabernacle" uses almost exactly the same language as the *Crede* to describe the canopy or shrine: "Oure bold kyng in Baliloun [read: Babiloun] nowe bildis vp a trone. All þe sete of þe sege was smaragdyns fyne … A tabernacle ouir þe trone tildid vp on loft." W.W. Skeat, ed., *The Wars of Alexander, an Alliterative Romance*, EETS e.s. 47 (London: Trübner, 1886; reprint 1973), l, 5645.

75 The adjectival form, "tabernaclid" (adj), is listed simply as "covered with a canopy."

76 Hudson, *SEWW*, 84. On shrine canopies, see Ben Nilson, *Cathedral Shrines of Medieval England* (Woodbridge, Suffolk: Boydell and Brewer, 1998), 40–41, 51.

77 Bruce Holsinger, "Lollard Ekphrasis: Situated Aesthetics and Literary History," *Journal of Medieval and Early Modern Studies*, 35 (2005): 82.

78 Holsinger, "Lollard Ekphrasis, 75.

79 On the transparency of poverty in the *Crede* – particularly as embodied in the suffering of Peres and his wife – see Kate Crassons, *The Claims of Poverty: Literature, Culture, and Ideology in Late Medieval England* (Notre Dame, IN: University of Notre Dame Press, 2010), 89–93, 109–13.

80 On the alabaster industry in late medieval England, see Marks, *Image and Devotion*, 228–9, 248, 251–3; see also Stanbury, *The Visual Object of Desire*, 27–8.

81 Shirley, *Fasciculi*, 429, emphasis added.

82 Shannon Gayk, *Image, Text, and Religious Reform in Fifteenth-Century England* (Cambridge: Cambridge University Press, 2010), 15–44.

83 We may understand this Wycliffite "poor man" as nothing but a rhetorical tool for shaming those who profited by a cult into better behavior and as having nothing to do with the "actual poor." Nevertheless, I think it is reasonable to assume that at least some Wycliffite authors cared about the disadvantaged members of society. On this issue, see Crassons, *The Claims of Poverty*, 140, who identifies Wycliffite polemic as "consciously employ[ing] poverty as a relativistic term." See also David Aers, "John Wyclif: Poverty and the Poor," *Yearbook of Langland Studies* 17 (2003): 57; and Margaret Aston," 'Caim's Castles': Poverty, Politics and Disendowment," in *The*

Church, Politics and Patronage in the Fifteenth Century, ed. R.B. Dobson (Gloucester: St Martin's Press, 1984); rpt. in Aston, *Faith and Fire: Popular and Unpopular Religion, 1350–1600* (London: Hambledon Press, 1993), 95–131; Helen Barr, *Socioliterary Practice in Late Medieval England* (Oxford: Oxford University Press, 2001), 128–57; and Anne Hudson, "Poor Preachers, Poor Men: Views of Poverty in Wyclif and His Followers," in *Häresie und vorzeitige Reformation im Spätmittelalter*, ed. František Šmahel and Elisabeth Müller-Luckner (Munich: Oldenbourg Wissenschaftsverlag, 1998), 41–53.

Coda: The Cultural Work of Relic Discourse

1 In addition to the stories in popular media, including those about John Paul II's uncongealed blood or the relic theft of Long Island – on which see the Introduction – see Caroline Walker Bynum, *Christian Materiality* (New York: Zone, 2011), a mass-market book; Charles Freeman, *Holy Bones, Holy Dust: How Relics Shaped the History of Medieval Europe* (New Haven, CT: Yale University Press, 2011); Peter Manseau, *Rag and Bone: A Journey Among the World's Holy Dead* (New York: Holt, 2009). The travelling exhibit *Treasures of Heaven: Saints, Relics, and Devotion in Medieval Europe*, as well as the exhibit Cynthia Hahn curated in New York City – entitled "Objects of Devotion and Desire" (http://www.objectsofdevotionanddesire.com) – indicate a continued interest in reliquaries as art objects. Scholarly interest has picked up apace: see Alexandra Walsham, ed., *Relics and Remains, Past and Present* Supplement 5 (2010); Seeta Chaganti, *The Medieval Poetics of the Reliquary* (Palgrave, 2008); and Cynthia Hahn's book, *Strange Beauty: Origins and Issues in the Making of Medieval Reliquaries 400–ca. 1204* (State Park: Pennsylvania State University Press, 2012). Unfortunately, *Strange Beauty* was not yet available when my book went to press.
2 Manseau, *Rag and Bone*, 13.
3 Bynum, *Christian Materiality*, 168.
4 On animated matter, see Sarah Stanbury, *The Visual Object of Desire in Late Medieval England* (Philadelphia: University of Pennsylvania Press, 2008), 15–17. Bynum makes similar arguments in *Christian Materiality*, 44, 105–9, 139–40, 145.
5 See Danyel M.R. Ferrari and Valentina A. Spalten, "Fragment/Composite" (http://www.objectsofdevotionanddesire.com/essays/fragmentcomposite.html), accessed 16 September 2011.
6 "Sacred Bones and Blood," *New York Review of Books* (August 18, 2011), 67.
7 For my discussion of this text, see chapter 5.

8 Lillian Swinburn, ed., *Lanterne of Liȝt*, EETS o.s. 151 (London: Kegan Paul, Trench, Trübner & Co., 1917), 43.

9 See, for instance, Shannon Gayk, " 'As Plouȝmen han preued': The Alliterative Work of a Set of Lollard Sermons," *Yearbook of Langland Studies* 20 (2006): 43–65.

10 Henry Noble MacCracken, ed., *The Minor Poems of John Lydgate*, EETS o.s. 107, 192, 2 vols. (London: Oxford University Press, 1911, 1934), II, 456–60. All citations are parenthetical and refer to this edition by line number. There are very few scholarly readings of this poem, and in general, commentary has focused on its didactic and antifeminist elements. See for instance Alan Renoir, "Attitudes toward Women in Lydgate's Poetry," *English Studies* 42 (1961): 1–14. For the manuscript context of this lyric, see Julia Boffey, "Short Texts in Manuscript Anthologies: The Minor Poems of John Lydgate in Two Fifteenth-Century Collections," in *The Whole Book: Cultural Perspectives on the Medieval Miscellany*, ed. Stephen G. Nichols and Siegfried Wenzel (Ann Arbor: University of Michigan Press, 1996), 69–82. MacCracken's edition does not include the introductory stanza. This stanza is not in all manuscript variants; it is the primary basis for Eve Salisbury's observation that the poem offers a "private, personal approach to the education of the young." See Eve Salisbury, ed., *The Trials and Joys of Marriage* (Kalamazoo, MI: Medieval Institute Publications, 2002), http://www.lib.rochester.edu/camelot/teams/salintro.htm, accessed 27 June 2010.

11 These lusty young images represent young, virile men. In such moments, it it evident that Lydgate is drawing from Chaucer's depiction of the Wife of Bath, who paints a similar picture of marriage and, like these wives, seeks out young bachelors. Lydgate's indebtedness to Chaucer's creation is clear throughout this poem. In the previous stanza, for example, the narrator complains that wives "hem reioise to see and be sayne, / And to seke sondry pilgremages" (99–100).

12 Brian Stock, *The Implications of Literacy: Written Language and Models of Interpretation in the Eleventh and Twelfth Centuries* (Princeton: Princeton University Press, 1983), 244.

Bibliography

Primary Sources

Manuscripts

Customary of the Shrine of St. Thomas, British Library, Add. MS 59616.
Cambridge Library MS Ee. 3.59.
York Minster MS Add. 2.
Edwards, A.S.G., ed. and intro., *The Life of St Edmund, King and Martyr: A Facsimile*. London: British Library, 2004.

Printed Texts

Adam of Eynsham. *Magna Vita Sancti Hugonis*. 2 vols. Edited by Decima L. Douie and Dom Hugh Farmer. New York: Thomas Nelson and Sons, 1961.
Althaus, Dudley. "Vial of Pope John Paul II's Blood Tours Mexico," *Houston Chronicle* (29 August 2011). : http://www.chron.com/news/article/Vial-of-Pope-John-Paul-II-s-blood-tours-Mexico-2141982.php. Accessed 21 September 2011.
Bannister, A.T., ed. *Register of Richard Mayew*. Hereford: Cantilupe Society Publications, 1919.
Bannister, A.T., ed. *Registrum Ade de Orleton, Episcopi Herefordensis, A.D. 1317–1327*. Hereford: Wilson and Phillips, 1907.
Barnum, Priscilla Heath, ed. *Dives and Pauper*. EETS o.s. 275, 280. 2 vols. London: Oxford University Press, 1976, 1980, 2004.
Barr, Helen, ed. *The Piers Plowman Tradition*. New York: Everyman, 1993.
Benoît de Saint-Maure. *Le roman de Troie*. Edited by Léopold Constans. Société des Anciens Textes Français. 6 vols. Paris: Firmin-Didot et Cie., 1904–12.

Blake, E.O., ed. *Liber Eliensis.* Camden Society Third Series. London: Offices of the Royal Historical Society, 1962.
Boccaccio, Giovanni. *Decameron.* Edited by Vittore Branca. Firenze: Le Monnier, 1951–2.
Boccaccio, Giovanni. *The Decameron.* Edited and translated by Mark Musa and Peter E. Bondanella. New York: Norton, 1977.
Bokenham, Osbern. *Legendys of Hooly Wummen.* Edited by Mary S. Serjeantson. EETS o.s. 206. London: Oxford University Press, 1938.
Caesarius of Heisterbach. *The Dialogue on Miracles.* Edited and translated by H. von E. Scott and C.C. Swinton Bland. 2 vols. London: George Routledge, 1929.
Capes, William W., ed. *Registrum Ricardi de Swinfield, Episcopi Herefordensis, A.D. 1283–1317.* Hereford: Wilson and Phillips, 1909.
Chaucer, Geoffrey. *The Riverside Chaucer.* Edited by Larry D. Benson. Boston: Houghton Mifflin, 1987.
Correale, R.M., and M. Hamel, eds. *Sources and Analogues of the Canterbury Tales.* Woodbridge, Suffolk: Boydell and Brewer, 2002.
Davies, John S., ed. *An English Chronicle of the Reigns of Richard II, Henry IV, Henry V, and Henry VI Written Before the Year 1471.* Camden Society First Series. London: Royal Society, 1856.
Dymmok, Roger. *Liber Contra Duodecim Errores et Hereses Lollardorum.* Edited by H.S. Cronin. London: Trübner, 1922.
Eadmer of Canterbury. *Lives and Miracles of Saints Oda, Dunstan, and Oswald.* Translated and edited by Andrew J. Turner and Bernard J. Muir. Oxford: Clarendon Press, 2006.
Erasmus, Desiderius. *Opera omnia Desiderii Erasmi Roterodami*, edited by L.-E. Halkin, F. Bierlaire, and R. Hoven. 20 vols. Amsterdam: North Holland, 1969–92.
Erasmus, Desiderius. *Collected Works of Erasmus.* Translated by R.A.B. Mynors, C.R. Thompson, et al. 84 vols. Toronto: University of Toronto Press, 1974–.
Fairweather, Janet, trans. ed. *Liber Eliensis.* Woodbridge, Suffolk: Boydell Press, 2005.
Foreville, Raymonde, and Gillian Keir, trans. eds. *The Book of Saint Gilbert.* Oxford: Oxford University Press, 1987.
Fowler, Joseph T., ed. *Extracts from the Account Rolls of the Abbey of Durham Cathedral.* 3 vols. Surtees Society 100. Durham: Published for the Surtees Society by Andrews & Co, 1899.
Fowler, Joseph T., ed. *The Life of St Cuthbert in English Verse, c. A.D. 1450.* Surtees Society 87. Durham: Published for the Surtees Society by Andrews & Co, 1891.

Fowler, Joseph T., ed. *Rites of Durham*. Surtees Society 107. Durham: Published for the Surtees Society by Andrews & Co, 1903.

Furnivall, F.J., and W.G. Stone, ed. and comp. *The Tale of Beryn*. EETS e.s. 105. London: Kegan Paul, Trench, Trübner & Co., 1909.

Geoffrey of Vinsauf. *Poetria nova*. Translated and edited by Margaret Nims. Toronto: PIMS, 1967.

Gerald of Wales. *Giraldi Cambrensis opera*. 8 vols. Edited by J.S. Brewer et al. Rolls Series 21. London: Longman, Green, Longman, and Roberts, 1861–91.

Gregory of Tours. *Glory of the Martyrs*. Translated and edited by Raymond Van Dam. Liverpool: Liverpool University Press, 1988.

Guibert of Nogent. *De sanctis et eorum pigneribus*. Edited by R.B.C. Huygens. Corpus Christianorum Continuatio Mediaevalis CXXVII. Turnholt: Brepols, 1993.

Guibert of Nogent. *Monodies and On the Relics of Saints: The Autobiography and a Manifesto of a French Monk from the Time of the Crusades*. Translated and edited by Joseph McAlhany and Jay Rubenstein. New York: Penguin, 2011.

Guido delle Colonne. *Historia destructionis Troiae*. Edited by Nathaniel Edward Griffin. Cambridge, MA: Medieval Academy of America, 1936.

Hamer, Richard, and Vida Russel, eds. *Supplementary Lives in Some Manuscripts of the Gilte Legende*. EETS o.s. 315. Oxford: Oxford University Press, 2000.

Hardyng, John. *The Chronicle of John Hardyng*. Edited by Henry Ellis. London: F.C. and J. Rivington, 1812.

Havergal, F.T. *Fasti Herefordenses and Other Antiquarian Memorials of Hereford*. Edinburgh: R. Clark, 1869.

Head, Thomas, ed. *Medieval Hagiography: An Anthology*. New York: Garland, 2000.

Herbert, John Alexander, ed. *Titus and Vespasian or Destruction of Jerusalem*. London: Roxburghe Club, 1905.

Heywood, John. *The Plays of John Heywood*. Edited by Richard Axton and Peter Happé. Cambridge: D.S. Brewer, 1991.

Horstmann, Carl, ed. *The Life of Saint Werburge of Chester*. EETS o.s. 88. Woodbridge, Suffolk: Boydell and Brewer, rpt. 2002.

Horstmann, Carl, ed. *Vita S. Etheldredae Eliensis*. In *Altenglische Legenden*, 282–307. Heilbronn: Gebr. Henninger, 1881.

Hudson, Anne, ed. *Selections from English Wycliffite Writings*. Cambridge: Cambridge University Press, 1978.

Hudson, Anne, ed. *The Works of a Lollard Preacher*. EETS o.s. 317. Oxford: Oxford University Press, 2001.

Jocelin of Brakelond. *The Chronicle of Jocelin of Brakelond*. Edited and translated by H.E. Butler. London: Thomas Nelson and Sons, 1949.

Knighton, Henry. *Knighton's Chronicle 1337–1396*. Edited and translated by G. H. Martin. Oxford: Clarendon Press, 1995.

Lacy, Norris J., ed. *Lancelot-Grail: The Old French Arthurian Vulgate and Post-Vulgate in Translation*. 5 vols. New York, Garland: 1993.

Langland, William. *Piers Plowman: A New Annotated Edition of the C-Text*. Edited by Derek Pearsall. Exeter: University of Exeter Press, 1978, rpt. 2008.

Langland, William. *The Vision of Piers Plowman: A Critical Edition of the B-Text*. Edited by A.V.C. Schmidt London: Everyman, 1978, rpt. 2001.

Lapidge, Michael, ed. *The Cult of St Swithun*. Winchester Studies Vol. 4.ii. Oxford: Oxford University Press, 2003.

Lawton, David A., ed. *Joseph of Arimathea: A Critical Edition*. New York: Garland Publishing, 1983.

Legg, J. Wickham, and W.H. St John Hope, ed. *Inventories of Christchurch Canterbury*. Westminster: Archibald Constable & Co, 1902.

Lovelich, Henry. *The History of the Holy Grail*. Edited by Frederick J. Furnivall. EETS e.s. 20, 24, 28, 30, and 95; 4 vols. London, UK: N. Trübner & Co.,1874–1905.

Lydgate, John. *John Lydgate's* Lives of Ss Edmund and Fremund *and the* Extra Miracles of St Edmund. Edited by Anthony Bale and A.S.G. Edwards. Heidelberg: Carl Winter, 2009.

Lydgate, John. *Lydgate's Troy Book*. Edited by Henry Bergen. EETS e.s. 97, 103, 106, 126. 4 vols. London: Kegan Paul, Trench, Trübner & Co, 1935.

Lydgate, John. *The Minor Poems of John Lydgate*. Edited by Henry Noble MacCraken, EETS o.s. 107, 192. 2 vols. London: Oxford University Press, 1911, 1934.

Lydgate, John. *The Lives of St. Edmund and St. Fremund*. Edited by Carl Horstmann. In *Altenglische Legenden*, 376–440. Heilbronn: Gebr. Henninger, 1881.

Malory, Thomas. *The Works of Sir Thomas Malory*. Edited by Eugène Vinaver. 3 vols. 3rd edition. Revised by P.J.C. Field. Oxford: Clarendon Press, 1990.

Masuccio Salernitano. *Novellino*. Translated and edited by W.G. Waters. London: Lawrence and Bullen, 1905.

Masuccio Salernitano. *Il Novellino*. Edited by Alfredo Mauro. Bari: Guis. Laterza & Figli, 1940.

Matthew, F.D., ed. *The English Works of Wyclif hitherto Unprinted*. EETS o.s. 74. Woodbridge, Suffolk: Boydell and Brewer, rpt. 1998.

Matthew of Paris. *Historia Anglorum*. Edited by Frederic Madden. 3 vols. London: Longmans, Green, Reader, and Dyer, 1866.

McSheffrey, Shannon, and Norman Tanner, trans. eds. *Lollards of Coventry 1486– 1522*. Camden Society Fifth Series. London: Cambridge University Press, 2003.

Medina, Jennifer. "California: Woman Arrested in Relic's Disappearance." *New York Times* (17 June 2011).

Medina, Jennifer. "Relic of Saint Disappears from Its Case Inside Church." *New York Times* (14 June 2011).

Meek, Elizabeth. *Historia destructionis Troiae*. Bloomington: Indiana University Press, 1974.

Mellows, W.T., ed. *The Chronicle of Hugh Candidus*. Oxford: Oxford University Press, 1949.

Mirk, John. *Festial*. Edited by Susan Powell. EETS o.s. 334. London: Oxford University Press, 2009.

More, Thomas. *A Dialogue Concerning Heresies*. Vol. 6 of *The Yale Edition of the Complete Works of St Thomas More*, edited by Thomas M.C. Lawler, Germain Marc'Hadour, and Richard C. Marius New Haven, CT, and London: Yale University Press, 1981.

Morse, Ruth, ed. *Saint Erkenwald*. Cambridge: D.S. Brewer; Totowa, NJ: Rowman and Littlefield, 1975.

Munro, John James, ed. *John Capgrave's Lives of St Augustine and St Gilbert of Sempringham, and a Sermon*. EETS o.s. 140. London: Kegan Paul, Trench, Trübner & Co., 1910; rpt. 1971.

Netter, Thomas. *Doctrinale Antiquitatum Fidei Catholicae Ecclesiae*. 3 vols. Edited by B. Blanciotti. Venice: Antonio Bassanese, 1757–9; rpt. Farnborough: Gregg, 1967.

Oliver, George, ed. *Lives of the Bishops of Exeter.* Exeter: William Roberts, Broadgate, 1861.

Orwell, George. "Politics and the English Language." http://mla.stanford.edu/Politics_&_English_language.pdf. Accessed 10 January 2011.

Pecock, Reginald. *Repressor of Overmuch Blaming of the Clergy*. Edited by C. Babington. 2 vols. London: Longman, Green, Longman, and Roberts, 1860, rpt. Elibrion Classics, 2005.

Raine, James, ed. *Historia Dunelmensis Scriptores Tres.* Surtees Society 9. London: Published for the Surtees Society by J.B. Nichols and Son, 1839.

Reginald of Durham. *Libellus de Admirandis Beati Cuthberti Virtutibus.* Edited by James Raine. Surtees Society 1. London: J. B. Nichols and Son, 1835.

Riley, H.T., ed. *Gesta abbatum monasterii sancti Albani*. 3 vols. London: Longman, 1867.

Robertson, James C., ed. *Materials for the History of Thomas Becket*. 7 vols. London: Longman, 1875–85.

Robinson, J. Armitage, ed. *Flete's History of Westminster Abbey*. Cambridge: Cambridge University Press, 1909.

Ross, Woodburn O., ed. *Middle English Sermons.* EETS o.s. 209. London: Oxford University Press, 1940.

Salisbury, Eve, ed. *The Trials and Joys of Marriage.* Kalamazoo, MI: Medieval Institute Publications, 2002.

Shirley, W.W., ed. *Fasciculi Zizaniorum Magistri Johannis Wyclif cum tritico.* Rolls Series 5. London: Longman, Brown, Green, Longmans, and Roberts, 1858; rpt. London: Kraus, 1965.

Simeon of Durham. *Histoira ecclesiae dunhelmensis.* 2 vols. Edited by Thomas Arnold. London: Longman, 1882–5.

Skeat, Walter W., ed. *Joseph of Arimathie: The Romance of the Seint Graal, or Holy Grail.* EETS o.s. 44. London: Trübner & Co, 1871, rpt. Felinfach: Llanerch, 1992.

Skeat, Walter W., ed. *The Wars of Alexander, an Alliterative Romance.* EETS e.s. 47. London: Trübner, 1886, rpt. 1973.

Stouck, Mary-Ann, ed. and trans. "A Reformer's View of the Cult of the Saints." In *Medieval Saints: A Reader*, edited by Mary-Ann Stouck, 595–7. Orchard Park, NY: Broadview Press, 1999.

Stow, John. *The Annales of England to 1605.* London, 1605, STC 23337.

Strawley, J.H., ed. and trans. *The Book of John de Schalby.* Lincoln Minster Pamphlets 2. Lincoln: Friends of Lincoln Cathedral, 1966.

Swinburn, Lillian, ed. *Lanterne of Liȝt.* EETS o.s. 151. London: Kegan Paul, Trench, Trübner & Co, 1917.

Tanner, Norman P., ed. *Heresy Trials in the Diocese of Norwich, 1428–31.* Camden Society Fourth Series. London: Royal Historical Society, 1977.

Thiofrid of Echternach. *Flores epytaphii sanctorum.* Edited by Michele Camillo Ferrari. Corpus Christianorum Continuatio Mediaevalis CXXXIII. Turnholt: Brepols, 1996.

Thomas of Monmouth. *The Life and Miracles of St William of Norwich.* Edited and translated by A. Jessopp and M.R. James. Cambridge: Cambridge University Press, 1896.

Thomas, A.H., and I.O. Thornley, eds. *Great Chronicle of London.* London: George W. Jones, 1938; rpt. Gloucester: Alan Sutton, 1983.

Tissier, André, ed. *Le Pardonneur, le Triacleur et la Tavernière. Recueil de farces.* Geneva: Librairie Droz, 1989.

van Bolland, J., et al., eds. "Miracula ex processu canonizationis." *Acta sanctorum* 1 Octobris, 610–705. http://acta.chadwyck.com.

Victricius of Rouen. *De laude sanctorum.* Edited by I. Mulders and R. Demeulenaere. CCSL 64. Turnhout: Brepols, 1985.

Victricius of Rouen. "In Praise of the Saints." Edited and translated by Phillipe Buc. In *Medieval Hagiography: An Anthology*, edited by Thomas Head, 31–51. New York: Routledge, 2001.

von Nolcken, Christina. "An Edition of Selected Parts of the Middle English Translation of the 'Rosarium Theologie.' " PhD diss., Oxford University, 1976.

von Nolcken, Christina, ed. *The Middle English Translation of the Rosarium Theologie: A Selection ed. From Cbr., Gonville and Caius Coll. MS 354/581*. Middle English Texts 10. Heidelberg: Carl Winter, 1979.

Walsingham, Thomas. *Historia anglicana*. Edited by H. T. Riley. Rolls Series 28. 2 vols. London: Longman, Green, Longman, Roberts, and Green, 1863.

Watkiss, Leslie, and Marjorie Chibnall, eds. *The Waltham Chronicle*. Oxford: Clarendon Press, 1994.

Wenzel, Siegfried, trans. ed. *Fasciculus morum: A Fourteenth-Century Preacher's Handbook*. University Park: Pennsylvania State University Press, 1989.

Whatley, E. Gordon., ed. and trans. *The Saint of London: The Life and Miracles of St Erkenwald*. Binghamton, NY: Medieval & Renaissance Texts & Studies, 1989.

Wilkins, David, ed. *Concilia Magnae Britanniae et Hiberniae, AD 466–1718*. 4 vols. London: R. Gosling, F. Gyles, T. Woodward, and C. Davis, 1737.

Wilmart, André, ed. "Edmeri Cantuariensis cantoris nova opuscula de sanctorum veneratione et obsecratione." *Revue des sciences religieuses* 15 (1935): 184–219, 354–79.

Wordsworth, C., ed. *Ceremonies and Processions of the Cathedral Church of Salisbury*. Cambridge: Cambridge University Press, 1901.

Wright, Thomas, ed. *Three Chapters of Letters Relating to the Suppression of the Monasteries*. Camden Society XXVI. London: John Bowyer Nichols and Son, 1843.

Wülfing, J. Ernst, ed. *The Laud Troy Book*. EETS o.s. 121, 122. London: Kegan Paul, Trench, Trübner & Co., 1902, 1903.

Wyclif, John. *De Eucharistia tractatus maior: Accedit tractatus de eucharistia et poenitentia sive de confessione*. Edited by Johann Loserth. London: Trübner, 1892.

Wyclif, John. *Iohannis Wyclif Sermones*. 2 vols. Edited by Johann Loserth and F.D. Matthew. London: Trübner, 1888.

Wyclif, John. *Tractatus de Ecclesia*. Edited by Johann Loserth and F.D. Matthew. London: Trübner, 1886.

Secondary Sources

Abou-El-Haj, Barbara. *The Medieval Cult of Saints: Formations and Transformations*. Cambridge: Cambridge University Press, 1994.

Abou-El-Haj, Barbara. "The Audiences for the Medieval Cult of Saints." *Gesta* 30, no. 1 (1991): 3–15. http://dx.doi.org/10.2307/767005.

Adair, John. *The Pilgrims' Way: Shrines and Saints in Britain and Ireland*. Hampshire, UK: BAS Printers, 1978.

Aers, David. *Chaucer, Langland and the Creative Imagination*. London: Routledge, 1980.

Aers, David. *Faith, Ethics and Church: Writing in England, 1360–1409*. Cambridge: D.S. Brewer, 2000.

Aers, David. "Faith, Ethics, and Community: Reflections on Late Medieval English Writing." *Journal of Medieval and Early Modern Studies* 28 (1998): 341–69.

Aers, David. "John Wyclif: Poverty and the Poor." *Yearbook of Langland Studies* 17 (2003): 55–72.

Aers, David, and Lynn Staley. *The Powers of the Holy: Religion, Politics, and Gender in Late Medieval English Culture*. University Park: Pennsylvania State University Press, 1996.

Anderson, Earl R. "'Ein Kind wird geschlagen': The Meaning of Malory's Tale of the Healing of Sir Urry." *Literature and Psychology* 49 (2003): 45–74.

Angenendt, Arnold. *Heilige und Reliquien: die Geschichte ihres Kultes vom frühen Christentum bis zum Gegenwart*. Munich: C.H. Beck, 1994.

Angenendt, Arnold. "Relics and Their Veneration." In *Treasures of Heaven: Saints, Relics, and Devotion in Medieval Europe*, edited by Martina Bagnoli, Holger A. Klein, C. Griffith Mann, and James Robinson, 19–28. New Haven, CT: Yale University Press, 2011.

Anitchkof, E. "Le Saint Graal et les rites eucharistiques." *Romania* 55 (1929): 174–94.

Armstrong, Dorsey. *Gender and the Chivalric Community in Malory's Morte d'Arthur*. Gainesville: University Press of Florida, 2003.

Ashley, Kathleen, and Pamela Sheingorn. *Writing Faith: Text, Sign and History in the Miracles of Sainte Foy*. Chicago: University of Chicago Press, 1999.

Aston, Margaret. " 'Caim's Castles': Poverty, Politics and Disendowment." In *The Church, Politics and Patronage in the Fifteenth Century*, edited by R.B. Dobson. Gloucester: St Martin's Press, 1984. Reprinted in Aston, *Faith and Fire: Popular and Unpopular Religion, 1350–1600*, 95–131. London: Hambledon Press, 1993.

Aston, Margaret. *England's Iconoclasts: Laws against Images*. Oxford: Clarendon Press, 1988.

Aston, Margaret. *Faith and Fire: Popular and Unpopular Religion 1350–1500*. London: Hambledon Press, 1993.

Aston, Margaret. *Lollards and Reformers: Images and Literacy in Late Medieval Religion*. London: Hambledon Press, 1984.

Atkinson, Stephen C.B. "Malory's Lancelot and the Quest of the Grail." In *Studies in Malory*, edited by James W. Spisak, 129–52. Kalamazoo, MI: Medieval Institute Publications, 1985.

Bagnoli, Martina, Holger A. Klein, C. Griffith Mann, and James Robinson, eds. *Treasures of Heaven: Saints, Relics, and Devotion in Medieval Europe*. New Haven, CT: Yale University Press, 2011.

Bailey, R.N. "St Cuthbert's Relics: Some Neglected Evidence." In *St Cuthbert, His Cult and His Community to AD 1200*, edited by Gerald Bonner, David Rollason, and Clare Stancliffe, 231–46. Woodbridge, Suffolk: Boydell and Brewer, 1989.

Bale, Anthony. *The Jew in the Medieval Book: English Antisemitisms 1350–1500*. Cambridge: Cambridge University Press, 2006.

Bale, Anthony. "Introduction." In *St Edmund, King and Martyr: Changing Images of a Medieval Saint*, edited by Anthony Bale, 1–25. York: York Medieval Press, 2009.

Bale, Anthony. "St Edmund in Fifteenth-Century London." In *St Edmund, King and Martyr: Changing Images of a Medieval Saint*, edited by Anthony Bale, 145–62. York: York Medieval Press, 2009.

Bale, Anthony. "Twenty-First Century Lydgate." *Modern Philology* 105, no. 4 (2008): 698–704. http://dx.doi.org/10.1086/595640.

Barber, Richard. *The Holy Grail: Imagination and Belief*. Cambridge, MA: Harvard University Press, 2004.

Barber, Richard. "Malory and the Holy Blood of Hailes." In *The Medieval Book and a Modern Collector*, edited by Takami Matsuda et al., 279–84. Cambridge: D.S. Brewer, 2004.

Barr, Helen. *Socioliterary Practice in Late Medieval England*. Oxford: Oxford University Press, 2001. http://dx.doi.org/10.1093/acprof:oso/9780198112426.001.0001.

Barr, Jessica. *Willing to Know God: Dreamers and Visionaries in the Later Middle Ages*. Columbus: Ohio State University Press, 2010.

Barrett, Illtud. "Relics of St Thomas Cantilupe." In *St. Thomas Cantilupe, Bishop of Hereford: Essays in His Honour*, edited by Meryl Jancey, 181–5. Hereford: Friends of Hereford Cathedral, 1982.

Barrett Jr, Robert W. *Against All England: Regional Identity and Cheshire Writing, 1195–1656*. Notre Dame, IN: University of Notre Dame Press, 2009.

Barron, W.R.J. "*Joseph of Arimathie* and the *Estoire del Saint Graal*." *Medium Ævum* 33 (1964): 184–94.

Bartlett, Robert. "The Hagiography of Angevin England." In *Thirteenth Century England V: Proceedings of the Newcastle upon Tyne Conference 1993*. Edited by P.R. Cross and S.D. Lloyd, 37–52. Woodbridge, Suffolk: Boydell Press, 1995.

Beckwith, Sarah. *Christ's Body: Identity, Culture, and Society in Late Medieval Writings*. London: Routledge, 1993.

Beckwith, Sarah. *Signifying God: Social Relation and Symbolic Act in the York Corpus Christi Plays*. Chicago: University of Chicago Press, 2001.

Belting, Hans. *Likeness and Presence: A History of the Image before the Era of Art*. Translated by Edmund Jephcott. Chicago: University of Chicago Press, 1994.

Benson, C. David. "Chaucer's Pardoner: His Sexuality and Modern Critics." *Mediaevalia* 8 (1982): 337–49.

Benson, C. David. *The History of Troy in Middle English Literature*. Woodbridge, Suffolk: D.S. Brewer, 1980.

Benson, C. David, and Elizabeth Robertson, eds. *Chaucer's Religious Tales*. Cambridge: D.S. Brewer, 1990.

Benson, Larry D. *Malory's Morte Darthur*. Cambridge: Harvard University Press, 1976.

Bertrand, Paul. "Authentiques de reliques: authentiques ou reliques?" *Le Moyen Âge* 112, no. 2 (2006): 363–74. http://dx.doi.org/10.3917/rma.122.0363.

Bethell, Denis. "The Making of a Twelfth-Century Relic Collection." In *Popular Belief and Practice: Papers Read at the Ninth Summer Meeting and the Tenth Winter Meeting of the Ecclesiastical History Society*, edited by G.J. Cuming and Derek Baker, 61–72. Cambridge: Cambridge University Press, 1972.

Blair, John. *The Church in Anglo-Saxon Society*. Oxford: Oxford University Press, 2005.

Blair, John. "St Frideswide's Monastery: Problems and Possibilities." *Oxoniensia* 53 (1988): 220–58.

Blaise, Albert. *Lexicon latinitatis Medii Aevi*. Turnholt: Brepols, 1975.

Blamires, Alcuin. "The 'Religion of Love' in Chaucer's *Troilus and Criseyde* and Medieval Visual Art." In *Word and Visual Imagination: Studies in the Interaction of English Literature and the Visual Arts*, edited by Karl Josef Höltgen, Peter M. Daly, and Wolfgang Lottes, 11–31. Erlangen: Universitätsbund Erlangen-Nürnberg, 1988.

Blanton, Virginia. *Signs of Devotion: The Cult of St Aethelthryth in Medieval England, 695–1615*. University Park: Pennsylvania State University Press, 2007.

Blick, Sarah. "Reconstructing the Shrine of St. Thomas Becket, Canterbury Cathedral." In *Art and Architecture of Late Medieval Pilgrimage in Northern Europe and the British Isles*, edited by Sarah Blick and Rita Tekippe, 405–41. Leiden: Brill, 2005.

Boardman, Phillip C. "Grail and Quest in the Medieval English World of Arthur." In *The Grail, the Quest, and the World of Arthur*, edited by Norris J. Lacy, 126–40. Cambridge: D.S. Brewer, 2008.

Boffey, Julia. "Short Texts in Manuscript Anthologies: The Minor Poems of John Lydgate in Two Fifteenth-Century Collections." In *The Whole Book:*

Cultural Perspectives on the Medieval Miscellany, edited by Stephen G. Nichols and Siegfried Wenzel, 69–82. Ann Arbor: University of Michigan Press, 1996.

Bogdanow, Fanni. "An Interpretation of the Meaning and Purpose of the Vulgate Queste del Saint Graal in the Light of the Mystical Theology of St Bernard." In *The Changing Face of Arthurian Romance: Essays on Arthurian Prose Romances in Memory of Cedric E. Pickford*, edited by Alison Adams, A.H. Diverres, et al., 23–46. Cambridge: D.S. Brewer, 1986.

Bonner, Gerald, David Rollason, and Clare Stancliffe, eds. *St Cuthbert, His Cult and His Community to AD 1200*. Woodbridge, Suffolk: Boydell and Brewer, 1989.

Bose, Mishtooni. "Reginald Pecock's Vernacular Voice." In *Lollards and Their Influence in Late Medieval England*, edited by Fiona Somerset, Jill C. Havens, and Derrick G. Pitard, 217–36. Woodbridge, Suffolk: Boydell Press, 2003.

Bose, Mishtooni, and J. Patrick Hornbeck II, eds. *Wycliffite Controversies*. Turnhout: Brepols, 2011.

Bozóky, Edina, and Anne-Marie Helvétius, eds. *Les reliques: objects, cultes, symboles: Actes du colloque international de l'université du Littoral-Côte d'Opale (boulogne-sur-Mer) 4–6 septembre 1997*. Turnhout: Brepols, 1999.

Bradstock, E.M. "The Juxtaposition of the 'Knight of the Cart' and 'The Healing of Sir Urry.' " *Journal of the Australasian Universities Modern Language Association* 50 (1978): 208–23.

Brantley, Jessica. *Reading in the Wilderness: Private Devotion and Public Performance in Late Medieval England*. Chicago: University of Chicago Press, 2007.

Braun, Joseph. *Die Reliquiare des christlichen Kultes und ihre Entwicklung*. Freiburg im Breisgau: Herder, 1940.

Brody, Saul N. "Making a Play for Criseyde: The Staging of Pandarus's House in Chaucer's *Troilus and Criseyde*." *Speculum* 73, no. 1 (1998): 115–40. http://dx.doi.org/10.2307/2886874.

Brown, Elizabeth A.R. "Death and the Human Body in the Later Middle Ages: The Legislation of Boniface VIII on the Division of the Corpse." *Viator* 12 (1981): 221–70.

Brown, Peter. *The Cult of the Saints: Its Rise and Function in Latin Christianity*. Chicago: University of Chicago Press, 1981.

Burger, Glenn. *Chaucer's Queer Nation*. Minneapolis: University of Minnesota Press, 2003.

Burger, Glenn. "Kissing the Pardoner." *PMLA* 107, no. 5 (1992): 1143–56. http://dx.doi.org/10.2307/462870.

Burnley, David. *Courtliness and Literature in Medieval England*. New York: Longman, 1998.

Butler, John. *The Quest for Becket's Bones: The Mystery of the Relics of St Thomas Becket of Canterbury*. New Haven, CT: Yale University Press, 1995.

Bynum, Caroline. "Bodily Miracles and the Resurrection of the Body in the High Middle Ages." In *Belief in History: Innovative Approaches to European and American Religion*, edited by Thomas Kselman, 68–106. Notre Dame, IN: University of Notre Dame Press, 1991.

Bynum, Caroline. "Why All the Fuss about the Body? A Medievalist's Perspective." *Critical Inquiry* 22, no. 1 (1995): 1–33. http://dx.doi.org/10.1086/448780.

Bynum, Caroline Walker. "The Blood of Christ in the Later Middle Ages." *Church History* 71, no. 4 (2002): 685–714. http://dx.doi.org/10.1017/S0009640700096268.

Bynum, Caroline Walker. *Christian Materiality: An Essay on Religion in Late Medieval Europe*. New York: Zone Books, 2011.

Bynum, Caroline Walker. *The Resurrection of the Body in Western Christianity, 200–1336*. New York: Columbia University Press, 1995.

Bynum, Caroline Walker. *Wonderful Blood: Theology and Practice in Late Medieval Northern Germany and Beyond*. Philadelphia: University of Pennsylvania Press, 2007.

Bynum, Caroline Walker, and Paula Gerson. "Body-Part Reliquaries and Body Parts in the Middle Ages." *Gesta* 36, no. 1 (1997): 3–7. http://dx.doi.org/10.2307/767274.

Camargo, Martin. "The Consolation of Pandarus." *Chaucer Review* 25 (1991): 214–28.

Camille, Michael. *The Gothic Idol: Ideology and Image-Making in Medieval Art*. Cambridge: Cambridge University Press, 1989.

Camp, Cynthia Turner. "Inventing the Past in Henry Bradshaw's *Life of St Werburge*." *Exemplaria* 23, no. 3 (2011): 244–67. http://dx.doi.org/10.1179/174963111X13009808981839.

Campbell, Kirsty. *The Call to Read: Reginald Pecock's Books and Textual Communities*. Notre Dame, IN: University of Notre Dame Press, 2010.

Cawsey, Kathy. "Disorienting Orientalism: Finding Saracens in Strange Places in Late Medieval English Manuscripts." *Exemplaria* 21, no. 4 (2009): 380–97. http://dx.doi.org/10.1179/175330709X449116.

Cespedes, Frank V. "Chaucer's Pardoner and Preaching." *English Literary History* 44, no. 1 (1977): 1. http://dx.doi.org/10.2307/2872523.

Chaganti, Seeta. *The Medieval Poetics of the Reliquary: Enshrinement, Inscription, Performance*. New York: Palgrave, 2008. http://dx.doi.org/10.1057/9780230615380.

Cherewatuk, Karen. "Malory's Launcelot and the Language of Sin and Confession." *Arthuriana* 16 (2006): 68–72.

Clark, Gillian. "Translating Relics: Victricius of Rouen and Fourth-Century Debate." *Early Medieval Europe* 10, no. 2 (2001): 161–76. http://dx.doi.org/10.1111/1468-0254.00083.

Clark, Gillian. "Victricius of Rouen: Praising the Saints." *Journal of Early Christian Studies* 7, no. 3 (1999): 365–99. http://dx.doi.org/10.1353/earl.1999.0071.

Coldstream, Nicola. "English Decorated Shrine Bases." *Journal of the British Archaeological Association* 129 (1976): 15–34.

Coldstream, Nicola. "The Medieval Tombs and the Shrine of Saint Thomas Cantilupe." In *Hereford Cathedral: A History*, edited by Gerald Aylmer and John Tiller, 322–30. London: Hambledon Press, 2000.

Cole, Andrew. *Literature and Heresy in the Age of Chaucer*. Cambridge: Cambridge University Press, 2008. http://dx.doi.org/10.1017/CBO9780511481420.

Cole, R.E.G. "Proceedings Relative to the Canonization of John de Dalderby, Bishop of Lincoln." *Associated Architectural Societies' Reports and Papers* 33 (1915): 243–76.

Cole, R.E.G. "Proceedings Relative to the Canonization of Robert Grosseteste, Bishop of Lincoln." *Associated Architectural Societies' Reports and Papers* 33 (1915): 1–34.

Collinson, Patrick, Nigel Ramsay, and Margaret Sparks, eds. *A History of Canterbury Cathedral*. New York: Oxford University Press, 1995.

Cooper, Helen. "Introduction." In *Chaucer and Religion*, edited by Helen Phillips, xi–xix. Cambridge: D.S. Brewer, 2010.

Cooper, Lisa, and Andrea Denny-Brown, eds. *The Arma Christi in Medieval and Early Modern Culture: Objects, Representation, and Devotional Practice*. Burlington, VT: Ashgate, 2013.

Copeland, Rita. "Chaucer and Rhetoric." In *The Yale Companion to Chaucer*, edited by Seth Lerer, 122–43. New Haven, CT: Yale University Press, 2006.

Copeland, Rita. "The Pardoner's Body and the Disciplining of Rhetoric." In *Framing Medieval Bodies*, edited by Sarah Kay and Miri Rubin, 138–59. Manchester: Manchester University Press, 1994.

Copeland, Rita. *Rhetoric, Hermeneutics, and Translation in the Middle Ages: Academic Traditions and Vernacular Texts*. Cambridge: Cambridge University Press, 1991. http://dx.doi.org/10.1017/CBO9780511597534.

Crassons, Kate. *The Claims of Poverty: Literature, Culture, and Ideology in Late Medieval England*. Notre Dame, IN: University of Notre Dame Press, 2010.

Cronin, H.S. "The Twelve Conclusions of the Lollards." *English Historical Review* 22 (1907): 292–304.
Crook, John. *The Architectural Setting of the Cult of Saints in the Early Christian West c.300–1200.* Oxford: Clarendon Press, 2000.
Crook, John. *English Medieval Shrines*. Woodbridge, Suffolk: Boydell Press, 2011.
Crook, John. "The Enshrinement of Local Saints in Francia and England." In *Local Saints and Local Churches in the Early Medieval West*, edited by Alan Thacker and Richard Sharpe, 189–224. New York: Oxford University Press, 2002.
Crook, John. "King Edgar's Reliquary of St Swithun." *Anglo-Saxon England* 21 (1992): 177–202. http://dx.doi.org/10.1017/S026367510000421X.
Crook, John. "St Swithun of Winchester." In *Winchester Cathedral: Nine Hundred Years, 1093–1993*, edited by John Crook, 57–68. Chichester, West Sussex: Phillimore, 1993.
Crook, John. "The Typology of Early Medieval Shrines." *Antiquaries Journal* 70, no. 1 (1990): 49–64. http://dx.doi.org/10.1017/S0003581500070293.
Daly, Patrick H. "The Process of Canonization in the Thirteenth and Early Fourteenth Centuries." In *St. Thomas Cantilupe, Bishop of Hereford: Essays in His Honour,* edited by Meryl Jancey, 125–36. Hereford: Friends of Hereford Cathedral, 1982.
D'Arcy, Anne Marie. *Wisdom and the Grail: The Image of the Vessel in the Queste del Saint Graal and Malory's Tale of the Sankgreal*. Dublin: Four Courts Press, 2000.
Davis, John F. "Lollards, Reformers and St Thomas of Canterbury." *University of Birmingham Historical Journal* 9 (1963): 1–15.
Delahoyde, Michael. " 'Heryng th'effect' of the Names in *Troilus and Criseyde.*" *Chaucer Review* 34, no. 4 (2000): 351–71. http://dx.doi.org/10.1353/cr.2000.0003.
de Man, Paul. *Allegories of Reading: Figural Language in Rousseau, Nietzsche, Rilke, and Proust*. New Haven, CT: Yale University Press, 1979.
Dickinson, J.C. *The Shrine of Our Lady of Walsingham*. Cambridge: Cambridge University Press, 1956.
Dierkens, Alain. "Du bon (et du mauvais) usage des reliquaires au Moyen Age." In *Les Reliques: objects, cultes, symboles. Actes du colloque international de l'Université du Littoral Cote d'Opal (Boulogne-sur-Mer) 4–6 septembre 1997*, edited by E. Bozóky and A.M. Helvétius, 239–52. Turnhout: Brepols, 1999.
Dinshaw, Carolyn. *Chaucer's Sexual Poetics*. Madison: University of Wisconsin Press, 1989.

Dinzelbacher, Peter. "Die 'Realpräesenz' der Heiligen in ihren Reliquiaren und Gräbern nach mittelalterlichen Quellen." In *Heiliegenverehrung in Geschichte und Gegenwant*, edited by Peter Dinzelbacher and Dieter Bauer, 115–74. Ostfildern: Schwabenverlag, 1990.

Donaldson, E. Talbot. "Chaucer's Three Ps: Pardoner, Pandarus, and Poet." *Michigan Literary Quarterly* 14 (1975): 282–301..

Donaldson, E. Talbot. *Speaking of Chaucer*. New York: Norton, 1970.

Dooley, Eugene A. *Church Law on Sacred Relics*. Canon Law Studies 70. Washington, DC: Catholic University of America Press, 1931.

Duffy, Eamon. "Sacred Bones and Blood." Review of Caroline Walker Bynum's *Christian Materiality*. In the *New York Review of Books* (18 August 2011): 66–8.

Duffy, Eamon. *The Stripping of the Altars: Traditional Religion in England c.1400–c.1500*. Rev. edition. New Haven, CT: Yale University Press, 2005.

Edwards, A.S.G. "John Lydgate's *Lives of SS Edmund and Fremund*: Politics, Hagiography and Literature." In *St Edmund, King and Martyr: Changing Images of a Medieval Saint*, edited by Anthony Bale, 133–44. York: York Medieval Press, 2009.

Edwards, Robert R. "Introduction." In *Troy Book: Selections*, edited by R. Robert Edwards, 1–25. Kalamazoo, MI: Medieval Institute Publications, 1998.

Emden, A.B. *A Biographical Register of the University of Oxford to A.D. 1500*. Vol. 1, *A–E*. Oxford: Clarendon Press, 1957.

Fehrenbacher, Richard W. "Al that which chargeth nought to seye." *Exemplaria* 9, no. 2 (1997): 341–69. http://dx.doi.org/10.1179/104125797790606556.

Ferrari, Danyel M.R., and Valentina A. Spalten. "Fragment/Composite." http://www.objectsofdevotionanddesire.com/essays/fragmentcomposite.html. Accessed 16 September 2011.

Ferrari, Michael. "Gold und Asche: Reliquie und Reliquiare als Medien in Thiofrid von Echternachs *Flores epytaphii sanctorum*." In *Reliquiare im Mittelalter*, edited by Bruno Reudenbach and Gia Toussaint, 61–74. Berlin: Akademie Verlag, 2005.

Ferrari, Michael. "Lemmata sanctorum: Thiofrid d'Echternach et le discours sur les reliques au XIIe siècle." *Cahiers de civilisation médiévale* 38, no. 151 (1995): 215–25. http://dx.doi.org/10.3406/ccmed.1995.2618.

Field, P.J.C. "Malory and the Grail." In *The Grail, the Quest, and the World of Arthur*, edited by Norris J. Lacy, 141–55. Cambridge: D.S. Brewer, 2008.

Finucane, Ronald C. "Cantilupe as Thaumatuge: Pilgrims and Their Miracles." In *St. Thomas Cantilupe, Bishop of Hereford: Essays in His Honour*, edited by Meryl Jancey, 137–44. Hereford: Friends of Hereford Cathedral, 1982.

Finucane, Ronald C. *Miracles and Pilgrims: Popular Beliefs in Medieval England*. 2nd ed. Totowa, NJ: Rowman and Littlefield, 1995.

Fleming, John. *Classical Imitation and Interpretation in Chaucer's Troilus*. Lincoln: University of Nebraska Press, 1990.

Fletcher, Alan. "Chaucer the Heretic." *Studies in the Age of Chaucer* 25 (2003): 53–121.

Fletcher, Alan. "The Preaching of the Pardoner." *Studies in the Age of Chaucer* 11 (1989): 15–35.

Fredeman, Jane C. "John Capgrave's Life of St. Gilbert of Sempringham." *Bulletin John Rylands University Library of Manchester* 55 (1972): 112–45.

Freeman, Charles. *Holy Bones, Holy Dust: How Relics Shaped the History of Medieval Europe*. New Haven, CT: Yale University Press, 2011.

Fyler, John M. "The Fabrications of Pandarus." *Modern Language Quarterly* 41, no. 2 (1980): 115–30. http://dx.doi.org/10.1215/00267929-41-2-115.

Ganim, John. "Lydgate, Location, and the Poetics of Exemption." In *Lydgate Matters: Poetry and Material Culture in the Fifteenth Century*, edited by Lisa H. Cooper and Andrea Denny-Brown, 165–83. New York: Palgrave, 2008.

Gayk, Shannon. " 'As Plouȝmen han preued': The Alliterative Work of a Set of Lollard Sermons." *Yearbook of Langland Studies* 20 (2006): 43–65.

Gayk, Shannon. *Image, Text, and Religious Reform in Fifteenth-Century England*. Cambridge: Cambridge University Press, 2010. http://dx.doi.org/10.1017/CBO9780511659058.

Geary, Patrick. *Furta Sacra: Thefts of Relics in the Central Middle Ages*. 2nd ed. Princeton, NJ: Princeton University Press, 1990.

Geary, Patrick. "Sacred Commodities: The Circulation of Medieval Relics." In *The Social Life of Things: Commodities in Cultural Perspective*, edited by Arjun Appadurai, 169–91. Cambridge: Cambridge University Press, 1986.

Gibson, Gail McMurray. *The Theater of Devotion: East Anglian Drama and Society in the Late Middle Ages*. Chicago: University of Chicago Press, 1989.

Gillespie, Vincent, and Kantik Ghosh, eds. *After Arundel: Religious Writing in Fifteenth-Century England*. Turnhout: Brepols, 2012.

Gillespie, Vincent. "Vernacular Theology." In *Middle English*, edited by Paul Strohm, 401–20. Oxford: Oxford University Press, 2007.

Goodich, Michael. *Miracles and Wonders: The Development of the Concept of Miracle, 1150–1350*. Williston, VT: Ashgate, 2007.

Goodich, Michael. "Reason or Revelation?: The Criteria for the Proof and Credibility of Miracles in Canonization Processes." In *Procès de canonisation au Moyen Âge:aspects juridiques et religieux*. Collection de l'école Française de Rome 340, edited by Gábor Klaniczay, 181–97. Rome: École française de Rome, 2004.

Goodich, Michael. *Violence and Miracle in the Fourteenth Century: Private Grief and Public Salvation*. Chicago: University of Chicago Press, 1995.

Grady, Frank. *Representing Righteous Heathens in Late Medieval England*. New York: Palgrave, 2005.

Gransden, Antonia. "The Alleged Incorruption of the Body of St Edmund, King and Martyr." *Antiquaries Journal* 74 (1994): 135–68. http://dx.doi.org/10.1017/S0003581500024410.

Green, Richard Firth. "Further Evidence for Chaucer's Representation of the Pardoner as a Womanizer." *Medium Ævum* 71 (2002): 307–9.

Green, Richard Firth. "The Pardoner's Pants (and Why They Matter)." *Studies in the Age of Chaucer* 15 (1993): 131–45.

Green, Richard Firth. "The Sexual Normality of Chaucer's Pardoner." *Mediaevalia* 8 (1982): 351–8.

Hahn, Cynthia. "Metaphor and Meaning in Early Medieval Reliquaries." In *Seeing the Invisible in Late Antiquity and the Early Middle Ages*, edited by Giselle de Nie, Karl F. Morrison, and Marco Mostert, 239–64. Utrecht Studies in Medieval Literacy 14. Turnhout: Brepols, 2005.

Hahn, Cynthia. "Narrative on the Golden Altar of Sant'Ambrogio in Milan: Presentation and Reception." *Dumbarton Oaks Papers* 53 (1999): 167–87. http://dx.doi.org/10.2307/1291799.

Hahn, Cynthia. "Seeing and Believing: The Construction of Sanctity in Early-Medieval Saints' Shrines." *Speculum* 72, no. 4 (1997): 1079–106. http://dx.doi.org/10.2307/2865959.

Hahn, Cynthia. *Strange Beauty: Origins and Issues in the Making of Medieval Reliquaries 400–circa 1204*. University Park: Pennsylvania State University Press, 2012.

Hahn, Cynthia. "The Voices of the Saints: Speaking Reliquaries." *Gesta* 36, no. 1 (1997): 20–31. http://dx.doi.org/10.2307/767276.

Hahn, Cynthia. "What Do Reliquaries Do for Relics?" *Numen* 57, no. 3 (2010): 284–316. http://dx.doi.org/10.1163/156852710X501324.

Hall, David. "The Sanctuary of St Cuthbert." In *St Cuthbert, His Cult and His Community to AD 1200*, edited by Gerald Bonner, David Rollason, and Clare Stancliffe, 425–36. Woodbridge, Suffolk: Boydell and Brewer, 1989.

Harris, Anne F. "Pilgrimage, Performance, and Stained Glass at Canterbury Cathedral." In *Art and Architecture of Late Medieval Pilgrimage in Northern Europe and the British Isles*, edited by Sarah Blick and Rita Tekippe, 243–81. Leiden: Brill, 2005.

Head, Thomas. *Hagiography and the Cult of Saints: The Diocese of Orléans, 800–1200*. Cambridge: Cambridge University Press, 1990. http://dx.doi.org/10.1017/CBO9780511562457.

Heath, Sidney. *Pilgrim Life in the Middle Ages*. London: Unwin, 1912.
Héliot, Pierre, and Chastang, Marie-Laure. "Quêtes et voyages de reliques au profit des églises françaises du Moyen Age." *Revue d'historie ecclésiastique* 59 (1964): 789–822.
Herrmann-Mascard, Nicole. *Les reliques des saints: Formation coutumière d'un droit. Société d'histoire du droit 6*. Paris: Éditions Klincksieck, 1975.
Hewitt, John. "The 'Keeper of Saint Chad's Head' in Litchfield Cathedral, and other Matters Concerning that Minster in the Fifteenth Century." *Archaeological Journal* 33 (1876): 72–82.
Hoffman, Donald. "Perceval's Sister: Malory's 'Rejected' Masculinities." *Arthuriana* 6 (1996): 72–83.
Holsinger, Bruce. "Lollard Ekphrasis: Situated Aesthetics and Literary History." *Journal of Medieval and Early Modern Studies* 35, no. 1 (2005): 67–90. http://dx.doi.org/10.1215/10829636-35-1-67.
Holsinger, Bruce and Elizabeth Robertson, eds. "Vernacular Theology and Medieval Studies." In *Literary History and the Religious Turn*, edited by Bruce Holsinger, 77–137. *English Language Notes* 44 (2006).
Howes, Laura L. "Chaucer's Criseyde: The Betrayer Betrayed." In *Reading Medieval Culture: Essays in Honor of Robert W. Hanning*, edited by Robert M. Stein and Sandra Pierson Prior, 324–43. Notre Dame, IN: University of Notre Dame Press, 2005.
Hudson, Anne. "Langland and Lollardy?" *Yearbook of Langland Studies* 17 (2003): 93–106.
Hudson, Anne. "Poor Preachers, Poor Men: Views of Poverty in Wyclif and His Followers." In *Häresie und vorzeitige Reformation im Spätmittelalter*, edited by František Šmahel and Elisabeth Müller-Luckner, 41–53. Munich: Oldenbourg Wissenschaftsverlag, 1998. http://dx.doi.org/10.1524/9783486594379.41.
Hudson, Anne. *The Premature Reformation: Wycliffite Texts and Lollard History*. Oxford: Clarendon Press, 1988.
Hughes, Jonathan. *Pastors and Visionaries: Religion and Secular Life in Late Medieval Yorkshire*. Woodbridge, Suffolk: Boydell and Brewer, 1988.
Ihle, Sandra Ness. *Malory's Grail Quest: Invention and Adaptation in Medieval Prose Romance*. Madison: Wisconsin University Press, 1983.
Jankulak, Karen. *The Medieval Cult of St Petroc*. Studies in Celtic History XIX. Woodbridge, Suffolk: Boydell and Brewer, 2000.
Jones, Christopher A. "Old English Words for Relics of the Saints." *Florilegium* 26 (2009): 85–129.
Jones, W.R. "Lollards and Images: The Defense of Religious Art in Later Medieval England." *Journal of the History of Ideas* 34, no. 1 (1973): 27–50. http://dx.doi.org/10.2307/2708942.

Jusserand, J.J. "Chaucer's Pardoner and the Pope's Pardoners." *Chaucer Society Essays* 13, no. 5 (1889): 423–36.

Justice, Steven. "Inquisition, Speech, and Writing: A Case from Late Medieval Norwich." In *Criticism and Dissent in the Middle Ages*, edited by Rita Copeland, 289–322. Cambridge: Cambridge University Press, 1996.

Kaiser, R. "Quêtes itinérantes avec des reliques pour financer la construction des églises (XIe–XIIe siècles)." *Le Moyen Âge* 101 (1995): 205–25.

Kamerick, Kathleen. *Popular Piety and Art in the Late Middle Ages: Image Worship and Idolatry in England, 1350–1500*. New York: Palgrave, 2002.

Kamowski, William. " 'Coillons,' Relics, Skepticism and Faith on Chaucer's Road to Canterbury: An Observation on the Pardoner's and the Host's Confrontation." *English Language Notes* 28 (1991): 1–8.

Kellogg, Alfred, and Louis A. Haselmayer. " 'Chaucer's Satire of the Pardoner.' *PMLA* 66 (1951): 251–77. Rpt." In *Chaucer, Langland, Arthur: Essays in Middle English Literature*, edited by Alfred Kellogg, 212–44. New Brunswick, NJ: Rutgers University Press, 1972.

Kemp, Eric W. *Canonization and Authority in the Western Church*. London: Oxford University Press, 1948.

Kennedy, Beverly. "Malory's Lancelot: 'Trewest Lover, of Synful Man.' " *Viator* 12 (1981): 409–56.

Kennedy, Edward Donald. "John Hardyng and the Holy Grail." In *Glatsonbury Abbey and the Arthurian Tradition*, edited by James P. Carley, 249–68. Cambridge: D.S. Brewer, 2001.

Knapp, Daniel. "The Relyk of a Seint: A Gloss on Chaucer's Pilgrimage." *English Literary History* 39, no. 1 (1972): 1–26. http://dx.doi.org/10.2307/2872288.

Knowles, David. *The Monastic Order in England: A History of Its Development from the Times of St. Dunstan to the Fourth Lateran Council, 940–1216*. 2nd ed. Cambridge: Cambridge University Press, 1963.

Knowles, David. *The Religious Orders in England*. 3 vols. Cambridge: Cambridge University Press, 1979.

Kolve, V.A. *Telling Images: Chaucer and the Imagery of Narrative II*. Stanford, CA: Stanford University Press, 2009.

Koopmans, Rachel. *Wonderful to Relate: Telling and Collecting Miracle Stories in High Medieval England*. Philadelphia: University of Pennsylvania Press, 2011.

Kraemer, Alfred Robert. *Malory's Grail Seekers and Fifteenth-Century English Hagiography*. New York: Peter Lang, 1999.

Kruger, Steven F. "Claiming the Pardoner: Toward a Gay Reading of Chaucer's Pardoner's Tale." In *Critical Essays on Geoffrey Chaucer*, edited by Thomas C. Stillinger, 150–72. New York: Prentice Hall, 1998.

Kruger, Steven F. *The Spectral Jew: Conversion and Embodiment in Medieval Europe*. Minneapolis: University of Minnesota Press, 2006.

Lacy, Norris J. "The Evolution and Legacy of French Prose Romance." In *The Cambridge Companion to Medieval Romance*, edited by Roberta L. Krueger, 167–82. Cambridge: Cambridge University Press, 2000. http://dx.doi.org/10.1017/CCOL0521553423.011.

Lagorio, Valerie M. ""The Evolving Legend of St Joseph of Glastonbury." *Speculum* 46 (1971): 209–31. Rpt." In *Glatsonbury Abbey and the Arthurian Tradition*, edited by James P. Carley, 55–81. Cambridge: D.S. Brewer, 2001.

Lagorio, Valerie M. "Joseph of Arimathea: The Vita of a Grail Saint." *Zeitschrift fur Romanische Philologie* 91, no. 1–2 (1975): 54–68. http://dx.doi.org/10.1515/zrph.1975.91.1-2.54.

Lamia, Stephen. "The Cross and the Crown, the Tomb and the Shrine: Decoration and Accommodation for England's Premier Saints." In *Decorations for the Holy Dead: Visual Embellishments on Tombs and Shrines of Saints*, edited by Stephen Lamia and Elizabeth Valdez del Álamo, 39–56. Tunhout: Brepols, 2002.

Lavezzo, Kathy. "The Minster and the Privy: Rereading the Prioress's Tale." *PMLA* 126, no. 2 (2011): 363–82. http://dx.doi.org/10.1632/pmla.2011.126.2.363.

Le Couter, J.D., and D.H.M. Carter. "Notes on the Shrine of St Swithun formerly in Winchester Cathedral." *Antiquaries Journal* 4 (1924): 359–70.

Lee, Jennifer M. "Searching for Signs: Pilgrims' Identity and Experience Made Visible in the *Miracula Sancti Thomae Cantuariensis*." In *Art and Architecture of Late Medieval Pilgrimage in Northern Europe and the British Isles*, edited by Sarah Blick and Rita Tekippe, 473–91. Leiden: Brill, 2005.

Leicester, H. Marshall, Jr " 'Synne Horrible': The Pardoner's Exegesis of His Tale, and Chaucer's." In *Acts of Interpretation: The Texts in Its Contexts, 700–1600: Essays on Medieval and Renaissance Literature in Honor of E. Talbot Donaldson*, edited by Mary J. Carruthers and Elizabeth D. Kirk, 25–50. Norman, OK: Pilgrim Books, 1982.

Lewis, C.S. *The Allegory of Love*. Oxford: Clarendon Press, 1936.

Lewis, C.S. "What Chaucer Really Did to *Il Filostrato*." *Essays and Studies* 17 (1932): 56–75. Reprinted in *Troilus and Criseyde*, edited by Stephen A. Barney, 451–64. New York: Norton, 2006.

Lewis, Katherine J. "Edmund of East Anglia, Henry VI and Ideals of Kingly Masculinity." In *Holiness and Masculinity in the Middle Ages*, edited by Patricia H. Cullum and Katherine J. Lewis, 158–73. Cardiff: University of Wales Press, 2004.

Lewis, Katherine J. "History, Historiography and Rewriting the Past." In *A Companion to Middle English Hagiography*, edited by Sarah Salih, 122–40. Cambridge: D.S. Brewer, 2006.

Leyerle, John. "The Heart and the Chain." In *The Learned and the Lewed*, Harvard English Studies 5, edited by Larry D. Benson, 113–45. Cambridge, MA: Harvard University Press, 1974.

Little, Katherine C. *Confession and Resistance: Defining the Self in Late Medieval England*. Notre Dame, IN: University of Notre Dame Press, 2006.

Loomis, Laura Hibbard. "The Holy Relics of Charlemagne and King Athelstan: The Lances of Longinus and St Mauricius." *Speculum* 25, no. 4 (1950): 437–56. http://dx.doi.org/10.2307/2849376.

Loomis, Roger Sherman. *The Grail: From Celtic Myth to Christian Symbol*. Princeton, NJ: Princeton University Press, 1963.

Loomis, Roger Sherman. "The Origin of the Grail Legends." In *Arthurian Literature in the Middle Ages: A Collaborative History*, edited by Roger Sherman Loomis, 274–94. Oxford: Clarendon Press, 1959.

Mahoney, Dhira B. "The Truest and Holiest Tale: Malory's Transformation of *La Queste del saint Graal*." In *The Grail: A Casebook*, edited by Dhira B. Mahoney, 379–96. New York: Garland, 2000.

Malden, A.R. *The Canonization of Saint Osmund*. Salisbury: Bennett Brothers, 1901.

Malo, Robyn. "Miracles of Justice." In *The Encyclopedia of Medieval Pilgrimage*, edited by Larissa J. Taylor et al., 438–40. Leiden: Brill, 2010.

Malo, Robyn. "The Pardoner's Relics (And Why They Matter the Most)." *Chaucer Review* 43, no. 1 (2008): 82–102. http://dx.doi.org/10.1353/cr.0.0005.

Malo, Robyn. "Shrine Keepers." In *The Encyclopedia of Medieval Pilgrimage*, edited by Larissa J. Taylor et al., 595–7. Leiden: Brill, 2010.

Mann, Jill. "Chance and Destiny in *Troilus and Criseyde* and the *Knight's Tale*." In *The Cambridge Companion to Chaucer*, 2nd ed., edited by Piero Boitani and Jill Mann, 93–111. Cambridge: Cambridge University Press, 2004. http://dx.doi.org/10.1017/CCOL0521815568.006.

Mann, Jill. "Chaucer and Atheism." *Studies in the Age of Chaucer* 17 (1995): 5–19.

Mann, Jill. *Chaucer and Medieval Estates Satire*. Cambridge: Cambridge University Press, 1973. http://dx.doi.org/10.1017/CBO9780511552977.

Mann, Jill. "Malory and the Grail Legend." In *A Companion to Malory*, edited by Elizabeth Archibald and A.S.G. Edwards, 203–20. Cambridge: D.S. Brewer, 1996.

Manseau, Peter. *Rag and Bone: A Journey among the World's Holy Dead*. New York: Holt, 2009.

Marks, Richard. *Image and Devotion in Late Medieval England*. Stroud, Gloucestershire: Sutton, 2004.

Marner, Dominic. *St Cuthbert: His Life and Cult in Medieval Durham*. Toronto: University of Toronto Press, 2000.

Marshall, Peter. *Religious Identities in Henry VIII's England*. Burlington, VT: Ashgate, 2006.

Mason, Arthur. *What Became of the Bones of St Thomas?* Cambridge: Cambridge University Press, 1920.

Masri, Heather. "Carnival Laughter in the Pardoner's Tale." *Medieval Perspectives* 10 (1995): 148–56.

Matarasso, Pauline Maud. "Introduction." In *The Quest of the Holy Grail*, translated and edited by Pauline Matarasso, 9–29. London: Penguin, 1969.

Matarasso, Pauline Maud. *The Redemption of Chivalry: A Study of the Queste del Saint Graal*. Geneva: Droz, 1979.

Mayr-Harting, Henry. "Functions of a Twelfth-Century Shrine: The Miracles of St Frideswide." In *Studies in Medieval History Presented to R.H.C. Davis*, edited by Henry Mayr-Harting and R.I. Moore, 193–206. London: Hambledon Press, 1985.

McAlpine, Monica. *The Genre of Troilus and Criseyde*. Ithaca, NY: Cornell University Press, 1978.

McAlpine, Monica. "The Pardoner's Homosexuality and How It Matters." *PMLA* 95, no. 1 (1980): 8–22. http://dx.doi.org/10.2307/461730.

McCormack, Frances M. "Chaucer and Lollardy." In *Chaucer and Religion*, edited by Helen Phillips, 35–40. Cambridge: D.S. Brewer, 2010.

McCormack, Frances M. *Chaucer and the Culture of Dissent: The Lollard Context and Subtext of the Parson's Tale*. Dublin: Four Courts Press, 2007.

McCulloh, John M. "The Cult of Relics in the Letters and Dialogues of Pope Gregory the Great: A Lexicographical Study." *Traditio* 32 (1976): 145–84.

McGerr, Rosemary P. *Chaucer's Open Books: Resistance to Closure in Medieval Discourse*. Gainesville: University of Florida Press, 1998.

McKenna, J.W. "Popular Canonization as Political Propaganda: The Cult of Archbishop Scrope." *Speculum* 45, no. 4 (1970): 608–23. http://dx.doi.org/10.2307/2855672.

Middle English Compendium Online. Ann Arbor: University of Michigan Digital Library Production Service. http://ets.umdl.umich.edu/m/mec/. Accessed 1 June 2010.

Mieszkowski, Gretchen. " 'The Least Innocent of All Innocent-Sounding Lines': The Legacy of Donaldson's Troilus Criticism." *Chaucer Review* 41, no. 3 (2007): 299–310. http://dx.doi.org/10.1353/cr.2007.0009.

Mieszkowski, Gretchen. *Medieval Go-Betweens and Chaucer's Pandarus*. New York: Palgrave, 2006.

Miller, Patricia Cox. " 'The Little Blue Flower Is Red': Relics and the Poetizing of the Body." *Journal of Early Christian Studies* 8, no. 2 (2000): 213–36. http://dx.doi.org/10.1353/earl.2000.0030.

Miller, Patricia Cox. "Relics, Rhetoric and Mental Spectacles in Late Ancient Christianity." In *Seeing the Invisible in Late Antiquity and the Early Middle Ages*, edited by Giselle de Nie, Karl F. Morrison, and Marco Mostert, 25–52. Utrecht Studies in Medieval Literacy 14. Turnhout: Brepols, 2005.

Minnis, Alastair. *Chaucer and Pagan Antiquity*. Woodbridge, Suffolk: Boydell and Brewer, 1982.

Minnis, Alastair. "Chaucer and the Queering Eunuch." *New Medieval Literatures* 6 (2003): 107–28.

Minnis, Alastair. "Chaucer's Pardoner and 'The Office of Preacher'." In *Intellectuals and Writers in Fourteenth Century Europe: the J.A.W. Bennett Memorial Lectures*, edited by Piero Boitani and Anna Torti, 88–119. Tübingen, Cambridge: Gunter Narr Verlag and D.S. Brewer, 1986.

Minnis, Alastair. "The Construction of Chaucer's Pardoner." In *Promissory Notes on the Treasury of Merits: Indulgences in Late Medieval Europe*, edited by Robert N. Swanson, 169–95. Leiden: Brill, 2006.

Minnis, Alastair. *Fallible Authors: Chaucer's Pardoner and the Wife of Bath*. Philadelphia: University of Pennsylvania Press, 2007.

Minnis, Alastair. "Once more into the breech: The Pardoner's prize *relyk*." In *Through a Classical Eye: Transcultural and Transhistorical Visions in Medieval English, Italian, and Latin Literature in Honour of Winthrop Wetherbee*, edited by R. F. Yeager and Andrew Galloway, 287–315. Toronto: University of Toronto Press, 2009.

Minnis, Alastair. "Reclaiming the Pardoners." *Journal of Medieval and Early Modern Studies* 33, no. 2 (2003): 311–34. http://dx.doi.org/10.1215/10829636-33-2-311.

Minnis, Alastair. *Translations of Authority in Medieval English Literature: Valuing the Vernacular*. Cambridge: Cambridge University Press, 2009. http://dx.doi.org/10.1017/CBO9780511575662.

Mireux, Marie-Danielle. "Guibert de Nogent et la critique du culte des reliques." *La piété populaire au Moyen Age* 1: 193–202. Actes du 99e congrès National des Sociétés Savantes Besançon 1954: Section de philologie et d'histoire jusqu'à 1610. 2 vols. Paris: Bibliothèque Nationale, 1977.

Modarelli, Michael. "Pandarus's 'Grete Emprise': Narration and Subjectivity in Chaucer's *Troilus and Criseyde*." *English Studies* 89, no. 4 (2008): 403–14. http://dx.doi.org/10.1080/00138380802011867.

Montgomery, Scott. "Exposure of Relics." In *The Encyclopedia of Medieval Pilgrimage*, edited by Larissa Taylor et al., 205–6. Leiden: Brill, 2010.

Morgan, Penelope E. "The Effect of the Pilgrim Cult of St Thomas Cantilupe on Hereford Cathedral." In *St. Thomas Cantilupe, Bishop of Hereford: Essays in His Honour*, edited by Meryl Jancey, 145–52. Hereford: Friends of Hereford Cathedral, 1982.

Murphy, J.J. "The Arts of Poetry and Prose." In *The Cambridge History of Literary Criticism*. Vol. 2, *The Middle Ages*, edited by Alastair Minnis and Ian Johnson, 42–67. Cambridge: Cambridge University Press, 2005.

Morris, Colin. "A Critique of Popular Religion: Guibert of Nogent on *The Relics of the Saints*." In *Popular Belief and Practice: Papers Read at the Ninth Summer Meeting and the Tenth Winter Meeting of the Ecclesiastical History Society*, edited by G.J. Cuming and Derek Baker, 55–60. Cambridge: Cambridge University Press, 1972.

Muscatine, Charles. "Chaucer's Religion and the Chaucer Religion." In *Chaucer Traditions: Studies in Honour of Derek Brewer*, edited by Ruth Morse and Barry Windeatt, 249–62. Cambridge: Cambridge University Press, 1990. http://dx.doi.org/10.1017/CBO9780511552984.019.

Nilson, Ben. *Cathedral Shrines of Medieval England*. Woodbridge, Suffolk: Boydell and Brewer, 1998.

Nilson, Ben. "The Medieval Experience at the Shrine." In *Pilgrimage Explored*, edited by J. Stopford, 95–122. Woodbridge, Suffolk: York Medieval Press, 1999.

Nissé, Ruth. "Grace under Pressure: Conduct and Representation in the Norwich Heresy Trials." In *Medieval Conduct*, edited by Kathleen Ashley and Robert L.A. Clark, 207–25. Minneapolis: University of Minnesota Press, 2000.

Nissé, Ruth. "Reversing Discipline: *The Tretise of Miracles Pleyinge*, Lollard Exegesis and the Failure of Representation." *Yearbook of Langland Studies* 11 (1997): 163–94.

Nolan, Maura. *John Lydgate and the Making of Public Culture*. Cambridge: Cambridge University Press, 2005. http://dx.doi.org/10.1017/CBO9780511483387.

Norton, Christopher. *Saint William of York*. York: University of York Medieval Press, 2006.

O'Neilly, J.G., and L.E. Tanner. "The Shrine of St Edward the Confessor." *Archaeologia* 100 (1966): 129–54. http://dx.doi.org/10.1017/S0261340900013734.

Osborn, Marijane. "Transgressive Word and Image in Chaucer's Enshrined *Coillons* Passage." *Chaucer Review* 37, no. 4 (2003): 365–84. http://dx.doi.org/10.1353/cr.2003.0015.

Owst, G.R. *Literature and Pulpit in Medieval England: A Neglected Chapter in the History of English Letters and of the English People*. Cambridge: Cambridge University Press, 1933.

Owst, G.R. *Preaching in Medieval England: An Introduction to Sermon Manuscripts of the Period, c. 1350–1450*. Cambridge: Cambridge University Press, 1926.

Patterson, Lee. *Chaucer and the Subject of History*. Madison: University of Wisconsin Press, 1991.

Patterson, Lee. "Chaucerian Confession: Penitential Literature and the Pardoner." *Medievalia et Humanistica* 7 (1976): 153–73.

Patterson, Lee. "Chaucer's Pardoner on the Couch: Psyche and Clio in Medieval Literary Studies." *Speculum* 76, no. 3 (2001): 638–80. http://dx.doi.org/10.2307/2903882.

Patterson, Lee. "The Parson's Tale and the Quitting of the Canterbury Tales." *Traditio* 34 (1978): 331–80.

Pauphilet, Albert. *Études sur la Queste del Saint Graal attribuée à Gautier Map*. Paris: E. Champion, 1921.

Pearsall, Derek. *John Lydgate*. London: Kegan Paul, 1970.

Phillips, Helen, ed. *Chaucer and Religion*. Cambridge: D.S. Brewer, 2010.

Pittock, Malcolm. "The Pardoner's Tale and the Quest for Death." *Essays in Criticism: A Quarterly Journal of Literary Criticism* 24 (1974): 107–23.

Platelle, Henri. "Guibert de Nogent et le *De pignoribus sanctorum*. Richesses et limites d'une critique médiévale des reliques." In *Les reliques: objects, cultes, symboles: Actes du colloque international de l'université du Littoral-Côte d'Opale (boulogne-sur-Mer) 4–6 septembre 1997*, edited by Edina Bozóky and Anne-Marie Helvétius, 109–21. Turnhout: Brepols, 1999.

Pugh, Tison. "Queer Pandarus? Silence and Sexual Ambiguity in Chaucer's *Troilus and Criseyde*." *Philological Quarterly* 80, no. 1 (2001): 17–35.

Radulescu, Raluca. *The Gentry Context for Malory's Morte Darthur*. Woodbridge: Boydell & Brewer, 2003.

Ramm, Ben. *Discourse for the Holy Grail in Old French Romance*. Cambridge: D.S. Brewer, 2007.

Rawcliffe, Carole. "Curing Bodies and Healing Souls: Pilgrimage and the Sick in Medieval East Anglia." In *Pilgrimage: The English Experience from Becket to Bunyan*, edited by Colin Morris and Peter Roberts, 108–40. Cambridge: Cambridge University Press, 2002.

Remensnyder, Amy. "Legendary Treasure at Conques: Reliquaries and Imaginative Memory." *Speculum* 71, no. 4 (1996): 884–906. http://dx.doi.org/10.2307/2865723.

Renoir, Alan. "Attitudes toward Women in Lydgate's Poetry." *English Studies* 42, no. 1–6 (1961): 1–14. http://dx.doi.org/10.1080/00138386108597093.

Reudenbach, Bruno, and Gia Toussaint, eds. *Reliquiare im Mittelalter*. Berlin: Akademie Verlag, 2005.

Rhodes, James F. "The Pardoner's *Vernycle* and His *Vera Icon*." *Modern Language Studies* 13, no. 2 (1983): 34–40. http://dx.doi.org/10.2307/3194485.

Richmond, Colin. "Religion and the Fifteenth-Century English Gentleman." In *The Church, Politics and Patronage in the Fifteenth Century*, edited by Barrie Dobson, 193–208. New York: St Martin's Press, 1984.

Richter, Michael. "Collecting Miracles along the Anglo-Welsh Border in the Early Fourteenth Century." In *Multilingualism in Later Medieval Britain*, edited by D.A. Trotter, 53–62. Cambridge: D.S. Brewer, 2000.

Riddy, Felicity. "Glastonbury, Joseph of Arimathea and the Grail in John Hardyng's Chronicle." In *Glatsonbury Abbey and the Arthurian Tradition*, edited by James P. Carley, 269–84. Cambridge: D.S. Brewer, 2001.

Riddy, Felicity. *Sir Thomas Malory*. Leiden: Brill, 1987.

Ridyard, S.J. " 'Condigna Veneratio': Post-Conquest Attitudes to the Saints of the Anglo-Saxons." *Anglo-Norman Studies* 9 (1986): 179–206.

Roberts, Marion E. "The Relic of the Holy Blood and the Iconography of the Thirteenth-Century North Transept Portal of Westminster Abbey." In *England in the Thirteenth Century: Proceedings of the 1984 Harlaxton Symposium*, edited by W. Mark Ormrod, 129–42. Woodbridge, Suffolk: Boydell and Brewer, 1985.

Robertson, D.W. *A Preface to Chaucer: Studies in Medieval Perspectives*. Princeton, NJ: Princeton University Press, 1962.

Robertson, Elizabeth, and Jennifer Jahner, eds. *Medieval and Early Modern Devotional Objects in Global Perspective: Translations of the Sacred*. New York: Palgrave, 2010.

Robeson, Lisa. "Writing as Relic." *Oral Tradition* 14 (1999): 430–46.

Rollason, David. "Relic-Cults as an Instrument of Royal Policy, *c*.900–*c*.1050." *Anglo-Saxon England* 15 (1986): 91–103. http://dx.doi.org/10.1017/S0263675100003707.

Rollason, David. *Saints and Relics in Anglo-Saxon England*. Cambridge, MA: Basil Blackwell, 1989.

Rosser, Gervase. "Sanctuary and Social Negotiation in Medieval England." In *The Cloister and the World: Essays in Medieval History in Honour of Barbara Harvey*, edited by John Blair and Brian Golding, 57–79. Oxford: Clarendon Press, 1996. http://dx.doi.org/10.1093/acprof:oso/9780198204404.003.0004

Rothkrug, Lionel. "German Holiness and Western Sanctity in Medieval and Modern History." *Historical Reflections. Reflexions Historiques* 15 (1988): 161–249.

Rothkrug, Lionel. "Popular Religion and Holy Shrines: Their Influence on the Origins of the German Reformation and Their Role in German Cultural Development." In *Religion and the People, 800–1700*, edited by J. Obelkevich, 20–86. Chapel Hill: University of North Carolina Press, 1979.

Rubenstein, Jay. *Guibert of Nogent: Portrait of a Medieval Mind*. New York: Routledge, 2002.

Rubenstein, Jay. "Liturgy against History: The Competing Visions of Lanfranc and Eadmer of Canterbury." *Speculum* 74, no. 2 (1999): 279–309. http://dx.doi.org/10.2307/2887048.

Rubin, Miri. *Corpus Christi: The Eucharist in Late Medieval Culture*. Cambridge: Cambridge University Press, 1991.

Salih, Sarah, ed. *A Companion to Middle English Hagiography*. Cambridge: D.S. Brewer, 2006.

Sanok, Catherine. *Her Life Historical: Exemplarity and Female Saints' Lives in Late Medieval England*. Philadelphia: University of Pennsylvania Press, 2007.

Scanlon, Larry, and James Simpson, eds. *John Lydgate: Poetry, Culture, and Lancastrian England*. Notre Dame, IN: University of Notre Dame Press, 2006.

Scase, Wendy. "The Audience and Framers of the Twelve Conclusions of the Lollards." In *Text and Controversy from Wyclif to Bale: Essays in Honor of Anne Hudson*, edited by Helen Barr and Ann M. Hutchison, 283–301. Turnhout: Brepols, 2005.

Scase, Wendy. *Reginald Pecock*. In Authors of the Middle Ages, edited by M.C. Seymour, Vol. 3 no. 8. Aldershot: Variorum, 1996.

Scattergood, John. "Pierce the Ploughman's Crede: Lollardy and Texts." In *Lollardy and the Gentry in the Later Middle Ages*, edited by Margaret Aston and Colin Richmond, 77–94. New York: St Martin's Press, 1997.

Schmitt, Jean-Claude. "Les reliques et les images. " In *Les reliques: objects, cultes, symboles: Actes du colloque international de l'université du Littoral-Côte d'Opale (boulogne-sur-Mer) 4–6 septembre 1997*, edited by Edina Bozóky and Anne-Marie Helvétius, 145–67. Turnhout: Brepols, 1999.

Scott, Kathleen L. *Later Gothic Manuscripts, 1390–1490*. 2 vols. London: H. Miller, 1996.

Sedgewick, G.G. "The Progress of Chaucer's Pardoner, 1880–1940." *Modern Language Quarterly* 1 (1940): 431–58.

Shichtman, Martin B. "Percival's Sister: Genealogy, Virginity, and Blood." *Arthuriana* 9 (1999): 11–20.

Shortell, Ellen M. "Dismembering Saint Quentin: Gothic Architecture and the Display of Relics." *Gesta* 36, no. 1 (1997): 32–47. http://dx.doi.org/10.2307/767277.

Sigal, Pierre André. *L'Homme et le miracle dans la France médiévale (XIe–XIIe siècle)*. Paris: Les Éditions du Cerf, 1985.

Sigal, Pierre André. "Les récits de miracles." In *Comprendre le XIIIe siècle*, edited by Pierre Guichard and Danièle Alexandre-Bidon, 133–44. Lyon: Presses Universitaires de Lyon, 1995.

Sigal, Pierre André. "Les Voyages de reliques aux onzième et douzième siècles." In *Voyage, quête, pèlerinage dans la littérature et la civilisation médiévales*, 73–104. Paris: Edition CUER, 1976.

Silvestre, Hubert. "Commerce et vol de reliques au Moyen Âge." *Revue Belge de Philologie et d'Histoire. Belgisch Tijdschrift voor Philologie en Geschiedenis* 30, no. 3 (1952): 721–39. http://dx.doi.org/10.3406/rbph.1952.2143.

Simpson, James. "Confessing Literature." *English Language Notes* 44 (2006): 121–6.

Simpson, James. *Reform and Cultural Revolution*. Oxford: Oxford University Press, 2002.

Sisk, Jennifer. "Lydgate's Problematic Commission: A Legend of St Edmund for Henry VI." *Journal of English and Germanic Philology* 109, no. 3 (2010): 349–75. http://dx.doi.org/10.1353/egp.0.0153.

Smith, Julia M.H. "Old Saints, New Cults: Roman Relics in Carolingian Francia." In *Early Medieval Rome and the Christian West: Essays in Honour of Donald A. Bullough*, edited by Julia M. H. Smith, 317–39. Leiden: Brill, 2000.

Smith, Julia M.H. "Oral and Written: Saints, Miracles, and Relics in Brittany, c. 850–1250." *Speculum* 65, no. 2 (April 1990): 309–43. http://dx.doi.org/10.2307/2864295.

Smith, Julia M.H. "Rulers and Relics c.750–c. 950: Treasure on Earth, Treasure in Heaven." In *Relics and Remains*, edited by Alexandra Walsham, *Past and Present* Supplement 5 (2010): 73–96. http://dx.doi.org/10.1093/pastj/gtq013

Smith, Mary Frances, Robin Fleming, and Patricia Halpin. "Court and Piety in Late Anglo-Saxon England." *Catholic Historical Review* 87, no. 4 (2001): 569–602. http://dx.doi.org/10.1353/cat.2001.0189.

Snoek, G.J.C. *Medieval Piety from Relics to the Eucharist: A Process of Mutual Interaction*. Leiden: Brill, 1995.

Somerset, Fiona. *Clerical Discourse and Lay Audience in Late Medieval England*. Cambridge: Cambridge University Press, 1998. http://dx.doi.org/10.1017/CBO9780511583070

Somerset, Fiona. " 'Hard is with seyntis forto make affray': Lydgate the 'Poet-Propagandist' as Hagiographer." In *John Lydgate*, edited by Larry Scanlon and James Simpson, 258–78. Notre Dame, IN: University of Notre Dame Press, 2006.

Southern, R.W. *Medieval Humanism*. New York: Harper and Row, 1970.

Spurrell, Mark. "The Promotion and Demotion of Whole Relics." *Antiquaries Journal* 80, no. 1 (2000): 67–85. http://dx.doi.org/10.1017/S0003581500050198.

Stanbury, Sarah. *The Visual Object of Desire in Late Medieval England*. Philadelphia: University of Pennsylvania Press, 2008.

Stanbury, Sarah. "The Voyeur and the Private Life in Troilus and Criseyde." *Studies in the Age of Chaucer* 13 (1991): 141–58.

Stanley, Arthur Penrhyn. *Historical Memorials of Canterbury*. New York: E.P. Dutton, 1911.

Stock, Brian. *The Implications of Literacy: Written Language and Models of Interpretation in the Eleventh and Twelfth Centuries*. Princeton, NJ: Princeton University Press, 1983.

Stock, Lorraine Kochanske. " 'Slydynge' Critics: Changing Critical Constructions of Chaucer's Criseyde in the Past Century." In *New Perspectives on Criseyde*, edited by Cindy L. Vitto and Marcia Smith Marzec, 11–36. Asheville, NC: Pegasus, 2004.

Stocker, David A. "The Mystery of the Shrines of St Hugh." In *St Hugh of Lincoln*, edited by H. Mayr-Harting, 89–124. Oxford: Clarendon Press, 1987.

Stocker, David A. "The Tomb and Shrine of Bishop Grosseteste in Lincoln Cathedral." In *England in the Thirteenth Century: Proceedings of the 1984 Harlaxton Symposium*, edited by W.M. Ormrod, 143–48. Woodbridge, Suffolk: Boydell and Brewer, 1985.

Storm, Melvyn. "The Pardoner's Invitation: Quaestor's Bag or Becket's Shrine?" *PMLA* 97, no. 5 (1982): 810–18. http://dx.doi.org/10.2307/462172.

Stouck, Mary-Ann. "Saints and Rebels: Hagiography and Opposition to the King in Late Fourteenth-Century England." *Medievalia et Humanistica* 24 (1997): 75–94.

Straker, Scott-Morgan. "Propaganda, Intentionality, and the Lancastrian Lydgate." In *John Lydgate: Poetry, Culture, and Lancastrian England*, edited by Larry Scanlon and James Simpson, 98–128. Notre Dame, IN: University of Notre Dame Press, 2006.

Strohm, Paul. *England's Empty Throne Usurpation and Textual Legitimation, 1399–1422*. New Haven, CT: Yale University Press, 1998.

Stroud, Daphne. "The Cult and Tombs of St Osmund at Salisbury." *Wiltshire Archaeological and Natural History Magazine* 78 (1984): 50–4.

Summit, Jennifer. "Troilus and Criseyde." In *The Yale Companion to Chaucer*, edited by Seth Lerer, 213–42. New Haven, CT: Yale University Press, 2006.

Sumption, Jonathan. *Pilgrimage: An Image of Mediaeval Religion*. London: Faber, 1975.

Sutton, Anne F. "Malory in Newgate: A New Document." *Library: The Transactions of the Bibliographical Society* 1 (2000): 243–62.

Swanson, Robert N. *Indulgences in Late Medieval England: Passports to Paradise?* Cambridge: Cambridge University Press, 2007.

Swanson, Robert N., and David Lepine. "The Later Middle Ages, 1268–1535." In *Hereford Cathedral: A History*, edited by Gerald Aylmer and John Tiller, 48–86. London: Hambledon Press, 2000.

Tatlock, J.S.P. "The English Journey of the Laon Canons." *Speculum* 8, no. 4 (1933): 454–65. http://dx.doi.org/10.2307/2855887.

Tatton-Brown, Tim. "The Burial Places of St Osmund." *Spire* 69 (1999): 19–25.

Tatton-Brown, Tim. "Canterbury and the Architecture of Pilgrimage Shrines in England." In *Pilgrimage:The English Experience from Becket to Bunyan*, edited by Colin Morris and Peter Roberts, 90–107. Cambridge: Cambridge University Press, 2002.

Thacker, Alan. "*Loca Sanctorum*: The Significance of Place in the Study of the Saints." In *Local Saints and Local Churches in the Early Medieval West*, edited by Alan Thacker and Richard Sharpe, 1–43. New York: Oxford University Press, 2002.

Thomas, Islwyn Geoffrey. "The Cult of Saints' Relics in Medieval England." PhD diss., University of London, 1974.

Thomson, John. *The Later Lollards, 1414–1520*. London: Oxford University Press, 1965.

Tiller, Kenneth J. " 'So precyously coverde': Malory's Hermeneutic Quest of the Sankgreal." *Arthuriana* 13, no. 3 (2003): 83–97.

Tucker, P.E. "A Source for the Healing of Sir Urry." *Modern Language Review* 50, no. 4 (1955): 490–92. http://dx.doi.org/10.2307/3719283.

Vance, Eugene. "Chaucer's Pardoner: Relics, Discourse, and Frames of Propriety." *New Literary History* 20, no. 3 (1989): 723–45. http://dx.doi.org/10.2307/469364.

van Os, Henk. *The Way to Heaven: Relic Veneration in the Middle Ages*. Baarn: De Prom, 2000.

Vauchez, André. *Sainthood in the Later Middle Ages*. Translated by Jean Birrell. Cambridge: Cambridge University Press, 1997.

Vincent, Nicholas. *The Holy Blood: King Henry III and the Westminster Blood Relic*. Cambridge: Cambridge University Press, 2001.

Vincent, Nicholas. "The Pilgrimages of the Angevin Kings of England, 1154–1272." In *Pilgrimage: The English Experience from Becket to Bunyan*, edited by Colin Morris and Peter Roberts, 12–45. Cambridge: Cambridge University Press, 2002.

Vincent, Nicholas. "Some Pardoners' Tales: The Earliest English Indulgences." *Transactions of the Royal Historical Society* 12, no. 12 (2002): 23–58. http://dx.doi.org/10.1017/S0080440102000026.

von Nolcken, Christina. "A 'Certain Sameness' and Our Response to It in English Wycliffite Texts." In *Literature and Religion in the Later Middle Ages:*

Philological Studies in Honor of Siegfried Wenzel, edited by R. Newhauser and John Alford, 191–208. Binghamton: Medieval and Renaissance Texts and Studies, 1995.

von Nolcken, Christina. "Another Kind of Saint: A Lollard Perception of John Wyclif." In *From Ockham to Wyclif*, edited by Anne Hudson and Michael Wilks, 429–43. Studies in Church History, Subsidia 5. Oxford: Basil Blackwell, 1987.

Wall, J. Charles. *Shrines of British Saints*. London: Methuen, 1905.

Walsham, Alexandra, ed. *Relics and Remains. Past and Present* Supplement 5 (2010).

Ward, Benedicta. *Miracles and the Medieval Mind: Theory, Record, and Event, 1000–1215*. 2nd ed. Philadelphia: University of Pennsylvania Press, 1987.

Watson, Nicholas. "Chaucer's Public Christianity." *Religion and Literature* 37 (2005): 99–114.

Watson, Nicholas. "Desire for the Past." *Studies in the Age of Chaucer* 21 (1999): 59–97.

Watson, Nicholas. "Vernacular Apocalyptic: on the *Lanterne of Liȝt*." *Revista Canaria de Estudios Ingleses* 47 (2003): 115–27.

Webb, Diana. *Medieval European Pilgrimage c.700–c.1500*. New York: Palgrave, 2002.

Webb, Diana. *Pilgrimage in Medieval England*. London: Hambledon and London, 2000.

Wenzel, Siegfried. "Chaucer's Pardoner and His Relics." *Studies in the Age of Chaucer* 11 (1989): 37–41.

Weston, Jessie L. *From Ritual to Romance*. New York: Doubleday, 1957.

Whitaker, Muriel. *Arthur's Kingdom of Adventure: The World of Malory's Morte Darthur*. Cambridge: D.S. Brewer, 1984.

Whitworth, Charles W. "The Sacred and Secular in Malory's *Tale of the Senkgreal*." *Yearbook of English Studies* 5 (1975): 19–29. http://dx.doi.org/10.2307/3507167.

Wieland, Gernot R. "The Hermeneutic Style of Thiofrid of Echternach." In *Anglo-Latin and Its Heritage: Essays in Honour of A.G. Rigg on His 64th Birthday*, edited by Siân Echard and Gernot R. Wieland, 27–47. *Journal of Medieval Latin* publications 4. Turnhout: Brepols, 2001.

Williams, Arnold. "Some Documents on English Pardoners, 1350–1400." In *Mediaeval Studies in Honor of Urban Tigner Holmes, Jr.*, edited by John Mahoney and John Esten Keller, 197–207. Chapel Hill: University of North Carolina Press, 1965.

Willis, R. *The Architectural History of Canterbury Cathedral*. London: Longman, 1845.

Willis, R. *The Architectural History of York Cathedral*. London: Office of the Archaeological Institute, 1848.

Wilson, Christopher. *The Shrines of St William of York*. York: Yorkshire Museum, 1977.

Windeatt, Barry. *Troilus and Criseyde*. Oxford: Oxford University Press, 1992.

Winstead, Karen. "Chaucer's Parson's Tale and the Contours of Orthodoxy." *Chaucer Review* 43 (2009): 239–59.

Winstead, Karen. *John Capgrave's Fifteenth Century*. Philadelphia: University of Pennsylvania Press, 2007.

Woodman, Francis. *The Architectural History of Canterbury Cathedral*. London: Routledge & Kegan Paul, 1981.

Yarrow, Simon. *Saints and Their Communities: Miracle Stories in Twelfth Century England*. Oxford: Clarendon Press, 2006.

Zacher, Christian. *Curiosity and Pilgrimage: The Literature of Discovery in Fourteenth- Century England*. Baltimore, MD: Johns Hopkins University Press, 1976.

Ziekowitz, Richard. "Sutured Looks and Homoeroticism: Reading Troilus and Pandarus Cinematically." In *Men and Masculinities in Chaucer's Troilus and Criseyde*, edited by Tison Pugh and Marcia Smith Marzec, 148–60. Cambridge: D.S. Brewer, 2008.

Zika, Charles. "Hosts, Procession, and Pilgrimage: Controlling the Sacred in Fifteenth-Century Germany." *Past & Present* 118, no. 1 (1988): 25–64. http://dx.doi.org/10.1093/past/118.1.25.

Index